FROMMER'S

COMPREHENSIVE TRAVEL GUIDE

COSTA RICA

by Karl Samson
with Jane Aukshunas

MACMILLAN • USA

About the Author: Karl Samson lives in the Pacific Northwest, but likes to escape that region's rainy winters by heading south to Costa Rica and other sunny Central American countries. *Frommer's Costa Rica, Guatemala & Belize* was his first guidebook to include Costa Rica. When at home he spends his time working on two Frommer guides to the Northwest as well as other books. **Jane Aukshunas,** who agreed to travel the world when she married Karl Samson, has become the organizational wizard of the several books the two have now written together.

MACMILLAN TRAVEL
A Simon & Schuster Macmillan Company
15 Columbus Circle
New York, NY 10023

ISBN 0-671-88368-2
ISSN 1077-890X

Design by Robert Bull Design
Maps by Ortelius Design

SPECIAL SALES
Bulk purchases (10+) copies of Frommer's travel guides are available to corporations at special discounts. The Special Sales Department can produce custom editions to be used as premiums and/or for sales promotion to suit individual needs. Existing editions can be produced with custom cover imprints such as corporate logos. For more information write to: Special Sales, Macmillan General Reference, 15 Columbus Circle, New York, NY 10023.

Manufactured in the United States of America

CONTENTS

LIST OF MAPS

COSTA RICA 4-5

SAN JOSÉ 48-49

WALKING TOUR—SAN JOSÉ 75

REGIONAL MAPS

WHAT THE SYMBOLS MEAN

 FROMMER'S FAVORITES—hotels, restaurants, attractions, and entertainments you should not miss

 SUPER-SPECIAL VALUES—really exceptional values

 FROMMER'S SMART TRAVELER TIPS—hints on how to secure the best value for your money

IN HOTEL AND OTHER LISTINGS

The following symbols refer to the standard amenities available in all rooms:

A/C air conditioning   TEL telephone   TV television
MINIBAR refrigerator stocked with beverages and snacks

The following abbreviations are used for credit cards:

AE American Express   DISC Discover   EU Eurocard
CB Carte Blanche   ER enRoute   MC MasterCard
DC Diners Club   V Visa

INVITATION TO THE READERS

In researching this book, I have come across many wonderful establishments, the best of which I have included here. I am sure that many of you will also come across appealing hotels, inns, restaurants, guest houses, shops, and attractions. Please don't keep them to yourself. Share your experiences, especially if you want to comment on places that have been included in this edition which have changed for the worse. You can address your letters to:

Karl Samson
Frommer's Costa Rica
c/o Macmillan Travel
15 Columbus Circle
New York, NY 10023

A DISCLAIMER

Readers are advised that prices fluctuate in the course of time and travel information changes under the impact of the varied and volatile factors that affect the travel industry. Neither the author nor the publisher can be held responsible for the experiences of readers while traveling. Readers are invited to write to the publisher with ideas, comments, and suggestions for future editions.

SAFETY ADVISORY

Whenever you're traveling in an unfamiliar city or country, stay alert. Be aware of your immediate surroundings. Wear a moneybelt and keep a close eye on your possessions. Be particularly careful with cameras, purses, and wallets, all favorite targets of thieves and pickpockets.

CHAPTER 1

GETTING TO KNOW COSTA RICA

Costa Rica—in Spanish, the name means "Rich Coast," and when the Spanish named this region, they felt that Costa Rica held great promise. In those days, gold and Indian souls, to convert and enslave, were the goal of the Spanish, and when Costa Rica yielded up little of either, the name became somewhat a misnomer as far as the Spanish were concerned. It took nearly 500 years for the Rich Coast to finally yield its true bounty—the green gold of its natural tropical beauty. The same dense forests, volcanic peaks, and rugged coastlines that created only impediments to Spanish settlement in Costa Rica are today attracting tens of thousands of visitors each year. They come to see some of Central America's most unspoiled forests and beaches, to learn about rain forests and cloud forests, and to go bird-watching and white-water rafting, horseback riding and diving.

Costa Rica is, and has been for many years, a relative sea of tranquility in a region that has been troubled by turmoil for centuries. When former Costa Rican president Oscar Arias Sánchez was awarded the Nobel Peace Prize for negotiating a peace settlement in Nicaragua in 1987, Costa Rica was able to claim credit for exporting a bit of its own political stability to the rest of Central America. For more than 100 years, Costa Rica has enjoyed a stable democracy and a relatively high standard of living for Latin America. The literacy rate is high, as are medical standards and facilities. Perhaps most significant, at least for proud Costa Ricans, is that this country does not have an army. Together these factors have led Costa Rica to be called the "Switzerland of Central America."

Costa Rica rightfully should be called Costas Ricas since it has two coasts, one on the Pacific Ocean and one on the Caribbean Sea. These two coasts are as different from one another as are the Atlantic and Pacific coasts of North America. The Pacific coast, which can be divided into three distinct regions (Guanacaste and the Nicoya Peninsula, the central coast, and the southern coast) is characterized by a rugged, though mostly accessible, coastline where mountains often meet the sea to create spectacular stretches of coastline. This coast varies from the dry sunny climate of the northwest to the hot, humid rain forests of the south. The Caribbean coast can be divided into two roughly equal stretches, half of which is only accessible by boat or small plane. This remote coastline is a vast flat plane laced with rivers and covered with rain forest. Farther south, along the stretch of coast accessible by car, there are uncrowded beaches and even a bit of coral reef. Between these two coasts lie mountains and forests, active volcanoes, and enough species of birds to keep avid bird-watchers busy for years.

Costa Rica has become acutely aware of the riches it has to offer tourists, and the country is undergoing phenomenal tourist-related growth. This rapid growth is

DID YOU KNOW . . . ?

- Costa Rica has the oldest democracy in Central America.
- San José, the capital, is farther south than Caracas, Venezuela.
- Costa Rica has no army, navy, air force, or marine corps.
- Costa Rica has 10% of the butterflies in the world and more than the entire African continent as well as more than 1,200 varieties of orchids and more than 800 species of birds.
- Isla del Coco, the largest uninhabited island in the world, is part of Costa Rica.
- You can see both the Caribbean Sea and the Pacific Ocean from the top of Costa Rica's Mount Chirripó.
- During an *arribada* more than 15,000 sea turtles may nest on the same beach over a period of only a few nights.
- In the rain forests of the Osa Peninsula it sometimes rains as much as 200 inches per year.

putting great strains on Costa Rica's natural resources and natural beauty. Though Costa Rica boasts of having preserved more than 10 percent of its surface area in national parks, outside those parks forests are rapidly being cut for lumber or converted into banana plantations. Though ecotourism has catapulted Costa Rica into the international limelight and attracted throngs of binocular-carrying visitors to its steamy jungles, vast stretches of beach are now being developed into massive mega-resorts with little regard for the impact such developments will have on the local environment or adjacent towns and villages. However, Costa Rica should remain for many years one of the most fascinating natural destinations in the Americas, and with political stability, an educated populace, and vast areas of wilderness, Costa Rica today truly is a rich coast.

1. GEOGRAPHY, HISTORY & POLITICS

GEOGRAPHY

Bordered on the north by Nicaragua and on the southeast by Panama, Costa Rica (19,530 square miles) is only slightly larger than Vermont and New Hampshire combined, with more than 750 miles of coastline on both the Caribbean Sea and the Pacific Ocean. Much of the country is mountainous, with three major ranges running northwest to southeast. Among these mountains are several volcanic peaks, some of which are still active. Between the mountain ranges fertile valleys, the largest and most populated of which is the Central Valley. With the exception of the dry Guanacaste region, much of Costa Rica's coastal area is hot and humid and covered with dense rain forests. The earliest Spanish settlers found the climate much more amenable in the highlands, and to this day most of the population lives in this region.

REGIONS IN BRIEF

The Central Valley The Central Valley is characterized by rolling green hills between 3,000 and 4,000 feet above sea level, where the climate has been described as "eternal spring." It is Costa Rica's primary agricultural region, with coffee farms making up the majority of landholdings. The rich volcanic soil of this region makes it ideal for growing almost anything. The country's earliest settlements were in this area, and today the Central Valley is a densely populated area laced with good roads and dotted with small towns. Surrounding the Central Valley are high moun-

IMPRESSIONS

Below us, at a distance of perhaps two thousand feet, the whole country was covered with clouds . . . the more distant clouds were lifted, and over the immense bed we saw at the same time the Atlantic and Pacific Oceans . . . This was the grand spectacle we had hoped . . . It is the only point in the world which commands a view of two seas . . .
—J. L. STEPHENS, *INCIDENTS OF TRAVEL IN CENTRAL AMERICA, CHIAPAS AND YUCATÁN*, 1841

FROMMER'S NATURE NOTES

Best Places to Bird-watch

As one of the world's foremost ecotravel destinations, Costa Rica is visited by thousands of avid bird-watchers each year. Every lodge outside of the city claims to have great bird-watching, and though bird-watching is dependent on numerous variables, some places just offer more opportunities to add to your life list. The following are lodges that I have found to offer superior bird-watching opportunities: Albergue de Montaña Savegre and Finca de Eddie Serano on the road to San Isidro de El General (both can almost guarantee sightings of resplendent quetzals); La Paloma Lodge in Drake Bay (where you can sit on the porch of your cabin as the avian parade goes by); Villa Blanca in San Ramon (on the edge of a cloud forest reserve where quetzals are often seen); Selva Verde Lodge, Chilamate (the rooms look straight into mostly undisturbed forest and the rain forest is just across the river); Lapa Rios on the Osa Peninsula (where I spotted two species of toucan parakeets, and hummingbirds before I ever made it in from the parking area); D'Galah Hotel in San José (the University of Costa Rica, an oasis of greenery in the city, is directly across the street).

Some of the best parks and preserves to visit include Monteverde Cloud Forest Reserve (resplendent quetzals and hummingbirds); Corcovado National Park (scarlet macaws); Caño Negro Wildlife Refuge (wading birds, including jabiru storks); Guayabo, Negritos and Pájaros Islands Biological Reserves in the Gulf of Nicoya (magnificent frigate birds and brown boobies); Palo Verde National Park (ibises, jacanas, storks, roseate spoonbills); Tortuguero National Park (great green macaws); and Rincon de la Vieja National Park (parakeets, curassows). Some good excursions to consider are the rafting float trips down the Corobicí near Liberia; boat trips to or at Tortuguero National Park; hikes in any cloud forest.

---

tains, among which are four volcanic peaks. Two of these, Poás and Irazú, are still active and have caused extensive damage during cycles of activity in the past two centuries. Much of the mountainous regions to the north and to the south of the capital of San José have been declared national parks to protect their virgin rain forests from logging.

Guanacaste and the Nicoya Peninsula This northwestern region of Costa Rica is the driest part of the country and has been likened to west Texas. Within this region is one of the last remnants of tropical dry forest left in Central America. Because the forest gives way to areas of savannah in Guanacaste, this is Costa Rica's "Wild West," where cattle ranching is the primary occupation. The Nicoya Peninsula is also the site of many of Costa Rica's sunniest and most popular beaches.

The Northern Zone This region lies to the north of San José and includes rain forests, cloud forests, the country's most active volcano (Arenal), Braulio Carillo National Park, and numerous remote lodges. Because this is one of the few regions of Costa Rica without any beaches, it primarily attracts people interested in nature. The northern zone also attracts windsurfers to Arenal Lake, which boasts some of the best windsurfing in the world.

The Central Pacific Coast The central Pacific coast is the most easily accessible coastline in Costa Rica, and consequently boasts the greatest number of beach resorts and hotels. Playa de Jacó is primarily a charter company destination attracting Canadian and German tourists, while Manuel Antonio caters to people seeking a bit more tranquility and beauty. This region is also the site of the highest peak in Costa Rica—Mount Chirripo—where frost is common.

COSTA RICA

NICARAGUA

Caribbean

Sea

PANAMA

Pacific

Ocean

Río San Juan

Santa Rosa

35

4

Chilamate

Aguas Zarcas

140

Quesada

141

Zarcero

San Ramón

Naranjo

Sarchi

Grecia

135

1

34

Bárcoles

Virilla

Escazú

209

San Ignacio

Poás Volcano

4

Barva Volcano

Alajuela

HEREDIA

SAN JOSÉ

Cartago

Orosi

Irazú Volcano

2

Braulio Carrillo National Park

CORDILLERA CENTRAL

Turrialba Volcano

Turrialba

San Miguel

Puerto Viejo

Río Sarapiquí

Barra del Colorado National Wildlife Refuge

Río Colorado

Tortuguero National Park

Barra del Colorado

Tortuguero

Tortuguero Canal

Guápiles

32

Siquirres

Río Reventazón

Río Pacuare

Río Reventazón

Limón

36

Cahuita

Playa Cahuita

Cahuita National Park

Bribri

Puerto Viejo

Río Telire

Cerro de la Muerte

Chirripó National Park

Cerro Chirripó

CORDILLERA DE TALAMANCA

Cerro Dúrika

Cerro Kámuk

Playa Esterillos

34

Quepos

Manuel Antonio National Park

Playa Manuel Antonio

San Isidro de el General

Playa Dominical

Playa Hermosa

Dominical

Pan American Hwy.

Coronado Bay

34

Palmar Norte

Sierpe

Río Sierpe

2

Piedras Blancas

San Vito

Caño Island

Drake

Osa Peninsula

Gulf

Dulce

Golfito

Corcovado National Park

Jiménez

Playa Zancudo

Zancudo

Pavonnes

Playa Tamales

Playa Carate

Airport ✈

The Caribbean Coast Most of the Caribbean coast is a wide, steamy lowland laced with rivers and blanketed with rain forests and banana plantations. The northern region of this coast is accessible only by boat or small plane and is the site of Tortuguero National Park, which is known for its nesting sea turtles and river-boat trips. The southern half of the Caribbean coast has several beautiful beaches, and as yet has few large hotels.

The South Pacific Coast This is one of Costa Rica's most remote and undeveloped regions. Much of the area is protected in Corcovado and La Amistad national parks. This is a hot, humid region characterized by rain forests and rugged coastlines.

HISTORY & POLITICS

DATELINE

- **13,000 B.C.** Earliest record of human inhabitants in Costa Rica.
- **1,000 B.C.** Olmec people from Mexico arrive in Costa Rica searching for rare blue jade.
- **1,000 B.C.–A.D. 1400** City of Guayabo is inhabited by as many as 10,000 people.
- **1502** Columbus discovers Costa Rica in September, landing at what is now Limón.
- **1519–1561** Spanish explore and colonize Costa Rica.
- **1563** City of Cartago is founded in Central Valley.
- **1737** San José is founded.
- **Late 1700s** Coffee is introduced as a cash crop.
- **1821** On September 15, Costa Rica, with the rest of Central America, gains independence from Spain.
- **1823** Capital is moved to San José.
- **1848** Costa Rica is proclaimed an independent republic.

(continues)

EARLY HISTORY Little is known of Costa Rica's history prior to its colonization by Spanish settlers. The pre-Columbian Indians who made their home in this region of Central America never developed the large cities or advanced culture that flowered farther north in what would become Guatemala, Belize, and Mexico. However, from scattered excavations around the country, primarily in the northwest, ancient artifacts have been unearthed that indicate a strong sense of aesthetics. Beautiful gold and jade jewelry, intricately carved grinding stones, and artistically painted terra-cotta ware point toward a highly skilled, if not large, population. The most enigmatic of these ancient relics are carved stone balls, some measuring several yards across and weighing many tons, that have been found along the southern Pacific coast. The purpose of these stone spheres remains a mystery: Some archeologists say that they may have been boundary markers; others think that they were celestial references. Still other scientists now claim that they are not manmade at all, but rather natural geological formations.

In 1502, on his fourth and last voyage to the New World, Christopher Columbus anchored just offshore from present-day Limón. Whether it was he who gave the country its name is open to discussion, but it was not long before the inappropriate name took hold. The earliest Spanish settlers found that, unlike the Indians farther north, the native population of Costa Rica was unwilling to submit to slavery. Despite their small numbers and scattered villages, they fought back against the Spanish. However, the superior Spanish firepower and the European diseases that had helped to subjugate the populations farther north conquered the natives. But when the fighting was finished, the settlers in Costa Rica found that there were no more Indians left to force into servitude. The settlers were forced to till their own lands, an exercise unheard of in other parts of Central America. Few pioneers headed this way because they could settle in Guatemala, where there was a large native work force. Costa Rica was nearly forgotten, as the Spanish crown looked elsewhere for riches to plunder and souls to convert.

It didn't take long for Costa Rica's few Spanish settlers to head for the hills, where they found rich volcanic soil and a climate that was less oppressive than in the lowlands. Cartago, the colony's first capital, was founded in 1563, but it would not be until the 1700s that more cities were founded in this agriculturally rich region. In the late 18th century, the first coffee plants were introduced, and because these plants thrived in the highlands, Costa Rica began to develop its first cash crop. Unfortunately, it was a long and difficult journey transporting the coffee to the Caribbean coast and thence to Europe, where the demand for coffee was growing.

FROM INDEPENDENCE TO THE PRESENT In 1821, Spain granted independence to its colonies in Central America. Costa Rica joined with its neighbors to form the Central American Federation, but in 1938 it withdrew to form a new nation and pursue its own interests, which differed considerably from those of the other Central American nations. By the mid-1800s, coffee was the country's main export. Land was given free to anyone willing to plant coffee on it, and plantation owners soon grew wealthy and powerful, creating Costa Rica's first elite class. Coffee plantation owners were powerful enough to elect their own representatives to the presidency.

This was a stormy period in Costa Rican history, and in 1856 the country was invaded by William Walker, a soldier of fortune from Tennessee who had grandiose dreams of presiding over a slavery state in Central America. Prior to his invasion of Costa Rica, he had invaded Baja California, and Nicaragua. The people of Central America were outraged by the actions of this man, who actually had backing from the U.S. president James Buchanan. The people of Costa Rica, led by their own president, Juan Rafael Mora, marched against Walker and chased him back to Nicaragua. Walker eventually surrendered to a U.S. warship in 1857, but in 1860 he attacked Honduras, claiming to be the president of that country. The Hondurans, who had had enough of Walker's shenanigans, promptly executed him.

Until 1890 coffee growers had to transport their coffee either by ox cart to the Pacific port of Puntarenas or by boat down the Río Sarapiquí to the Caribbean. In the 1870s, a progressive president proposed a railway from San José to the Caribbean coast to facilitate the transport of coffee to European markets. It took nearly 20 years for this plan to reach fruition and more than 4,000 workers lost their lives constructing the railway, which passed through dense jungles and rugged mountains on its journey from the Central Valley to the coast. It was under the direction of the project's second chief engineer, Minor Keith, that a momentous deal was made with the government of Costa Rica: In order to continue the financially strapped project, Keith had struck on the idea of using the railway right-of-way (land on either side of the tracks) as banana plantations. The export of this crop would help to finance the railway, and in exchange Keith would get a 99-year lease on 800,000 acres of land with a 20-year tax deferment. In 1878 the first bananas were shipped from Costa Rica, and in 1899 Keith and a partner formed the United Fruit Company, a company that would eventually become the largest landholder in Central America and cause political disputes and wars throughout the region.

In 1889 Costa Rica held what is considered the first free election in Central American history. The opposition candidate won the election, and the control of the government passed from the hands of one political party to those of another without bloodshed or hostilities. Thus Costa Rica established itself as the region's only true democracy. In 1948 this democratic process was challenged by a former president (who had been president from 1940 to 1944), Rafael Angel Calderón, who lost a bid at a second term in office by a narrow margin. Calderón, who had the backing of Communist labor unions, refused to yield the country's leadership to the rightfully elected

DATELINE

- **1856** Battle of Santa Rosa; Costa Ricans defeat the United States, who backed proslavery advocate William Walker.

- **1870s** First banana plantations are formed.

- **1889** First election is won by an opposition party, establishing democratic process in Costa Rica.

- **1899** The United Fruit Company is founded by railroad builder Minor Keith.

- **1948** After aborted revolution, Costa Rican army is abolished.

- **1987** President Oscar Arias Sánchez is awarded the Nobel Peace Prize for orchestrating the Central American Peace Plan.

president Otillio Ulate, and a revolution ensued. Calderón was eventually defeated. In the wake of this crisis, a new constitution was drafted; among other changes, it abolished Costa Rica's army so that such a revolution could never happen again.

Peace and democracy have become of tantamount importance to Costa Ricans since the revolution of 1948. When Oscar Arias Sánchez was elected president in 1986, his main goal was to seek a solution to the ongoing war in Nicaragua, and one of his first actions was to close down Contra bases inside Costa Rica and enforce Costa Rica's position of neutrality. In 1987 Sánchez won the Nobel Peace Prize for initiating a Central American peace plan aimmed at settling the war in Nicaragua.

Costa Rica's 100 years of nearly uninterrupted democracy have helped make it the most stable economy in Central America. This stability and adherence to the democratic process are a source of great pride to Costa Ricans. They like to think of their country as a "Switzerland of Central America" not only because of its herds of dairy cows but also because of its staunch position of neutrality in a region that has been torn by nearly constant civil wars and revolutions for more than 200 years.

2. CULTURAL & SOCIAL LIFE

Art Though the pre-Columbian cultures of Costa Rica were small compared to those of the Mayas, Aztecs, and Incas, they did leave the country with an amazing wealth of artistically designed artifacts. Gold and jade jewelry, painted terra-cotta pots, and carved stone sculptures and grinding stones from this period can be seen in several San José museums. Since the Spanish Conquest, Costa Rica's artists have followed European artistic styles. The Museo de Arte Costarricense exhibits works by the country's better-known artists of the last 400 years, with most of the artistic movements of those years represented.

Architecture The pre-Columbian peoples of Costa Rica left few signs of their habitation. The excavations at Guayabo, little more than building foundations and paved streets, are the country's main archeological site. Numerous earthquakes over the centuries have destroyed most of what the Spanish built. One such earthquake, in 1910, halted the construction of a cathedral in Cartago, the ruins of which are now a peaceful park in the middle of town. The ruins of another church, the oldest in Costa Rica, can be found near the village of Ujarrás in the Orosi Valley. This church was built in 1693 and abandoned in 1833 when the village was flooded. The central plaza in Heredia has a historic church built in 1796, and also on this square is an old fortress tower known as El Fortín.

Religion Costa Ricans on the whole are devout Roman Catholics. The patron saint of Costa Rica is **Neustra Señora de Los Angeles** (Our Lady of the Angels) who has a Byzantine-style church dedicated to her in Cartago. In the church is a shrine which contains a tiny figure of La Negrita, the Black Virgin, to whom miraculous healing powers have been attributed. The walls of the shrine are covered with a fascinating array of tiny silver images left as thanks for cures affected by La Negrita. August 2 is the day dedicated to her, when thousands of people walk from San José to Cartago in devotion to this powerful statue.

The People When the first Spaniards arrived in Costa Rica, the small Indian population was further reduced by wars and disease until they became a minority. Consequently, most of the population of Costa Rica today is of pure Spanish

IMPRESSIONS

We, the people of Costa Rica, believe that peace is much more than the absence of hostility among men and nations . . . To us peace is the only ideal that, once achieved, will give us the right to call ourselves . . . human beings.
—Oscar Arias, Former Costa Rican President and Nobel Peace Prize Laureate

FROMMER'S NATURE NOTES
Sea Turtles

Few places in the world have as many sea turtle nesting sites as Costa Rica. Up and down both coasts, five species of these huge marine reptiles come ashore at specific times of year to dig nests in the sand and lay their eggs. Sea turtles are endangered throughout the world due to overhunting, accidental deaths in fishing nets, development on beaches formerly used as nesting areas, and the collection and sale (often illegally) of their eggs. International trade in sea turtle products is already prohibited by most countries (including the United States), but sea turtle numbers continue to dwindle.

Among the species of sea turtles that nest on Costa Rica's beaches are olive Ridley (known for their mass egg-laying migrations known as *arribadas*), leatherback, hawksbill, green, and Pacific green turtles. Excursions to see nesting turtles have become common, and though these tours are fascinating, please make sure that you and your guide do not disturb the turtles. Any light source (other than red-tinted flashlights) can confuse female turtles and cause them to return to the sea without laying their eggs. In fact, as more and more development takes place on the Costa Rican coast, the lights created by hotels may cause the number of nesting turtles to drop. Luckily most of the nesting beaches have been protected as national parks. The following are the main places to see nesting sea turtles: Santa Rosa National Park (near Liberia), Las Baulas National Marine Park (near Tamarindo), Ostional National Wildlife Refuge (near Playa Nosara), Cocovado National Park (on the Osa Peninsula), Tortuguero National Park (on the northern Caribbean coast).

descent, and it is not at all surprising to see blond Costa Ricans. However, there are still some remnant Indian populations on reservations around the country. On the Caribbean coast, there is also a substantial population of English-speaking black Créoles who came over from Jamaica to work on the railroad and in the banana plantations. They have never moved far inland, preferring the humid lowlands to the cool Central Valley. For the most part, these different groups coexist without friction.

Costa Ricans, who are also known as *Ticos*, have a high literacy rate and nearly 50% of the work force is women. There is a large, working middle class, and there is not the gross disparity between rich and poor that you see in other Central American countries.

Performing Arts & Evening Entertainment   One of the very first things that Costa Ricans did with their newfound coffee wealth in the mid-19th century was to build an opera house. The elite were upset that opera singers were bypassing their country when they toured the Americas. Today that opera house is known as the Teatro Nacional and is as popular as it was 100 years ago. Hardly a night goes by that some performance isn't held in the stately theater.

However, despite San José's interest in classical music, mariachi, marimba, and salsa music have a firm grip on the hearts of all Ticos. In San José there are several 24-hour restaurants where mariachi and marimba music can be heard live and for free at any hour of the day or night. Discos specializing in salsa music are also common throughout the country. While down on the Caribbean coast, reggae and soca music are also popular.

Sports & Recreation   Soccer is the national sport of Costa Rica, but baseball, polo, squash, and handball are also popular. Costa Rica has less than half a dozen golf courses, including the Cariari Hotel and Country Club in San José, Los Reyes at Guacima in Alajuela, the Costa Rican Country Club in Escazú, and the Tango

Mar golf course on the Nicoya Peninsula. Sportfishing is very popular here, and the waters in and around Costa Rica abound with everything from trout and tarpon to sailfish and marlin. There are fishing tournaments throughout the year and fishing boats for hire on both coasts.

Surfing is another sport that has caught on in a big way in Costa Rica. There are excellent surfing waves at various points on both costs, and many hotels offer off-season discounts to surfers.

3. FOOD & DRINK

Very similar to other Central American cuisines, Costa Rican food is not especially memorable. Perhaps this is why there is so much international food available throughout the country. However, if you really want to save money, you'll find that Costa Rican food is always the cheapest food available. It is primarily served in sodas, Costa Rica's equivalent of diners.

FOOD
MEALS & DINING CUSTOMS

Rice and beans are the basis of Costa Rican meals. At breakfast, they're called *gallo pinto* and come with everything from eggs to steak to seafood. At lunch or dinner, rice and beans go by the name *casado* (which also means "married"). A casado usually comes with cabbage-and-tomato salad, fried plantains (a type of banana), and a meat dish of some sort.

Dining hours in Costa Rica are flexible: Many restaurants in San José are open 24 hours, a sign that Ticos are willing to eat at any time of the night or day. However, expensive restaurants tend to open for lunch between 11am and 2pm and for dinner between 6pm and midnight.

THE CUISINE

Appetizers *Bocas* are served with drinks in most bars. Often the bocas are free, but even if they aren't, they're very inexpensive. Popular bocas include *gallos* (stuffed tortillas), ceviche, and tamales.

Soups Black-bean soup, *sopa negra*, is a creamy soup with a poached or boiled egg soaking in the broth. It is one of the most popular of Costa Rican soups and shows up on many menus. *Olla de carne* is a delicious soup made with beef and several local vegetables, including chayote, ayote, yuca, and plantains, all of which have textures and flavors similar to various winter squashes. *Sopa de mondongo* is made with tripe, the stomach of a cow, which some love and others find disgusting. *Picadillo* is a vegetable stew with a little bit of meat in it. It's often served as a side dish with a *casado*.

Sandwiches & Snacks Ticos love to snack, and there are a large variety of tasty little sandwiches and snacks available on the street, at snack bars, and in sodas. *Arreglados* are little meat-filled sandwiches, as are *tortas*, which are served on little rolls with a bit of salad tucked into them. *Gallos* are tortillas stuffed with meat, beans, or cheese. Tacos, tamales, and empanadas also are quite common.

Meat Costa Rica is beef country, one of the tropical nations that has converted much of its rain-forest land to pastures for raising beef cattle. Consequently, beef is cheap and plentiful, although it may be a bit tougher than you are used to. Spit-roasted chicken is also very popular here and is surprisingly tender.

Seafood Costa Rica has two coasts, and as you would expect, there is plenty of seafood available everywhere in the country. *Corvina* (sea bass) is the most commonly served fish, and it is prepared innumerable ways, including as *ceviche*, a sort of marinated salad. Surprisingly, although Costa Rica is a major exporter of shrimp and lobster, both are very expensive here. In fact, shrimp is often more expensive than lobster. The reason is that most of the shrimp and lobster are exported, causing them to be very expensive at home.

Vegetables On the whole, you will find vegetables surprisingly lacking in the meals you are served in Costa Rica. The standard vegetable with any meal is a little pile of shredded cabbage topped with a slice or two of tomato. For a much more satisfying and filling salad, order *palmito* (hearts of palm salad). Hearts of palm are considered a delicacy in most places because an entire palm tree (albeit a small one) must be cut down to extract the heart. The heart is a bit like the inner part of an artichoke—many leaves layered around one another. These leaves are chopped into large pieces and served with other fresh vegetables, a salad dressing on top. Even here, where the palms are plentiful, palmito is relatively expensive. If you want something more than this, you'll have to order a side dish such as *picadillo*, a stew of vegetables with a bit of meat in it. Most people have a hard time thinking of *plátanos* (plantains) as vegetables, but these giant relatives of bananas are sweet and require cooking before they can be eaten. Fried plátanos are one of my favorite dishes. *Yuca* (manioc root) is another starchy staple vegetable of Costa Rica.

One more vegetable worth mentioning is the *pejibaye*, a form of palm fruit that looks like a miniature orange coconut. Boiled Pejibayes are frequently sold from carts on the streets of San José. When cut in half, a pejibaye reveals a large seed surrounded by soft, creamy flesh and looks a bit like an avocado. You can eat it like an avocado, too, by just scooping the flesh out.

Fruits Costa Rica has a wealth of delicious tropical fruits. The most common are mangoes (season begins in May), papayas, pineapples, and bananas. Other less well-known fruits inlcude the *marañon*, which is the fruit of the cashew tree and has orange or yellow glossy skin; the *granadilla* or *granada* (passion fruit); the *mamón chino*, which Asian travelers will immediately recognize as the rambutan; and the *carambola* (star fruit). When ordering *ensalada de fruita* (fruit salad) in a restaurant, make sure that it is made with fresh fruit and does not come with ice cream and Jell-O (unless that is what you want). What a shock I had when I first received a bowl of canned fruit covered with Jell-O cubes and three scoops of ice cream!

Desserts *Queque seco*, which literally translates as "dry cake," is the same as pound cake. *Tres leches* cake on the other hand is so moist you almost need to eat it with a spoon. *Flan de coco* is a sweet coconut flan. There are many other sweets available, many of which are made with milk and raw sugar (rich and sweet).

COSTA RICAN MENU TERMS

Bocas Appetizers
Casado Lunch or dinner meal consisting of rice, beans, a main dish, and fried plantains
Ceviche Marinated seafood salad
Corvina Sea bass
Gallo pinto Breakfast dish consisting of rice, beans, and eggs or meat
Horchata Fresco made with rice flour and cinnamon
Palmito Hearts of palm salad
Pinolillo Fresco made with roasted corn flour
Plátanos Plantains, similar to bananas
Frescos Water- or milk-based drinks made in a blender with fresh fruit
Tortas Small sandwiches

DRINKS
WATER & SOFT DRINKS

Although water in most of Costa Rica is said to be safe to drink, visitors often become ill shortly after arriving in Costa Rica. Play it safe and stick to bottled water, which is readily available. *Aqua mineral,* or simply *soda,* is sparkling water in Costa Rica. It's inexpensive and refreshing. Most major brands of soft drinks are also available.

FROMMER'S NATURE NOTES
The Resplendent Quetzal

Revered by the pre-Columbian cultures throughout Central America, the resplendent quetzal has been called the most beautiful bird on earth. Ancient Aztec and Maya Indians believed the quetzal protected them in battle, and even the bird's brilliant breast plumage has an Indian legend to explain it: When Spanish conquistador Pedro de Alvarado defeated Maya chieftain Tecun Uman in 1524 near what is today the town of Quezaltenango, Guatemala, the Maya chief was mortally wounded in the chest. Tecun Uman's protector quetzal covered the dying chieftain's body, and when, upon Tecun Uman's death, the quetzal arose, the once white-breasted bird had a blood-red breast. So integral a part of Guatemalan culture is the quetzal that its name is given to that country's currency.

About the size of a robin, the males of this species have brilliant red breasts; iridescent emerald green heads, backs, and wings; and white tail feathers complemented by a pair of iridescent green tail feathers that are nearly two feet long. These birds live only in the dense cloud forests that cloak the higher slopes of Central America's mountains. Throughout their range, quetzals are endangered, and though many areas of cloud forest have been preserved as habitat for these beautiful birds, researchers have recently discovered that the birds do not spend their entire lives within the cloud forest. After nesting, between March and July, quetzals migrate down to lower slopes in search of food. These lower slopes have not been preserved in most cases, and now conservationists are trying to salvage enough lower elevation forests to help the quetzals survive. Hopefully, enough land will soon be set aside to assure the perpetuation of this magnificent species of bird.

Though for many years, Monteverde Cloud Forest Preserve was the place to see quetzals, throngs of people crowding the preserve's trails now make it difficult to see any wildlife. Other places where you are more likely to see quetzals are in the Los Angeles Cloud Forest Reserve near San Ramon, on the Cerro de la Muerte between San José and San Isidro de El General, in Tapantí National Wildlife Refuge, and in Chirripó National Park.

Frescos, a bit like milkshakes, are my favorite drinks in Costa Rica. They are usually made with fresh fruit and milk or water. Among the more common fruits used are mangoes, papayas, blackberries (*moras*), and pineapples. Some of the more unusual frescos are *horchata* (made with rice flour and a lot of cinnamon) and *pinolillo* (made with roasted corn flour). The former is wonderful; the latter requires an open mind. Order *un fresco de leche sin hielo* if you are trying to avoid untreated water.

BEER, WINE & LIQUOR

The German presence in Costa Rica over the years has produced several fine beers, which are fairly inexpensive. Heineken also is available. Costa Rica distills a wide variety of liquors, and you'll save money by ordering these rather than imported brands. Imported wines are available at reasonable prices in the better restaurants throughout the country. You can save a bit of money by ordering a South American wine rather than a European one. Café Rica and Salicsa are two coffee liqueurs made in Costa Rica; the former is very similar to Kahlua, and the latter is a cream coffee liqueur. Both are delicious.

4. RECOMMENDED BOOKS & FILMS

BOOKS

Some of the books mentioned below may be difficult to track down in U.S. bookstores, but you'll find them all in abundance in Costa Rica's bookstores. Buy them during you trip to deepen your Costa Rica experience, or bring them home with you to illuminate your memories.

GENERAL *The Costa Ricans* (Prentice Hall Press, 1987), by Richard, Karen, and Mavis Biesanz, is a well-written account of the politics and culture of Costa Rica.

To learn more about the life and culture of Costa Rica's Talamanca Coast, an area populated by Afro-Caribbean people whose forebears immigrated from Caribbean islands in the early 19th century, pick up a copy of *What Happen: A Folk-History of Costa Rica's Talamanca Coast* (Publications in English, 1993) by Paula Palmer. Or, for a look at the perspective of the indigenous people of the Talamanca region, read Palmer, Sanchez, and Mayorga's *Taking Care of Sibo's Gifts: An Environmental Treatise from Costa Rica's Kekoldi Indigenous Reserve* (Editorama, 1991).

The Costa Rica Reader (Grove Press, 1989), edited by Marc Edelman and Joanne Kenen, is a collection of essays on Costa Rican topics. For insight into Costa Rican politics, economics, and culture, this weighty book is invaluable. *Costa Rica: A Traveler's Literary Companion* (Whereabouts Press, 1994), edited by Barbara Ras and with a forward by Oscar Arias Sánchez, is a collection of short stories by Costa Rican writers and is organized by region of the country.

NATURAL HISTORY *Costa Rica National Parks* (Editorial Heliconia, Fundacion Neotropica, 1988), by Mario A. Boza, is published in Madrid and available in both hardbound and softcover editions. It is a beautiful picture book of Costa Rica's national parks. Each of the country's national parks is represented by several color photos and a short description of the park in Spanish and English. *Costa Rica's National Parks and Preserves* (The Mountaineers, 1993), by Joseph Franke, is similar but with fewer photos. *The Illustrated Geography of Costa Rica* (Trejos Hermanos) is also a hardcover book full of wonderful photos and makes a good memento of your trip.

Dr. Donald Perry's fascinating *Life Above the Jungle Floor* (Don Perro Press, 1991) is an account of Perry's research into the life of the tropical rain-forest canopy. Perry is well known for the cable-car network he built through the rainforest treetops so that he could study this area of great biological and botanical activity.

Lessons of the Rainforest (Sierra, 1990), edited by Suzanne Head and Robert Heinzman, is a collection of essays by leading authorities in the fields of biology, ecology, history, law, and economy who look at the issues surrounding tropical deforestation. *A Guide to the Birds of Costa Rica* (Christopher Helm Ltd, 1991), by F. Gary Stiles and Alexander Skutch, is an invaluable guide to identifying the many birds you see during your stay. It is often available for examination at nature lodges.

Other interesting natural-history books that will give you a look at the plants and animals of Costa Rica include *Sarapiquí Chronicle* (Smithsonian Institution Press, 1991) by Allen Young; *Costa Rica Natural History* (University of Chicago Press, 1983) by Daniel Janzen; *Butterflies of Costa Rica* (Princeton University Press, 1987) by Philip DeVries; and *Orquideas de Costa Rica* (Editorial UCR) by Rafael Rodriguez, Dora Mora, Maria Barahona, and Norris Williams.

FILM

1492—Conquest of Paradise (1993), starring Gerard Depardieu, is the story of Christopher Columbus's discovery of the Americas and was filmed at several locations in Costa Rica, including the Pacific and Caribbean coasts, Jacó and Limón.

CHAPTER 2

PLANNING A TRIP TO COSTA RICA

Costa Rica is one of the fastest-growing tourist destinations in the Americas, and as the number of people visiting Costa Rica has increased, so too has the need for pretrip planning. When is the best time to go to Costa Rica? The cheapest time? Should I rent a car and what will it cost? Where should I go in Costa Rica? What are the hotels like? How much should I budget for my trip? These are just a few of the important questions that this chapter will answer for you so you can be prepared when you arrive in Costa Rica.

1. INFORMATION, ENTRY REQUIREMENTS & MONEY

SOURCES OF INFORMATION

In the United States, you can get information on Costa Rica by contacting the **Costa Rica Brochure Service** (tel. toll free 800/327-7033), a representative of the **Costa Rican Tourist Board (I.C.T., or Instituto Costarricense de Turismo)** in the United States.

Once you are in Costa Rica, you'll find an I.C.T. information center desk at Juan Santamaría International Airport (to the left before you go up the stairs after clearing Customs). If you do not have a room reservation, the helpful folks here will call around to try to find you one. The main tourist information center is beneath the Plaza de la Cultura, Calle 5 between Avenida Central and Avenida 2 (tel. 222-1090 or 223-8423) in downtown San José. The staff here is particularly helpful. They even have photo albums filled with pictures from various lodges around the country, so you can get an idea of what places look like before you decide to go.

ENTRY REQUIREMENTS

DOCUMENTS

SECURING & RENEWING YOUR U.S. PASSPORT Passport applications are available from authorized post offices, clerks of court, or passport agencies. It is also possible to request an application—Form DSP-11 for a new passport or DSP-82 for a renewal—by mail, from Passport Services, Office of Correspondence, Department of State, 1425 K St. NW, Washington, DC 20522-1075. The back of the application gives the addresses of 13 agencies that can process the applications, including Boston, Chicago, Honolulu, Houston, Los Angeles, Miami, New Orleans, New York City, Philadelphia, San Francisco, Seattle, Stamford, Conn., and Washington, D.C. Be forewarned that lines are long in these agencies, and you can get a passport more quickly and easily from a post office or courthouse. (Processing usually takes four weeks in either case.)

The passport application must be accompanied by proof of U.S. Citizenship: an old passport, a certified copy of your birth certificate complete with registrar's seal, a report of birth abroad, or naturalized citizenship documents. In addition, a driver's license, employee identification card, military ID, or student ID card with photo is acceptable.

The application must be accompanied by two identical recent two- by two-inch photos, either color or black-and-white with a white background. Look in the *Yellow Pages* of your telephone book for places that take passport photos and expect them to be expensive (up to $9 for two).

First-time applicants age 18 and older pay $65 ($55 plus a $10 first-time processing fee); under 18 and the fee is $40 ($30 plus a $10 first-time fee). Parents or guardians may apply for children under 13, presenting two photos for each child. Children 14 years and older must apply in person. Anyone 16 years or older who has an expired passport issued no more than 12 years ago may reapply by mail, submitting the old document with new photos and pink renewal form DSP-82. You must send a check or money order for $55; there is no additional processing fee. Adult passports are valid for 10 years; children's passports, for 5 years.

If your passport is lost or stolen, you must submit form DSP-64 in person to reapply. There is a $10 processing fee.

The booklet "Your Trip Abroad" (publication no. 044-000-02335-1) provides general information about passports and is available for $1.25 per copy from the U.S. Government Printing Office, Superintendent of Documents, P.O. Box 371954, Pittsburgh, PA 15250-7954 (tel. 202/783-3238 8am to 4pm eastern time; fax 202/512-2250).

For recorded passport information, or to report a lost or stolen passport, call 202/647-0518.

TOURIST VISAS If you are a citizen of the United States, Canada, Great Britain, or Northern Ireland, you may visit Costa Rica for a maximum of 90 days. No visa is necessary, but you must have a valid passport (U.S. citizens can use an original certified birth certificate and a driver's license, though this is an inconvenience when cashing traveler's checks, renting a car, or returning to the United States). If you are a citizen of the Republic of Ireland, a visa, valid passport, and round-trip ticket are required, and you can stay for only 30 days. Citizens of New Zealand or Australia need a valid passport, but no visa to enter Costa Rica, and can stay for 30 days. If you want to extend your visa, you will need to apply to the Department of Immigration with your passport.

If you overstay your visa or entry stamp, you will have to pay around $50 for an exit visa. If you need to get an exit visa, talk to a travel agent in San José. They can usually get the exit visa for you for a small fee. If you want to stay longer than the validity of your entry stamp or visa, the easist thing to do is cross the border into Panama or Nicaragua for 72 hours and them reenter Costa Rica on a new entry stamp or visa.

THE COLÓN, THE U.S. DOLLAR & THE BRITISH POUND

In late 1993, there were approximately 148 colónes to the American dollar, or 223 colónes to the British pound. However, because the colón has been in a constant state of devaluation, expect this rate to have changed somewhat by the time you arrive. Because of this devaluation and the accompanying inflation, this book lists prices in U.S. dollars only.

Colónes	U.S. $	U.K. £	Colónes	U.S. $	U.K. £
5	0.035	0.02	1,000	7.0	4.0
10	0.07	0.04	5,000	35.0	20.0
25	0.175	0.1	10,000	70.0	40.0
50	0.35	0.2	25,000	175.0	100.0
75	0.525	0.3	50,000	350.0	200.0
100	0.7	0.4	75,000	525.0	300.0
200	1.4	0.8	100,000	700.0	400.0
300	2.1	1.2	200,000	1,400.0	800.0
400	2.8	1.6	300,000	2,100.0	1,200.0
500	3.5	2.0	500,000	3,500.0	2,000.0
750	5.25	3.0	1,000,000	7,000.0	4,000.0

If you need a visa or have other questions about Costa Rica, you can contact any of the following Costa Rican embassies: in the **United States,** 2114 S St. NW, Washington, DC 20008 (tel. 202/234-2945); in **Canada,** 135 York St., Suite 208, Ottawa, Ontario K1N 5T4 (tel. 613/562-2855); in **Great Britain,** 14 Lancaster Gate, London, England W2 3LH (tel. 71-723-1772). Residents of Northern Ireland use the embassy in London. There are no embassies in Australia or New Zealand.

MONEY

CASH & CURRENCY The unit of currency in Costa Rica is the colón ($¢$). In late 1993, there were approximately 148 colónes to the American dollar, but because the colón has been in a constant state of devaluation, expect this rate to have changed somewhat by the time you arrive. Because of this devaluation and accompanying inflation, this book lists prices in U.S. dollars only.

The colón is divided into 100 centimos. There are coins of 50 and 100 centimos and 1, 2, 5, 10, and 20 colónes. There are notes in denominations of 50, 100, 500, 1,000, and 5,000 colónes. You might also encounter a special issue 5-colón bill that is a popular gift and tourist souvenir. It is valid currency, although it sells for much more than its face value.

TRAVELER'S CHECKS Traveler's checks can be readily changed at hotels and banks. The exchange rate at banks is sometimes slightly higher than at hotels, but it can take a very long time to change money at a bank, and therefore it is not recommended.

CREDIT CARDS Major international credit cards accepted readily at hotels throughout Costa Rica include American Express, MasterCard, and VISA. The less expensive hotels tend to take cash only. Many restaurants and stores also accept credit cards. Before paying for a hotel with your credit card, check to see if the policy is to charge extra (from 5% to 8%) for credit cards.

WHAT THINGS COST IN SAN JOSÉ — U.S. $

Taxi from the airport to the city center	12.00
Local telephone call	.03
Double at Hotel Herradura (very expensive)	$125.00
Double at Hotel Grano de Oro (moderate)	$69.00
Double at Hotel Bienvenido (budget)	$19.00
Lunch for one at Café de Teatro Nacional (moderate)	9.50
Lunch for one at Soda La Central (budget)	3.50
Dinner for one, without wine, at El Balcon de Europa (expensive)	16.50
Dinner for one, without wine, at La Cocina de Leña (moderate)	12.25
Dinner for one, without wine, at Pollos Gallo Pinto (budget)	5.45
Bottle of beer	.85
Coca-Cola	.85
Cup of coffee	.60
Roll of ASA 100 Kodacolor film 24 exposures	5.85
Admission to the Jade Museum	Free
Movie ticket	2.05
Ticket at Teatro Melico Salazar	4.05

2. WHEN TO GO—CLIMATE, HOLIDAYS & EVENTS

CLIMATE Costa Rica is a tropical country and has distinct wet and dry seasons. However, some regions are rainy all year and others are very dry and sunny for most of the year. Temperatures vary primarily with elevation, not with season. On the coasts it is hot all year, while up in the mountains, it can be cool at night any time of year. In the highest elevations (10,000 to 12,000 feet), frost is common.

Average Monthly Temperatures and Rainfall in San José

	Jan	Feb	Mar	Apr	May	June	July	Aug	Sept	Oct	Nov	Dec
Temp (°F)	66	66	69	71	71	71	70	70	71	69	68	67
Temp (°C)	19	19	20.5	21.5	21.5	21.5	21	21	21.5	20.5	20	19.5
Days of Rain	1	0	1	4	17	20	18	19	20	22	14	4

Generally speaking, the rainy season (or "green season," as the tourism industry has begun calling it) is from May to mid-November. Costa Ricans call this wet time of year their winter. The dry season, considered summer by Costa Ricans, is from mid-November to April. In Guanacaste, the dry northwestern province, the dry season lasts several weeks longer than in other places. Even in the rainy season, days often start sunny, with rain falling in the afternoon and evening. On the Caribbean coast, especially south of Limón, you can count on rain all year round, although this area gets less rain in September and October than the rest of the country gets. The best time of year to visit is in December and January, when everything is still green from the rains, but the sky is clear. However, advantages to traveling to Costa Rica in the rainy season are that prices are lower, the country is greener, and there are fewer tourists. Rain doesn't usually fall all day long, and when it does, it's a good opportunity to climb into a hammock and catch up on your reading.

HOLIDAYS Because Costa Rica is a Roman Catholic country, most of its holidays and celebrations are church related. The major celebrations of the year are Christmas, New Year's, and Easter, which are all celebrated for several days. Keep in mind that Holy Week (Easter Week) is the biggest holiday time in Costa Rica and many families head for the beach (this is the last holiday before school starts). Also there is no public transportation on Holy Thursday or Good Friday. Official holidays in Costa Rica include: January 1 (New Year's Day), March 19 (St. Joseph's Day), Thursday and Friday of Holy Week, April 11 (Juan Santamaría's Day), May 1 (Labor Day), June 29 (Saints Peter and Paul's Day), July 25 (annexation of the province of Guanacaste), August 2 (Virgin of Los Angeles's Day), August 15 (Mother's Day), September 15 (Independence Day), October 12 (Discovery of America), December 8 (Immaculate Conception of the Virgin Mary), December 25 (Christmas Day), December 31 (New Year's Eve).

COSTA RICA
CALENDAR OF EVENTS

JANUARY

☐ **Fiesta of Santa Cruz,** Santa Cruz, Guanacaste. A religious celebration honoring the Black Christ of Esquipulas (a famous Guatemalan statue) features folk dancing, marimba music, and bullfights. Mid–January.

FEBRUARY

☐ **Fiesta of the Diablitos,** Rey Curré village near San Isidro de El General. Boruca Indians wearing wooden devil and bull masks perform dances representative of the Spanish conquest of Central America. Fireworks displays, Indian handcrafts market. Date varies.

MARCH

☐ **Día del Boyero** (Ox Cart Drivers' Day), San Antonio de Escazú. Colorfully painted ox carts parade through this suburb of San José and local priests bless the oxen. Second Sunday.

APRIL

☐ **Holy Week** (week before Easter). Religious processions are held in cities and towns throughout the country. Dates vary from year to year (between late March and early April).

☐ **Juan Santamaría Day,** Alajuela. Costa Rica's national hero is honored with parades, concerts, and dances. April 11.

MAY

☐ **Carrera de San Juan,** The country's biggest marathon, runs through the mountains from the outskirts of Cartago to the outskirts of San José. May 17.

JULY

☐ **Fiesta of the Virgin of the Sea,** Puntarenas. A regatta of colorfully decorated boats carrying a statue of Puntarenas's patron saint. A similar festival is held at Playa de Coco. Saturday closest to July 16.

☐ **Annexation of Guanacaste Day,** Liberia. Tico-style bullfights, folk dancing, horseback parades, rodeos, concerts, and other events in celebration of this region becoming part of Costa Rica. July 24.

AUGUST

☐ **Día de San Ramon,** San Ramon. More than two dozen statues of saints from various towns are brought to San Ramon where they are paraded through the streets. August 31.

☐ **Fiesta of the Virgin of Los Angeles,** Cartago. This is the annual pilgrimage day of the patron saint of Costa Rica, and many people walk from San José to the basilica in Cartago. August.

SEPTEMBER

☐ **Costa Rica's Independence Day,** all over the country. Nighttime parades of children. September 15.

OCTOBER

☐ **Fiesta del Maiz,** Upala. A celebration of corn with beauty queens wearing outfits made from corn plants. October 12.

☐ **Limón Carnival,** Limón. A smaller version of Mardi Gras complete with floats and dancing in the streets. Commemorates Columbus's discovery of Costa Rica. Week of October 12.

DECEMBER

☐ **Festejos Populares,** San José. Bullfights, a horseback parade (El Tope), a carnival with street dancing and floats, and an amusement park at the fairgrounds in Zapote. On the night of December 31, there is a dance in the Parque Central. Last week of December.

☐ **Día de la Polvora,** San Antonio de Belen and Jesus Maria de San Mateo. Fireworks displays to honor Our Lady of the Immaculate Conception. December 8.

☐ **Fiesta de la Yeguita,** Nicoya. A statue of the Virgin of Guadalupe is paraded through the streets accompanied by traditional music and dancing. December 12.

☐ **Fiesta de los Negritos,** Boruca. Boruca Indians celebrate the feast day of their patron saint, the Virgin of the Immaculate Conception, with costumed dances and traditional music. December 8.

☐ **Las Posadas,** throughout the country. Children and carolers go door to door seeking lodging to re-enact Joseph and Mary's search for a place to stay. Starting December 15.

3. HEALTH, INSURANCE & OTHER CONCERNS

HEALTH Vaccinations No vaccinations are required for a visit to Costa Rica, unless you are coming from an area where yellow fever exists. However, because sanitation is generally not as good as it is in developed countries, you may be exposed to diseases for which you may wish to get vaccinations: typhoid, polio, tetanus, and infectious hepatitis (gamma globulin). If you are planning to stay in major cities, you stand little risk of encountering any of these diseases, but if you venture out into remote regions of the country, you stand a higher risk.

Malaria is found in the lowlands on both coasts. Although it is rarely found in urban areas, it is still a problem in remote wooded regions, and in 1993, there was a malaria outbreak in Playa Jacó. Malaria prophylaxes are available, but several have side effects and others are of questionable effectiveness. Consult your doctor or your local health board as to what is currently considered the best preventative treatment for malaria. Be sure to ask whether a recommended drug will cause you to be hypersensitive to the sun. It would be a shame to come down here for the beaches and then never be able to go out in the sun. Because malaria-carrying mosquitoes come out only at night, you should do as much as possible to avoid being bitten by mosquitoes after dark. If you are in a malarial area, wear long pants and long sleeves, use insect repellent, and sleep under a mosquito net or burn mosquito coils (similar to incense, but with a pesticide). Of greater concern may be an outbreak of dengue fever that occurred in 1993. Dengue fever is similar to malaria, and is spread by a daytime mosquito. This mosquito seems to be most common in lowland urban areas, and Liberia and Limón were the worst hit cities in Costa Rica. If you should develop a high fever accompanied by nausea, diarrhea, or vomiting during or shortly after a visit to Costa Rica, consult a physician and explain that you have been in a country with both malaria and dengue fever. Many people are convinced that taking B-complex vitamins daily will help prevent mosquitoes from biting you.

Costa Rica has been relatively free from the cholera epidemic that has spread through much of Latin America in recent years. This is largely due to an extensive public awareness campaign that has promoted good hygiene and increased sanitation. Your chances of contracting cholera while you're here are very slight. However, it is still advisable to avoid *ceviche*, a raw seafood salad, if it has any shellfish in it. Shellfish are known carriers of cholera.

Riptides Many of Costa Rica's beaches have riptides, strong currents that can drag swimmers out to sea. A riptide occurs when water that has been dumped on the shore by strong waves forms a channel back out to open water. These channels have strong currents. If you get caught in a riptide, you can't escape the current by swimming toward shore; that is the equivalent of swimming upstream in a river. To break free of the current, swim parallel to shore, and use the energy of the waves to help you get back to the beach.

INSURANCE Before leaving on your trip, contact your health-insurance company and find out whether your insurance will cover you while you are away. If not, contact a travel agent and ask about travel health-insurance policies. A travel agent can also tell you about trip insurance to cover cancellations or loss of baggage. If you have homeowner's or renter's insurance, you may be covered against theft and loss even while you are on vacation. Be sure to check this before taking out additional insurance. Some credit cards provide trip insurance when you charge an airline ticket, but be sure to check with your credit-card company. If you decide that your current insurance is inadequate, you can contact your travel agent for information on various types of travel insurance, including insurance against cancellation of a prepaid tour should this become necessary. The following companies offer various types of travel insurance: **Teletrip** (Mutual of Omaha), P.O. Box 31685, Omaha, NE 68131 (tel. toll free 800/228-9792); **Wallach and Co., Inc.,** P.O. Box 480, Middleburg, VA 22117-0480 (tel. toll free 800/237-6615); or **Access America, Inc.,** P.O. Box 90315, Richmond, VA 23286-4991 (tel. toll free 800/424-3391 or 800/284-8300).

WHAT TO PACK Clothing Costa Rica is a tropical country, so to stay comfortable, bring lightweight, natural-fiber clothing. In the rainy season an umbrella, not a raincoat (which is too hot), is necessary. Nights at any time of year can be cool in San José and in the mountains, so also bring a wool sweater or jacket. Good walking shoes are a must if you plan to visit any of the national-park rails (though you may also want to rent rubber boots in some parks). If you will be traveling to exceptionally humid areas, such as the Osa Peninsula or south of Limón on the Caribbean coast, you might consider bringing a pair of nylon shorts and a nylon tank top, as these fabrics can be washed and dried quickly.

Other Items A bathing suit is a must, and a mask and snorkel come in handy. Insect repellent is invaluable, and I have heard that citronella-based repellents, available at natural-food stores, are sometimes more effective than chemical repellents. Sunscreen, an absolute necessity, is available in Costa Rica but is more expensive than in the United States. Be sure to have waterproof sunscreen if you plan to go rafting. Bring plenty of film and spare batteries for your camera. A water-filter straw, available in camping supply stores, is a convenient way to be sure you always have purified water to drink. The straws are inexpensive and disposable. A Swiss army knife almost always comes in handy at some point in a trip, as does a small sewing kit. Bring along a couple of plastic bags of different sizes for that unexpected rain shower when you might be out walking with your camera or other items you wouldn't want to get wet.

4. TIPS FOR THE DISABLED, SENIORS, SINGLES, FAMILIES & STUDENTS

FOR THE DISABLED In general, there are few handicapped-accessible buildings in Costa Rica. In San José, sidewalks are crowded and uneven. Few hotels offer handicapped-accessible accommodations, and there are neither public buses or private vans for transporting disabled individuals. It is difficult for a person with disabilities to get around in Costa Rica.

Mobility International USA, P.O. Box 10767, Eugene, OR 97440 (tel. 503/343-1284), is a membership organization that promotes international educational exchanges for people of all disabilities and ages. In the past they have had trips to Costa Rica and may again in the future. For a $20 membership you can receive their quarterly newsletter and access to their referral service ($10 newsletter only). Also available is a video tape that recounts the story of two exchange groups between Costa Rica and the United States.

FOR SENIORS Many airlines now offer senior-citizen discounts, so be sure to ask about these when making reservations. Due to its temperate climate, stable government, low cost of living, and friendly *pensionado* program, Costa Rica is popular with retirees from North America. There are excellent medical facilities in San José, and plenty of community organizations to help retirees feel at home. If you would like to learn more about retiring in Costa Rica, contact the **Costa Rican Pensionado Office** in San José (tel. 506/223-1733 extension 244 or 264).

Elderhostel, 75 Federal St., Boston, MA 02110 (tel. 617/426-7788), offers very popular study tours to Costa Rica. To participate in an Elderhostel program, either you or your spouse must be at least 60 years old. Great bird-watching trips and lectures on Costa Rican culture and history are some of the more interesting aspects of these trips.

FOR SINGLES   You'll pay the same penalty here that you would elsewhere: Rooms are more expensive if you aren't traveling in a pair. If you are looking for someone to travel with, **Travel Companions Exchange,** P.O. Box 833, Amityville, NY 11701-0833 (tel. 516/454-0880), provides listings of possible travel companions categorized under such headings as special interests, age, education, and location. It costs a minimum of $36 for a six-month membership and subscription to the service. It is also possible to subscribe to the organization's bimonthly newsletter without becoming a member. The newsletter costs $24 for a six-month subscription.

FOR FAMILIES   Hotels in Costa Rica occasionally give discounts for children under 12 years old, and sometimes young children under 3 or 4 years are allowed to stay for free. Don't look for the same type of discounts that you find in the United States.

FOR STUDENTS   Costa Rica is the only country in Central America with a network of hostels that are affiliated with the International Youth Hostel Federation. Ask at the **Toruma Youth Hostel,** Avenida Central between calles 29 and 31, San José (tel. 224-4085) for information on hostels at Rara Avis in Horquetas, Chilamate, La Fortuna, Lake Arenal, San Isidro, Jacó Beach, Liberia, and Rincón de la Vieja National Park. In San José, there is also a student travel agency: **OTEC,** Edificio Ferencz, 2nd floor, Calle 3 between avenidas 1 and 3, 275 meters north of the National Theater (tel. 255-0554 or 222-0866). If you already have an **international student identity card,** you can use your card to get discounts on airfares, hostels, national and international tours and excursions, car rentals, and store purchases. If you don't have one, stop by the OTEC office with a passport or other identification that shows you are under 35 years old, proof of student status, and two passport photos; for about $10, they'll prepare an ID card for you.

Students interested in a working vacation in Costa Rica should contact the **Council on International Educational Exchange (C.I.E.E.),** 205 E. 42nd St., New York, NY 10017 (tel. 212/661-1414 or 212/661-1450). This organization also issues official student identity cards and has offices all over the United States. They also recently published *Smart Vacations: The Traveler's Guide to Learning Adventures Abroad* (St. Martin's Press, 1993), a directory of companies, organizations, and schools offering educational travel programs.

5. ALTERNATIVE/ADVENTURE TRAVEL

LANGUAGE PROGRAMS   There are several schools in the San José area that offer Spanish language courses, and many people come to Costa Rica with the intention of learning Spanish. Courses are of varying lengths and intensiveness, and often include cultural activities and day excursions. The Spanish schools can also arrange for homestays with a middle-class Tico family, an experience that will help you to speak only Spanish in your daily life. Classes are intensive and often one-on-one. Listed below are some of the larger and more popular Spanish-language schools, with approximate costs. Contact the schools for the most current price information.

Forester Instituto Internacional, Apdo. 6945-1000, San José, Costa Rica (tel. 506/225-3155, 225-0135, or 225-1649; fax 506/225-9236), is located 75 meters south of the Automercado in the Los Yoses district of San José. Prices for a four-week language course range from about $500 without homestay to about $900 with homestay.

Central American Institute for International Affairs (ICAI), Apdo. 10302, San José, Costa Rica (tel. 506/233-8571; fax 506/221-5238), offers a four-week Spanish-language immersion program, along with a homestay, for $895. They also offer courses in Central American studies and other topics. In the United States, contact the Language Studies Enrollment Center, P.O. Box 5095, Anaheim, CA 92814 (tel. 714/527-2918; fax 714/826-8752).

Centro Lingüístico Conversa, Apdo. 17-1007, Centro Colón, San José, Costa Rica (tel. 506/221-7649; fax 506/233-2418), provides a most attractive environment for studying Spanish at its El Pedregal farm 10 miles west of San José. A four-week course here, including room and board, costs $1,340 for one person and $2,530 for a married couple.

Costa Rican Language Academy, Avenida Central across from Calle 25B and the Pizza Hut (Apdo. 336-2070), San José (tel. 506/233-8914 or 221-1624; fax 506/233-8670), offers three, four, or five hours of daily Spanish instruction in one to four week packages. Four hours per day for four weeks will cost $900, including homestay.

Instituto Interamericano de Idiomas (Intensa), Calle 33 between avenidas 5 and 7 (Apdo. 8110-1000), San José (tel. 506/224-6353 or 225-6009; fax 506/253-4337), offers two- to four-week programs. A four-week, four-hour-per-day program with homestay costs $845.

Instituto Universal de Idiomas, Apdo. 751-2150, Moravia (tel. 506/257-0441 or 233-2980; fax 506/223-9917), is located on Avenida 2 at the corner of Calle 9. Conveniently located, it charges $750 for a four-week course (only three hours per day) with homestay.

Pura Vida Instituto, Avenida 3 between calles 8 and 10, Heredia (tel. 506/237-0387; fax 506/237-0387). The weekly cost here includes five days of school, and seven days of room and board with a Costa Rican family.

La Escuela Idiomas D'Amore, Apdo. 67, Quepos (tel. 506/777-1143, 777-0543, or in the United States, 213/851-2739 or 414/781-3151), is situated in the lush surroundings of Manuel Antonio. Four weeks of classes for four hours per day costs $550; with homestay the cost is $785.

LATIN DANCE If you are interested in learning or polishing up your salsa or merengue, San José is a good place to do so. When you feel confident enough, you try out what you've learned at some of the area nightclubs. Dance schools in the San José area include **Academia de Bailes Latinos,** Avenida Central and Calle 25B, across from Pizza Hut (tel. 221-1624 or 233-8914); **Malecon,** Calle 17 between avenidas 2 and 4 (tel. 222-3214); and **Danza Viva,** 75 meters south of the Higueron, San Pedro (tel. 253-3110).

STUDY PROGRAMS **Institute for Central American Development Studies (ICADS),** Apdo. 3-2070 Sabanilla, San José (tel. 506/225-0508; fax 506/234-1337), offers internship and research opportunities in Costa Rica in the areas of environment, agriculture, and women's studies. They also offer an intensive Spanish-language program. Their address in the United States is: Dept. 826, P.O. Box 025216, Miami, FL 33102-5216.

Centro Creativo, Apdo. 597-6150, Santa Ana (tel. 282-6556), is located 20 minutes by car or taxi from San José. Art classes and workshops are offered here, along with holistic health services, a small bed-and-breakfast, and a daytime café. Prices vary depending on activity; call to find out when activities are offered.

ECOTOURISM & ADVENTURE TRAVEL Ecotourism (from the term "ecological tourism") is the word these days in Costa Rica. With the growing awareness of the value of tropical forests and the interest in visiting rain forests, dozens of lodges and tour companies have sprung up to cater to tourists interested in enjoying the natural beauties of Costa Rica. These lodges are usually situated in out-of-the-way locations, sometimes deep in the heart of a forest and sometimes on a farm with only a tiny bit of natural forest. However, they all have one thing in common: they cater to environmentally aware people with an interest in nature. Horseback riding, rafting, kayaking, hiking, and bird-watching are among the popular activities offered at these lodges.

Some U.S. tour operators that offer adventure-tour packages to Costa Rica include **International Expeditions Inc.**, One Environs Park, Helena, AL 35080 (tel. 205/428-1700, or toll free 800/633-4734); **Journeys International, Inc.**, 4011 Jackson Rd., Ann Arbor, MI 48103 (tel. 313/665-4407, or toll free 800/255-8735); **Mountain Travel•Sobek**, 6420 Fairmount Ave., El Cerrito, CA 94530 (tel. 510/527-8100, or toll free 800/227-2384); **Wilderness Travel**, 801 Allston Way, Berkeley, CA 94710 (tel. 510/548-0420, or toll free 800/368-2794); **Overseas Adventure Travel**, 349 Broadway, Cambridge, MA 02139 (tel. 617/876-0533, or toll free 800/221-0814); and **Costa Rica Connection**, 75 Oso St., San Luis Obispo, CA 93401 (tel. 805/543-8823, or toll free 800/345-7422).

In addition to the above-mentioned companies, many environmental organizations, including the Sierra Club, Nature Conservancy, and the Audubon Society, also offer trips to Costa Rica.

There are also dozens of tour companies in San José that offer nature-related tours ranging from one-day rafting trips to week-long adventures. Among the most popular multiday soft adventure trips to Costa Rica are trips to Tortuguero National Park (lowland Caribbean rain forests and rivers), white-water rafting trips, trips to Monteverde or another cloud forest area, and trips to the Osa Peninsula (lowland Pacific rain forest and beaches). Also growing in popularity are nature-oriented cruises on the *Temptress*, a small cruise ship that plies the waters off Costa Rica's Pacific coast.

Because these tours are sometimes held only when there are enough interested people or on set dates, it pays to contact a few of the companies and find out what they might be doing when you plan to be in Costa Rica. For information on day trips out of San José, see the "Easy Excursions" section of Chapter 3. The following is a list of some of the larger companies that offer adventure-travel or eco-travel trips:

Costa Rica Expeditions, Calle Central and Avenida 3, Apdo. 6941, San José (tel. 506/257-0766 or 222-0333; fax 257-1665), offers tours to Monteverde Cloud Forest Reserve, Tortuguero National Park, and Corcovado National Park, as well as white-water rafting trips and other excursions.

Costa Rica Sun Tours, Apdo. 1195-1250, Escazú (tel. 506/255-2011 or 255-3418; fax 506/255-4410), specializes in small country lodges for nature-oriented travelers.

Geotur, Apdo. 469 Y-1011, San José (tel. 506/234-1867; fax 506/253-6338), offers tours of Braulio Carrillo National Park, Carara Biological Reserve, Cahuita National Park, and other destinations.

Pura Natura, Avenida 7 between Calle 1 and Calle Central (Apdo. 7126-1000), San José (tel. 506/255-0011 or 255-2055; fax 506/255-2155), offers one- to five-day hiking, mountain-biking, and horseback-riding trips that are among the most adventurous of any available in Costa Rica. You can hike through Corcovado National Park or up to the peak of Mount Chirripó, among other trips.

If your interest is in rafting or sea kayaking, contact **Rios Tropicales,** Apdo. 472-1200, Pavas (tel. 506/233-6455; fax 506/255-4354). This company operates several 1- to 10-day raft trips, as well as sea kayaking and mountain-biking trips.

Tikal Tour Operators, Apdo. 6398-1000, San José (tel. 506/257-1480; fax 506/223-1916), offers rafting, diving, and volcano trips and visits to Braulio Carrillo National Park, Rincón de la Vieja National Park, Monteverde, and other parks.

FISHING VACATIONS Costa Rica offers some of the best fishing in the Americas. Among the game fish along the country's two coasts are tarpon, snook, marlin, and sailfish. There is also good fishing for rainbow bass in Lake Arenal. In the regional chapters I have mentioned sports-fishing companies in various locations. However, if you want to learn more about fishing in Costa Rica and arrange a fishing vacation, contact **Sportfishing Costa Rica,** Apdo. 115-1150, La Uruca (tel. 506/238-2726 or 238-2729).

There are numerous fishing lodges throughout the country, though the best known are along the northern Caribbean coast where the tarpon fishing is some of the best in the world. Among these lodges are the following: **Isla del Pesca Tarpon and Snook Fishing Resort,** Apdo. 8-4390-1000, San José (tel. 506/223-4560 or 221-6673); **Silver King Lodge,** Rainforest Excursions, 1107 East Lemon St., Tarpon Springs, FL 34689 (tel. in Costa Rica 506/288-1403); and the **Rio Colorado Lodge,** 12301 North Oregon Ave., Tampa, FL 33612 (tel. 813/931-4849, or toll free 800/243-9777).

CRUISES   One other interesting option is to take a cruise on the *Temptress.* This small cruise ship plies the waters off Costa Rica's Pacific coast from Santa Rosa National Park in the north to Corcovado National Park in the south. The ship usually anchors in remote, isolated, and very beautiful spots. Each day you have an option of a natural-history tour or a recreational and cultural tour. For information, contact **Temptress Cruises,** 1600 NW LeJeune, Suite 301, Miami, FL 33126 (tel. 305/871-2663 or [in Costa Rica] 506/220-1679, or toll free 800/336-8423).

Alternatively, you could charter a sailboat through **Veleros del Sur Sail Boat Chartering,** Apdo. 13-5400, Puntarenas (tel. 506/661-1320 or 661-3880).

ECOLOGICAL ORGANIZATIONS   Below are some organizations that are working on ecology and sustainable development projects. Contact them if you are interested in volunteering or would like to support them by becoming a member of their organization.

Arbofilia, Apdo. 512-1100, Tibas, Costa Rica (tel. 506/235-5470; fax 506/240-8832), operates programs wherein biologists and farmers work together to reclaim land that has been badly damaged by deforestation. Farming without chemicals is encouraged.

Tsuli Tsuli, Audubon Society of Costa Rica, Apdo 4910-1000, San José (tel. 506/240-8775), operates programs that work for river reforestation, wildlife protection, pollution control, and ecotourism. If you would like to become a member, contact the Audubon Society in San José.

ASCONA, Apdo. 8-3790-1000, San José (tel. 506/222-2296 or 222-2288; fax 506/253-4963), promotes sensible natural-resource development and welcomes volunteers and donations, which can be made through the World Wildlife Fund, 1250 24th St. NW, Washington, DC 20037 (tel. 202/293-4800).

Monteverde Conservation League, Apdo. 10581-1000, San José (tel. 506/645-5003; fax 506/645-5104). Based in Monteverde, the League has purchased more than 44,000 acres of rain forest and has ongoing programs of education and reforestation with communities who live adjacent to protected areas.

Neotropica Foundation, Apdo. 236-1002, Paseo del los Estudiantes, San José (tel. 506/253-2130), advocates sustainable development in buffer zones near national parks and helps communities secure title for rain-forest areas in return for a commitment to protect those areas. In the United States, contact the Nature Conservancy (tel. 703/841-4199; fax 703/841-4880).

Organization for Tropical Studies, Apdo. 676, San José (tel. 506/40-6696), represents several Costa Rican and U.S. universities. This organization's mission is to promote research, education, and the wise use of natural resources in the tropics. Research facilities include La Selva Biological Station near Braulio Carrillo National Park.

---

6. GETTING THERE

BY PLANE

It takes between 3 and 7 hours to fly to Costa Rica from most U.S. cities, and as Costa Rica becomes more and more popular with North American travelers, more flights are being added to San José's Santamaría International Airport. The following airlines currently serve Costa Rica from the United States, using the gateway cities listed.

American Airlines (tel. toll free 800/433-7300) has daily flights from Miami and Dallas/Fort Worth. **Aviateca** (Guatemalan) (tel. toll free 800/327-9832) flies from Los Angeles, Houston, Miami, and New Orleans. **Continental** (tel. toll free 800/231-0856) offers flights daily from Houston. **Lacsa** (Costa Rican) (tel. toll free 800/225-2272) has service from New York, Miami, New Orleans, Los Angeles, and San Francisco. **Mexicana** (tel. toll free 800/531-7921) has flights from New York, Denver, Miami, Dallas/Fort Worth, San Antonio, San José (California), and San Francisco, although with these flights it is necessary to spend a night in Mexico. If you travel from Chicago and Los Angeles with them, you can get to San José in one day. **Sahsa** (Honduran) (tel. toll free 800/327-1225) flies from Miami, New Orleans, and Houston. It is sometimes possible to make a direct connection from Houston, but from the first two cities it is necessary to stay overnight in Honduras. **Taca** (El Salvadoran) (tel. toll free 800/535-8780) offers flights from Los Angeles, San Francisco, Chicago, Houston, New Orleans, Miami, Washington, and New York. **United Air Lines** (tel. toll free 800/241-6522) and **Aero Costa Rica** (tel. toll free 800/237-6274) both have flights from Miami. From Europe, you can take **Iberia** (tel. toll free 800/772-4642) from Spain or **LTU International Airways** (tel. toll free 800/888-0200) from Germany. These latter two airlines both stop in Miami. Coming from the United Kingdom, you can take American Airlines direct to Miami and then on to Costa Rica, or Continental Airlines through Newark to Miami and then on to Costa Rica. Other alternatives are British Airways direct to Miami and then transferring to a different airline, or Delta Airlines through Atlanta to Miami and then to a different airline.

REGULAR AIRFARES In recent years airfares have been very unstable. Several major carriers have gone out of business, and the recession has had an adverse effect on airfares. Such instability makes it very difficult to quote an airline ticket price. APEX (advance-purchase excursion) ticket prices seem to be similar with each airline, but first-class ticket prices can have a wide variation. At press time, an APEX ticket or a coach ticket from New York to San José was running between $650 and $790; from Los Angeles between $570 and $730. First class from New York was about $1,680, and from Los Angeles was about $2,100. On rare occasions, special fares may be offered at rock bottom prices, but don't count on it. Regardless of

---

Ⓕ FROMMER'S SMART TRAVELER: AIRFARES

1. Check the ticket brokers' ads in the Sunday travel sections of major-city newspapers. These tickets can be $100 to $200 cheaper than the lowest standard airfares.
2. Keep tuned in to fare wars. Ticket prices to Central American destinations are sometimes cut drastically. If your schedule is flexible, you may be able to save quite a bit of money.
3. Try getting a discounted ticket from your departure city to one of the Central American gateway cities (Miami, New Orleans, Houston, or Los Angeles), and combine this with a discount ticket from one of those cities on to Costa Rica.
4. Shop all the airlines that fly to Costa Rica, including the small Central American airlines that travel agents don't usually check.
5. You'll usually save money if you take a "milk run" (flight that makes several stops) rather than a direct flight.
6. Always ask for the lowest-priced fare, which will usually be a mid-week departure.

how much the cheapest ticket costs when you decide to fly, you can bet it will have some restrictions. It will almost certainly be non-refundable, and you may have to pay within 24 hours of making a reservation. You'll likely have to buy the ticket in advance (anywhere from one week to 30 days). You will also likely have to stay over a weekend and limit your stay to 30 days or less.

TICKET BROKERS/CONSOLIDATORS You can shave a little bit off these ticket prices by purchasing your ticket from what is known as a ticket broker or consolidator. These ticketing agencies sell discounted tickets on major airlines; although the tickets have as many, and sometimes more, restrictions than an APEX ticket, they can help you save money. You'll find ticket brokers' listings—usually just a column of destinations with prices beside them—in the Sunday travel sections of major city newspapers. You'll almost never get the ticket for the advertised price, but you will probably get it for less than the airline would sell it to you.

BY BUS

Bus service runs regularly from both Panama City, Panama, and Managua, Nicargua. From Panama City it is a 20-hour, 900-kilometer trip; buses leave Panama City daily at 8pm. For more information, call the Tica Bus Company (tel. 506/221-8954 or 221-9229). From Managua it is 11 hours and 450 kilometers to San José. Buses leave Managua Monday through Saturday at 6:30 or 7am. For more information, call the Tica Bus Company, above, or Sirca Company (tel. 506/222-5541 or 223-1464).

BY CAR

It is possible to travel to Costa Rica by car, but it can be difficult, especially for U.S. Citizens. The Interamerican Highway (also known as the Panamerican Highway) passes through El Salvador, Honduras, and Nicaragua after leaving Guatemala and before reaching Costa Rica. All three of these countries can be problematic for travelers because of the continuing internal strife and visa formalities. If you do decide to undertake this adventure, take the gulf-coast route from the border crossing at Brownsville, Texas, as it involves traveling the least number of miles through Mexico.

Contact **Sanborn's Insurance Company,** 2009 S. 10th St., McAllen, TX 78501 (tel. 210/686-0711), located about 1½ hours from Brownsville. They can supply you with trip insurance for Mexico and Central America—insurance is not available after you have left the United States—and an itinerary. Sanborn's also has branches at other U.S./Mexico border crossings.

Don't drive at night because of the danger of being robbed by bandits, and drink only bottled drinks. If you want to consult a good guidebook, look up *Drive the Pan-Am Highway to Mexico and Central America* by Audrey and Raymond Pritchard, available through P.O. Box 526770, Miami, FL 33152.

BY SHIP

More than 200 cruise ships stop each year in Costa Rica, calling at Limón on the Caribbean coast and at Puerto Caldera on the Pacific coast. Cruise lines that offer stops in Costa Rica include Cunard, Royal Caribbean, Holland American, Princess, Regency, and Royal Cruise. Contact a travel agent to find out more about these cruise lines.

PACKAGE TOURS

It is sometimes cheaper to purchase an airfare-and-hotel package rather than just an airline ticket. This is especially true if airfares happen to be in a high period and if you will be traveling with a companion. The best way to find out about these package tours is to contact a travel agent.

Some companies that specialize in travel to Costa Rica include **Costa Rica Experts,** 3166 North Lincoln Ave., Chicago, IL 60657 (tel. 312/935-1009); **Tourtech,** 17780 Fitch St., Suite 110, Irvine, CA 92714 (tel. toll free 800/882-2636); and **Holbrook Travel,** 3540 NW 13th St., Gainsville, FL 32609 (tel. 904/377-7111 or toll free 800/451-7111). Some Canadian companies specializing in tours to Costa Rica include **Via Nova-America,** 4571 Rue St. Denis, Montréal, P.Q. H2J 2I4 (tel. 514/847-9279); and **Onisac International,** 221-2002 Quebec Ave., Saskatoon, Sask. S7K 5G6 (tel. 306/652-4410).

Once you are in Costa Rica, there are dozens of tour companies that will arrange overnight and longer tours to remote lodges that cater to ecotourists. For information on some of these companies, see the "Alternative/Adventure Travel" section above.

7. GETTING AROUND

BY PLANE

Surprisingly, getting around by air is one of the best ways to get around Costa Rica. Because the country is quite small, the flights are short and not too expensive. The domestic airlines of Costa Rica are **Sansa,** Calle 24 between Avenida Central and Avenida 1 (tel. 506/233-3258 or 233-0397) which offers a free shuttle bus from their downtown office to the airport, and **Travelair,** (tel. 506/232-7883 or 220-3054) which charges more for flights to the same destinations, but is popular because it is more reliable. Flights last between 20 and 50 minutes. Travelair operates from Pavas Airport, 4 miles from San José, and Sansa operates from the Juan Santamaría International Airport.

In the high season, between December and May, be sure to book reservations well in advance. If you plan to return to San José, buy a round-trip ticket as they tend to be less expensive than two one-way tickets.

BY BUS

This is by far the best way to visit most of Costa Rica. Buses are inexpensive, well maintained, uncrowded, and they go nearly everywhere. There are three types of buses. Local buses are the cheapest and slowest; they stop frequently and are generally a bit dilapidated. Express buses run between San José and most beach towns and major cities; they sometimes only operate on weekends and holidays. A few luxury buses and minibuses drive to destinations frequented by foreign tourists. For details on how to get to various destinations from San José, see the "Getting There" heading of each section in the regional chapters.

BY CAR

CAR RENTALS   Renting a car in Costa Rica is not something to be entered into lightly. Costa Rica has the second highest accident rate per capita in the world. In addition, since all rental cars in Costa Rica bear special license plates, they are readily identifiable to thieves. Nothing is ever safe in a car in Costa Rica, although parking in guarded parking lots helps. The tourist plates also signal police that they can extort money from unwary tourist motorists. Never pay money directly to a police officer who stops you for any traffic violation. Before driving off with a rental car, be sure that you inspect the exterior and point out to the rental company representative every tiny scratch, dent, tear, or any other damage. It is a common practice with Costa Rican car-rental companies to claim that you owe payment for damages the company finds when you return the car.

On the other hand, renting a car allows you much greater freedom to explore remote areas of the country. Several people have written to me to say that they feel visitors should always rent four-wheel-drive vehicles. I have always rented a regular car, and though there are roads I can't drive down, I have always managed to get around just fine (including to Monteverde). If, after weighting the alternatives, you decide you want to rent a car, read on.

Avis, Budget, Hertz, National, and Thrifty car-rental agencies all have offices in Costa Rica. You will save somewhere between $35 and $75 per week on a car rental if you make a reservation in your home country at least one week before you need the car. The least-expensive National car available rents for about $230 per week, plus insurance (total of around $320) in San José, but if you book this same car in advance from the United States, you can get it for $194 per week, plus insurance (total of around $285). To rent a car in Costa Rica, you must be at least 21 years old and have a valid driver's license and a major credit card in your name. See the "Getting Around" section of Chapter 3 for details on renting a car in San José. Cars can also be rented in Quepos, Jacó, and Limón.

GASOLINE Regular gasoline is what is most readily available in Costa Rica. Most rental cars take regular. When going off to remote places, try to have as full a gas tank as possible—in very small towns, you can sometimes get gasoline from enterprising families who sell it by the liter from their houses. Look for hand-lettered signs that say "gasolina."

ROAD CONDITIONS Most roads are in fairly good condition, with the exception of unpaved roads in the rainy season, which can be rutted, slippery, and difficult to negotiate. If possible, before you rent a vehicle, find out about the road conditions to see if it is necessary to have a four-wheel-drive to get to your destination. Some paved roads are badly potholed, so stay alert for the invisible pothole riding in the shadows. An especially bad example is the road from San Isidro de General to Cartago over the Cerro de la Meurte. Route numbers are rarely used on road signs in Costa Rica, though there are frequent signs listing the number of kilometers to various towns or cities.

DRIVING RULES A foreign driver's license is valid for the first three months that you are in Costa Rica. Seat belts are required for driver and passengers. Motorcyclists must wear a helmet. Highway police use radar, so keep to the speed limit if you don't want to get pulled over. Speeding tickets can be charged to your credit card for up to a year after you leave the country if they are not paid before leaving.

MAPS Car rental agencies and the I.C.T. information centers (see "Information, Entry Requirements, and Money," at the beginning of this chapter) at the airport and in downtown San José have adequate road maps. Other sources in San José are The Bookshop, Avenida 1 between calles 1 and 3 (tel. 221-6847); Libreria Lehmann, Avenida Central between calles 1 and 3 (tel. 223-1212); and Jimenez & Tanzi, Calle 3 between avenidas 1 and 3 (tel. 233-8033).

BREAKDOWNS If your car should break down and you are unable to get off the road, check to see if there is a reflective triangle in the trunk. If not, place a pile of leaves and/or tree branches in the road 100 feet on either side of the car to warn approaching drivers.

BY FERRY

There are four different ferries operating across the Gulf of Nicoya. Three are car ferries: one across the Rio Tempisque, one from Puntarenas to Playa Naranjo, and one from Puntarenas to Paquera. The passenger ferry runs from Puntarenas to Paquera. For more detailed information, see Chapter 4, "Guanacaste and the Nicoya Peninsula," and Chapter 6, "The Central Pacific Coast."

HITCHHIKING

Although buses go to most places in Costa Rica, they can be infrequent in the remote regions, and consequently, local people often hitchhike to get to their destination sooner. If you are driving a car, people will frequently ask you for a ride. If you are hitching yourself, keep in mind that if a bus doesn't go to your destination, there probably aren't too many cars going there either. Good luck.

LOCATING ADDRESSES

There are no street addresses in Costa Rica, at least not often. Addresses are given as a set of coordinates such as "Calle 3 between Avenida Central and Avenida 1." Many addresses include additional information such as the number of meters or *varas* (an old Spanish measurement roughly equal to a yard) from a specified intersection or some other well-known landmark. Often the additional information is only useful if you are familiar with the area. In San José, many addresses use distances from the Coca-Cola bottling plant that once stood near the market. The bottling plant is long gone, but the address descriptions remain. In outlying neighborhoods, addresses can become long directions such as "50 meters south of the old church, then 100 meters east, then 20 meters south." Luckily for the visitor, most addresses are straightforward.

SUGGESTED ITINERARIES

HIGHLIGHTS

The following are the main tourist destinations in Costa Rica: San José; Manuel Antonio National Park; Jacó Beach; the beaches of the Nicoya Peninsula; Monteverde Cloud Forest Reserve (or another cloud-forest region); Tortuguero National Park; Irazú Volcano; Poás Volcano; Arenal Volcano and Arenal Lake; The Osa Peninsula; jungle lodges throughout the country; Cahuita/Peurto Viejo; and Dominical.

PLANNING YOUR ITINERARY

If You Have One Week

Day 1: Visit the museums and the National Theater in San José.
Day 2: Make an excursion to the Orosi Valley, Lankester Gardens, and Irazú Volcano.
Days 3 and 4: Travel to Monteverde (or another cloud forest region) and spend a day exploring the cloud forest.
Days 5 and 6: Head to one of the many Pacific coast beaches.
Day 7: Return to San José.

If You Have Two Weeks

Day 1: Visit the museums and the National Theater in San José.
Days 2 and 3: Make an excursion to the Orosi Valley, Lankester Gardens, and Irazú Volcano one day and go rafting on the other.
Days 4 and 5: Travel to Monteverde (or another cloud forest area) and explore the cloud forest.
Days 6 and 7: Travel to Lake Arenal to see the eruptions of Arenal Volcano, soak in some hot springs, and maybe go to Caño Negro National Wildlife Refuge.
Days 8: Explore Rincon de la Vieja or Santa Rosa National Park.
Day 9, 10, 11, and 12: Spend these days relaxing on a beach or perhaps explonng the Corcovado Peninsula.

FROMMER'S FAVORITE
COSTA RICA EXPERIENCES

A Night at San José's Teatro Nacional Built in the late 19th century with money raised through a tax on coffee exports, this classic opera house is still staging the best cultural performances in the country.

A Day of White-Water Rafting Costa Rica offers some of the best white-water rafting opportunities in the world. The water is warm, the mountains are green, and the rapids are as rough as you want.

Cruising the Tortuguero Canals North of Limón, on the Caribbean coast, there are no roads, only canals through the wilderness. A boat trip through the canals to Tortuguero Naitonal Park is as thrilling as exploring the Amazon.

A Hike Through a Cloud Forest The mountain-top cloud forests of Costa Rica are home to an amazing diversity of plants and animals, including the resplendent quetzal, one of the world's most beautiful birds.

Bird-Watching Almost anywhere in Costa Rica, you are likely to see colorful and unfamiliar birds. The sight of a quetzal or a scarlet macaw are enough to turn anyone into an avid bird-watcher.

Hiking Through the Rain Forest There are rain forests all over Costa Rica and all of them are fascinating. A walk through one of these forests with a knowledgeable guide can teach you much about rain forest ecology.

Swimming on Deserted Beaches Costa Rica has 735 miles of coastline, which means it isn't too difficult to find a stretch of beach with nearly no one else on it. No matter what your taste in beaches, you're sure to find one to match your dreams.

Soaking in the Hot Springs at Tabacon This is actually a hot river that flows down off of Arenal Volcano. The crystal-clear water flows through a lush, forested valley.

Days 13 and 14: Fly to Tortuguero National Park and spend a day there, returning the next day by boat and bus.

If You Have Three Weeks

If you have three weeks, you can spend more time on the beach, perhaps several different beaches. With this much time, you can easily visit both coasts. You could also do trips to two or three different remote lodges in different parts of the country. You might even consider doing a week-long cruise along the Pacific coast.

Themed Choices

The most common choice for a themed vacation in Costa Rica is to make it a naturalist tour by visiting as many of the national parks and private nature reserves as you can in the amount of time available. Another possible theme would be to sample as many of the different beaches as you can.

8. WHERE TO STAY

Costa Rica is in the midst of a massive tourism boom. Almost weekly new hotels open up around the country. The past few years have seen the opening of the first mega-resorts, including an all-inclusive beach resort where even cocktails are included in the rates. Even as this book was being researched construction was continuing on several new large resorts on the Nicoya Peninsula. At this time, however, there are still few hotels or resorts offering the sort of luxurious accommodations you'll find in Hawaii or the Caribbean. Yes, there are hotels of international standards, but Costa Rica is not yet a luxury resort destination.

The country's strong point is its moderately priced hotels. In the $60 to $90 price range, you'll find comfortable accommodations almost anywhere in the country. However, within this price range, room size and quality vary quite a bit. Don't expect the uniformity you find in the United States in this price range. There are also quite a few good deals for less than $60.

At the opposite end of the accommodations spectrum, bed-and-breakfast inns have also been proliferating. Though the majority of these are in the San José area, you will now find B&Bs (often gringo owned and operated) throughout the country. Another welcome hotel trend in the San José area is the renovation and conversion of old homes into small hotels. Most of these hotels are in the Barrio Amon district of downtown San José, and though there is a problem with noise and exhaust fumes in this neighborhood, they have more character than any other hotels in the country. You'll also find similar hotels in the Paseo Colón district.

Costa Rica has been riding the ecotourism wave and there are now small nature-oriented ecolodges throughout the country. These lodges offer opportunities to see wildlife (including sloths, monkeys, and hundreds of species of birds) and learn about tropical forests. They range from Spartan facilities catering primarily to scientific researchers to luxury accommodations that are among the finest in the country. Keep in mind that though the nightly room rates at these lodges are often quite moderate, the price of a visit starts to climb when you throw in transportation (often on chartered planes), guided excursions, and meals. Also, just because your travel agent can book a reservation at most of these lodges does not mean they're not remote. Think long and hard about whether you really want to put up with hot, humid weather (no air-conditioning), biting insects, waits in the sun for transportation, and strenuous hikes to see wildlife.

A couple of uniquely Costa Rican accommodation types you may encounter are the apartotel and the cabina. An apartotel is just what it sounds like, an apartment hotel, where you'll get a full kitchen and one or two bedrooms. Cabinas are Costa Rica's version of cheap vacation lodging. They are very basic, very inexpensive, and are often cinder-block buildings divided into small rooms. Occasionally you'll find a cabina where the units are actually cabins, but these are a rarity. Cabinas often have clothes-washing sinks and kitchenettes, since they cater primarily to Tico families on vacation.

Please note that room rates listed in this book do not include the 14.3% room taxes. These taxes will add considerably to the cost of your room. I have separated hotel listings throughout this book into several broad categories. In the San José chapter these categories are: Very Expensive—above $125 a night; Expensive—$90 to $125; Moderate—$60 to $90; Inexpensive—$30 to $60; Budget—under $30. Throughout the rest of the book the categories are: Very Expensive—above $125; Expensive—$80 to $125; Moderate—$35 to $80; and Budget—under $35.

9. WHERE TO DINE

Though Costa Rica is experiencing a hotel construction boom, there does not seem to be a parallel boom in new restaurants. San José remains the unquestioned gastronomic capital of the country, and here you can find the cuisines of the world served with formal service at moderate prices. There are several excellent French and Italian restaurants around the San José area, as well as Peruvian, Japanese, Swiss, and Spanish establishments. Costa Rica is a major producer and exporter of beef, and consequently, San José also has plenty of good steakhouses. At the most expensive restaurant in San José, you'll have to drink a lot of wine to spend more than $40 on dinner.

Unfortunately, outside of San José quality meals are a rarity, even at the most popular beaches. In fact, many beach resorts are so remote that you have no choice but to eat in the hotel's dining room, and on other beaches, the only choices aside from the hotel dining rooms are cheap local places or overpriced tourist traps serving indifferent meals. At remote jungle lodges, the food is usually served buffet- or family-style and is often quite good. However, meals at these lodges hinge almost entirely on who is doing the cooking. I hesitate to recommend food in such lodges because the cook I had when I visited may be long gone by the time you arrive.

If you're looking for cheap eats, you'll find them in little restaurants known as "sodas," which are the equivalent of a diner in the United States. At a soda you'll have lots of choices: rice and beans with steak, rice and beans with fish, rice and beans with chicken. You get the picture. The Tico standards of rice and beans are the norm and are served at three meals a day. Also, though there is plenty of seafood available throughout the country, at sodas it all-too-often is served fried.

Costa Ricans love to eat, and they love to have a view when they eat. Almost anywhere you go in the country, if there is a view, there will be a restaurant taking advantage of it. If you are driving around the country, don't miss an opportunity to dine with a view at some little roadside restaurant. The food may not be fantastic, but the view will be.

I have separated restaurant listings throughout this book into three price categories based on the average coast of a meal, including tax and service charge but not including beer or wine. The categories are as follows: Expensive—more than $15; Moderate—$8 to $15; Budget—less than $8. Whenever you eat out, keep in mind that there is an 11% sales tax. You may also find that a service charge of 10% has been added to your bill, which makes tipping unnecessary.

10. WHAT TO BUY

Buy coffee. If you're a coffee drinker or if you know some coffee drinkers (I guess that's all of us), then be sure to stock up on fresh-roasted coffee beans before you head home. Café Britt is the coffee you'll see sold in hotels and souvenir shops all over the country. Sure, it's good coffee, but it's also overpriced. If you go into the central market in downtown San José or a grocery store anywhere in the country, you'll find coffee at much lower prices. Just be sure you're buying whole beans. Costa Rican grinds are much finer than U.S. grinds and often have sugar mixed right in to the coffee. Costa Rica also produces its own coffee liqueur (Café Rica), including a creme liqueur (Salicsa), both of which are quite inexpensive. These are best purchased in a liquor store or a grocery store. In duty-free shops at the airport, you'll pay more for either of these local liqueurs. Salsa Lizano, a flavorful green sauce used the same way we use steak sauce here in the north, is another comestible worth bringing home with you.

Costa Rica is not known for its handcrafts, though it does have a town—Sarchí—that is filled with handcraft shops. So scant are the country's handcraft offerings that many shops sell Guatemalan clothing, Panamanian appliquéed textiles, El Salvadoran painted wood souvenirs, and Nicaraguan rocking chairs. There is quite a bit of wood carving being done in the country, but it is, for the most part, either tourist-souvenir wooden bowls, napkin holders, and the like, or elegant and expensive art pieces. Sarchí is best known as the home of the colorfully painted Costa Rican oxcart, reproductions of which are manufactured in various scaled-down sizes. There is also a lot of furniture made in Sarchí.

A few other items worth keeping an eye out for include reporductions of pre-Columbian gold jewelry and carved stone figurines. The former are available either in solid gold, silver, or gold plated. The latter, though interesting, are extremely heavy.

 COSTA RICA

American Express   American Express (tel. 223-3644) has a counter in San José at the Banco de San José on Calle Central between avenidas 3 and 5. It's open Monday through Friday from 8am to 4pm.

Business Hours   Banks are usually open Monday through Friday from 9am to 3pm. Offices are open Monday through Friday from 8am to 5pm (closed for two hours at lunch). **Stores** are open Monday through Saturday from 9am to 7pm (many close for an hour at lunch). Bars are open until 1 or 2am. Many restaurants stay open 24 hours, while other close between meals.

Camera/Film   Most types of film, except Kodachrome, are available. However, prices are higher than in the United States.

Climate   See "When to Go," in this chapter.

Crime   See "Safety," below.

Currency   See "Information, Entry Requirements, and Money," in this chapter.

Customs   You can bring in half a kilo of tobacco products, three liters of liquor, and two cameras duty-free.

Documents Required   See "Information, Entry Requirements, and Money," in this chapter.

Driving Rules   See "Getting Around," in this chapter.

Drug Laws   Drug laws in Costa Rica are strict, so stay away from marijuana and cocaine. You'll also need a prescription from a doctor or lab results to have a prescription filled in Costa Rica.

Drugstores   A drugstore in Costa Rica is a *farmacia*. You'll find at least one in nearly every town.

Electricity   The standard in Costa Rica is the same as in the United States: 110 volts.

Embassies/Consulates   The following embassies and consulates are located in San José: **United States Consulate,** in front of Centro Commercial, on the road to Pavas (tel. 220-3939 or, after 4pm, 220-3127); **Canadian Embassy,** Calle 3 and Avenida Central (tel. 255-3522); **British Embassy,** Paseo Colón between calles 38 and 40 (tel. 221-5566).

Emergencies   For an **ambulance** call 221-5818; to report a **fire** call 118; to contact the **police** call 117, or 127 outside cities.

Etiquette   Ticos tend to dress conservatively and treat everyone very respectfully. Both sexes shake hands.

Hitchhiking   This is permitted and is fairly common. If you're trying to get to remote parks or volcanoes, however, there usually isn't much traffic on such roads. Buses, which are quite inexpensive, go almost everywhere in the country.

Holidays   See "When to Go," in this chapter.

Information   See "Information, Entry Requirements, and Money," in this chapter. Also see individual city sections for local information offices.

Language   Spanish is the official language of Costa Rica. *Berlitz Latin-American Spanish Phrasebook and Dictionary* (Berlitz Guides, 1992) is probably the best phrasebook to bring with you.

Laundry   Laundromats are few and far between in Costa Rica, more common are expensive hotel laundry services. For listings of laundromats, see individual city and town sections.

Liquor Laws   Alcoholic beverages are sold every day of the week throughout the year, with the exception of two days before Easter and the two days before and after a presidential election.

Mail   A letter or postcard to the United States costs 30¢ and takes about one week. A post office is called a *correo* in Spanish. You can get stamps at the post office, newsstands, or gift shops in large hotels. If you are sending mail to Costa Rica it can take as much as a month to get to the more remote corners of the country. Plan ahead. Also, many hotels now have mailing addresses in the United States. Always use this address when writing from North America or Europe.

Maps   The Costa Rican Tourist Board (I.C.T.), (see "Information, Entry Requirements, and Money," in this chapter), can usually provide you with good maps of both Costa Rica and San José. Other sources in San José are The Bookshop, Avenida 1 between calles 1 and 3 (tel. 221-6847); Libreria Lehmann, Avenida Central between calles 1 and 3 (tel. 223-1212); and Jimenez & Tanzi (tel. 233-8033).

Newspapers/Magazines   There are three Spanish-language dailies in Costa Rica and one English-language weekly, the *Tico Times*. In addition, you can get *Time, Newsweek*, and several U.S. newspapers at hotel gift shops and a few of the bookstores in San José.

Passports   See "Information, Entry Requirements, and Money," in this chapter.

Pets   If you want to bring your cat or dog, be sure it has current vaccinations against rabies and distemper, and take along the documentation to prove it.

Police   The number for the Policia de Transity is 227-7150 or 227-8030.

Radio/TV   There are about 10 TV channels and satellite TV from the United States. There are more than 100 radio stations on the AM and FM dials.

Restrooms   These are know as *sanitarios* or *servicios sanitarios*. They are marked *damas* (women) and *hombres* or *caballeros* (men).

Safety   Though most of Costa Rica is very safe, Costa Rica is known for its pickpockets. Never carry a wallet in your back pocket. In fact, never carry anything of value in pants' pockets or in a daypack on your back. A woman should keep a tight grip on her purse (keep it tucked under your arm). Be sure not to leave valuables in your hotel room. Don't park a car on the street in Costa Rica, especially in San José; there are plenty of public parking lots around the city.

Because all rental cars have special plates, they are easily spotted by thieves who know that such cars are likely to be full of expensive camera equipment, money, and so on. Don't ever leave anything of value in a car parked on the street, not even for a moment. Public intercity buses are also frequent targets of stealthy thieves. Never check your bags into the hold of a bus if you can avoid it. If this cannot be avoided, keep your eye on what leaves the hold any time the bus stops. If you put your bags in an overhead rack, be sure you can see the bag at all times. Try not to fall asleep.

For safety while swimming, see the information "Riptides" and "Health, Insurance, and Other Concerns," above.

Taxes   All hotels charge 14.3% tax. Restaurants charge 11% tax and also add on a 10% service charge, for a total of 21% more on your bill. There is an airport departure tax of $6.75.

Telephone/Telex/Fax   Costa Rica has an excellent phone system, with a dial tone similar to that heard in the United States. As of March 1993, all phone numbers in Costa Rica have seven digits. If you run across an old six-digit number, check the phone book or try calling the operator to find out what the new number is. There is one telephone book for all of Costa Rica which includes both white and yellow pages. A pay phone costs 5 colónes (2¢) and most phones take 5-, 10-, or 20-colón coins, though some take 5-colón coins only. For making calling card and collect calls, you can reach an AT&T operator by dialing 114, MCI by dialing 162, Sprint by dialing 163, Bell by dialing 161, and a Costa Rican operator by dialing 0 (pay phones require a coin deposit). The Costa Rican telephone system allows direct international dialing but it is expensive. You can make international phone calls, as well as send telexes and faxes, from the I.C.E office, Avenida 2 between calles 1 and 3, in San José. The office is open daily from 7am to 10pm.

The Western Union office (tel. 257-1150) is on Calle 9 between avenidas 2 and 4 in San José, and along with telegram service also offers a quick way to wire money. Radiográfica (tel. 287-0087), at Calle 1 and Avenida 5 in San José, has telex, telegram, and fax service.

Time   Costa Rica is on Central Standard Time, six hours behind Greenwich mean time.

Tipping   Tipping is not necessary in restaurants, where a 10% service charge is always added to your bill (along with an 11% tax). If service was particularly good, you can leave a little at your own discretion, but it is not mandatory. Porters and bellhops get around 60¢ per bag. You don't need to tip a taxi driver unless the services has been superior—a tip is not usually expected.

Tourist Offices   See "Information, Entry Requirements, and Money," in this chapter. Also see specific cities.

Visas   See "Information, Entry Requirements, and Money," in this chapter.

Water   Though the water in San José is said to be safe to drink, outside of this city water quality varies. Because many tourists do get sick within a few days of arriving in Costa Rica, I recommend playing it safe and sticking to bottled drinks as much as possible and avoiding ice.

CHAPTER 3

SAN JOSÉ

San José is a city built on coffee. This is not to say that the city runs on bottomless pots of java. No, San José was built on the profits of the coffee export business. Between the airport and downtown you pass by coffee farms, and glancing up from almost any street in the city you can see, on the volcanic mountains that surround San José, a patchwork quilt of farm fields, most of which are planted with the *grano de oro* (golden bean), as it is known here. San José was a forgotten backwater of the Spanish empire until the first shipments of the local beans made their way to the sleepy souls in Europe late in the 19th century. Soon, San José was riding high on this vegetable gold. Coffee planters, newly rich and craving culture, imposed a tax on themselves in order to build the Teatro Nacional, San José's most beautiful building. Coffee profits also built the city a university. Today, you can smell the coffee roasting as you wander the streets near the central market, and in any café or restaurant you can get a hot cup of sweet, milky café con leche to remind you of the bean that built San José.

Why does coffee grow so well around San José? It's the climate. The Central Valley, in which the city sits, has a perfect climate. At 3,750 feet above sea level, San José enjoys springlike temperatures year round. It is this pleasant climate and the beautiful views of lush green mountainsides that make San José a memorable city to visit. Sure, there are ugly buildings (earthquakes over the years brought down most of the city's traditional architecture), traffic congestion (both vehicular and pedestrian), and exhaust fumes, but all you have to do is glance up at those mountains to know that this is the most beautiful capital city in Central America. And if a glance isn't enough for you, you'll find that it's extremely easy to get out into the countryside from San José. Within an hour or two, you can climb a volcano, go white-water rafting, hike through a cloud forest, and stroll through a butterfly garden, among many other activities.

San José is also the most cosmopolitan city in Central America. Costa Rica's stable government and San José's climate have, over the years, attracted people from all over the world. One result has been the amazing variety of cuisines available in the city's restaurants. Another more recent result has been the proliferation of small hotels in renovated historic buildings. Together these restaurants and hotels provide visitors with a greater variety of options than are to be found anywhere between Mexico City and Bogotá.

WHAT'S SPECIAL ABOUT SAN JOSÉ

Museums
> The Gold Museum, the largest collection of pre-Columbian gold jewelry and ornaments in the Americas.
> The Jade Museum, an equally impressive collection of pre-Columbian jade artifacts and jewelry.
> The National Museum of Costa Rica, an excellent collection of pre-Columbian artifacts.

Parks/Gardens
> Lankester Gardens, near Cartago, with hundreds of species of orchids on display.

Religious Shrines
> The Basilica de Nuestra Senora de Los Angeles, in Cartago, with a statue of La Negrita that is said to heal the sick.
> Also in Cartago, the ruins of a church that have been turned into a park.

Activities
> Myriad active day trips, including white-water rafting, horseback riding, forest hikes, biking trips, hot-air ballooning, and many others.

Natural Spectacles
> Two volcanoes near San José (Poás and Irazú) with roads to their rims.

After Dark
> San José's Teatro Nacional, a stately old opera house with performances almost nightly.
> El Pueblo, a shopping, dining, and entertainment complex with nearly a dozen bars, discos, nightclubs, and even a roller-skating rink.

Zoos
> The Serpentarium, a reptilian zoo with dozens of Costa Rica's poisonous snakes on display.
> Spirogyra Butterfly Garden, The Butterfly Farm, and Butterfly Paradise, three butterfly gardens around the San José area.
> Zoo Ave, a private bird zoo near Alajuela.

Shopping
> Fresh-roasted Costa Rican coffee, available for as little as $1 per pound.

1. ORIENTATION

ARRIVING

BY PLANE   Juan Santamaría International Airport (tel. 441-0744 for 24-hour airport information) is located near the city of Alajuela, about 20 minutes from downtown San José. A taxi into town will cost around $12, and a bus only 40¢. The Alajuela–San José buses run frequently and drop you on Avenida 2 between Calle 12 and Calle 14. There are several car-rental agencies located at the airport, although if you are planning on spending a few days in San José, a car is a liability. If you are heading off to the beach immediately, it is much easier to pick up your car here than at a downtown office. You'll find the car-rental offices and the bus and taxi stands up the stairs and to the left after you clear Customs.

You have several options for changing money when you arrive at the airport.

You can get colónes at the money-changing kiosk just before the immigration desks. There is also a bank in the departures hall. It's open Monday through Friday from 9am to 2pm. When the banks are closed, there are usually official money changers (with badges) working inside the terminal. Outside the terminal, you may be approached by unofficial money changers. Though black-market money changing is illegal, it is quite common.

BY BUS If you arrived in Costa Rica overland and are coming to San José for the first time by bus, where you disembark depends on where you are coming from. Bus companies have their offices all over downtown San José. To find out where you will be dropped off, see the "Getting There" section of Chapter 2.

TOURIST INFORMATION

There is an **I.C.T. (Instituto Costarricense de Turismo)** desk at Juan Santamaría International Airport, open daily from 8am to 9pm, where you can pick up maps and brochures before you head into San José. You'll find the desk on the left before you come to the stairs that lead up to street level from the Customs inspection counter. The main tourist information center is at the Plaza de la Cultura, on Calle 5 between Avenida Central and Avenida 2 (tel. 222-1090), beside the entrance to the underground Gold Museum. The people here are very helpful. This office is open Monday through Friday from 9am to 5pm and Saturday from 9am to 1pm.

CITY LAYOUT

MAIN ARTERIES & STREETS Downtown San José is laid out on a grid. *Avenidas* (avenues) run east and west, while *calles* (streets) run north and south. The center of the city is at **Avenida Central** and **Calle Central.** To the north of Avenida Central, the avenidas have odd numbers beginning with Avenida 1; to the south, they have even numbers beginning with Avenida 2. Likewise, calles to the east of Calle Central have odd numbers, and those to the west have even numbers. The main downtown artery is **Avenida 2,** which merges with Avenida Central on either side of the downtown area. West of downtown, Avenida Central becomes **Paseo Colón,** which ends at Sabana Park and feeds into the highway to Alajuela, the airport, and the Pacific coast. East of downtown, Avenida Central leads to San Pedro and then to Cartago and the Interamerican Highway heading south. Calle 3 will take you out of town to the north and put you on the road to the Caribbean coast.

FINDING AN ADDRESS This is one of the most confusing aspects of visiting San José in particular and Costa Rica in general. There are no street addresses, at least not often. Addresses are given as a set of coordinates such as "Calle 3 between Avenida Central and Avenida 1." It is then up to you to locate the building within that block, keeping in mind that the building could be on either side of the street. Many addresses include additional information, such as the number of meters or *varas* (an old Spanish measurement roughly equal to a yard) from a specified intersection or some other well-known landmark. These landmarks are what become truly confusing for visitors to the city because they are often landmarks only if you have lived in the neighborhood all your life. The classic example of this is the Coca-Cola plant, one of the most common landmarks used in addresses in the blocks surrounding San José's main market. It refers to a Coca-Cola bottling plant that once stood in this area. Unfortunately, the edifice is long gone, but the address descriptions remain. In outlying neighborhoods, addresses can become long directions such as "50 meters south of the old church, then 100 meters east, then 20 meters south." Luckily for the visitor, most downtown addresses are straightforward. Oh, if you're wondering how mail deliverers manage, you'll be reassured to know that nearly everyone in San José uses a post office box. This is called the *apartado* system, and is abbreviated Apdo. on mailing addresses.

NEIGHBORHOODS IN BRIEF

San José is sprawling. Today it is divided into dozens of neighborhoods known as *barrios*. Most of the listings in this chapter fall within the main downtown area, but there are a few outlying neighborhoods you will need to know about.

Downtown This is San José's busiest area and is where you'll find most of the city's museums. There are also many tour companies, restaurants, and hotels downtown. Unfortunately, traffic noise and exhaust fumes make this one of the least pleasant parts of the city. Streets and avenues are usually bustling and crowded with pedestrians and vehicular traffic.

Barrio Amon/Barrio Atoya These two neighborhoods are the site of the greatest concentration of historic buildings in San José, and in the past few years, enterprising entrepreneurs have been renovating the old buildings and turning them into hotels. If you're looking for character and don't mind the noise and exhaust fumes, this neighborhood makes a good base for exploring the city.

Paseo Colón Paseo Colón, a wide boulevard west of downtown, is an extension of Avenida Central and ends at Sabana Park. It has several good, small hotels and numerous excellent restaurants. This is also where many of the city's rental-car agencies have their offices. Because this area is really part of downtown, I have not treated it as a separate area in the hotel and restaurant listings.

San Pedro/Los Yoses Located east of downtown San José, this neighborhood is home to the University of Costa Rica. There are numerous college-type bars and restaurants all around the edge of the campus and several good restaurants and small hotels.

Escazú Located in the hills west of San José, Escazú is a suburb with a small-town atmosphere. Although it's only 15 minutes from San José by taxi, it seems much farther away because of its relaxed atmosphere. Many bed-and-breakfast establishments are located here.

2. GETTING AROUND

BY BUS Bus transportation around San José is cheap—the fare is usually less than 15¢. The most important buses are those running east and west along Avenida 2 and Avenida 3. The Sabana–Cementerio bus runs from Sabana Park to downtown and is one of the most convenient buses to use. San Pedro buses will take you out of downtown heading east. You'll find a bus stop for the outbound Sabana–Cementerio bus across the street from Costa Rica Expeditions on Avenida 3 near the corner of Calle Central. These buses don't run very frequently, and their stops are far apart. Considering this and the congestion on Avenida 3, you'll find that it is generally easier to walk to your destination if it is closer than Sabana Park. Buses are always boarded from the front, and the bus drivers can make change. Be especially mindful of your wallet, purse, or other valuables since pickpockets often work the crowded buses. The Alajuela–San José buses that run in from the airport cost 40¢.

BY TAXI Although taxis in San José have meters *(marías)*, the drivers sometimes refuse to use them, so occasionally you'll have to negotiate the price. However, always try to get them to use the meter first. The official rate at press time is around 55¢ for the first kilometer and around 25¢ for each additional kilometer. If you have a rough idea of how far it is to your destination, you can estimate how much it should cost from these figures. You'll find taxis in front of the Teatro Nacional (high prices) and around the Parque Central at Avenida Central and Calle Central. Taxis in front of hotels usually charge more than others. You can also get a cab by calling 235-9966 or 254-5847.

ON FOOT Downtown San José is very compact. Nearly every place you might want to go is within an area 15 blocks by 4 blocks. Because of the traffic congestion, you'll often find it faster to walk than to take a bus or taxi. Avenida Central is a pedestrians-only street for several blocks around Calle Central.

BY MOTORCYCLE Motorcycles rent for about the same amount as cars, $35 a day or $210 a week. Due to poor road conditions and the difficulty of driving in Costa Rica, they are not recommended unless you are an experienced rider. Companies renting motorcycles include **Moto Rental,** Avenida 1 between calles 30 and 32 (tel. 257-1065) and **La Aventura Rent a Moto,** Avenida 10 at Calle 8 (tel. 233-6629).

BY CAR It will cost you around $40 per day to rent a car in Costa Rica, unless you make a reservation before you leave home. If you do decide to rent a car, and pick it up in downtown San José, be prepared for some very congested streets. The following international companies have desks at Juan Santamaría International Airport, as well as offices downtown: **Avis Rent A Car** (tel. toll free 800/331-1212; tel. at airport 442-1321; tel. in downtown San José 232-9922); **Budget Rent A Car** (tel. toll free 800/527-0700; tel. at airport 441-4444; tel. in downtown San José 223-3284); **Hertz Rent A Car** (tel. toll free 800/654-3131; tel. at airport 221-1818; tel. in downtown San José 223-5959); and **National Car Rental** (tel. toll free 800/227-7368; tel. at airport 441-6533; tel. in downtown San José 233-4044). **Thrifty Car Rental** has an office in downtown San José (tel. 255-4141 or toll free 800/367-2277).

You will save somewhere between $35 and $75 per week on a car rental if you make a reservation in your home country at least one week before you need the car. The least-expensive National car available rents for about $230 per week, plus insurance (total of around $320) in San José, but if you book this same car in advance from the United States, you can get it for $194 per week, plus insurance (total of around $285). Though it is possible at some rental-car agencies to waive the insurance charges, you will have to pay all damages before leaving the country if you are in an accident. Even if you do take the insurance, you will have a deductible of between $500 and $750. At some agencies you can buy additional insurance to lower the deductible.

There are dozens of other rental-car agencies in San José, including the following: **Adobe Rent a Car,** Calle 7 between avenidas 8 and 10 (tel. 221-5425); **Hola! Renta Car,** west of Hotel Irazú, La Uruca, San José (tel. 231-5666); **Elegante Rent A Car,** Calle 10 between avenidas 13 and 15 and Paseo Colón at Calle 34 (tel. 233-8605 or toll free 800/582-7432); and **Tico Rent A Car,** Calle 10 between avenidas 13 and 15 or Paseo Colón between calles 24 and 26 (tel. 222-8920 or 223-9642).

FAST FACTS: SAN JOSÉ

American Express American Express (tel. 223-3644) has a counter in the Banco de San José on Calle Central between avenidas 3 and 5. It's open Monday through Friday from 8am to 4pm.

Babysitters Your only chance for a babysitter in San José is to check with your hotel.

Bookstores The Bookshop, Avenida 1 between calles 1 and 3 (tel. 221-6847) has a wide selection of English-language newspapers, magazines, and books; it's open Monday through Saturday from 9am to 7pm and Sunday from 9am to 3pm. For used books in English, stop by Book Traders (tel. 255-0508), open Monday through Saturday from 9am to 5pm. It's located above the Pizza Hut on Avenida 1 between calles 3 and 5, and has another location (which is open on Sundays) just down the street on Avenida 1 between calles 5 and 7.

Car Rentals See "Getting Around," in this chapter.

Climate See "When to Go," in Chapter 2.

Country Code The country code for San José is 506.

Crime See "Safety," below.

Currency Exchange The best thing to do is to change money at your hotel. If they can't do this for you, they can direct you to a private bank where you won't have to stand in line for hours. Avoid changing money on the street.

Dentist If you need a dentist while in San José, your best bet is to call your embassy, which will have a list of recommended dentists.

Doctor Contact your embassy for information on doctors in San José.

Drugstores Farmacia Fischel, Avenida 3 and Calle 2, is across from the main post office (tel. 223-0909). Open Monday through Saturday from 8am to 7pm.

Embassies/Consulates See "Fast Facts: Costa Rica," in Chapter 2.

Emergencies In case of fire dial 118; for the police dial 117; for an ambulance dial 128 or 221-5818.

Eyeglasses Optica Jiménez, Avenida 2 and Calle 3 (tel. 222-0233 or 233-4417) is open Monday through Saturday from 8am to noon and 2 to 6pm.

Hairdressers/Barbers El Toque Nuevo, Avenida 2 between calles 1 and 3 in Edificios Los Arcados (tel. 222-0877) is open Monday through Saturday from 9am to 7pm. It services both men and women.

Holidays See "When to Go," in Chapter 2.

Hospitals Clinica Biblica, Avenida 14 between Calle Central and Calle 1 (tel. 223-6422 or, for emergencies, 257-0466), is conveniently located close to downtown and has several English-speaking doctors.

Information See "Orientation," above in this chapter.

Laundry/Dry Cleaning Sixaola, Avenida 2 between calles 7 and 9 (tel. 221-2111), open Monday through Friday from 7am to 6pm and Saturday from 8am to 1pm, is one of the only places downtown to get clothes cleaned. Unfortunately, their prices are quite high. Ask at your hotel—most offer a laundry service, though these too are expensive.

Libraries The National Library is at the corner of Avenida 3 and Calle 15.

Lost Property If you lose something in San José, consider it gone.

Luggage Storage/Lockers Most hotels will store luggage for you while you are traveling around the country. Sometimes there is a charge for this service.

Newspapers/Magazines The *Tico Times* is Costa Rica's English-language weekly paper and serves both the expatriate community and tourists. You can also get the *International Herald Tribune, USA Today, Time,* and *Newsweek* as well as other English-language publications. You'll find these publications in hotel gift shops and in bookstores selling English-language books.

Photographic Needs Film is very expensive in Costa Rica, so bring as much as you will need. You can buy film and other photographic equipment at Dima, Avenida Central between calles 3 and 5 (tel. 222-3969), which is open Monday through Friday from 9am to 5pm and Saturday from 8am to noon. I recommend that you wait to have your film processed at home.

Police Dial 117 for the police.

Post Office The main post office (*correo*) is on Calle 2 between avenidas 1 and 3. It's open Monday through Friday from 7am to 10pm, and Saturday from 8am to noon for purchasing stamps. For mailing packages, hours are Monday through Friday from 8am to 5pm.

Radio/TV There are about 10 TV channels, plus satellite TV from the United States. There are dozens of AM and FM radio stations in San José.

Religious Services The *Tico Times* has a listing of churches in San José. You can also ask at the tourist office for a list of the city's churches, or ask at your hotel. The following are a number of suggestions for English-language services: Episcopal Church of the Good Shepherd (tel. 222-1560); reformed Jewish services at B'Nai Israel (tel. 225-8561); Catholic mass at the International Chapel of St. Mary at the Hotel Herradura complex; Christian Fellowship services (tel. 228-0594); International Baptist Church (tel. 224-9424); Quaker services (tel. 233-6168).

Restrooms These are known as *sanitarios* or *servicios sanitarios*. They are marked *damas* (women) and *hombres* or *caballeros* (men).

Safety Never carry anything you value in your pockets or purse. Pickpockets and purse slashers are rife in San José, especially on public buses, in the markets, or near a hospital. Leave your passport, money, and other valuables in your hotel safe, and only carry as much as you really need when you go out. If you do carry anything valuable with you, keep it in a moneybelt or special passport bag around your neck. Day packs are a prime target of brazen pickpockets throughout the city. Also, be advised that the Parque Central is not a safe place for a late-night stroll.

Other precautions include walking around corner vendors, not between the vendor and the building. The tight space between the vendor and the building is a favorite spot for pickpockets. Never park a car on the street, and never leave anything of value in a car, even if it's in a guarded parking lot. Don't even leave your car by the curb in front of a hotel while you dash in to check on your reservation. With these precautions in mind you should have a safe visit to San José. Also see "Safety" in "Fast Facts: Costa Rica," in Chapter 2.

Shoe Repair Ask at your hotel for the repair shop nearest you.

Taxes All hotels charge 14.3% tax. Restaurants charge 11% tax and also add on a 10% service charge, for a total of 21% more on your bill. There is an airport departure tax of $6.75.

Taxis See "Getting Around," earlier in this chapter.

Telegrams/Telexes You can send telegrams and telexes from the I.C.E. office on Avenida 2 between calles 1 and 3 (open daily from 7am to 10pm) or from the Western Union office (tel. 257-1150), Calle 9 between avenidas 2 and 4.

Telephones Pay phones are not as common in San José as they are in North American cities. When you do find one, whether on the street or in a restaurant or hotel lobby, it may take coins of various denominations or it may take only 5-colón coins. A call within the city will cost 5 colónes. Pay phones are notoriously unreliable, so it may be better to make calls from your hotel, though you will likely be charged around 100 colónes per call.

Useful Telephone Numbers For the exact time, call 112.

Water The water in San José is said to be perfectly fine to drink. Residents of the city will swear to this. However, frequent complaints about intestinal illnesses by tourists make me a bit skeptical about San José's water. If you want to be cautious, drink bottled water and *frescos* made with milk instead of water. *Sin hielo* means "no ice."

Weather The weather in San José (including the Central Valley) is usually temperate, never getting extremely hot or cold. May to November is the rainy season, though the rain usually falls in the afternoon and evening.

3. ACCOMMODATIONS

As the capital of Costa Rica, San José has a wide variety of hotels, ranging from luxury resorts to budget pensions charging only a few dollars a night. However, these two extremes are the exceptions, not the norm. The vast number of hotels, and the best deals, are to be found in the $30-to-$90 price range. Within this range you'll find restored homes that have been turned into small hotels and bed-and-breakfasts. You will also find modern hotels with swimming pools and exercise rooms, and older downtown business hotels. When considering where to stay in San José, you should take into consideration how long you plan to stay, what you expect to do while you're here, and whether or not you want to be in the heart of the city or out in the suburbs.

Downtown hotels, many of which are in beautifully restored homes, though convenient to museums, restaurants, and shopping, are often very noisy. Many people are also bothered by the exhaust fumes here in downtown. If you want clean air and a peaceful night's sleep, consider staying out in the suburbs. Escazú is quiet and has great views, while Los Yoses is fairly close in yet still quiet. If you have rented a car, I recommend that you don't stay at a downtown hotel because parking is often expensive and the traffic congestion is trying, to say the least. If you plan to take some day tours, you can just as easily arrange these from a hotel outside downtown.

In the past few years, dozens of bed-and-breakfast inns have opened up around the San José area. Most are in residential neighborhoods that are quieter, though less convenient, than downtown locations. You can find out about many B&Bs by contacting the **Costa Rica Bed & Breakfast Group** (tel. 506/223-4168 or 228-9200).

If you plan to be in town for a while or are traveling with family or several friends, you may want to consider staying in an apartotel. As the name implies these are a cross between an apartment and a hotel. You can rent by the day, but you get a furnished apartment with full kitchen.

A word about laundry service at hotels: Laundry is charged by the piece and prices are ludicrous. My wife and I did a quick tally of our dirty clothes and came up with something like $75 for a load of laundry. Rinse out your own clothes if possible, or take them to a laundromat.

The price categories used below are defined as follows (for a double room): Very Expensive—$125 and up; Expensive—$90 to $125; Moderate—$60 to $90; Inexpensive—$30 to $60; Budget—$30 and under. However, please keep in mind that the $14.3% hotel-room tax, which adds quite a bit to the price of a room, is not included in rates listed below. If you have set $90 as your total daily room budget, you will want to look for a hotel charging between $75 and $80 per night before the tax.

DOWNTOWN SAN JOSÉ

EXPENSIVE

AUROLA HOLIDAY INN, Avenida 5 and Calle 5 (Apdo. 7802-1000), San José. Tel. 506/223-7233. Fax 506/255-1036. 188 rms, 16 suites, A/C TV TEL
$ Rates: $102–$110 single; $112–$120 double; $142–$400 suite single, $152–$400 suite double. AE, DC, MC V. **Parking:** Free.

This is downtown San José's only high-rise deluxe hotel and is situated directly across the street from the attractive Parque Morazan. If familiarity in a foreign country is a comfort to you, this is the place to stay. Unfortunately, you may have to put up with less than gracious service from a staff that seems to be overworked. The hotel has been around for quite a few years, but a recent renovation added new carpets, new elevators, and key-card locks. Try to get one of the upper-floor rooms on the north side for one of the best views in the city.

Dining/Entertainment: The Mirador, up on the 17th floor, is the Aurola's top restaurant and serves good continental and international fare. The view is the best in San José. There is also a casino on this same floor. Just off the lobby is the more casual Tropicana, which serves an impressive, though pricey, breakfast buffet. Bar La Palma overlooks the lobby and Parque Morazan. There is also a snack bar adjacent to the pool.

Services: Room service, laundry service, car-rental desk, travel agency, tour desk.

Facilities: Indoor pool, hot tub, saunas, exercise room, gift shop, executive center.

COROBICÍ HOTEL & SPA Autopista General Canas, Sabana Norte (Apdo. 2443-1000), San José. Tel. 506/232-8122, 232-0618, or toll free (in the U.S.) 800/227-4274. Fax 506/231-5834. 177 rms, 26 suites. A/C TV TEL SAFE
$ Rates: $107 single; $117–$135 double; $150–$375 suite. AE, DC, MC, V. **Parking:** Free.

 FROMMER'S SMART TRAVELER: HOTELS

1. Always remember to ask what the total cost of a room will be with the taxes added in. Currently the room tax is a whopping 14.3%, which adds a sizeable chunk to your hotel bill.
2. Visit in the rainy season (May to November) when rates are usually lower.
3. If you are traveling on a tight budget, consider taking a room with a shared bath, which will save you a considerable amount of money.
4. You'll also save money if you take a room with a fan instead of air conditioning. In most parts of the country, a fan is really all that's necessary, and air-conditioned rooms often have problems with mildew.
5. To avoid a frantic hotel search, make a reservation for your first night in town, especially if you're arriving after dark.
6. Keep your eyes open for new hotels; the tourism industry is booming in Costa Rica and newer hotels offer good values.
7. Always ask for a room away from the street if you are staying in downtown San José. Traffic noises here can be horrendous.

Located just past the end of Paseo Colón and on the edge of Parque La Sabana, the Corobicí is more convenient than the resorts out by the airport, but is rather sterile and austere both inside and out. The lobby is a vast expanse of marble floor faced by blank walls, though the modern art deco furnishings lend a bit of character. Guest rooms, however, are quite modern and confortable, with good beds and walls of glass through which most floors get good views of the valley and surrounding mountains. Joggers will find that the proximity of Parque La Sabana makes this a good choice.

Dining/Entertainment: Perhaps the hotel's greatest attributes are its restaurants. Fuji serves authentic Japanese meals amid equally authentic surroundings. La Gondola serves good Italian food. These two restaurants are open for lunch and dinner only. At El Tucan Coffee Shop, you can get an inexpensive meal throughout the day. The Guacamaya is a quiet lobby bar, while the Pub Bar is a bit more lively and features karaoke music. There is also a casino.

Services: 24-hour room service, valet/laundry service, downtown shuttle ($2 per person each way), tour desk, car-rental desk.

Facilities: The Corobicí claims to have the largest health spa in Central America. You'll find a well-equipped exercise room, sauna, hot tub, and aerobics classes. However, you'll have to pay an additional $10 for the use of these facilities. The hotel's outdoor pool is rather small and uninviting. Other facilities include a beauty parlor and a gift shop.

HOTEL L'AMBIANCE, 949 Calle 13 (Apdo. 1040-2050), San José (in the U.S.: C/O INTERLINK, 179, P.O. Box 526770, Miami, FL 33152). Tel. 506/222-6702. Fax 506/223-0481. 7 rms, 1 suite. TV TEL

$ Rates: $70 single; $90 double; $110 suite single, $140 suite double. No credit cards.
Parking: Nearby.

L'Ambiance is a beautifully restored stucco building with a central courtyard patio reminiscent of old Spain, and is about the closest you'll come to colonial luxury in Costa Rica. The building is on a quiet street only a few blocks from the heart of downtown San José, so you get both the convenience of the city and the quiet of a suburban location. Tile floors in the halls and on the veranda surrounding the courtyard provide a touch of old Costa Rica, while European and North American antiques add a bit of international flavor. Guest rooms have high ceilings and either hardwood floors or carpeting. There is a mix of antique and modern furnishings, and though there is no air conditioning, overhead fans manage to keep the rooms cool. Rooms vary in size.

Dining/Entertainment: The hotel's dining room/bar is a surprising contrast to the rest of the hotel. Potted plants and white lattice walls give it a greenhouse feel. The menu, which changes regularly, offers a limited selection of well-prepared continental dishes. Prices are quite reasonable.

Services: Concierge service, laundry service.

PARQUE DEL LAGO HOTEL, Avenida 2 between calles 40 and 42 (Apdo. 624-1007), San José (in the U.S.: P.O. Box 025216-1634, Miami, Fl 33102-5216). Tel. 506/222-1577, or toll free (in the U.S.) 800/663-8889. Fax 506/223-1617. 30 rms, 9 suites, A/C TV TEL SAFE

$ Rates: $60–$95 single; $60–$110 double; $115–$200 single suite, $130–$200 double suite. VIP level rooms at additional charge. AE, MC, V. **Parking:** Free.

Located less than a block from Parque La Sabana, this new luxury hotel is set up with business travelers in mind. Beautifully designed, the hotel incorporates Italian marble, antique Costa Rican tile floor, and ornate colonial-styled number plaques beside each guest-room door. Room sizes and styles vary, but in the standard rooms you'll find such amenities as minibars, coffeemakers, and clock-radios. There are also marble-topped desks and café tables. Light sleepers will appreciate the double glass on all the windows. Suites offer the same luxurious styling as well as considerably more room. The third floor, which has the best views, is the VIP floor. Though there are a few rooms here for $60, most are considerably more expensive, so I am including the listing in this category rather than in the "Moderate" category.

Dining/Entertainment: There is no restaurant in the hotel, but there are several nearby.

Services: Airport shuttle, secretarial services, concierge service, sports-equipment rentals.

Facilities: Business center, coin laundry, gift shop, art gallery.

MODERATE

AMSTEL AMÓN, Avenida 13 and Calle 5 (Apdo. 4192-1000), San José. Tel. 506/222-4622. Fax 506/233-3329. 75 rms, 15 suites. TV TEL SAFE

$ Rates: $75 single or double; $90–$120 suite. AE, MC, V. Parking: Free.

This hotel was still under construction when I was last in town, but it looked like it was going to be quite nice. It is located on the north edge of the Barrio Amón historic neighborhood, and though the building is new, it fits in architecturally with other older buildings in the area. This hotel should not be confused with the older Amstel Morazan, which is a few blocks away and is rather noisy at night. This new Amstel hotel is off the bus route and away from the nightclubs so it should be a bit quieter. Rooms are likely to feature plenty of modern amenities. A restaurant, bar, and casino were all part of the restaurant's plan, and services should include a tour desk, car-rental desk, and laundry service. There were also plans to have an exercise room, hot tub, business center, gift shop, and beauty parlor.

BRITANNIA HOTEL, Calle 3 and Avenida 11 (Apdo. 3742-1000), San José. Tel. 506/223-6667. Fax 506/223-6411. 24 rms. TV TEL SAFE

$ Rates (including Tico breakfast): $73–$97 single; $85–108 double. AE, DC, MC, V. **Parking:** Nearby.

Of the many hotels that have been created from restored old houses in downtown San José, this is the most luxurious. The big, pink building, with its wraparound veranda, is unmistakable and is certainly one of the most attractive old houses in the neighborhood. In the lobby, tile floors, stained-glass clerestory windows, a brass chandelier, and reproduction Victorian decor all help set a tone of tropical luxury. Along with restoring the old home, the owners have built a three-story addition, which is separated from the original building by a narrow atrium. Rooms in the original home have hardwood floors and furniture. High ceilings and fans help keep these rooms cool. In the deluxe rooms, you'll find a hairdryer and basket of toiletries in the bathroom. Though the streetside rooms have double glass, light sleepers will still want to avoid these rooms. The quietest rooms are those toward the back of the addition. In what was once the wine cellar, you'll find a casual restaurant. The buffet breakfast is served in the adjacent skylit room. Afternoon tea and happy-hour drinks are also served. There is room service, and the hotel has an airport shuttle.

LA CASA VERDE DE AMÓN, Calle 7 and Avenida 9 no. 910, San José (in the U.S.: Dept. 1701, P.O. Box 025216, Miami, FL 33102-5216). Tel. 506/223-0969. 5 rms, 2 suites. TV TEL

$ Rates (including continental breakfast): Dec 1–Apr 30, $65–$72 single or double, $86 suite; May 1–Nov 30, $55–$65 single or double, $72 suite. AE, MC, V. **Parking:** Nearby.

This tropical Victorian house was built around 1910 and was completely renovated between 1989 and 1992. There are beautiful old tile and polished hardwood floors throughout the building, which give the house a patrician air. Off the lobby, there is a small patio and open-air breakfast room. Up on the second floor, there is a large central seating area with a 110-year-old baby grand piano and stained-glass clerestory windows at the top of the high ceiling. These windows bathe this room in a beautiful blue light. Rooms are all different, but most are furnished with antiques. Some have their original porcelain fixtures and brass faucets, which means you may find a bathtub or only a shower in your bathroom. One of the two suites is huge, with a high ceiling, king beds, and a separate seating area. All the rooms have clock-radios, but unfortunately, it is likely that traffic noises will wake you in the morning if you have a room on the streetside of the hotel. The hotel offers airport transfers.

D'RAYA VIDA, Apdo. 493-1000, San José (in the U.S.: P.O. Box 025216-1638, Miami, FL 33102-5216). Tel. 506/223-4168. Fax 506/223-4157. 5 rms (2 with private bath).

$ Rates (including full breakfast): Nov–Apr, $65 single, $85 double; May–Oct, $50 single, $65 double. AE, MC, V. **Parking:** Free.

This little bed-and-breakfast is so secluded that it seems to be in a world all its own, yet it is in downtown San José. To find the inn, go east on Avenida 9, then turn left on Calle 17. In 100 meters, turn left on Avenida 11. Follow this road to the dead end at the inn's front gate. Behind the gate, in a shady old garden, is a miniature villa. The restored old stucco home is furnished with the owners' eclectic collection of crafts from around the world, and in the living room, you'll find a grand piano and fireplace. (Sounds like a B&B up north, doesn't it?) Guest rooms are all different. One of the upstairs rooms has its own private balcony, while the other has an unusual four-poster bed. My favorite rooms, however, are the two downstairs, which have private bathrooms. One is decorated with masks from around the world, and the other has Indian art and a fountain just outside. Be forewarned, however, that there is an active railroad track right next to the house, although trains only run during the day. D'Raya Vida offers free airport pick-up.

FLEUR DE LYS HOTEL, Calle 13 between avenidas 2 and 6, 50 meters south of the Plaza de la Democracia (Apdo. 10736-1000), San José. Tel. 506/225-3939 or 224-0505. Fax 506/253-6934. 20 rms, 1 suite. TV TEL

$ Rates: $65 single; $70 double; $80–$95 suite. AE, DC, MC, V. **Parking:** Nearby.

Located close to the National Museum and Plaza de la Cultura, the Fleur de Lys is a restored mansion that has been painted an eye-catching pink. Inside, the historic mansion is less ostentatious. The lobby and hallways feature polished hardwoods and old tiles, while in the guest rooms, each of which is different, there are modern furnishings. The standard rooms tend to be cramped, so if you need space, you may want to opt for a suite. All the rooms are decorated with unusual original artworks that give this hotel a character unique in San José. Carpeting and modern tiled bathrooms with comtemporary fixtures assure you of the creature comforts. The most unusual room is the master suite, which has black lacquer furnishings, a cordless phone, halogen lamps, a black-tile bathroom, and a tiny sunroom off the bedroom.

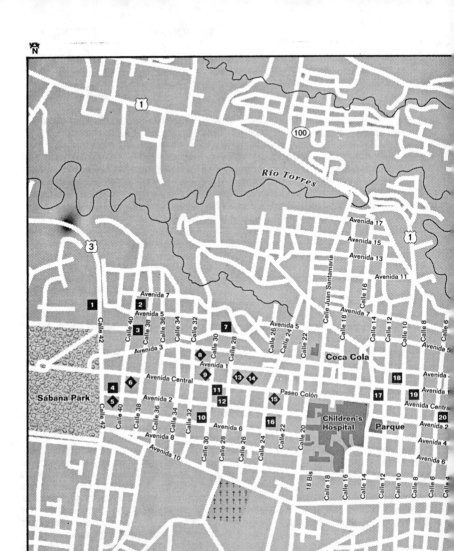

ACCOMMODATIONS:

Amstel Amón **29**
Apartotel Castilla **16**
Apartotel San José **58**
Aurola Holiday Inn **32**
Britannia Hotel **26**
Casa Morazan **33**
La Casa Verde de Amón **28**
Coffee Garden Inn **59**
Corobicí Hotel & Spa **1**
D'Raya Vida **40**

Fleur de Lys Hotel **55**
Gran Hotel Costa Rica **46**
Hotel Alameda **17**
Hotel Bienvenido **18**
Hotel Cacts **7**
Hotel Del Rey **47**
Hotel Diplomat **20**
Hotel Don Carlos **34**
Hotel Dunn Inn **31**
Hotel Edelweiss **39**
Hotel Ejecutivo Napoleon **3**

Hotel Europa **21**
Hotel Grano de Oro **10**
Hotel Johnson **19**
Hotel L'Ambiance **38**
Hotel Le Bergerac **61**
Hotel Petite Victoria **12**
Hotel Ritz and Pension Continental **24**
Hotel Rosa Del Paseo **11**
Hotel Santo Tomas **25**
Hotel Torremolinos **2**
Hotel Villa Tournon **30**

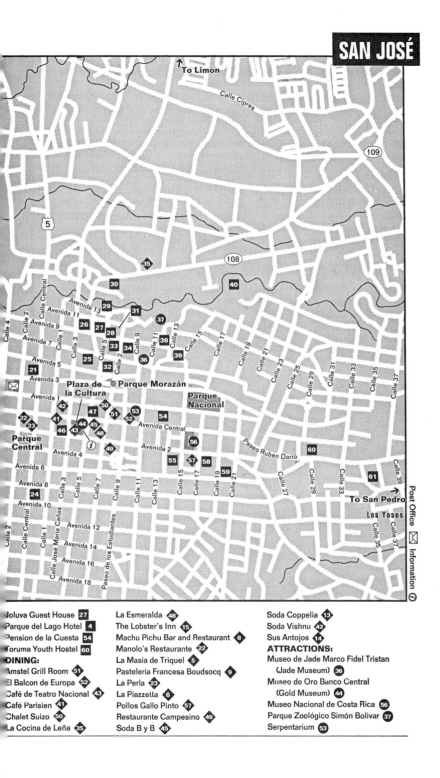

SAN JOSÉ

Joluva Guest House 27
Parque del Lago Hotel 4
Pension de la Cuesta 54
Toruma Youth Hostel 60
DINING:
Amstel Grill Room 51
El Balcon de Europa 52
Café de Teatro Nacional 43
Café Parisien 41
Chalet Suizo 50
La Cocina de Leña 35

La Esmeralda 48
The Lobster's Inn 15
Machu Pichu Bar and Restaurant 8
Manolo's Restaurante 22
La Masia de Triquel 5
Pasteleria Francesa Boudsocq 9
La Perla 23
La Piazzetta 6
Pollos Gallo Pinto 57
Restaurante Campesino 49
Soda B y B 45

Soda Coppelia 13
Soda Vishnu 42
Sus Antojos 14
ATTRACTIONS:
Museo de Jade Marco Fidel Tristan (Jade Museum) 36
Museo de Oro Banco Central (Gold Museum) 44
Museo Nacional de Costa Rica 56
Parque Zoológico Simón Bolivar 37
Serpentarium 53

 FROMMER'S COOL FOR KIDS: HOTELS

Cariari Hotel & Country Club *(see p. 59)* Not only is there a big pool that the kids will love, but there's a babysitting service that allows Mom and Dad some time to themselves.

Hotel Herradura *(see p. 60)* The large grounds give the kids plenty of space to run off excess energy.

Apartotel Castilla and Apartotel San José *(see p. 52)* These two places both provide apartment-style accommodations complete with kitchens, which are a definite plus when you've got fussy kids to feed.

This room is definitely worth the extra expense. There is an elegant little Italian restaurant off the lobby and a bar in a front room with a streetside terrace.

GRAN HOTEL COSTA RICA, Avenida 2 between calles 1 and 3, San José. Tel. 506/221-0796 or 221-4000. Fax 506/221-3501. 109 rms, 8 suites. TV TEL SAFE
$ Rates: $51 single; $68 double; $75 triple; $66–$150 single suite, $77–$180 double suite. AE, MC, V. **Parking:** Nearby.
Though the Gran Hotel Costa Rica can claim the best location of any downtown hotel, it does not, unfortunately, offer rooms to match the prestigious location or name. Though most of the guest rooms here are fairly large, they have not been updated in a couple of decades, giving them a generally run-down feel, especially in the bathrooms.
The Café Parisien is the hotel's greatest attribute, and it is memorable not so much for its food as for its atmosphere. The restaurant is an open-air patio that overlooks all the vendors, street musicians, and activity of the Plaza de la Cultura. On the opposite side of the lobby, there is a small and very casual casino. The hotel also maintains a tour desk and gift shop, and it offers laundry service.

HOTEL DEL REY, Avenida Central and Calle 5 (Apdo. 6241-1000), San José. Tel. 506/221-7272 or 257-3130. Fax 506/221-0096. 104 rms, 3 suites. TV TEL SAFE
$ Rates: $55–$75 single; $68–$75 double; $75–$85 triple; $125 suite. AE, MC, V. **Parking:** Nearby.
This is one of the newest larger hotels to open in downtown San José and it offers the amenities and services of other downtown choices of this size. The difference is that most of the Del Ray's competitors haven't been upgraded in the past 20 or 30 years. You can't miss the Del Rey; it's an attractive pink corner building with vaguely colonial styling. The lobby continues the facade's theme with pink-tile floors and stone columns. Inside there are carved hardwood doors for every guest room. Behind these impressive doors, you'll find wall-to-wall carpeting and hardwood furniture. The rooms very in size and comfort. There are quiet interior rooms that have no windows, and larger rooms with windows (but also street noises). The hotel has its own casino, as well as a large, casual dining room and a bar with a sportfishing theme.

HOTEL EJECUTIVO NAPOLEON, Calle 40 between avenidas 3 and 5 (Apdo. 8-6340), San José. Tel. 506/223-3252, 223-3282, or 222-2278. Fax 506/222-9847. 27 rms, 1 suite. TV TEL
$ Rates (including continental breakfast): $65–$75 single; $75–$85 double. AE, MC, V. **Parking:** Free.
This hotel out at the west end of Paseo Colón near Parque La Sabana, is small and quiet and offers many of the amenities of a larger, less personal hotel. The rooms here are fairly large, and though they have older furnishings, they are still quite comfortable. Carpeting, big new TVs, and modern bathrooms all help to balance

out the shortcomings of the furniture. Though it is rarely necessary, air conditioning is available in some rooms. Ask for a room away from the street if you're a light sleeper.

What gives this hotel a good measure of appeal is its courtyard garden and swimming pool. There is a breakfast room and bar in the lobby, and a second, smaller bar beside the swimming pool. The hotel also maintains a tour desk and has laundry service.

HOTEL GRANO DE ORO, Calle 30 no. 251, between avenidas 2 and 4, 150 meters south of Paseo Colón (Apdo. 1157-1007, Centro Colón), San José (in the U.S.: P.O. Box 025216-36, Miami, FL 33102-5216). Tel. 506/255-3322. Fax 506/221-2782. 35 rms, 2 suites. TV TEL SAFE
$ Rates: $64–$80 single; $69–$85 double; $115 suite. AE, MC, V (add 6% surcharge). **Parking:** Free.

San José boasts dozens of old homes that have been converted into hotels, but few offer the luxurious accommodations or professional service that can be found at the Grano de Oro. Located on a quiet side street of of Paseo Colón, this small hotel offers a variety of room types to fit most budgets and tastes. Personally, I like the patio rooms, which have French doors opening onto private patios. However, if you want a room with plenty of space, ask for one of the deluxe rooms, which have large, modern, tiled baths with big tubs. Throughout all the guest rooms, you'll find attractive hardwood furniture, including old-fashioned wardrobes in some rooms. For additional luxuries, you can stay in one of the suites, which have whirlpool tubs. The hotel's patio garden restaurant serves excellent international meals and some of the best desserts in the city, and when it comes time to relax you can soak in a hot tub or have a drink in the rooftop lounge, which has a commanding view of San José.

HOTEL IRAZÚ, Autopista General Cañas, San José. Tel. 506/232-4811 or 220-1441. Fax 506/232-4549. 336 rms, 1 suite. TV TEL
$ Rates: $50–$77 single; $61–$88 double; $180 suite. AE, MC, V. **Parking:** Free.
If you like the feel of luxury resorts but can't afford what they charge for a room, then the Irazú might just be the answer. At the Irazú, rates are surprisingly low, but then the rooms aren't exactly luxurious. The more expensive rooms are those with air conditioning, while some of the less expensive standard rooms have balconies. The Irazú is popular with international conferences and always seems to be busy, which means service can sometimes be lackluster. However, you can lounge around the pool—large and set in a grassy courtyard, it's the hotel's greatest asset—or play tennis on the lighted courts to your heart's content, and when you want to go downtown, you can hop on the free shuttle.

There's a casual coffee shop off the lobby and a tropical motif bar that overlooks the swimming pool. Unfortunately, food is indifferently prepared. The Irazú also has one of the largest casinos in San José. The Irazú's other amenities include a sauna, massages, a beauty salon, room and laundry service, and free local phone calls; it maintains a gift shop, tour desk, travel agency, and car-rental desk.

HOTEL ROSA DEL PASEO, 2862 Paseo Colón (Apdo. 287-1007), San José. Tel. 506/257-3213, 257-3258, or 257-3225. Fax 506/223-2776. 20 rms, 1 suite. TV TEL MINIBAR SAFE
$ Rates (including continental breakfast): Nov–Mar, $70 single, $80 double, $90 triple, $130 suite; Apr–Oct, $60 single, $70 double, $80 triple, $120 suite. DC, MC, V. **Parking:** Nearby.
This hotel is housed in one of San José's most beautiful old stucco homes, but unfortunately it is right on busy Paseo Colón. If you should be so unfortunate as to get one of the front guest rooms, I don't think you would be able to sleep at all. However, if you get a room in back, you should be well insulated from the noise. Built more than 110 years ago, this old home underwent a complete renovation and modernization a few years ago and is now richly appointed and surprisingly evocative of 19th-century Costa Rica. There are beautiful details—transoms, ornate stucco door frames, polished hardwood floors—throughout the hotel. Reproduction antique

and wicker furnishings evoke both the tropics and the past century.

There is no restaurant on the premises, but snacks and cold meals are available. You'll also find 24-hour bar/beverage service, laundry service, airport transportation, a craft shop, and an art gallery.

INEXPENSIVE

APARTOTEL CASTILLA, Calle 24 between avenidas 2 and 4 (Apdo. 944-1007), San José. Tel. 506/222-2131. Fax 506/221-2080. 15 apts. TV TEL

$ Rates: $33.40 single; $40.05 double; $48.35 triple; $56.60 quad. AE, MC, V. **Parking:** Free.

Though this place has been around for years and the furniture is a bit dated and rather basic, you certainly get plenty of room. There is also the convenience of having your own kitchen, which can help save money, and daily maid service. There are parquet floors throughout, and small tiled bathrooms. In the bedrooms, you'll find twin beds only. The back apartments are particularly quiet.

Apartotel Castilla is located about halfway down Paseo Colón, which makes it convenient both to downtown (a 15-minute walk) and dozens of restaurants in all price ranges.

APARTOTEL SAN JOSÉ, Avenida 2 between calles 17 and 19 (P.O. Box 4192-1000), San José, Tel. 506/222-0455. Fax 506/233-3329. 12 apts. TV TEL

$ Rates: $46 single; $53–$60 double; $58–$65 triple. MC, V. **Parking:** Free.

Operated by the same company that runs the Amstel hotels, this apartotel is located across the street from the National Museum. As at the Castilla, the furnishings are older (from the 1960s and 1970s), so the apartments look a bit dated, but there is of course plenty of space. Because you're on a side street off of Avenida 2, it is fairly quiet. This place is a bit more expensive than the Castilla, but it is more convenient to downtown museums and restaurants. A laundry/valet service is available.

CASA MORAZAN, Calle 7 and Avenida 9 (Apdo. 10063-1000), San José. Tel. 506/257-4175. Fax 506/221-3826. 10 rms, 1 suite. A/C TV TEL

$ Rates (including continental breakfast): Nov 15–Mar 15, $40–$75 single, $50–$85 double, $100 suite; Mar 16–Nov 14, $40–$60 single, $40–$75 double, $75 suite. MC, V. **Parking:** Nearby.

The Barrio Amon district of downtown San José has seen a rapid proliferation of hotels in the past few years, and this is another of the better ones. The interior styling is very modern, with art deco accents throughout. Guest rooms are carpeted and many have king-size beds. The bathrooms are of average size but have modern fixtures. The big business suite offers plenty of space for small meetings and such. This hotel had just opened up when I visited and there were plans to add a small dining room serving a limited menu. Unfortunately, most of the rooms get quite a bit of traffic noise.

HOTEL ALAMEDA, Avenida Central between calles 12 and 14 (Apdo. 680) San José. Tel. 506/223-6333 or 221-3045. Fax 506/222-9673. 52 rms. TV TEL

$ Rates: $33.25 single; $42.90 double. AE, DC, MC, V. **Parking:** Nearby.

This is another of San José's large old hotels, but a remodeled lobby gives the hotel a very modern feel. The rooms here are of medium size, with carpeting, older furniture, small tiled baths, and plenty of closet space. There are large windows so the rooms are bright, but the windows also let in the street noises. There's a large restaurant on the second floor. The menu features international and Costa Rican dishes at prices ranging from about $3.35 to $14.80. There is also room service and a laundry and dry-cleaning service.

HOTEL DIPLOMAT, Calle 6 between Avenida Central and Avenida (Apdo. 6606-1000), San José. Tel. 506/221-8133 or 221-8744. Fax 506/233-7474. 29 rms (all with bath). TEL

$ Rates: $25.50 single; $37 double. AE, MC, V. **Parking:** Nearby.

It's easy to miss the entrance to this hotel. Watch for it on the east side of the street. The lobby is narrow, and the front door is fairly nondescript. The carpeted rooms are rather small but comfortable nonetheless, and some rooms on the upper floors have nice views of the mountains. The tiled baths are clean, and the water is hot. For $3 extra per night you can get a TV. If you get too claustrophobic in your room, there is a sitting area on each floor. The Diplomat seems to be popular with North American retirees and businesspeople. The hotel's restaurant is a very attractive dark room with pink tablecloths, flowers on every table, and pastel walls. For those seeking an intimate place for dinner, try one of the tiny booths for two. Prices range from $2 for a sandwich to $15 for a lobster dinner.

HOTEL DON CARLOS, 779 Calle 9 between avenidas 7 and 9 (in the U.S.: Dept. 1686, P.O. Box 025216, Miami, FL 33102-5216). Tel. 506/ 221-6707. Fax 506/255-0828. 25 rms, 6 suites.

$ Rates (including continental breakfast): $40–$50 single; $50–$60 double. AE, MC, V. **Parking:** Nearby.

⭐ If you are looking for a small hotel that is unmistakenly tropical and hits at the days of the planters and coffee barons, this is the place for you. Located in an old residential neighborhood only blocks from the business district, the Don Carlos is popular with both vacationers and businesspeople. A large pre-Columbian reproduction of a carved-stone human figure stands outside the front door of this gray hotel, which was a former president's mansion. Inside you'll find many more pre-Columbian stone reproductions, as well as orchids, ferns, palms, and parrots. The wicker furniture in the lounge and the small courtyard leading to a sunny deck with a bubbling fountain tempt guests to relax in the tropical breezes after a day of exploring the capital. Most of the rooms are quite large, and each is a little different from the others. In case you're interested, the paintings throughout the hotel are for sale. The gift shop here is one of the largest in San José and is the best in the country. The complimentary breakfast and moderately priced meals are served in the Pre-Columbian Lounge. Unfortunately, many people can't tolerate the traffic noises here.

HOTEL DUNN INN, Calle 5 and Avenida 11 (Apdo. 1584-1000), San José. Tel. 506/222-3232 or 222-3426. Fax 506/221-4596. 27 rms, 1 suite.

$ Rates (including continental breakfast): $45.75 single or double; $55.75 triple; $89.25 suite. V. **Parking:** Nearby.

Located in the Barrio Amon historic neighborhood, the Dunn Inn is among the better small hotels in the area. Part of the hotel is housed in a century-old mansion, while other rooms are in a new wing. This hotel offers quiet sophistication at reasonable rates. The courtyard of the old mansion has been partially covered and turned into the dining room and bar, which, if you have a room directly above, can be a bit noisy at night. Orchids and bromeliads hang from the brick walls, and a fountain bubbles away beside a huge philodendron vine. Some of the rooms have the original hardwood flooring and some are carpeted. The new wing has some very nice rooms with exposed brick walls. Although it is quite a bit more expensive than the normal rooms, the one suite is quite luxurious with a whirlpool bath, minibar, hardwood and carpeted floors, potted bromeliads, dual sinks, a lot of sunshine in the bathroom, and paneled walls.

HOTEL EDELWEISS, Avenida 9 between calles 13 and 15, 100 meters east of the Condovac offices, San José. Tel. 506/221-9702. Fax 506/222-1241. 16 rms. TEL

$ Rates (including continental breakfast): $45 single; $55–$65 double. MC, V. **Parking:** Nearby.

Up at the top of the hill on Avenida 9, you'll find another renovated and converted old home that is now a pleasant, small hotel. There's lots of polished hardwood throughout the hotel, including floors and furniture in many of the the guest rooms. Rooms vary in size, and those in front are very noisy. In the center of the building is an unusual little bar under a translucent roof.

HOTEL EUROPA, Calle Central between avenidas 3 and 5 (Apdo. 72), San José. Tel. 506/222-1222. Fax 506/221-3976. 72 rms, 3 suites. A/C TV TEL

$ Rates: $50–$60 single; $50–$65 double; $120 suite. AE, MC, V. **Parking:** Nearby.

This is one of San José's older business hotels, and its modest rates and sophisticated service make it popular with both business and leisure travelers. The clientele tends to be a bit older than at many of the smaller and more modern hotels around town. Linoleum halls lead to small, carpeted rooms with old TVs. On each floor, you'll find a big lounge by the elevator. The fact that the hotel has a small swimming pool tucked away in the back is a definite plus in this downtown location. A formal little restaurant off the lobby offers impeccable service, though prices seem a bit high for Costa Rica.

HOTEL PETITE VICTORIA, Paseo Colón, Costado Oeste Sala Garbo, San José. Tel. 506/233-1812 or 233-1813. Fax 506/233-1938. 15 rms (all with bath).

$ Rates: May–Nov, $39.35 single, $48.15 double; Dec–Apr, $48.15–$74.35 single, $52.50–$74.35 double. AE, MC, V. **Parking:** Free.

One of the oldest houses in San José, this tropical Victorian home was once the election campaign headquarters for Oscar Arias Sánchez, Costa Rica's former president who won a Nobel Peace Prize. Today, after extensive remodeling and restoration, it is an interesting little hotel that offers a historic setting at inexpensive rates. The big front porch is perfect for sitting and taking in the warm sun, while inside a circular banquette sits in the middle of a tile-floored lobby. Guest rooms have high ceilings and fans to keep the air cool and medium-to-large tiled bathrooms. Inside, walls are made of wood, so noise can be a bit of a problem, but this is a small price to pay for such old-fashioned elegance. Tour arrangements and laundry service are also offered. When I last visited, a patio restaurant was under construction and there were plans to add several new, less expensive rooms with shared bathrooms.

HOTEL SANTO TOMAS, Avenida 7 between calles 3 and 5, San José. Tel. 506/255-0448. Fax 506/22-3950. 20 rms.

$ Rates (including continental breakfast): $49.50–$75 single: $55–$85 double; $85–$95 triple (5% discount on entire stay after three consecutive days). Credit cards accepted for room reservation guarantee only. **Parking:** Nearby.

Even though it is on an otherwise nondescript street, this converted mansion is a real jewel inside. Built around 100 years ago by a coffee baron, the house was once slated to be bulldozed in order to expand the Aurola Holiday Inn's parking lot. Under the direction of American Thomas Douglas, the old mansion has been restored to its former grandeur. The first thing that you see when you walk through the front door is the beautiful carved-wood desk that serves as the reception area. Throughout the guest rooms you'll find similar pieces of exquisitely crafted antique reproductions made here in Costa Rica from rare hardwoods. The hardwood floors throughout most of the hotel are original and were made from a type of tree that has long since become almost impossible to find. The rooms vary in size, but most are fairly large and have a small table and chairs. Skylights in some bathrooms will brighten your morning, and queen-size beds will provide a good night's sleep. Maps of Costa Rica hang on the walls of all the guest rooms so you can get acquainted with the country. There are a couple of patio areas, as well as a TV lounge and combination breakfast room and outdoor bar. Laundry service and a baggage storage room are available.

HOTEL TORREMOLINOS, Calle 40 and Avenida 5 bis (Apdo. 114-1017), San José. Tel. 506/222-5266 or 222-9129. Fax 506/255-3167. 71 rms, 14 suites. TV TEL

$ Rates: $45 single; $55 double; $65 triple; $75–$85 suite. AE, MC, V. **Parking:** Free.

If you want to be close to downtown, have a pool, and not spend a fortune for a room, this is your best choice. Located at the west end of Paseo Colón, the Torremolinos is on a fairly quiet street and is built around a colorful and well-tended garden that makes the hotel's pool a wonderful place to while away an afternoon. The rooms are simply furnished and have plenty of space. Most also, for some strange reason, feature Egyptian artwork on the walls. Besides having a nice pool and gardens, the hotel has an exercise room and sauna, a moderately priced restaurant serving international dishes, a lobby bar, and room service.

HOTEL VILLA TOURNON, Calle 3, 200 meters north of Avenida 13 (Apdo. 6606-1000), San José. Tel. 506/233-6622. Fax 506/222-5211. 80 rms, 1 suite. TV TEL

$ Rates: $50–$60 single; $55–$65 double; $70–$80 suite. AE, MC, V. **Parking:** Free.

Formerly the Hotel Bougainvillea, this was one of San José's earlier luxury hotels. Today the styling and furnishings are a bit dated, but the prices are so reasonable that it is a great choice for those who care more about having access to a swimming pool than they do about the quality of the furniture in their room. Some of the rooms here have parquet floors while others (more expensive) have carpeting. The less expensive rooms have two twin beds, while for a bit extra you can get a room with two doubles. There's a large restaurant serving international dishes, plus a small bar. Hotel amenities include room service and a car-rental desk. El Pueblo, a restaurant, entertainment, and shopping complex is only a block away, and downtown is also walkable (in daylight hours).

PENSION DE LA CUESTA, 1332 Cuesta de Nuñez, Avenida 1 between calles 11 and 15. Tel. 506/255-2896. Fax 506/223-2272. 8 rms (none with private bath).

$ Rates (including continental breakfast): $25 single; $35 double. MC, V.

Though these prices may seem a bit steep for a room without a private bathroom, this little bed-and-breakfast is definitely worth considering. It is owned by an artist from the Guanacaste province of Costa Rica, and original artwork abounds. The building itself is a classic example of a tropical wood-frame home and has been painted an eye-catching pink with blue-and-white trim. The rooms are a bit dark and are very simply furnished, but there is a very sunny and cheery sunken lounge-court area in the center of the house. You'll find this hotel on the hill leading up to the Parque Nacional.

BUDGET

COFFEE GARDEN INN, 75 meters east of the northeast corner of the Corte Suprema de Justicia, San José. Tel. 506/221-6191. 6 rms (all with shared bath).

$ Rates (including Tico breakfast): Dec–Mar, $30 single, $35 double; Apr–Nov, $20 single, $25 double. No credit cards.

This newer home was recently converted into a bed-and-breakfast inn and though none of the guest rooms have private bathrooms, this lack is made up for by the presence of a small swimming pool in the back garden. You just won't find a hotel with a pool for this little money anywhere else in San José. There is also a small bar and restaurant, so you have all the amenities of a bigger hotel under this one small roof. Rooms are fairly basic, but antiques in public areas lend the B&B a touch of class. This place is popular with students and younger travelers.

HOTEL BIENVENIDO, Calle 10 between avenidas 1 and 3 (Apdo. 389-2200), San José. Tel. 506/221-1872. 48 rms (all with bath).

$ Rates: $9.50 single; $19 double; $28.50 triple. No credit cards.

This very basic hotel is one of the most popular in the city with travelers on a tight budget. The rooms are clean, though a bit dark, and there is always ample hot water. The hotel was created from an old movie theater, and there are still a few architectural details remaining from the building's former incarnation. This place fills up by early afternoon in the high season, so call ahead for a reservation and ask for a quiet room in the back.

HOTEL CACTS, 2845 Avenida 3 bis between calles 28 and 30 (Apdo. 379-1005), San José. Tel. 506/221-2928 or 221-6546. Fax 506/221-8616. 18 rms (14 with private bath).

$ Rates (including continental breakfast): $27.15 single with bath; $27.15 double without bath, $30.60 double with bath; $34.11 triple without bath, $39.40 triple with bath. No credit cards.

⭐ This is one of the most interesting and unusual budget hotels I've ever seen, housed in an attractive tropical contemporary home on a business and residential street. You reach the reception area via a flight of outside steps that lead past a small garden area. Once inside, you are in a maze of halls on several levels (the house is built on a slope). My favorite room is the huge bi-level family room with its high beamed ceiling. The Cacts has been in the midst of an ambitious expansion for several years now and by the time you arrive you may find a rooftop terrace dining area and quite a few more rooms in various price ranges.

HOTEL JOHNSON, Calle 8 between Avenida Central and Avenida 2, (Apdo. 6638-1000), San José. Tel. 506/223-7633 or 223-7827. Fax 506/222-3683. 57 rms, 3 suites (all with bath).

$ Rates: $10.90–$13.65 single; $13.65–$15.45 double; $16.35–$18.20 triple; $23.60 suite (for five). DC, MC, V.

The lobby of this large, centrally located hotel is on the second floor. You'll find the hotel patronized primarily by Costa Rican businesspeople and families, but it is a good choice for any budget traveler. In the lobby there is a TV and several lounge chairs, and on each of the residence floors above there is a sitting area. The rooms have tile floors and open onto a narrow air shaft that lets in a bit of light and noise from other rooms. Bathrooms are relatively clean and roomy. Most rooms come with twin beds (you might want to test a few beds if you're picky about mattresses). There's a bar and a dining room where you can get inexpensive meals. The special of the day goes for $2.50, while à la carte meals run from $3.50 to $5.50.

HOTEL RITZ AND PENSION CONTINENTAL, Calle Central between avenidas 8 and 10 (Apdo. 6783-1000), San José. Tel. 506/222-4103. Fax 506/222-8849. 27 rms (5 with bath).

$ Rates: $5.60–$10.50 single without bath, $14.65 single with bath; $9.80–$15.55 double without bath, $19.30 double with bath; $12.80–$21.35 triple without bath, $24.25 triple with bath; $15.15 quad without bath, $24.25 with bath. AE, MC, V.

These two side-by-side budget hotels are under the same management and together have rooms to fit most budget travelers' needs. There is even a travel agency and tour company on the first floor, so you can arrange all of your travels around Costa Rica without leaving the hotel. Rooms vary greatly in size and comfort levels, but all tend to be dark and a bit musty. Bathrooms are a bit old and showers have showerhead heaters that just barely work. If the first room you see isn't to your liking, just ask to see another in a different price category. The current owners are Swiss, so you'll probably meet quite a few Swiss travelers if you stay here.

JOLUVA GUESTHOUSE, 936 Calle 3B between avenidas 9 and 11, San José. Tel. 506/223-9901 or (in the U.S.) 619/298-7965. Fax 619/294-2418. 8 rms (6 with private bath). TV

$ Rates (including continental breakfast): $25 single without bath, $30 single with bath; $30 double without bath, $40 double with bath. MC, V.

Though you can find a less expensive hotel, there are few in this price range that offer the old-fashioned architectural detail of the Joluva. There are old tile and hardwood floors throughout, and high ceilings (and in one room, beautiful plasterwork on the ceiling). However, the rooms are small and a bit dark, with windows that open into a covered courtyard. The breakfast room has skylights, which help brighten it a bit.

TORUMA YOUTH HOSTEL, Avenida Central between calles 29 and 31, San José. Tel. 506/224-4085. 105 beds (all with shared bath).

$ Rates (including continental breakfast): $5.40–$8.25 per person per night with an IYHF card; $6.70–$9.45 without IYHF card. No credit cards.

This attractive old building, with its long veranda, is the largest hostel in Costa Rica's system of official youth hostels. Although it is possible to find other accommodations around town in this price range, any such room would not likely be as clean. The atmosphere here is convivial and will be familiar to anyone who has hosteled in Europe. The large lounge in the center of the building has a high ceiling and a great deal of light. The dorms have four to six beds per room. There is an inexpensive restaurant adjacent to the hotel, and if you want, you can store luggage here for 35¢ per day.

SAN PEDRO/LOS YOSES

MODERATE

HOTEL LE BERGERAC, 50 S. Calle 35 (Apdo. 1107-1002), San José. Tel. 506/234-7850. Fax 506/225-9103. 16 rms TV TEL SAFE

$ Rates (including continental breakfast): Dec 1–Apr 30, $68–$88 single or double; May 1–Nov 30, $58–$78 single or double. Corporate rates available. AE, MC, V. **Parking:** Free.

With all the sophistication and charm of a small French inn, the Hotel Le Bergerac has ingratiated iself with business travelers and members of various diplomatic missions. What these visitors have found (and what you too will find should you stay here) is a tranquil environment in a quiet suburban neighborhood, spacious and comfortable accommodations, personal service, and gourmet French meals. The owners of the hotel, who are from the United States and France, have a total of 27 years of hotel experience, which accounts for the professionalism with which this hotel is operated. The hotel is comprised of two houses with a courtyard garden in between. Almost all of the rooms are quite large, and each is a little different. My favorite rooms are those with private patios. Some rooms have king beds, and in the old master bedroom, you'll find a little balcony. In the evenings candlelight and classical music set a relaxing and romantic mood, and gourmet French meals are available for guests.

INEXPENSIVE

D'GALAH HOTEL, Calle Masis, 100 meters past Calle La Cruz (Apdo. 208-2350), San José. Tel. 506/234-1743 or 253-7539. 30 rms. TV TEL

$ Rates: $30 single; $42–$53 double. AE, MC, V. **Parking:** Free.

If you have come to Costa Rica to bird-watch, the D'Galah Hotel is definitely where you should stay when you're in San José. Directly across the street from the hotel is the University of Costa Rica, which is an oasis of greenery that attracts many species of birds. Joggers will also appreciate this location and the pleasant trails on campus. Rooms are a bit old fashioned and dark, but for the most part are quite spacious and acceptable if you aren't too demanding. The largest rooms are those with kitchenettes and sleeping lofts. The newest rooms have carpets and private little patios. Amenities include a small swimming pool, a sauna, and a breakfast room.

ESCAZÚ

EXPENSIVE

TARA RESORT HOTEL, Apdo. 1459-1250, Escazú. Tel. 506/228-6992. Fax 506/228-9651. 30 suites and bungalows. TV TEL

$ Rates: $85–$185 single or double. AE, MC, V. **Parking:** Free.

Located one kilometer south of the village of San Antonio de Escazú (follow the signs), Tara is perched high on a mountainside overlooking the entire Central Valley and surrounding volcanic peaks. The view is breathtaking and so is the setting. Anyone who has ever seen *Gone With the Wind* will immediately recognize this as a reproduction of the movie's Tara, the plantation home of Scarlett O'Hara. Antebellum southern grandeur has been lovingly re-created here in Costa Rica much to the delight of anyone with the finances to spend a night or two here. Room rates are high, but every room is a suite or bungalow. The suites are all part of the main house and each has its own balcony (try to get one overlooking the valley). Rooms vary in size, but in the larger rooms you might find a seating area, a big bathroom with two sinks, a tub, a heat lamp, and perhaps even two balconies. Furnishings are traditional American styles that fit right in with the architecture.

Dining/Entertainment: The Atlanta Dining Gallery is an elegant setting for fine meals; unfortunately, the windows do not do justice to the view. In the evenings there is live jazz and piano music. Meals are often served on the large back patio, which has an unobstructed view of the valley.

Services: Free airport transportation, horseback riding.

Facilities: Outdoor swimming pool, hot tub, sauna, various lawn and indoor games, conference facilities.

MODERATE

COSTA VERDE INN, Apdo. 89, Escazú (in the U.S.: Dept. 305, Box 025216, Miami, FL 33102). Tel. and Fax 506/228-4080. 8 rms (6 with private bath).

$ Rates (including full breakfast): Nov 1–Apr 15, $45 single without bath, $55 single with bath; $52 double without bath, $64 double with bath; $57 triple without bath, $89 triple with bath. Apr 16–Oct 31, lower rates apply. MC, V (add 8% surcharge). **Parking:** Free.

If you're a tennis player or someone who values peace and quiet, the Costa Verde Inn is an excellent choice. This sprawling, modern home incorporates flagstone and stone walls throughout and has a vaguely colonial feel. A large and lush garden, complete with lighted tennis court, surrounds the inn. My favorite rooms are the two by the tennis courts, one of which has a sunken stone-floored shower. Other rooms have hardwood floors, and in all the rooms you'll find king-size beds. Common areas include a large living room with fireplace and a wide tiled patio that overlooks the garden. Throughout the inn, you'll see old black-and-white photos that have been hand colored. Ask the innkeeper about the photographer who took these pictures. You can also find out here about various excursions around the country, including the inn's own bicycle trip down a volcano. The inn offers airport pickups.

INEXPENSIVE

HOTEL MIRADOR PICO BLANCO, Apdo. 900 Escazú. Tel. 506/289-6197 or 289-5189. 23 rms.

$ Rates: $40 single; $50 double; $65 triple. AE, MC, V. **Parking:** Free.

If you'd like a room with a view but can't afford the prices charged at most mountainside inns around the area, check out this cozy and casual hotel. There's nothing fancy about the rooms here, though the hotel was being renovated when I last visited, and some of the rooms were newer and more comfortable than others. There's an absolutely fabulous view from most rooms and from the dining room and terrace. Some rooms have high ceilings that give the rooms the appearance of spaciousness, and almost all have balconies (albeit small ones). The restaurant is a popular and inexpensive spot, probably the cheapest view restaurant in the valley. A taxi up here from the airport will cost you about $15.

BUDGET

FOREST B&B, HOSTEL-HOTEL, 1300 meters east of Intex building, Casa no. 78, Bello Horizonte, Escazú. Tel. 506/228-0900. 35 beds.

$ Rates: $15 per person. AE, MC, V (plus 7% surcharge).

If you're on a backpacker's budget but don't want to stay in downtown San José, where all the budget hotels seem to be, consider staying at this converted home. Located on a large lot in a quiet residential neighborhood east of downtown Escazú, the Forest B&B offers Spartan accommodations in a luxurious, modern home. Out in the garden there's a pool (that never gets very warm), and inside there's some exercise equipment. Guests can use the huge kitchen.

HEREDIA/ALAJUELA/AIRPORT AREA

VERY EXPENSIVE

CARIARI HOTEL & COUNTRY CLUB, Autopista General Cañas, Ciudad Cariari (Apdo. 737-1007 Centro Colón), San José. Tel. 506/239-0022, or toll free (in the U.S.) 800/227-4274. Fax 506/239-2803 or 239-0285. 220 rms, 24 suites. A/C TV TEL

$ Rates: $115 single; $125–$165 double; $200–$375 suite. AE, MC, V. **Parking:** Free.

Located about halfway into San José from the airport, the Cariari is the only resort hotel in the Central Valley with its own golf course, and as such is a must for golfers vacationing in Costa Rica. The Cariari, with its use of stone walls, an open-air lobby, and lush garden plantings, also has more of a tropical feel than the city's other luxury hotels. However, the landscaping is not as impeccably manicured as that at the Herradura (see below), nor is the hotel itself as elegant. Many of the guest rooms were recently remodeled, and all have plenty of space. The basic rooms have king beds and small baths. Poolside rooms are quite a bit more expensive, and though they have minibars, hairdryers, and safes, they seem a bit overpriced. All in all the rooms lack the sort of quality furnishings and styling that you would expect in this price range. Try to get an upper-floor room; those on the lower floor tend to be a bit dark.

Dining/Entertainment: Los Vitrales is the hotel's most formal restaurant and serves well-prepared French and continental fare. For more casual meals, there is Las Tejas, where there's a breakfast buffet. For seafood and cocktails there is the tropical, open-air atmosphere of Los Mariscos, which also has live Latin and jazz music in the evenings. More entertainment is provided by the hotel's casino, which is open nightly until 2am.

Services: 24-hour room service, complimentary city shuttle, tour desk, car-rental desk, golf lessons and club rentals, babysitting, massage.

Facilities: The large pool is surrounded by plenty of patio space and lots of lounge chairs and has a swim-up bar. In addition to the 18-hole golf course, there are 10 tennis courts, a pro shop, a health club with saunas, whirlpool tubs, an exercise room, a game room, and a swimming pool. Other facilities include a gift shop, beauty parlor, and barber shop.

FINCA ROSE BLANCA COUNTRY INN, Apdo. 41-3009, Santa Bárbara de Heredia. Tel. 506/269-9392. Fax 506/269-9555. 8 suites.

$ Rates (including full breakfast): $102–$180 single; $120–$200 double. AE, V. **Parking:** Free.

⭐ This is another of those Central Valley lodges that is difficult to find but well worth searching out. If the cookie-cutter rooms of international resorts leave you cold, then perhaps the fascinatingly unique rooms of this unusual inn will be more your style. Finca Rosa Blanca is an architectural confection set amid the lush green hillsides of a coffee plantation. Square corners seem to have been prohibited in the design of this beautiful home. There are turrets and curving walls of glass, arched windows, and a semicircular built-in couch. Everywhere the glow of polished hardwood contrasts with the blindingly white stucco walls. The best way I can describe the architecture of this inn is as 21st-century pueblo.

Inside is original artwork everywhere. Each room is decidely different and unique. There's the black-and-white room with a patio and bed made from coffee-tree wood. Another room has a bed built into a corner and a handmade tub with windows on two sides. The view is fabulous. If breathtaking bathrooms are your idea of the ultimate luxury, then consider splurging on the master suite, which has a stone waterfall that cascades into a tub in front of a huge picture window. This suite also has a spiral staircase that leads to the top of the turret. In addition to breakfast, a five-course gourmet dinner is available for $25 per person. There is an honor bar for guests.

Dining/Entertainment: For $25 per person you can arrange to have a five-course gourmet dinner served in the small dining room. Be sure to reserve early because the dinning room has limited seating. In a tiny space off of the living room, there is an honor bar tucked into a reproduction of a typical Costa Rican ox cart.

Services: Car rentals and guide services can be arranged through the hotel.

HOTEL HERRADURA, Autopista General Cañas, Ciudad Cariari (Apdo. 7-1880), San José. Tel. 506/239-0033. Fax 506/239-2292. 234 rms, 24 suites. A/C TV TEL

$ Rates: $115–$180 single; $125–$180 double; $180–$795 suite. AE, DC, MC, V. **Parking:** Free.

Big and sprawling, the Herradura is the most impeccably designed and maintained of San José's resort hotels. It is also the city's largest conference center, and as such is often bustling with businesspeople. However, despite the crowds, service here never seems to falter. The gardens here are the most beautiful of any hotel in the city—exquisitely manicured. The superior rooms (there are no standards) could definitely stand new fabrics, are rather small, and have no views to speak of from their balconies. Bathrooms in these rooms are small and the plastic countertops have seen a few forgotten cigarettes. The deluxe rooms, on the other hand, are very attractive and luxurious. The walls of glass let in plenty of light and usually a good view ($10 extra for pool-view rooms). There are balconies and marble-topped café tables, and in the bathrooms, there are green marble counters, phones, and hairdryers.

Dining/Entertainment: For quiet dining, there is Sakura, a Japanese restaurant with an indoor garden setting. For continental fare and entertainment with your meal, try Bon Vivant, which books a wide variety of entertainers. Casual meals, including buffets, are available at the 24-hour Tropicala coffee shop. Bambolleo is a lounge that offers piano music and light snacks. In addition to the entertainers who perform at Bon Vivant, there are also shows at Tiffany's Club, the hotel's disco and nightclub. There's live Latin dance music most nights. Gamblers can spend their time at the elegant Casino Krystal.

Services: 24-hour room service, city shuttle, car-rental desk, tour desk, babysitting.

Facilities: The Herradura's main swimming pool (there are three) is the largest and most attractive in San José, with a beachlike patio, a swim-up bar, tiled café tables in the water, and attractive landscaping around the edges of the pool. The resort's 18-hole golf course, 10 tennis courts, pro shop, and health club are the same ones that are used by the Cariari Hotel (see above). Other facilities include a gift shop and a small exercise room.

EXPENSIVE

SAN JOSÉ PALACIO, Autopista General Cañas (Apdo. 458-1150), San José. Tel. 506/220-2034 or 220-2035. Fax 506/220-2036. 254 rms, 24 suites. A/C TV TEL MINIBAR SAFE

$ Rates: $110–$120 single; $115–$125 double; $155–$375 suite. AE, DC, MC, V. **Parking:** Free.

Owned by the Barcelo company, the developer of the controversial Tambor project on the Nicoya Peninsula, the Palacio tries very hard to live up to its name. This is as luxurious a hotel as you will find in Costa Rica. The Palacio is not as far out of town as the Cariari or Herradura, and so it is more convenient for exploring downtown San José. The hilltop location assures good views from nearly every room. Business travelers and conferences seem to be the bulk of the business here.

Rooms are very modern and all have angled walls of glass to take in the superb views. Furnishings are of the highest quality, and in some rooms there are even leather chairs. If you choose to stay in one of the executive rooms, you'll receive a continental breakfast and afternoon coffee.

Dining/Entertainment: Ambar is the hotel's premiere dining room, and the creative continental cuisine is reasonably priced and among the best in town. Anfora is a larger and more casual dining room that does an impressive, though expensive, lunch buffet. El Bosque is the hotel's main lounge and is adjacent to the small casino.

Services: Room service, massages, car-rental desk, travel agency, babysitting.

Facilities: Free-form pool with adjacent grill and piano bar, exercise room, sauna, two tennis courts, three racquetball/squash courts, shopping arcade, barber shop, beauty parlor.

MODERATE

HOTEL BOUGAINVILLEA, Apdo. 69-2120, San José. Tel. 506/240-8822. Fax 506/240-8484. 44 rms. TV TEL

$ Rates: $65 single; $75 double. AE, MC, V. **Parking:** Free.

The Hotel Bougainvillea is an excellent choice if you are looking for a reasonably priced hotel in a quiet residential neighborhood not far from downtown. The hotel offers most of the amenities of the more expensive resort hotels around the valley, but charges considerably less. The views across the valley from this hillside location are beautiful, and the gardens of the hotel are beautifully designed and well tended. Guest rooms, though they lack any Costa Rican style, are as predictable as those in any international hotel. Rooms are carpeted and have small triangular balconies oriented to the views. Though there is no air-conditioning, there are fans, and temperatures are rarely too hot here. The hotel's dining room features continental dishes, with flambéed Delmonico steak being one of the specialities. Prices here are quite reasonable. There is also a quiet bar just off the lobby and room service. A complimentary downtown shuttle bus will take you in and out of town. The hotel's swimming pool is in its own private, walled garden and is quite attractive. There are also tennis courts and a jogging trail.

---

4. DINING

San José has an amazing variety of restaurants serving cuisines of the world in all price ranges. You'll never pay much for even the best meal in Costa Rica. In fact, the highest price you can pay in the entire country is around $40 per person for an extravagant six- or seven-course meal. Most restaurants fall in the moderate category. Quality and presentation are both quite high, and service in the better restaurants is usually very formal (quite a switch for anyone accustomed to snide waiters in chic eateries).

For a true deal head to a *soda,* the equivalent of a diner in the United States, where you can get good, cheap, and filling Tico food. Rice and beans are the staples here and show up at breakfast, lunch, and dinner. Rice and beans are called *gallo pinto* when served for breakfast and may come with anything from fried eggs to steak. At lunch and dinner those very same rice and beans are called a *casado,* (which means "married") and are served with a salad of cabbage and tomatoes, fried bananas, and steak, chicken, or fish. Gallo pinto might cost $2, and a casado might cost $2.70.

Another favorite of Ticos, and tourists, is the *fresco.* A fresco is a bit like a fresh fruit milkshake without the ice cream, and when made with mangos, papayas, bananas or any of the other delicious tropical fruits of Costa Rica, it is pure ambrosia. Frescos are also made with water (*con agua*), but these are not nearly as good as those made with milk (*con leche*) and despite all assurances that the water in San José is safe to drink, you're better off avoiding it as much as possible.

For the following listings I considered a restaurant expensive if a meal without wine or beer would be more than $15. Moderate restaurants serve complete dinners for between $8 and $15, and budget listings are those where you can get a complete meal for less than $8. Also, you should note that in the price ranges for the following restaurants, the highest prices are almost always for shrimp or lobster dishes.

Other fish and meat dishes are always considerably less expensive. If you want to save money on a meal, skip the wine, which is almost always imported and expensive.

DOWNTOWN

EXPENSIVE

EL BALCÓN DE EUROPA, Calle 9 between avenidas Central and 1. Tel. 221-4841.
Cuisine: CONTINENTAL. **Reservations:** Recommended.
$ Prices: Appetizers $4.40–$5.10; main courses $5.10–$15.35. No credit cards.
Open: Sun–Fri noon–10pm.

⭐ Open since 1908, El Balcón de Europa is one of San José's most popular restaurants. What atracts people from all walks of life to this restaurant is outstanding service, gourmet Italian food, and cheese. You may have noticed a lack of cheese in other parts of Costa Rica, but not here. The centerpiece of the restaurant is a table covered with imported European cheeses (at room temperature) and an array of fresh-baked desserts. Take a seat and immediately a basket of two types of bread and breadsticks arrives accompanied by a sample plate of cheeses. There are many different pastas on the menu served in a variety of tasty sauces, mostly cream-based. For an entrée, try the unusual piccatine al limone, a paper-thin steak cooked in lemon sauce. To accompany your meal there is a limited selection of wines from Europe, California, and South America.

CHALET SUIZO, Avenida 1 between calles 5 and 7. Tel. 222-3118.
Cuisine: SWISS. **Reservations:** Not required.
$ Prices: Appetizers $2.40–$14.90; main courses $5.75–$23.30. AE, DC, MC, V.
Open: Daily lunch 11:30am–2:15pm; dinner 6pm–midnight.

You can't miss this Swiss restaurant, which is done up on the outside to look like a Swiss chalet unceremoniously wedged into the middle of a nondescript downtown block lined with shops. Inside it's all dark and cozy. The menu is very Swiss, and includes such dishes as beef or cheese fondue, raclette, and various meat dishes served with sauerkraut. However, there are also quite a few decidedly non-Alpine shrimp and fish dishes on the menu.

THE LOBSTER'S INN, Paseo Colón at Calle 24 (opposite Mercedes-Benz). Tel. 223-8594.
Cuisine: SEAFOOD. **Reservations:** Not required.
$ Prices: Appetizers $3.20–$18.20; main courses $6.60–$22.25. AE, DC, MC, V.
Open: Lunch Mon–Sat 11am–3pm; dinner Mon–Sat 5:30–10:30pm, Sun 11am–10:30pm.

Located on Paseo Colón in a neighborhood where there are other restaurants of similar quality, this one stands out for its delicious seafood, which is fresh off the restaurant's own fishing fleet. One taste of the creme of shrimp soup, which comes loaded with shrimp, will prove it. Try shrimp en brochette, or choose from about 10 different preparations of corvina (sea bass), including corvina with plenty of garlic or in a caper sauce. A specialty is the (very large) lobster dinner. Red tablecloths, heavy colonial furniture, and hanging ferns are father formal, brightened by aquariums full of large fish—carp, gars, and oscars (to look at, not to eat). Portions are generous and the service, by waiters in red ties and cummerbunds, is friendly and thoughtful. To end your meal, choose from a cart full of cordials. Occasionally there is live music in the evening.

LA MASIA DE TRIQUEL, corner Avenida 2 and Calle 40, across from the Parque del Largo Hotel. Tel. 221-5073 or 232-3584.
Cuisine: SPANISH. **Reservations:** Recommended on weekends.
$ Prices: Appetizers $3.50–$14.90; main courses $6.10–$21.65. AE, DC, MC, V.
Open: Lunch Tues–Sat noon–2pm, Sun noon–4pm; dinner Tues–Fri 6:30–11pm, Sat 7–11pm.

Located in an aging white stucco house only a block from Parque La Sabana, La Masia de Triquel is San José's finest Spanish restaurant. Service is extremely formal and the clientele comes from the city's upper crust. Though Costa Rica is known for its beef, here you'll also find such meats as lamb, quail, and rabbit. Seafood dishes include the usual shrimp and lobster, but also squid and octopus. However, there is really no decision to be made when perusing the menu: Start with a big bowl of gazpacho and then spend the rest of the evening enjoying all the succulent surprises you'll find in a big dish of paella.

LA PIAZZETTA, Paseo Colón near Calle 40 (opposite Banco de Costa Rica). Tel. 222-7896 or 221-8451.
    Cuisine: ITALIAN. **Reservations:** Recommended.
$ **Prices:** Appetizers $3.25–$11.50; pastas $3.25–$14.90; main courses $5.75–$28.40. MC, V.
    Open: Lunch Mon–Sat noon–2pm; dinner Mon–Sat 6:30–11pm.

With an amazingly long menu and service by waiters in suits and bow ties, this Italian restaurant hearkens back to the Italian restaurants of old in the United States, when southern Italian cooking was still an exotic ethnic cuisine.

The menu includes quite a few *risotto* (rice) dishes, which is a surprise, since most Italian restaurants in Costa Rica stick to spaghetti. There also are some other unexpected dishes that make appearances here, including smoked salmon, lobster, and truffles. Salads are colorful and artistically arranged. Try *baugna cauda*, anchovies and peppers in an olive-oil–based broth, if you're in no fear of a coronary. For dessert, sample a classic chocolate mousse, or tiramisu—don't ask what it is, you'll find out. It's good.

MODERATE

AMSTEL GRILL ROOM, Avenida 1 and Calle 7. Tel. 222-4622.
    Cuisine: CONTINENTAL/COSTA RICAN. **Reservations:** Not required.
$ **Prices:** Appetizers: $2.05–$12.20; main courses $5.60–$16.90. AE, MC, V.
    Open: Daily 6:30–11am, 11:30am–3pm, and 6–10pm.

Ask anyone in San José for a restaurant recommendation and this hotel dining room is always near the top of the list. For years the Grill Room has maintained its high standards. The atmosphere is one of quiet sophistication with white-jacketed waiters moving unobtrusively between the tables making sure that everyone is happy. Businesspeople and well-dressed matrons are the primary customers, but tourists in more casual attire receive the same careful attention. Lunch here is a real bargain and the most popular meal of the day. For between $4.90 and $6.45 you can order the special of the day or the deluxe special of the day, which may include entrées such as corvina meunière or sirloin steak. Soup or salad and a dessert round out the meal. Should you choose to order à la carte, try one of the choice steaks of Costa Rican beef or fresh shrimp.

CAFÉ DE TEATRO NACIONAL, Teatro Nacional, Avenida 2 between calles 3 and 5. Tel. 223-4488.
    Cuisine: CONTINENTAL. **Reservations:** Not required.
$ **Prices:** Sandwiches and soups $2.50–$4.65; main courses $5–$8.35. MC, V.
    Open: Mon–Sat 11am–6pm.

This is one of my favorite places to eat in all of San José. Even if there is no show at the Teatro Nacional during your visit, you can enjoy a meal or a cup of coffee here and soak up the neoclassical atmosphere. The theater was built in the 1890s from the designs of European architects, and the art nouveau chandeliers, ceiling murals, and marble floors and tables are purely Parisienne. There are changing art displays by local artists to complete the très chic café atmosphere. The menu includes such continental dishes as quiche, Hungarian goulash soup, and wiener schnitzel, but the main attactions here are the specialty cakes and tortes which are displayed in a glass case. Ice cream dishes are raised to a high art form here with names such as passionate love and spaghetti ice cream. The ambience is

**FROMMER'S SMART TRAVELER:
RESTAURANTS**

1. Always remember that an 11% tax and 10% service charge are added to the price of dinner. Your total bill will be 21% higher than the prices you see on the menu.
2. If you want to save money, eat at sodas, the Costa Rican equivalent of a diner. Gallo pinto is the national breakfast and is always quite cheap, while casados offer similar flavors and savings at lunch and dinner.
3. Keep an eye on the bar tab. Liquor and wine are pricey, while beer is as cheap as soft drinks.
4. Always ask what frescos a restaurant has. These are fresh fruit drinks the likes of which you will rarely ever find at home.

classic French café, but the marimba music drifting in from outside the open window will remind you that you are still in Costa Rica.

CAFE PARISIEN, Gran Hotel Costa Rica, Avenida 2 between calles 1 and 3. Tel. 221-4011.
  Cuisine: INTERNATIONAL. **Reservations:** Not required.
  $ Prices: Sandwiches $1.90–$5.10; appetizers $1.50–$6.65; main courses $5.50–$18.25. AE, MC, V.
  Open: Daily 24 hours.
The Gran Hotel Costa Rica is hardly the best hotel in San José, but it does have a picturesque patio café right on the Plaza de la Cultura. A wrought-iron railing, white columns, and arches create an Old World atmosphere, and on the plaza all around the café marimba bands perform and vendors sell handcrafts. It's open 24 hours a day and there is almost no hour when there isn't something interesting going on in the plaza. Stop by for the breakfast buffet ($6.75 to $8.15) and fill up as the plaza vendors set up their booths; peruse the *Tico Times* over coffee while you have your shoes polished; or simply bask in the tropical sunshine while you sip a beer. Lunch and dinner buffets are also offered for about $8.80.

LA COCINA DE LEÑA, El Pueblo. Tel. 255-1360.
  Cuisine: COSTA RICAN. **Reservations:** Not required.
  $ Prices: $5.40–$18.95. AE, DC, MC, V.
  Open: Daily lunch 11:30am–3pm; dinner 6–11:30pm.
Located in the unusual El Pueblo shopping, dining, and entertainment center. La Cocina de Leña (The Wood Stove) has a rustic feel to it. There are stacks of firewood on shelves above the booths, long stalks of bananas hanging from pillars, tables suspended by heavy ropes from the ceiling, and most unusual of all—menus printed on paper bags. Though almost every restaurant in Costa Rica offers tipico meals, few serve the likes of green banana or hearts of palm ceviche. After such unusual appetizers you might wonder what would come next. Perhaps oxtail stew served with yuca and plátano might appeal to you; if not, there are plenty of steaks and seafood dishes on the menu. *Chilasuilas* are delicious tortillas filled with fried meat. Black-bean soup with egg is a Costa Rican standard and is well done here, and the corn soup with pork is equally satisfying. For dessert there is très leches cake as well as the more unusual sweetened *chiverre*, which is a type of squash that looks remarkably like a watermelon.

MACHU PICHU BAR AND RESTAURANT, Calle 32 between avenidas 1 and 3. Tel. 222-7384.
  Cuisine: PERUVIAN/CONTINENTAL. **Reservations:** Not required.
  $ Prices: Appetizers $1.70–$9.30; main courses $3.50–$11.50. No credit cards.
  Open: Daily 8am–10pm.
Located just off Paseo Colón near the Kentucky Fried Chicken, Machu Pichu is an unpretentious little restaurant that has become one of the most popular places in San

José. The menu is primarily seafood (especially sea bass), and consequently most dishes tend toward the upper end of the menu's price range, but all are well worth the price. The soups are good, and several of my favorite entrées are *causa Limeña*, which is lemon-flavored mashed potatoes stuffed with shrimp, *aji de gallina*, a dish of chopped chicken in a fragrant cream sauce, and octopus with garlic butter. Be sure to ask for one of the specialty drinks.

BUDGET

LA CASA DEL LAGO, at the north end of the lake in Parque la Sabana. No phone.
   Cuisine: COSTA RICAN. **Reservations:** Not accepted.
$ **Prices:** All items $1.50–$3.05. No credit cards.
   Open: Tues–Sun 11am–5pm.
On Sundays this little restaurant and the patio outside are filled with Tico families enjoying their day in the park. It's not surprising, because the view here, of the lake, a large fountain, and Pico Blanco in the distance, is one of the best in the city. Another advantage is that it is close to the Museum of Art and makes a good stop for finger foods such as burgers or fried chicken, or something more substantial such as a casado, fish with garlic, or pork chops. Counter service is fast, and they serve interesting *naturales* (fruit juices) such as naranjilla and mora.

LA ESMERALDA, Avenida 2 between calles 5 and 7. Tel. 221-0530.
   Cuisine: COSTA RICAN. **Reservations:** Not required.
$ **Prices:** Main courses $3.35–$7.80. AE, DC, MC, V.
   Open: Mon–Sat 11am–5am.
No one should visit San José without stopping in at La Esmeralda at least once, the later at night the better. This is much more than just a restaurant serving Tico food: It is the Grand Central Station of Costa Rican mariachi bands. In fact, mariachis and other bands from throughout Central America and Mexico hang out here every night waiting for work. While they wait they often serenade diners in the cavernous open-air dining hall of the restaurant. Friday and Saturday nights are always the busiest, but you'll probably hear lots of excellent music any night of the week. The classic Tico food is quite good. Try the coconut flan for dessert.

MANOLO'S RESTAURANTE, Avenida Central between calles 0 and 2. Tel. 221-2041.
   Cuisine: COSTA RICAN. **Reservations:** Not required.
$ **Prices:** All items $3–$9.15. MC, V.
   Open: Daily 11am–10pm upstairs; 24 hours downstairs.
Upstairs on a busy corner on Avenida Central, you'll find this roomy restaurant popular with Ticos and tourists alike. You can view the action in the street below, or catch the live folk-dance performance which is staged nightly. The open kitchen serves up steaks and fish, but there is also a popular buffet that includes several tipico dishes, such as platános and black-bean soup for $5.10. Downstairs you'll find Manolo's Churreria, a good place for a quick sandwich—and they have espresso.

PASTELERIA FRANCESA BOUDSOCQ, Calle 30 at Paseo Colón. Tel. 222-6732.
   Cuisine: PASTRIES. **Reservations:** Not required.
$ **Prices:** $1.05–$2.75. No credit cards.
   Open: Mon–Sat 8am–7pm, Sun 8am–6:30pm.
Ticos love their pastries and bakeries, and pastry shops abound all over San José. However, this little place on Paseo Colón is one of the best I've found. They have savory meat-filled pastries that make good lunches, as well as plenty of unusual sweets that are great afternoon snacks. There are only a couple of tables here.

LA PERLA, Avenida 2 and Calle Central. Tel. 222-7492.
   Cuisine: INTERNATIONAL. **Reservations:** Not accepted.
$ **Prices:** Main courses $1.30–$7.45, MC, V.

Open: Daily 24 hours.

It's easy to walk right past this place (I did) the first time you try to find it. The entrance is right on the corner looking across to Parque Central, and the restaurant itself is a little bit below street level. This place isn't long on atmosphere but the food is good and the portions are large. The special here is *paella*, a Spanish rice-and-seafood dish for only $5.60. Other good choices are *sopa de mariscos*, which is a seafood soup with mussels and clams in a delicious broth, or *huevos à la ranchera*, which is prepared a bit differently than in Mexico and makes a filling meal any time of the night or day. Be sure to try a delicious fresco, made with water or milk and fresh fruit whirred in a blender. *Mora* (blackberry) is my favorite.

POLLOS GALLO PINTO, one block south of the National Museum (Calle 17, between avenidas 2 and 6). Tel. 257-4437.
   Cuisine: COSTA RICAN. **Reservations:** Not accepted.
$ Prices: Main courses $1.35–$5.45.
   Open: Daily 11am–10pm.

★ Jorge Zuñiga, owner of this family-run restaurant, made a great success of his former eating establishment, Restaurante Campesino, and now brihis touch to Pollos Gallo Pinto. What's the big attraction? Chickens roasted over coffee-root fires, enticing you with their mouth-watering fragrance. And that's not all—accompanying each order of tender bird (which comes in quarter-, half-, and whole-chicken servings) are crunchy salads, french fried potatoes, refried beans, and little homemade tortillas with that wood-smoked flavor. Even if you aren't very hungry, the food here is sure to whet your appetite.

RESTAURANTE CAMPESINO, Calle 7 between avenidas 2 and 4. Tel. 222-1170.
   Cuisine: COSTA RICAN. **Reservations:** Not accepted.
$ Prices: Whole chicken $5.05; half chicken $2.65. MC, V.
   Open: Daily 10am–midnight.

This little restaurant serves delicious chicken, which is not surprising since chicken is just about all they serve. The secret of this delectable chicken is in the wood fire over which the chicken is roasted. Depending on how hungry you are, you can get a quarter, half, or full chicken; and you might also try the palmito (hearts of palm) salad. You can't miss this place—watch for the smoking chimney high above the roof, or at street level watch for the window full of chickens roasting over an open fire.

SODA B Y B, Calle 5 and Avenida Central. Tel. 222-7316.
   Cuisine: COSTA RICAN. **Reservations:** Not accepted.
$ Prices: Sandwiches $1–$3.10; breakfasts $1.15–$2.25. MC, V.
   Open: Mon–Fri 8:30am–10pm, Sat 9am–10pm.

Located on the corner across from the Tourist Information Center on the Plaza de la Cultura, this spot is popular with downtown shoppers and office workers. Service is good, prices (and noise level) are low, and the food is surprisingly good for a sandwich shop. Slide into a high-backed wooden booth and order the *chalupa de pollo B y B*—it's a sort of tostada piled high with chicken salad and drenched with sour cream and guacamole.

SODA COPPELIA, Paseo Colón between calles 26 and 28. Tel. 223-8013.
   Cuisine: COSTA RICAN. **Reservations:** Not accepted.
$ Prices: Main courses $1.70–$3.15. No credit cards.
   Open: Mon–Sat 6am–7pm.

If you're looking for a filling, cheap, and quick breakfast in the Paseo Colón area, I recommend this soda. You'll find it near the movie theater. The wooden booths and a few tables on a covered walkway (noisy) are frequently full of local business-people because the meals are so reasonably priced, such as steak for $2.90. For lighter fare, try the burgers, sandwiches, or some of the good-looking pastries such as flaky empanadas or carrot bread.

SODA VISHNU, Avenida 1 between calles 1 and 3. Tel. 222-2549.
Cuisine: VEGETARIAN. **Reservations:** Not accepted.
$ Prices: Main courses $1.05–$2.95. No credit cards.
Open: Mon–Sat 7am–9pm, Sun 9am–7pm.

Vegetarians may find themselves eating all their meals at this bright and modern natural-foods eatery. There are booths for two or four people and photo murals on the walls. At the cashier's counter you can buy natural cosmetics, honey, and bags of granola. However, most people just come for the filling *plato de dia* that includes soup, salad, veggies, an entree, and dessert for around $2.10. There are also bean burgers and cheese sandwiches on whole wheat bread. There is another Vishnu around the corner on Calle 3 between Avenida Central and Avenida 1.

SUS ANTOJOS, Paseo Colón between calles 26 and 28 (across from the Ambassador Hotel). Tel. 222-9086.
Cuisine: MEXICAN. **Reservations:** Not required.
$ Prices: Main courses $2.25–$7.45. AE, MC, V.
Open: Daily 11:30am–10pm.

Located down some steps in the Paseo Colón neighborhood, this cozy place serves a dozen types of tacos, or *antojitos* (little bits to mix and match), and you can watch the cook making tortillas and grilling meats on the huge griddle in the open kitchen. We tried *chilasquiles de pollo*, chicken baked with a layer of cheese, tomato, and sour cream, and *entremes ranchero*, a little bit each of steak, pork chops, salad, beans, and guacamole, and both were tasty and well-prepared. One of the renowned margaritas is a good accompaniment to just about anything on the menu.

SAN PEDRO/LOS YOSES

EXPENSIVE

LE CHANDELIER, 100 meters west and 100 meters south of the I.C.E. office in San Pedro. Tel. 225-3980.
Cuisine: FRENCH. **Reservations:** Recommended.
$ Prices: Appetizers $6–$11; main courses $6.75–$24.35 lunch, $10.30–$25.35 dinner; fixed-price lunch $15.90, fixed-price dinner $33.80. AE, MC, V.
Open: Lunch Mon–Fri 11:30am–2pm; dinner Mon–Sat 6:30–11pm.

Sounds like a nice place. Located in a large older house in a quiet residential neighborhood east of downtown San José, Le Chandelier is one of the most elegant restaurants in town. The neighborhood, landscaping, and architectural styling give it the feel of an older Hollywood or Beverly Hills restaurant. The menu includes delicious renditions of French classics such as onion soup, escargots bourguignon, and chicken à l'orange. There are also such less familiar and unexpected dishes as tenderloin with cranberry sauce, carpaccio with smoked salmon and palmito, and roast duck in green pepper sauce. The set dinner is a true feast and might start with an appetizer of carpaccio, followed by gratin of Camembert with shrimp, sorbet, tournedos in cabernet sauvignon and green pepper, cheese and fruit, and a dessert of tiramisu This is one of the few restaurants in San José with a no-smoking room.

MODERATE

PIZZERIA IL POMODORO, 100 meters north of the church of San Pedro. Tel. 224-0966. Also at Escazú de la Residencia, 100 meters west of the U.S. Embassy.
Cuisine: ITALIAN. **Reservations:** Not accepted.
$ Prices: Pizzas $2.70–$5 small, $5.25–$8.10 large. MC, V.
Open: Mon–Fri 11am–11pm, Sat–Sun 11am–midnight.

This casual place a couple of blocks from the University of Costa Rica campus in San Pedro is popular with students. There are great pizzas as well as calzones,

FROMMER'S COOL FOR KIDS: RESTAURANTS

Manolo's Restaurante *(see p. 65)* The kids can get burgers, sandwiches, and milkshakes, and they may even enjoy the evening folk-dance performance.

La Casa del Lago *(see p. 65)* Located in the center of Parque la Sabana, this casual place serves fried chicken and burgers, and the kids can run around the park until they're exhausted.

foccacia, pastas, and risotto. With its old wooden tables and walls and checkerboard floor, this place looks as if it's been here for ages. The bar is popular in the evenings.

RESTAURANT AVE FÉNIX, 175 meters west of the church of San Pedro. Tel. 225-3362.

Cuisine: CHINESE. **Reservations:** Not required.

$ Prices: Appetizers $1.55–$2.45; main courses $4.05–$13.20. DC, MC, V.

Open: Sun–Thurs 11am–11pm, Fri–Sat 11am–midnight.

There are dozens of Chinese restaurants around San José and aside from the fact that they're good places to get some fresh vegetables (lacking from most Tico-style meals), there isn't much to recommend them. Ave Fénix is an exception. Though the restaurant itself isn't fancy, the meals are well-prepared and flavorful. In addition to standard dishes, you'll also find some Szechuan preparations. If it's mango season, try the unusual chicken with mango.

BUDGET

SPOON, one block south of Apartotel Los Yoses. Tel. 224-0328 or 253-1331. Also located 25 meters east of the Plaza de la Cultura.

Cuisine: PASTRIES. **Reservations:** Not accepted.

$ Prices: Sandwiches and pastries $1–$3. DC, MC, V.

Open: Daily 8am–10pm.

Popular with expatriate North American and Europeans living in Los Yoses, Spoon is one of San José's legendary pastry shops. It's always busy, but if you're lucky you can get a seat at one of the glass-topped tables that are made with old sewing machine treadles. The names on the long menu probably won't mean much to you so either pick a few items at random or go over to the cases full of tasty looking pastries and point out to the server what you'd like.

ESCAZÚ

EXPENSIVE

ATLANTA DINING GALLERY, Tara Resort Hotel, 600 meters south of the San Antonio de Escazú cemetary. Tel. 228-6992.

Cuisine: CONTINENTAL. **Reservations:** Recommended.

$ Prices: Appetizers $3.05–$7.45; main courses $7.10–$20.15. AE, MC, V.

Open: Breakfast daily 7–11am; lunch daily 11am–3pm; dinner Sun–Thurs 6–10pm, Fri–Sat 6–11pm.

For elegance, excellent service, delicious food, and fabulous views, you just can't beat the Atlanta Dining Gallery. Located in a reproduction antebellum mansion, this place is straight out of the deep south, except for that view of the Central Valley out the windows. Elegant dark-wood furnishings and a hardwood floor set the tone, but it is the view that keeps grabbing your attention. Scarlett O'Hara never had it so good. Most nights of the week such dishes as filet mignon with mushrooms, shrimp scampi, chicken with a mango and avocado sauce, and corvina with a red pepper and wine sauce, accompany the views. However, Sunday night is all-you-can-eat pasta night (for only $5.75). A tempting assortment of desserts accompanies a choice of after-dinner apéritifs and cognacs.

EL TULÁ RESTAURANTE, 200 meters west of the Periférico Los Anonos, San Rafael de Escazú. Tel. 228-0053.
   Cuisine: ITALIAN. **Reservations:** Recommended on weekends.
$ **Prices:** Appetizers $4.40–$12.20; pasta $5.40–$8.10; main courses $6.80–$18.95. AE, DC, MC, V.
   Open: Lunch Tues–Sun noon–2:30pm; dinner Tues–Sat 7–11pm, Sun 7–10pm.
Escazú is one of San José's wealthiest suburbs, and this is where locals head when they want good Italian food. El Tulá is a tony place by Costa Rican standards and has surprisingly contemporary decor. Waiters wear white jackets and bow ties, so there's no question of how you should dress. Though the exterior of the building is rather nondescript, the interior is quite attractive, with hardwood floors and pink tablecloths in the dining room. If the weather is good, you can eat out on the terrace.

   In addition to Italian standards, you'll find such flavorful offerings as corvina with basil and an unusual meal of noodles in a fondue dish. Friday and Saturday evenings there is a very popular buffet dinner.

MODERATE

EL CHÉ, 100 meters south of the Escazú/Santa Ana crossroad. Tel. 228-1598.
   Cuisine: STEAK. **Reservations:** Recommended for large groups.
$ **Prices:** Appetizers $1.40–$4.40; main courses $6.70–$8.80. AE, MC, V.
   Open: Lunch Mon–Fri noon–3pm; dinner Mon–Fri 6–11pm, Sat–Sun 11am–11pm.
This small neighborhood place is owned by a former Argentinian, who likes to play '60s rock 'n' roll music in his restaurant. Charcoal-broiled *lomita* (sirloin steak) is the raison d'être for this place. The steak is so tender that you can cut it with a fork (possibly because of the secret marinade). While waiting for your very fine steak, order some mouth-watering appetizers such as parsley/garlic sauce that you can pile onto crunchy french bread, pickled onions, a spicy and flavorful *chorizzo* (sausage), or a hearts of palm salad. Enjoy your meal outside on the patio or indoors in a comfortable atmosphere with red tablecloths and candles.

SPECIALTY DINING

STREET FOOD On almost every street corner in downtown San José you'll find a fruit vendor. If you're lucky enough to be in town between April and June you can sample more varieties of mangoes than you ever knew existed. I like buying them already cut up in a little bag. They cost a little more this way but you don't get nearly as messy. Be sure to try a green mango with salt and chili peppers. That's the way they seem to like mangoes best in the steamy tropics—guaranteed to wake up your taste buds.

   Another common street food that you might be wondering about is called *pejibaye*, a bright orange palm nut about the size of a small apple. They are boiled in big pots on carts. You eat them in much the same way you would an avocado, and they taste a bit like squash.

LATE NIGHT/24 HOURS San José has quite a few all-night restaurants including La Perla, La Esmeralda, and Café Parisien, all of which are described above. Another popular place, which is almost exclusively for men, is the Soda Palace on Avenida 2 and Calle 2 (see "Evening Entertainment," below, for more information).

5. ATTRACTIONS

As are most of the cities of Central America, San José is crowded, congested, and smoggy. Most visitors to the country try to get out of town as fast as possible so they can spend more time on the beach or off in the rain forests. However, there are quite a few attractions here in the city to keep you busy for a while, and if you start doing day trips out of the city, you can spend quite a few days here. Some of the best and most modern museums in Central America are here in San José, and together these museums have a wealth of fascinating pre-Columbian artifacts.

SUGGESTED ITINERARIES

IF YOU HAVE ONE DAY Start your day on the Plaza de la Cultura. Visit the Gold Museum (if it is a Saturday or Sunday) and see if you can get tickets for a performance that night at the Teatro Nacional. From the Plaza de la Cultura stroll up Avenida Central to the Museo Nacional. After lunch head over to the Jade Museum if you have the energy for one more museum. After all this culture, a stroll through the chaos of the Mercado Central is in order. Try dinner at La Cocina De Leña before going to the Teatro Nacional. After the performance you absolutely must swing by La Esmeralda for some live mariachi music before calling it a day.

IF YOU HAVE TWO DAYS Follow the itinerary above. On Day Two visit the Serpentarium or the Spirogyra Butterfly Garden, do a bit of shopping, and then head out Paseo Colón to the Museo de Arte Costarricense.

IF YOU HAVE THREE DAYS Follow the itinerary for the two days outlined above. On Day Three, head out to Irazú Volcano, Orosi Valley, Lankester Gardens, and Cartago. Start your day at the volcano and work you way back toward San José.

IF YOU HAVE FIVE DAYS Follow the itinerary for three days outlined above. Then spend Days Four and Five on other excursions from San José. You can go white-water rafting, hiking in a cloud forest, or horseback riding for a day if you are an active type. If you prefer less strenuous activities, try a cruise around the Gulf of Nicoya and a trip to the Rain Forest Aerial Tram.

THE TOP ATTRACTIONS

MUSEO DE ARTE COSTARRICENSE, Calle 42 and Paseo Colón, Parque la Sabana este. Tel. 222-7155 or 222-7932.
This small museum at the end of Paseo Colón in Parque la Sabana was formerly an airport terminal. Today, however, it houses a collection of works in all media by Costa Rica's most celebrated artists. On display are many exceptionally beautiful pieces in a wide range of artistic styles, demonstrating how Costa Rican artists have interpreted the major European artistic movements. In addition to the permanent collection of sculptures, paintings, and prints, there are regular temporary exhibits. If the second floor is open during your visit, be sure to go up and have a look at the conference room's unusual bas-relief walls, which chronicle the history of Costa Rica from pre-Columbian times to the present with evocative images of the people. On weekends local artists sell their work out on the plaza in front of the museum.
Admission: $2.05; Sun free (donation is suggested).
Open: Daily 10am–5pm. **Bus:** Sabana–Cementerio.

MUSEO DE JADE MARCO FIDEL TRISTAN [Jade Museum], Avenida 7 between calles 9 and 9B, 11th Floor, INS Building. Tel. 223-5800, ext. 2584.
Among the pre-Columbian cultures of Mexico and Central America, jade was the most valuable commodity, worth more than gold. This modern museum displays a huge collection of jade artifacts from throughout Costa Rica's pre-Columbian archeological sites. Most of the jade pieces are large pendants that were

parts of necklaces and are primarily human and animal figures. A fascinating display illustrates how the primitive peoples of this region carved this extremely hard stone. Most of the jade pieces date from 330 B.C. to A.D. 700.

There is also an extensive collection of pre-Columbian polychromed terra-cotta vases, bowls, and figurines. Some of these pieces are amazingly modern in design and exhibit a surprisingly advanced technique. Particuarly fascinating is a vase that incorporates real human teeth, and a display that shows how jade was imbedded in human teeth merely for decorative reasons. Most of the identifying labels and explanations are in Spanish but there are a few in English.

Before you leave be sure to check out the splendid view of San José from the lounge area.

Admission: Free.

Open: Mon–Fri 8am–3:30pm. **Bus:** Any bus to downtown.

MUSEO DE ORO BANCO CENTRAL [Gold Museum], Calle 5 between Avenida Central and Avenida 2. Tel. 223-0528.

Located directly beneath the Plaza de la Cultura, this unusual underground museum houses one of the largest collections of pre-Columbian gold in the Americas. On display are more than 20,000 troy ounces of gold in more than 2,000 objects. The sheer number of small pieces can be overwhelming; however, the unusual display cases and complex lighting systems show off every piece to its utmost. This museum also includes a gallery for temporary art exhibits and a numismatic and philatelic museum.

Admission: Free.

Open: Fri 1–5pm, Sat–Sun 10am–5pm. **Bus:** Any bus to downtown.

MUSEO NACIONAL DE COSTA RICA, Calle 17 between Avenida Central and Avenida 2. Tel. 257-1433.

Costa Rica's most important museum is housed in a former army barracks that was the scene of fighting during the civil war of 1948. You can still see hundreds of bullet holes on the turrets at the corners of the building. Inside this traditional Spanish-style courtyard building, you will find displays on Costa Rican history and culture from pre-Columbian times to the present. In the pre-Columbian rooms, you'll see a 2,500-year-old jade carving that is shaped like a seashell and etched with an image of a hand holding a small animal. Among the most fascinating objects unearthed at Costa Rica's numerous archeological sites are many *metates* or grinding stones. This type of grinding stone is still in use today throughout Central America. However, the ones on display here are more ornately decorated than those that you will see anywhere else. Some of the metates are the size of a small bed and are believed to have been part of funeral rites. A separate vault houses the museum's small collection of pre-Columbia gold jewelry and figurines. In the courtyard, you'll see some of Costa Rica's mysterious stone spheres.

Admission: 70¢.

Open: Tues–Sat 8:30am–4:30pm, Sun 9am–4:30pm. **Bus:** San Pedro.

MUSEO NACIONAL DE CIENCIAS NATURALES "LA SALLE," across from the southwest corner of Parque la Sabana. Tel. 232-1306.

Before heading out to the wilds of the Costa Rican jungles, you might want to stop by this natural-history museum and find out more about the animals you might be seeing. There are stuffed and mounted anteaters, monkeys, tapirs, and many others. However, the collection includes animals from all over the world as well. There are also 1,200 birds and 12,500 insects displayed. A collection of 13,500 seashells is another highlight.

Admission: 70¢ adults, 35¢ children.

Open: Mon–Fri 8am–3pm, Sat 8am–noon, Sun 9am–4pm. **Bus:** Escazú or Pavas from Avenida 1 and Calle 18.

MUSEO DE ENTOMOLOGIA, University of Costa Rica, School of Music, San Pedro. Tel. 253-5323, ext. 5042.

The tropics have produced the world's greatest concentrations and diversity of insects, and here at this small museum you can see more than one million mounted

insects from around the world. The butterfly collection is the star attraction here.
Admission: $2.05.
Open: Mon–Fri 1–4:45pm. **Bus:** San Pedro from Avenida 2 between calles 5 and 7.

MORE ATTRACTIONS

PARQUE ZOOLÓGICO SIMÓN BOLÍVAR, Avenida 11 and Calle 11. Tel. 233-6701.
I don't think I have ever seen a sadder zoo than this little park tucked away beside the polluted Río Torres. It is a shame that a country that has preserved so much of its land in national parks would ignore this zoo. The cages here are only occasionally marked, and many are dirty and small. The collection includes Asian, African, and Costa Rican animals. For many years, there have been plans to build a new zoo with more modern displays, but as yet nothing has happened.
Admission: 55¢.
Open: Daily 8am–4pm. **Bus:** Any bus to downtown, then walk.

SERPENTARIUM, Avenida 1 between calles 9 and 11. Tel. 255-4210.
The tropics abound in reptiles and amphibians, and the Serpentarium is an excellent introduction to all that slithers and hops through the jungles of Costa Rica. The live snakes, lizards, and frogs are kept in beautiful, large terrariums that simulate their natural environments. Poisonous snakes make up a large part of the collection with the dreaded fer-de-lance pit viper eliciting the most gasps from enthralled visitors. Also fascinating to see are the tiny, billiantly colored poison arrow frogs. Iguanas and Jesus Christ lizards are two of the more commonly spotted of Costa Rica's reptiles, and both are represented here. Also on display is an Asian import—a giant Burmese python, which is one of the largest I have ever seen. This little zoological museum is well worth a visit, especially if you plan to go bashing about in the jungles. It will help you identify the numerous poisonous snakes you'll want to avoid.
Admission: $2.05.
Open: Daily 9am–6pm. **Bus:** Any bus to downtown.

SPYROGYRA BUTTERFLY GARDEN, 100 meters east and 100 meters south of El Pueblo Shopping Center. Tel. 222-2937.
Butterflies have been likened to self-propelled flowers, so it comes as no surprise that butterfly gardens are becoming all the rage throughout the tropics these days. If you'd like to find out why, drop in here at Spyrogyra. Though this butterfly garden is smaller and less spectacular than the other two listed below, it is a good introduction to the life cycle of butterflies. You'll find Spyrogyra near El Pueblo, a 30-minute walk from the center of San José.
Admission: $4.
Open: Wed–Mon 9am–4pm. **Bus:** Calle Blancos bus from Calle 3 and Avenida 5.

ATTRACTIONS OUTSIDE OF SAN JOSÉ

THE BUTTERFLY FARM, in front of Los Reyes Country Club, La Guácima de Alajuela. Tel. 438-0115.
At any given time, you may see around 30 of the 80 different species of butterflies raised at this butterfly farm south of Alajuela. The butterflies live in a large enclosed garden similar to an aviary, and flutter about the heads of visitors during tours of the gardens. When we visited we saw glittering blue morphos and a butterfly that mimics the eyes of an owl. In the demonstration room you'll see butterfly eggs, caterpillars, and pupae. Among the latter, there are cocoons trimmed in a shimmering gold color and cocoons that mimic a snake's head in order to frighten away predators. The farm also offers a bee tour during which you can observe bees at work in glass observation hives.

Admission: $9 adults, $4 children ages 4–12, $6 students. Group rates available. **Open:** Daily 9am–5pm. **Bus:** San Antonio/Ojo de Agua on Avenida 1 between calles 20 and 22.

BUTTERFLY PARADISE, on the road from San Joaquín to Santa Barbara, 1 kilometer north, and 350 meters west, on the right-hand side. Tel. 221-2015 or 224-1095.

This butterfly garden is similar to the other two and offers the same experience— a guided walk through the screened-in butterfly garden. You'll see dozens of beautiful butterflies and learn all about their feeding, mating, and egg-laying habits. In the museum collection there are more butterflies to marvel over, and many other insects as well.

Admission: $6.75 adults, $3.40 children ages 3–12.

Open: Daily 9am–4pm. **Bus:** First take a bus to Heredia from Calle 1 between avenidas 7 and 9 in San José. In Heredia, transfer to a bus bound for either San Joaquín or Santa Barbara. In San Joaquín, you can get a taxi.

CAFÉ BRITT FARM, north of Heredia on the road to Barva. Tel. 260-2748.

Though bananas are the main export of Costa Rica, people are far more interested in the country's second most important export—coffee. Café Britt is one of the leading brands of coffee here, and the company has put together an interesting tour and stage production at its farm, which is 20 minutes outside of San José. Here, you'll see how coffee is grown. You'll also visit the roasting plant to learn how a coffee "cherry" is turned into a delicious roasted bean. Tasting sessions are offered for the visitor to experience the different qualities of coffee. There is also a store here where you can buy very reasonably priced coffee. Call the above number for the tour, which includes pick-up at your hotel.

Admission: $15 adults, $7.50 children under age 12.

Open: Tours Dec–Apr, daily 9am, 11am, and 3pm; May–Oct, Mon–Sat 10am, Sun 10am and 12pm. Store open daily 8am–5pm.

LANKESTER GARDENS, Paraíso de Cartago. Tel. 551-9877.

There are more than 1,200 varieties of orchids in Costa Rica, and no less than 800 species are on display at this botanical garden in Cartago province. Created in the 1940s by English naturalist Charles Lankester, the gardens are now administered by the University of Costa Rica. The primary goal of the gardens is to preserve the local flora, with an emphasis on orchids and bromeliads. Paved trails wander from open, sunny gardens into shady forests. In each environment, different species of orchids are in bloom. There are free guided tours, or you can wander on your own.

Admission: $2.05.

Open: Daily 8am–3pm. **Bus:** Cartago bus from San José, then the Paraíso bus from the south side of the Parque Central in Cartago.

MUSEO JOYAS DEL TRÓPICO HUMEDO [Jewels of the Rain Forest], 100 meters east of the cemetery of Santa Domingo de Heredia. No phone.

Far more than just another bug collection, this exhibit takes the position that insects are works of art, tiny tropical jewels. The displays are artistically arranged and include more than 50,000 arthropods and insects (including thousands of different butterflies) collected from around the world by former Oregon biologist Richard Whitten and his wife Maggie.

Admission: $4.05 adults, 70¢ children under age 12.

Open: Tues–Sun 9am–1pm and 2–5pm. **Bus:** At Calle 1 between avenidas 7 and 9, take the Heredia/Tibás/Santo Domingo bus, then taxi from Santo Domingo.

ZOO AVE, La Garita, Alajuela. Tel. 433-9140.

Dozens of scarlet macaws, several different species of toucans, and other brilliantly colored birds from Costa Rica and around the world make this place an exciting one to visit. Bird-watching enthusiasts will be able to get a closer look at birds they may have seen in the wild. Look out for the 12-foot-long crocodile.

Admission: $4.75.

Open: Daily 9am–5pm. **Bus:** Catch an Alajuela bus on Avenida 2 between calles 12 and 14. In Alajuela, transfer to a bus for Atenas and get off at Zoo Ave before you get to La Garita.

WALKING TOUR — DOWNTOWN SAN JOSÉ

Start: Plaza de la Cultura.
Finish: Plaza de la Cultura.
Time: Allow a full day for this tour, though most of your time will be spent touring the three museums mentioned.
Best Time: Friday, when the maximum number of museums will be open.
Worst Time: Monday, when some museums may be closed.

Because San José is so compact, it's possible to visit nearly all of the city's major sites in a single day's walking tour. Begin your tour on the Plaza de la Cultura, perhaps after having breakfast at the Gran Hotel Costa Rica.

Begin by walking to the:

1. **Teatro Nacional,** which faces the entrance to the Gran Hotel Costa Rica. Be sure to take a walk around inside this baroque masterpiece. The café here is another great place to have a meal or a pastry and coffee. Next door is the:
2. **Gold Museum,** which is built beneath the Plaza de la Cultura to the left of the Teatro Nacional. This museum houses the largest collection of pre-Columbian gold in Central America. From the Gold Museum, walk two blocks west on Avenida 2 to reach the:
3. **National Cathedral,** a neoclassical structure with a tropical twist. The roof is tin, and the ceiling is wood. A statue of the Virgin Mary is surrounded by neon stars and a crescent moon. Diagonally across the street is the:
4. **Melico Salazar Theater.** This theater has an impressive pillared facade, though the interior is not nearly as ornate. Continue west on Avenida 2 and turn right on Calle 6. In two blocks, you will be in the:
5. **Mercado Central,** a fragrant (not necessarily pleasantly so) district of streets crowded with produce vendors. A covered market, with its dark warren of stalls, takes up an entire block and is the center of activity. Beware of pickpockets in this area. Head back toward the Teatro Nacional on Avenida 1, and in seven blocks you will come to an excellent place for lunch.

REFUELING STOP One of the best lunches in San José is at the **Amstel Grill Room,** Avenida 1 and Calle 7. White-jacketed waiters attend to your every need. The cuisine is American, continental, and Costa Rican, and the prices are reasonable.

After lunch head over to the corner of Avenida 1 and Calle 9 where you'll find the:

6. **Serpentarium.** This indoor zoo offers a fascinating look at the reptiles and amphibians of Costa Rica and other parts of the world. When you leave the Serpentarium, head north on Calle 9 and you will come to:
7. **Parque Morazán,** a classically designed park that was restored to its original configuration in 1991. This is a good place for people-watching. At the center of the park is a large bandstand modeled after a music temple in Paris. Across the street from the west side of the park you'll find:
8. **Suraska,** a handcrafts shop with a good selection of products made from local woods, as well as ceramics and jewelry. Retrace your steps back to the far side of the park and across the street to the north you will see the:

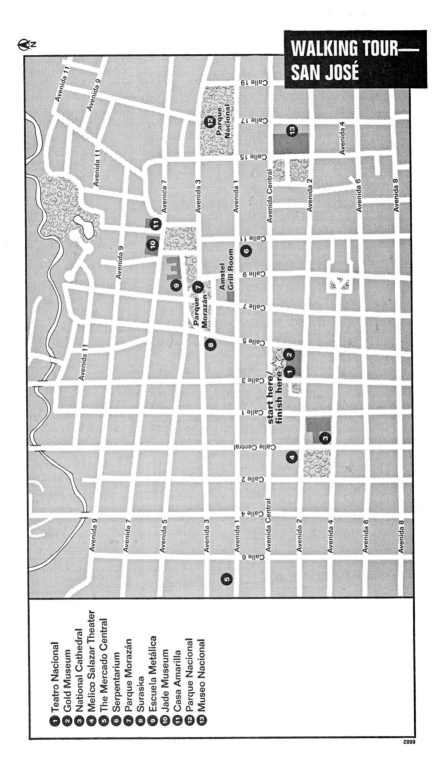

WALKING TOUR—
SAN JOSÉ

N

Avenida 11
Avenida 9
Calle 19
Calle 17
Parque Nacional ⑫
Calle 15
Avenida 11
⑬
Avenida 4
Avenida 11
Avenida 7
Avenida 3
Avenida 1
Avenida Central
Avenida 2
Avenida 6
Avenida 8
⑪
⑩
Avenida 9
Calle 11
⑥
Calle 9
Amstel Grill Room
⑨ ⑦
Parque Morazán
Calle 7
Avenida 11
⑧
Calle 5
① ②
①
Calle 3
③
start here/ finish here
Calle 1
Calle Central
④
Calle 2
Calle 4
Avenida Central
Avenida 9
Avenida 7
Avenida 5
Avenida 3
Avenida 1
Avenida 2
Avenida 4
Avenida 6
Avenida 8
Calle 6
⑤

① Teatro Nacional
② Gold Museum
③ National Cathedral
④ Melico Salazar Theater
⑤ The Mercado Central
⑥ Serpentarium
⑦ Parque Morazán
⑧ Suraska
⑨ Escuela Metálica
⑩ Jade Museum
⑪ Casa Amarilla
⑫ Parque Nacional
⑬ Museo Nacional

9. Escuela Metálica, Avenida 5 and Calle 9, which is one of the most unusual buildings in the city. It is made of metal panels that are bolted toegether, and was manufactured in Europe late in the 19th century. One block north, on Avenida 7, you'll come to the:

10. Jade Museum, which is located in a high-rise office building. The cool, dark exhibit halls are filled with jade pendants, and there are also great views of the city. Across Calle 11 from the Jade Museum is the:

11. Casa Amarilla, which is an attractive old building that now houses the Ministry of Foreign Affairs. This building, along with the park directly across the street, were donated to Costa Rica by Andrew Carnegie. From here, walk back up the hill (east) to Calle 15 and turn right. Ahead of you, at the corner of Avenida 3, you will see the:

12. Parque Nacional, which has an impressive monument to the nations that defeated Tennesseean William Walker's attempt to turn Central America into a slave state in the 19th century. Across Avenida 1 is a statue of Juan Santamaría, who gave his life to defeat Walker. If you continue south on Calle 17, you will find the:

13. Museo Nacional de Costa Rica, between Avenida Central and Avenida 2. This museum is housed in a former army barracks that still shows signs of the 1948 revolution. Inside the Costa Rica's largest collection of pre-Columbian art and artifacts. After touring the museum, you need only head west on Avenida Central or Avenida 2 and in seven blocks you will be back at the Plaza de la Cultura.

ORGANIZED TOURS

There are literally dozens of tour companies operating in San José, and the barrage of advertising brochures can be quite intimidating. There really isn't much reason to take a tour of San José since it is so compact—you can easily visit all the major sites on your own. However, if you want to take a city tour, which will run you about $18, here are some companies: **Otec Tours,** Edeficio Ferencz, Calle 3 between avenidas 1 and 3, Apdo. 323-1002, San José (tel. 255-0554, 222-0866, or 24-hour line 225-2500); **TAM,** Calle 1 between Avenida Central and Avenida 1 (tel. 222-2642 or 222-2732); **Vic-Vic Tours,** Calle 3 between avenidas 5 and 7 (tel. 233-3435); and **Swiss Travel Service,** (tel. 231-4055), which has several offices around San José including locations in the lobbies of the Hotel Corobicí and the Hotel Amstel.

SPECIAL/FREE EVENTS

San José is a conservative city and doesn't stage many public festivals or events. Those it does have are strictly religious in nature: The days between Christmas and New Year's and the week prior to Easter are the city's two top periods of celebration. During these times there are parades, dances, and other special events.

On Sundays throughout the year there are often free classical music concerts on the Parque Central and the Parque Morazán.

SPORTS/RECREATION

Parque la Sabana, formerly San José's airport, is the city's center for sports and recreation. Here you'll find everthing from jogging trails and soccer fields to the National Stadium. For information on horseback riding, hiking, and white-water rafting trips from San José, see "Easy Excursions," at the end of this chapter.

If you like to swim and would like to spend an afternoon relaxing in a spring-fed swimming pool, head out to **Ojo de Agua,** which is just beyond the airport near Alajuela. The crystal-clear waters are cool and refreshing, and even if it seems a bit chilly in San José, it is always several degrees warmer out here. Admission is 70¢ and there are express buses from San José Monday through Saturday both in the morning and in the afternoon. These buses depart from Avenida 1 between calles 20 and 22.

You can even bungee jump in Costa Rica now. If you want to try this daring sport, contact **Tropical Bungee** (tel. 255-4354) or **No Fear Bungee** (tel. 643-3338). These two companies charge between $40 and $60 for your first jump and $20 to $25 for subsequent jumps on the same day.

6. SAVVY SHOPPING

In Costa Rica, you probably won't be overwhelmed by the desire to buy things the way you might be in other countries that have indigenous handcrafts, but there are a few interesting and unique items to buy. For lack of their own handcrafts, Costa Rica does a brisk business of selling crafts and clothes imported from Guatemala.

THE SHOPPING SCENE

Shopping in San José centers around by the parallel streets of Avenida Central and Avenida 2, from about Calle 14 in the west to Calle 13 in the east. For several blocks east of the Plaza de la Cultura, Avenida Central is a pedestrians-only street where you'll find store after store of inexpensive clothes for men, women, and children.

Most shops in the downtown district are open Monday through Saturday from about 8:30am to noon and from 2 to 6pm. You'll find that some shops close for lunch while others remain open. When you do purchase something, you'll be happy to find that there is no sales tax.

There are several markets around downtown San José, but by far the largest is the Mercado Central, which is located between Avenida Central and Avenida 1 and calles 6 and 8. Inside this dark maze of stalls you'll find all manner of vendors. Although this is primarily a food market, you can find a few vendors selling Costa Rican souvenirs. Be especially careful about your wallet or purse because this area is frequented by very skillful pickpockets. All the streets surrounding the Mercado Central are jammed with produce vendors selling from small carts or loading and unloading trucks. It is always a hive of activity, with crowds of people jostling for space on the streets. In the hot days of the dry season, the aromas can get quite heady.

International laws prohibt purchasing endangered wildlife—visitors to Costa Rica should not buy any wildlife or plants, even if it is legal. The Audubon Society does not tolerate sales of any kind of sea turtle products (including jewelry), wild birds, lizard or snake skin, coral, or orchids (except those grown commercially).

Just in case you discover when you get home that the photos you took on your trip don't capture the beauty of Costa Rica, you might want to buy one of the picture books on Costa Rica mentioned in the "Recommended Books and Films" section of Chapter 1.

SHOPPING A TO Z

ART GALLERIES

AMIR ART GALLERY, Calle 5 between avenidas 1 and 3. Tel. 255-3261.
This gallery carries original artworks in a variety of mediums featuring Central American themes. It also has a second location: Avenida 5 between calles 3 and 5.

GALLERIA ANDROMEDA, Calle 9 at Avenida 9. Tel. 223-3529.
This small, personal gallery features national artists of good quality. There are usually prints and paintings by several artists on display, and prices are very reasonable.

JEWELRY

ESMERALDAS Y DISEÑOS, Avenida Las Americas, Sabana Norte, from the Restaurante Chicote, 100 meters north, 50 meters west and 150 meters north. Tel. 231-4808 or 231-5428.

Notice the location given above for this jewelry store—it is truly a classic San José address. You'll find here copies of pre-Columbian jewelry designs in gold, and jewelry including semiprecious stones from Brazil and emeralds from Columbia.

LA GRAN JOYA [The Big Jewel], Paseo Colón on the west side of Toyota. Tel. 233-1433.

This jewelry store, located downtown, is a specialist in diamonds, emeralds, sapphires, and rubies. They also engrave emeralds and other stones, and carry jade, silverware, and watches.

LEATHER

MALETY, Avenida 1 between calles 1 and 3. Tel. 221-1670.

The quality of leather products found in Costa Rica is not as good as in North America and prices are high, but take a look and see for yourself. This is one of the outlets in San José where you can shop for locally produced leather bags, briefcases, purses, wallets, and other such items. A second store is located on Calle 1 between Avenida Central and Avenida 2.

LIQUORS

Café Rica, similar to Kahlua, and Salicsa, a cream liqueur, are two delicious liqueurs made from coffee in Costa Rica. You can buy these liqueurs in government liquor stores and tourist shops, but just about the best prices I have seen are at the supermarket chain **Mas X Menos.** There are Mas X Menos outlets on Paseo Colón and Avenida Central on the east end of town, just below the Museo Nacional de Costa Rica.

MARKETS

MERCADO CENTRAL, between Avenida Central and Avenida 1 and calles 6 and 8. No phone.

This rabbit warren of a market sells primarily food, but you can also find some interesting local household goods, tools, and the usual souvenirs. A good place for people-watching, but also keep an eye on your wallet or purse. On Sundays, only a few vendors are open.

FASHIONS [WOMEN'S]

ANGIE THEOLOGOS'S GALLERY, San Pedro; call for directions. Tel. 225-6565.

Angie makes sumptuous handcrafted jackets from handwoven and embroidered Guatemalan textiles. Her work also includes boleros, and T-shirts made with Panamanian molas (appliquéd panels). Her colorful gallery of clothing may soon be located at the airport as well.

COFFEE

Two words of advice—buy coffee. Buy as much as you can carry. Coffee is probably the best shipping deal in all of Costa Rica. Although the best Costa Rican coffee is supposedly shipped off to North American and European markets, it is hard to beat coffee that is roasted right in front of you. Café Britt is the big name in Costa Rican coffee, but is not necessarily the best, though it is the most expensive. For good flavor and value, visit Café Trebol, on Calle 8 between Avenida Central and Avenida 1, which is highly recommended as a place to buy coffee. They'll pack the beans for you in whatever size bag you want. Be sure to ask for whole beans; Costa Rican grinds are too fine for standard coffee filters. Best of all is the price: One pound of coffee sells for about $1! It makes a great gift and keeps for a long time in your refrigerator or freezer. If you should happen to buy prepackaged coffee in a supermarket in Costa Rica, be sure the package is marked *puro;* otherwise, it will likely be mixed with a good amount of sugar—the way Ticos like it.

HANDCRAFTS

If your interest is in handcrafts, there are many places for you to visit. The most appealing artisan's maket is the daily one on the Plaza de la Cultura. Prices here tend to be high and bargaining is necessary, but there are some very nice items for sale. If you prefer to do your craft shopping in a flea-market atmosphere, head over to **La Casona** on Calle Central between Avenida Central and Avenida 1. Also be sure to visit the excellent **Annemarie Souvenir Shop** in the lobby of the Hotel Don Carlos.

Several other shops around San José sell a wide variety of crafts—from the truly tacky to the divinely inspired. Here are some of the places to look for such items.

ANNEMARIE SOUVENIR SHOP, Calle 9 between avenidas 7 and 9. Tel. 221-6063.

⭐ Tucked into the lobby of the Hotel Don Carlos, this shop has an amazing array of wood products, leather goods, papier-maché figurines, paintings, books, cards, posters, and jewelry, to mention just a few of the things you'll find here. Don't miss this shopping experience.

ASOCIACIÓN NACIONAL PRO DESARROLLO DE LA ARTESANIA (ANDA), Avenida Central between calles 5 and 7. Tel. 233-3340.

If you're looking for Guatemalan clothing and they're asking too much on the Plaza de la Cultura, you might try this shop in the center of town. They also carry masks, carved gourds, T-shirts, and other souvenir-type items.

ATMÓSFERA, Calle 5 between avenidas 1 and 3. Tel. 222-4322.

⭐ This place has high-quality Costa Rican arts and crafts, from naive paintings and sculpture to skilled turned-wood bowls. It consists of several small rooms on two floors, so be sure you explore every nook and cranny—you'll see stuff here that is not available anywhere else in town.

LA GALERIA, Calle 1 between Avenida Central and Avenida 1. Tel. 221-3436.

This small store features some of the best of modern Costa Rican handcrafts. There is a fine selection of wood carvings and gold and silver pre-Columbian jewelry reproductions, paintings and prints with Latin American themes, metalware, and rugs. The little boxes and bowls of native Costa Rican hardwoods are particularly attractive.

LAS GARZAS HANDICRAFT MARKET, in Moravia, 100 meters south and 50 meters east from the Red Cross Station. Tel. 236-0037.

This artisan's market is a short ride out of San José, and includes more than 25 shops which sell wood, metal, and ceramic crafts, among a large variety of other items.

MAGIA, Calle 5 between avenidas 1 and 3. Tel. 233-2630.

What you'll notice here is that almost everything is made of wood. The shop is filled with elegant, thin bowls of native hardwood, a big selection of wooden boxes, mirrors framed in wood and very handsome handmade furniture. All items are high quality, created by artisans under the guidance of designer J. Morrison.

MAYA-QUICHE, Avenida Central between calles 5 and 7. Tel. 223-5030.

Located across the street from the handcraft shop ANDA (in the Galería Central Ramírez Valido shopping mall), this shop sells handcrafts from Central American countries, including gaily painted boxes, letters, and animals from El Salvador and molas from Panama.

MERCADO DE ARTESANOS CANAPI, Calle 11 and Avenida 1. Tel. 221-3342.

The most unusual crafts for sale here are the brightly painted miniature oxcarts that are almost the national symbol. These oxcarts are made in the small town of Sarchí, which is mentioned under "Easy Excursions" in this chapter. This store also carries a wide variety of typical Costa Rican handcrafts, including large, comfortable woven-rope hammocks; reproductions of pre-Columbian gold jewelry and pottery bowls; coffee-wood carvings; and many other carvings from rare Costa Rican hardwoods.

MERCADO NACIONAL DE ARTESANÍAS, Calle 11 and Avenida 4 Bis. Tel. 221-5012.
Located only a couple of blocks away from the above-mentioned Mercado de Artesanos CANAPI store, this shop offers similar crafts at similar prices.

SURASKA, Calle 5 and Avenida 3. Tel. 222-0129.
If you haven't been impressed with the quality of Costa Rican handcrafts, save your money for a visit to this store. Among the selections here are ceramics, mobiles, and jewelry. Of particular note are the wood carvings of North American artist Barry Biesanz, who turns out exquisite pieces of finely worked hardwood. Be forewarned, however, that these pieces are expensive.

7. EVENING ENTERTAINMENT

To find out about the entertainment scene in San José, pick up a copy of the *Tico Times* (English) and *La Nación* (Spanish). The former is a good place to find out where local expatriates are hanging out; the latter's "Viva" section has extensive listings of everything from discos to movie theaters to live music.

THE PERFORMING ARTS

LAURENCE OLIVIER THEATER, Avenida 2 and Calle 28. Tel. 223-1960.
Located next to the Sala Garbo in the Paseo Colón neighborhood, this modern theater features plays in both English and Spanish by various local theater groups.
Prices: $3–$5. **Bus:** Sabana–Cementerio.

TEATRO MELICO SALAZAR, Avenida 2 between Calle Central and Calle 2. Tel. 221-4952.
Just a few blocks away from the Teatro Nacional, and directly across the street from the Parque Central, is this 1920s neoclassical theater. Though the facade is far more impressive than the interior, it is still a grand old theater. "Fantasia Folclórico," which features modern dance, pantomime, and traditional dances that together tell the history of Costa Rica, is staged every Tuesday night at 8pm. The box office is open daily from 9am to noon and from 2 to 8pm.
Prices: $4.05–$10.15. **Bus:** Sabana–Cementerio.

TEATRO NACIONAL, Avenida 2 between calles 3 and 5. Tel. 221-1329.
⭐ Financed with a self-imposed tax on coffee exports, this grand baroque theater was completed in 1897. Muses representing Music, Fame, and Dance gaze off into the distance from the roof, while statues of Beethoven and Calderón de la Barca flank the entrance. The lobby is simple and elegant. Marble floors, frescoes, and gold-framed Venetian mirrors offer cultured Ticos a grand foyer in which to congregate prior to performances by the National Symphony Orchestra, ballet companies, opera companies, and all the other performers who keep this theater busy almost every night of the year. Within the hall itself, there are three tiers of seating amid an elegant gilt-and-plasterwork decor, and of course the wealthy patrons have their private box seats. Marble staircases are lined with sculptures; the walls are covered with murals and changing art exhibits. The symphony season begins in late April, shortly before the start of the rainy season, and continues on until November. The Café de Teatro Nacional, just off the lobby, is open Monday

through Saturday and is the most elegant café in the city. The theater box office is open Monday through Saturday from 9am to noon and 1:30 to 5pm.

Prices: Tour tickets $2.40; tickets for performances $1.35–$6.10; purchasers of cheaper tickets must use side entrance. **Bus:** Sabana–Cementerio.

THE CLUB & MUSIC SCENE

Salsa is the music of young people in San José, and on any weekend you can join the fun at half a dozen or more high-decibel nightclubs around town. The "Viva" section of the *La Nación* newspaper has weekly performances schedules. A couple of performing groups (*grupos*) to watch for are "Marfil" and "Los Brillanticos."

The best place to sample San José's nightclub scene is in El Pueblo, a shopping, dining, and entertainment complex done up like an old Spanish village. It's just across the river to the north of town. The best way to get here is by taxi; all the drivers know El Pueblo well. Within the alleyways that wind through El Pueblo are a dozen or more bars, clubs, and discos. There is even a roller-skating rink. **Cocoloco** (tel. 222-8782) features nightly "fiestas," and **Discoteque Infinito** (tel. 233-0988) has three different ambiences under one roof. Manhattan is a piano bar, and the **Tango Bar** is just what its name implies.

LIVE MUSIC

AKELARE, Calle 21 between avenidas 4 and 6. Tel. 223-0345.

This popular club is located in a renovated old house near the Museo Nacional. There are many rooms in which to check out the action, as well as a garden out back. There are frequent live music performances by hot Costa Rican groups.

LA ESMERALDA, Avenida 2 between calles 5 and 7. Tel. 221-0530.

A sort of mariachi Grand Central Station, La Esmeralda is a cavernous open-air restaurant and bar that stays open 24 hours a day. In the evenings, mariachi bands park their vans out front and wait to be hired for a moonlight serenade or perhaps a surprise party. While they wait, they often wander into La Esmeralda and practice their favorite melodies. If you've never been serenaded at your table before, this place is a must.

KEY LARGO, Calle 7 between avenidas 1 and 3. Tel. 221-0277.

Housed in one of the most beautiful old buildings in San José, Key Largo is elegant and expensive and the best-known nightclub in Costa Rica. It's worth a visit just to see the interior of the building, but be forewarned—this is known as San José's number-one prostitute hangout.

DISCOS

SALSA 54, Calle 3 between avenidas 1 and 3. No phone.

This is the place to go to watch expert salsa dancers and to try some yourself. You might even run into a Latin dance class here.

LAS TUNAS, Sabana North, 500 meters west of I.C.E. office. Tel. 231-1802.

This happening place serves Mexican food and barbecue, but where it really cooks is in the bar and discotheque, where live Costa Rican pop music is featured weekly.

THE BAR SCENE

The best part of the varied bar scene in San José is something called a *boca,* the equivalent of a *tapa* in Spain, a little dish of snacks that arrives at your table when you order a drink. In most bars, the bocas are free; but in some, where the dishes are more sophisticated, you'll have to pay for the treats. Also, with the exception of Key Largo, drinks are reasonably priced at 85¢ to $3.40.

CHARLESTON, Avenida 4 between calles 7 and 9. Tel. 255-3993.

Jazz lovers will enjoy this relaxed bar, which has a 1920s theme. Great recorded jazz music plays on the stereo all day and night. There are occasional live bands.

EL CUARTEL DE LA BOCA DEL MONTE, Avenida 1 between calles 21 and 23. Tel. 221-0327.
This very popular bar is reputed to have the best bocas in San José, although you'll have to pay for them. Their cocktails are also famous. Just look around and see what sort of amazing concoctions people are drinking and ask for whichever one strikes your fancy.

NASHVILLE SOUTH, Calle 5 between avenidas 1 and 3. Tel. 233-1988.
As it name implies, this is a country-and-western bar. It's very popular with homesick expatriates and has a friendly atmosphere and fun music.

RIO, Avenida Central, Los Yoses. Tel. 253-5088.
This bar and restaurant is close to the University of Costa Rica, and consequently attracts a younger clientele. At night Rio is always packed to overflowing with the wealthy and the wanna-be's of San José.

RISA'S BAR, Calle 1 between Avenida Central and Avenida 1. Tel. 223-2803.
This second-floor bar is in a beautiful old building in the heart of downtown San José. There's a big dug-out canoe over the bar, but the exposed brick walls and the U.S. rock videos give Risa's a very North American urban atmosphere. The music is loud!

SHAKESPEARE BAR, Avenida 2 and Calle 28. No Phone.
Located next to the Sala Garbo movie theater, this classy little spot frequently has live jazz on the weekends. It's a good place to meet after a movie or a show at the Laurence Olivier Theater next door.

SODA PALACE, Calle 2 and Avenida 2. Tel. 221-3441.
Mostly a men's hangout, this dingy but brightly lit bar hardly lives up to its name, but is a Costa Rican institution. It opens directly onto busy Avenida 2 and is open 24 hours a day. Men of all ages sit at the tables conversing loudly and watching the world pass by. You never know what might happen at the Palace. Mariachis stroll in, linger for a while, then continue on their way. Legend has it that the revolution of 1948 was planned right here.

A GAY BAR

LA TORRE, Calle 7 between Avenida Central and Avenida 1. No phone.
Popular with gays and straights as well, this club plays music that will make you want to dance.

MORE ENTERTAINMENT

MOVIE THEATERS Even if you aren't interested in what's playing at one of the downtown theaters, it's worth the $1.75 to $2 admission just to gain entrance to one of these old palaces. The screens are huge, most movies are in English with Spanish subtitles, and on a weeknight you might have the theater almost to yourself. Check the "Viva" section of *La Nación* or the *Tico Times* for movie listings and times.

Sala Garbo, 100 meters south of the Pizza Hut on Paseo Colón (tel. 222-1034) shows foreign films, sometimes with English subtitles.

GAMBLING CASINOS Gambling is legal in Costa Rica, and there are casinos at virtually every major hotel. In most of these hotel casinos, you'll need to get dressed up; but at the casino in the lobby of the Gran Hotel Costa Rica, at Calle 3 between Avenida Central and Avenida 2, on the Plaza de la Cultura, there doesn't seem to be any dress code.

8. NETWORKS & RESOURCES

FOR STUDENTS The University of Costa Rica is located north of the church in San Pedro, which is an eastern suburb of San José. If you're looking to meet other college students check with the university administrative office or try hanging out in some of the many bars in this neighborhood.

Costa Rica is the only country in Central America with a network of hostels that are affiliated with the International Youth Hostel Federation. Ask at the **Toruma Youth Hostel,** Avenida Central between calles 29 and 31 (tel. 224-4085) in San José, for information on hostels. There is also a student travel agency: **OTEC,** Edificio Ferencz, 2nd floor, Calle 3 between avenidas 1 and 3, 275 meters north of the Teatro Nacional (tel. 255-0554 or 222-0866) where you can get an international student identity card for discounts on airfares, hostels, national and international tours and excursions, car rentals, and store purchases.

FOR GAY MEN & LESBIANS The International Gay and Lesbian Association (tel. 234-2411) is a place to contact for information and weekly meetings.

FOR WOMEN Costa Rican men may occasionally hiss at you (an attention-getting device) on the street, but if you ignore them they will leave you alone. On the whole, Ticos are very well mannered.

Casa de la Nueva Mujer (House of the New Woman) is a meeting place, a pension, and a place to hang out. Women visitors can stay here for less than $10 a night. They also offer Spanish courses and specialized trips for women visiting Costa Rica. Tours include day trips to such places as Irazú Volcano and multi-day trips to Santa Rosa National Park. They are 250 meters north and 100 meters east of the La Cosecha market on Sabanilla's main street (tel. 225-3748).

FOR SENIORS Elderhostel, 75 Federal St., Boston, MA 02110 (tel. 617/ 426-7788), offers very popular study tours to Costa Rica. To participate in an Elderhostel program, either you or your spouse must be at least 60 years old.

9. EASY EXCURSIONS

San José makes an excellent base for exploring the beautiful Meseta Central and the surrounding mountains, and in fact it is possible to explore much of the country on day tours from San José. Probably the best way to make the most of these excursions is on guided tours, though if you rent a car, you'll have greater independence. There are also some day trips that can be done by public bus. Below is information on many of the day tours that are offered by tour companies in San José. I have arranged these by type of activity. In addition to the tours listed below, there are many other tours, some of which combine two or three different activities or destinations. Companies offering a wide variety of primarily nature-related day tours out of San José include **Costa Rica Expeditions** (tel. 257-0766 or 222-0333), **Costa Rica Sun Tours** (tel. 255-3418), **Geotour** (tel. 234-1867 or 224-1899), **Otec Tours** (tel. 255-0554 or 222-0866), and **Swiss Travel Service** (tel. 231-4055).

Before signing on for a tour of any sort, find out how much time is spent in transit and eating lunch and how much time is actually spent doing the primary activity. I've had a complaint about the Carara Biological Reserve tours, which spend most of their time on the road or in Jacó Beach.

RECREATIONAL DAY TRIPS

BICYCLING Narrow mountain roads with spectacular views make for some great, though strenuous, bicycling in Costa Rica. As yet there are only a few companies offering cycling trips, however. **Rios Tropicales** (tel. 233-6455) offers a day-long mountain-bike trip to Tapantí National Park. Most of the riding on this trip is downhill, and there are numerous opportunities to bird-watch and explore nature trails. The cost of $70 includes transportation, use of cycling equipment, breakfast, and lunch. Rios Tropicales also offers multi-day biking and rafting trips.

When I was last in Costa Rica, the **Costa Verde Inn** (tel. 228-4080) in Escazú had just begun offering downhill volcano rides similar to those offered in Hawaii. These rides start at the top of Poás Volcano and roll for 18 kilometers down the slopes of the volcano. The tour costs $65 and includes lunch, transportation, and use of bicycles and gear. You can also add a visit to Heredia and the Café Britt coffee farm for an additional $14.

Other companies offering bicycling trips include **El León Viajero** (tel. 23-9398), which has three different tours ranging in price from $65 to $85.

CRUISES Several companies offer cruises to remote islands in the Gulf of Nicoya, and these excursions include gourmet buffet meals and stops at deserted (until your boat arrives) beaches. Companies offering these trips include **Calypso Tours** (tel. 233-3617), **Bay Island Cruises** (tel. 239-4951 or 239-4952), **Costa Sol Tropical Cruises** (tel. 239-2000), **Sea Ventures** (tel. 257-2904 or 257-3097), and **Fantasia** (tel. 255-0791). The cruises cost $70 and include transportation from San José to Puntarenas and back. Most of these companies offer various sunset cruises and dinner cruises. Calypso Tours also offers catamaran sailing trips around the Gulf of Nicoya for $79.

A FLOWER FARM If you're a flower fancier and would like to visit a tropical flower farm, contact **Adventours of Costa Flores** (tel. 220-1311). Costa Flores is the largest tropical-flower farm in the world and grows more than 600 varieties of tropical flowers. Strikingly beautiful heliconias are the main produce of this farm. A trip to the farm, including transportation and lunch, costs $70.

HIKING If you do not plan to visit Monteverde or one of Costa Rica's other cloud-forest reserves, consider doing a day tour to a cloud forest. Guided hikes through these misty, high-altitude forests provide an opportunity to visit one of the tropics' most fascinating habitats. Bird-watching and a chance to learn about the ecology of the cloud forest are the main attraction of these trips. One of the most popular and highly recommended hiking tours is to the Los Angeles Cloud Forest Reserve. This tour is operated by **Hotel Villablanca** (tel. 228-4603) and includes a three-hour guided walk through the cloud forest. The cost is $70, which includes transportation, breakfast, and lunch. Hiking tours through the cloud forest on Barva Volcano are offered by **Jungle Trails** (tel. 255-3486) for $75 per person. This trip offers a chance to see the resplendent quetzal. Another cloud forest day hike is offered by **Senderos de Iberoamérica** (tel. 255-2859). This trip takes you to the Los Juncos Biological Reserve for a total of five hours of guided walks. Transportation, breakfast, and lunch are all included in the $70.

HORSEBACK RIDING If you enjoy horseback riding, you have your choice of many fascinating locations near San José for day-long trips. The going rates for a day trip out of San José to go horseback riding is around $70 per person, including transportation, lunch, and a four-hour guided ride. **L.A. Tours** (tel. 221-4501) offers rides through pastures and along the beach. **Sacramento Horseback Ride** (tel. 237-2116 or 237-2441) offers rides through mountain forests and pastures. Great view! **Viajes Alrededor del Mundo** (tel. 221-3060 or 222-5005) offers a trip through the cloud forest on the flank of Poás Volcano. The ride visits two different waterfalls. **El León Viajero** (tel. 233-9398) offers three different horseback-riding tours, each in a different part of the country.

HOT-AIR BALLOONING One of the most fascinating ways to see Costa Rica is from a balloon floating above the forest. Hot-air balloon rides are offered by **Serendipity Adventures** (tel. 450-0318), though only one of their three trips is a day trip. Prices, including transportation and brunch, are $285 for one person, $235 per person for a group of two or three people, and $195 per person for groups of four or five people. Other trips include overnight accommodations and are more expensive.

PRE-COLUMBIAN RUINS Though Costa Rica lacks such massive pre-Columbian archeological sites as can be found in Guatemala or Honduras, it does have Guayabo National Monument, a small excavated town, which today is but a collection of building foundations, cobbled streets, and the like. **Senderos de Iberoamérica** (tel. 255-2859) offers trips to the monument to see Costa Rica's most extensively excavated pre-Columbian archeological site for $70 per person.

RAFTING, KAYAKING & RIVER TRIPS Cascading down from Costa Rica's mountain ranges are dozens of tumultuous rivers, several of which have become very popular for white-water rafting and kayaking. For between $65 and $90, you can spend a day rafting through lush tropical forests. Longer trips are also available. Some of the more reliable rafting companies are **Costa Rica Expeditions** (tel. 257-0766), **Rios Tropicales** (tel. 233-6455), and **Costaricaraft** (tel. 225-3939). If I had to choose just one day trip to do out of San José, it would be a white-water rafting trip. Rios Tropicales also offers sea-kayaking trips in Curú Bay ($85) and three different sea-kayaking trips from Manuel Antonio (see Chapter 6, "The Central Pacific Coast," for details on these latter trips).

There are also some raft and boat trips on calmer waters. These trips usually focus on the wildlife and scenery along the river. **Panamericana de Viajes** (tel. 223-4567) offers a trip they call the "Crocodile Adventure." On this leisurely float, you'll have ample opportunities to photograph the Tarcoles River's many crocodiles. The trip costs $75 and includes transportation, breakfast, and lunch.

Uno Travel Services (tel. 253-7589 or 253-6759) offers tours that include a boat trip down the Sarapiquí River, a quiet river fed by clear mountain streams. The scenery along this river is a combination of rain forest and farms. These tours include a stop at either Poás Volcano ($95 per person) or Arenal Volcano ($115 per person). You can also kayak the Sarapiquí River. Trips are offered by **Rancho Leona,** La Virgen de Sarapiquí, Heredia (tel. 761-1019). For $80 you get a day of kayaking plus two nights lodging in shared accommodations (bunks) at the ranch's private hostel. Lunch on the day of your kayak trip is included in the price, but other meals are not. Be sure to ask about getting there when making a reservation.

Perhaps the best-known river tours are those that go up to Tortuguero National Park. Though it is possible to do this tour as a day trip out of San José, it is a long and expensive day. You're much better off doing it as a one- or two-night trip. See Chapter 8, "The Caribbean Coast," for details.

RAIN FOREST AERIAL TRAM By the time you arrive in Costa Rica, you should be hearing all about the Rain Forest Aerial Tram. The tramway was under construction on a private reserve bordering Braulio Carillo National Park when we were last in Costa Rica. The tramway is the dream of rain-forest researcher Dr. Donald Perry, whose cable-car system through the forest canopy at Rara Avis helped him to spend years studying and writing about that little-known, yet most important, aspect of the rain-forest environment. The tramway will take visitors on a 90-minute ride through the rain forest tree tops, where they will have a chance to glimpse the complex web of life that makes these forests so unique. The cost for tours, including transportation from San José, is expected to be around $70. Check with any tour operator in San José to find out more about this excursion.

TRAIN EXCURSIONS For many years the most popular excursion from San José was the so-called jungle train which chugged to Limón amid rugged and remote scenery. This train no longer operates, but a section of the track is still used for a railroad excursion known as the "Banana Train." This excursion is operated by **Swiss Travel Service** (tel. 231-4055) and includes a tour of a banana plantation and a short trip in restored narrow-gauge railway cars. The "Green Train" is a similar excursion operation by **TAM Tours** (tel. 222-2642 or 222-2732). Either trip will cost you $70.

VOLCANO TRIPS Poás, Irazú, and Arenal volcanoes are three of Costa Rica's most popular destinations. For more information on the Arenal Volcano, see Chapter 5, and for more information on Poás and Irazú, see below. Numerous tour companies in San José offer trips to all three volcanoes, and though the trips to Poás and Irazú take only half a day, the trips to Arenal take all day. I don't recommend these latter trips because you arrive when the Arenal is hidden by clouds and leave before the night's darkness shows off the volcano's glowing eruptions. Tour companies offering trips to Poás and Irazú include **Costa Rica Expeditions** (tel. 257-0766 or 222-0333); **Costa Rica Sun Tours** (tel. 255-3418); **Otec Tours** (tel. 255-0554 or 222-0866); **Swiss Travel Service** (tel. 231-4055). Prices range from $28 for a half-day trip to $55 for a full-day trip.

CARTAGO, THE OROSI VALLEY & IRAZÚ VOLCANO

Located about 15 miles southeast of San José, Cartago is the former capital of Costa Rica. Founded in 1563, it was Costa Rica's first city—and was in fact its only city for almost 150 years. Irazú Volcano rises up from the edge of town, and although it is quiescent these days, it has not always been so peaceful. Earthquakes have damaged Cartago repeatedly over the years, so that today there are few colonial buildings left standing. However, in the center of the city are the ruins of a large church that was destroyed in 1910, before it was ever finished. Construction was abandoned after the quake, and today the ruins are a neatly manicured park.

Cartago's most-famous building, however, is the **Basilica de Nuestra Señora de Los Angeles** (the Basilica of Our Lady of the Angels), which is dedicated to the the patron saint of Costa Rica and stands on the east side of town. Within the walls of this Byzantine-style church is a shrine containing the tiny figure of La Negrita, the Black Virgin, which is nearly lost amid its ornate altar. This statue was found at a spring that now bubbles up at the rear of the church on the right side. Miraculous healing powers have been attributed to La Negrita, and over the years thousands of pilgrims have come to the shrine seeking cures for their illlnesses and difficulties. The walls of the shrine are covered with a fascinating array of tiny silver images left as thanks for cures affected by La Negrita. Amid the plethora of diminutive arms and legs, there are also hands, feet, hearts, lungs, kidneys, eyes, torsos, breasts, and—peculiarly—guns, trucks, beds, and planes. There are even dozens of sports trophies which I assume were left in thanks for helping teams win big games. August 2 is the day dedicated to La Negrita. On this day thousands of people walk from San José to Cartago in devotion to this powerful statue.

If you'd like to soak in a warm-water swimming pool, head four kilometers south of Cartago to Aguas Calientes. A few kilometers east out of Cartago, you'll find Lankester Gardens, a botanical garden known for its orchid collection. See "Attractions," above, for details.

Buses for Cartago leave San José frequently from Calle 5 and Avenida 18. The length of the trip is 45 minutes; the fare is about 45¢.

Located 32 kilometers north of Cartago, 11,260-foot-tall Irazú Volcano is one of Costa Rica's more-active volcanoes, although at this time it is dormant. It last erupted on March 19, 1963, on the day that President John F. Kennedy arrived in Costa Rica. The eruption showered ash on the Meseta Central for months after, destroying crops and collapsing roofs, but enriching the soil. There is a good paved road right to the rim of the crater, where a desolate expanse of gray sand nurtures few plants and the air smells of sulfur. If you arrive early enough, you may be treated to a view of both the Pacific Ocean and the Caribbean Sea. There are also magnificent views of the fertile Meseta Central and Orosi Valley as you drive up from Cartago. Clouds descend by noon, so schedule your trip up here as early in the day as possible. From the parking area, a short trail leads to the rim of the volcano's two craters, their walls a maze of eroded gullies feeding onto the flat floor far below. This is a national park and is officially open only from 8am to 4pm, but there is nothing to stop you from visiting earlier. Don't forget to wear warm clothes. This may be the tropics, but it's cold up at the top. In the busy season, the admission of $1.35 is charged. On you way back down, stop for breakfast at **Restaurant Linda Vista** (tel. 225-5808). It's on the right as you come down the mountain. Located at an elevation of 10,075 feet, it claims to be the highest restaurant in Central America; there are walls of windows looking out over the valley far below. A hearty Tico breakfast of gallo pinto with ham will cost about $2.40.

Buses leave for Irazú Volcano Saturday, Sunday, and holidays from Avenida 2 between calles 1 and 3 (in front of the Gran Hotel Costa Rica). The fare is around $4.90 and the trip takes about 1½ hours. To make sure the buses are running, phone 272-0651. If you are driving, head northeast out of Cartago toward San Rafael, then continue driving uphill toward the volcano, passing the turnoffs for Cot and Tierra Blanca en route.

The **Orosi Valley,** southeast of Cartago and frequently visible from the top of Irazú, is called the most beautiful valley in Costa Rica. The Reventazon River meanders through this steep-sided valley until it collects in the lake formed by the Cach Dam. There are scenic overlooks near the town of Orosi, which is at the head of the valley, and in Ujarrás, which is on the banks of the lake. Near Ujarrás are the ruins of Costa Rica's oldest church, whose tranquil gardens are a great place to sit and gaze at the surrounding mountains. Across the lake is a popular recreation center, called Charrarra, where you'll find a picnic area, swimming pool, and hiking trails. In the town of Orosi there is a colonial church built in 1743. A small museum here displays religious artifacts.

It would be difficult to explore this whole area by public bus, since this is not a densely populated region. However, there are buses from Cartago to the town of Orosi. During the week, these buses run every half hour and leave from a spot one block east and three blocks south of the church ruins in Cartago. Saturday and Sunday, a bus runs every hour from the same vicinity and will drop you at the Orosi lookout point. The trip takes 30 minutes, and the fare is 30¢. If you are driving, take the road to Paraíso from Cartago, head toward Ujarrás, continue around the lake, then pass through Cach and on to Orosi. From Orosi, the road leads back to Paraíso. There are also guided day tours of this area from San José.

POÁS VOLCANO

This is another active volcano accessible from San José in a day trip. It is 58 kilometers from San José on narrow roads that wind through a landscape of fertile farms and dark forests. As at Irazú, there is a paved road right to the top. The volcano stands 8,800 feet tall and is located within a national park, which preserves not only the volcano but also dense stands of virgin forest. Poás's crater is nearly a mile across and is said to be the second-largest crater in the world. Geysers in the crater sometimes spew steam and muddy water 600 feet into the air, making this the largest geyser in the world. There is an information center where you can see a slide show about the volcano, and there are marked hiking trails through the cloud forest that rings the crater. About 20 minutes from the parking area, along a forest trail, is an overlook onto beautiful Botos Lake, which has formed in one of the volcano's extinct craters.

Because the sulfur fumes occasionally become dangerously strong at Poás, the park is sometimes closed to the public. Before heading out for the volcano, contact the tourist office to make sure that the park is open. The admission fee is $1.35.

There is an excursion bus on Sunday leaving from Calle 12 and avenidas 2 and 4 at 8:30am and returning at 2:30pm. The fare is $3.65 for the round-trip. The bus is always crowded, so arrive early. Other days, take a bus to Alajuela, then a bus to San Pedro de Poás. From there you will have to hitchhike or take a taxi ($20 round-trip), which makes this alternative as costly as a tour. All the tour companies in San José offer excursions to Poás, although they often don't arrive until after the clouds have closed in. If you're traveling by car, head for Alajuela and continue on the main road through town toward Varablanca. Just before reaching Varablanca, turn left toward Poasito and continue to the rim of the volcano.

HEREDIA, ALAJUELA, GRECIA, SARCHÍ & ZARCERO

All of these cities and towns are northwest of San José and can be combined into a long day trip, perhaps in conjunction with a visit to Poás Volcano.

Heredia was founded in 1706. On its central park stands a colonial church dedicated in 1763. The stone facade leaves no questions as to the age of the church, but the altar inside is decorated with neon stars and a crescent moon surrounding a statue of the Virgin Mary. In the middle of the palm-shaded park is a music temple, and across the street, beside several tile-roofed municipal buildings, is the tower of an old Spanish fort. Of all the cities in the Meseta Central, this is only one that has even the slightest colonial feeling to it.

Alajuela is one of Costa Rica's oldest cities, and is located only 19 kilometers from San José. Although it is an attractive little city filled with parks, there isn't much to see or do here. The **Juan Santamaría Historical Museum,** Avenida 3 between Calle Central and Calle 2 (tel. 442-1838), commemorates Costa Rica's national hero, who gave his life defending the country against a small army led by William Walker, a U.S. citizen who invaded Costa Rica in 1856. Walker was trying to set up a slave state in Central America. Open Tuesday through Sunday from 8am to 6pm; admission is free.

From Alajuela, a narrow, winding road leads to the town of **Grecia,** which is noteworthy for its unusual metal church, which is painted a deep red and has white gingerbread trim. The road to Sarchí is to the right as you go around the church.

Sarchí is Costa Rica's main artisan's town. It is here that the colorfully painted miniature oxcarts you see all over Costa Rica are made. Oxcarts such as these were once used to haul coffee beans to market. Today, though you may occasionally see oxcarts in use, most are purely decorative. However, they remain a well-known symbol of Costa Rica. In addition to miniature oxcarts, many other carved wooden souvenirs are made here with rare hardwoods from the nation's forests. There are dozens of shops in town, and all have similar prices. The other reason to visit Sarchí is to see its unforgettable church. Built between 1950 and 1958, the church is painted pink with aquamarine trim and looks strangely like a child's birthday cake.

Beyond Sarchí, on picturesque roads lined with cedar trees, you will find the town of **Zarcero.** In a small park in the middle of town is a menagerie of topiary sculptures (sculpted shrubs) that includes a monkey on a motorcycle, people and animals dancing, an ox pulling a cart, and a man wearing a top hat. It is well worth the drive to see this park.

The road to Heredia turns north off the highway from San José to the airport. To reach Alajuela from Heredia, take the scenic road that heads west through the town of San Joaquín. To continue on to Sarchí, it is best to return to the highway south of Alajuela and drive west toward Puntarenas. Turn north to Grecia and then west to Sarchí.

TURRIALBA

This attractive little town 53 kilometers east of San José is best known as the starting and ending point for popular white-water rafting trips. However, it is also worth a visit if you have an interest in pre-Columbian history or botany. **Guayabo National Monument** is one of Costa Rica's only pre-Columbian sites that is open to the public. It's located 19 kilometers northeast of Turrialba and preserves a townsite that dates to between 1000 B.C. and A.D. 1400. Archeologists believe that Guayabo may have had a population of as many as 10,000 people, but there is no clue yet as to why the city was eventually abandoned only shortly before the Spanish arrived in the New World. Excavated ruins at Guayabo consist of paved roads, aqueducts, stone bridges, and house and temple foundations. There are also grave sites and petroglyphs. The monument is open daily from 8am to 3pm, and admission is $1.35.

Botanists and gardeners may want to pay a visit to the **Center for Agronomy Research and Development (CATIE)**, which is located five kilometers southeast of Turrialba on the road to Siquerres. This center is one of the world's foremost facilities for research into tropical agriculture. Among the plants on CATIE's 2,000 acres are hundreds of varieties of cacao and thousands of varieties of coffee. The plants here have been collected from all over the world. In addition to trees used for food and other purposes, there are also plants grown strictly for ornamental purposes. CATIE is open Monday through Friday from 7am to 4pm. For information on guided tours, phone 556-6431.

While you are in the area, don't miss an opportunity to spend a little time at **Turrialtico** (tel. 556-1111) an open-air restaurant and small hotel high on a hill overlooking the Turrialba Valley. The view from here is one of the finest in the country, with the lush green valley far below and volcanoes in the distance. Meals are quite inexpensive and a room will cost you only $20. This place is popular with rafting companies who bring groups here for meals and for overnights before, after, and during multi-day rafting trips.

GUANACASTE & THE NICOYA PENINSULA

Guanacaste province, in northwestern Costa Rica, is the nation's sunniest and driest region. The rainy season here starts later and ends earlier, and overall it is more dependably sunny here than in other parts of the country. Combine this climate with a coastline that stretches from the Nicaraguan border to the southern tip of the Nicoya Peninsula and you have an equation that yields beach bliss. Beautiful beaches abound along this coastline. Some are pristine and deserted, some are lined with luxury resort hotels, and still others are backed by little villages where you can still get a room for under $30. These beaches vary from long, straight stretches of sand to tiny coves bordered by rocky headlands. Whatever your passion in beaches, you're likely to find something that comes close to perfection.

There is, however, one caveat. During the dry season, when sunshine is most reliable, the hillsides in Guanacaste turn browner than the chaparral of southern California. Dust from dirt roads blankets the trees in many areas and the vistas are far from tropical. However, if you can't tolerate the least bit of rain on your holiday in the sun, the beaches up here are where you'll want to be.

On the other hand, if you happen to visit this area in the rainy season, the hillsides are a beautiful, rich green, but you will have clouds and rain to deal with. If you want your beaches backed by greenery, and you're coming down between December and May, head south or over to the other side of the country. The beaches of the south Pacific coast and the Caribbean coast are much lusher and have more of a tropical feel, though they also are more humid and rainy.

Guanacaste is also Costa Rica's "wild west," a dry landscape of cattle ranches and cowboys, who are known as *sabaneros*, a name that derives from the Spanish word for savannah or grassland. This is big country, with big views and big sky. If it weren't for those rain-forest clad volcanoes in the distance, you might swear you were in Texas. However, Guanacaste hasn't always looked this way. At one time this land was covered with a dense, though fairly dry, forest that was cut for lumber to create pasturelands for grazing cattle. Today, that dry tropical forest exists only in remnants preserved in several national parks. Up in the mountains, in Rincón de la Vieja National Park, not only will you find forests and wildlife, but you'll also find hot springs and bubbling mudpots similar to those in Yellowstone National Park in the United States.

WHAT'S SPECIAL ABOUT GUANACASTE & THE NICOYA PENINSULA

Beaches

Playa Conchal, which is formed from crushed seashells.

Playa Flamingo, one of the whitest beaches on this coast.

The beaches of Ostional National Wildlife Refuge, almost always deserted.

Parks/Gardens

Rincón de la Vieja, site of numerous hot springs, steam vents, and bubbling mudpots.

Santa Rosa and Guanacaste national parks, which include some of the last tropical dry forests in Central America.

Cabo Blanco Absolute Nature Preserve, with its howler monkeys and deserted beaches.

Natural Spectacles

Every year, hundreds of thousands of turtles lay their eggs on beaches in Santa Rosa National Park.

Nesting turtles on Playa Grande, near Tamarindo.

Activities

Sportfishing for billfish off the northwest coast.

Scuba diving to experience the brilliant underwater life around the Bat Islands.

Rafting float trips on the Corbicí River.

Hot surfing at Tamarindo and at Witch's Rock in Santa Rosa National Park.

1. LIBERIA

232 kilometers NW of San José; 133 kilometers NW of Puntarenas

GETTING THERE **By Air** The airstrip in Liberia was recently expanded to accommodate commercial international flights, but at the time of publishing, flights were not yet going into Liberia.

By Bus Express buses leave San José daily at 7, 9, and 11:30am and 1, 3, 4, 6, and 8pm from Calle 14 between avenidas 1 and 3. Duration: 4 hours. Fare: $3.60. From Puntarenas, buses leave at 5:30, 7, and 9:30am and noon. Duration: 2 hours. Fare $2.10.

By Car Take the Interamerican Highway west out of San José, and follow the signs for Nicaragua. It takes about four hours to get to Liberia.

DEPARTING The Liberia bus station is on the edge of town 200 meters north and 100 meters east of the main intersection on the Interamerican Highway. Express buses for San José leave daily at 4:30, 6, and 7:30am and 12:30, 2, 4, 6, and 8pm. To reach Monteverde take any Puntarenas or San José bus leaving before 1pm. Get off at the Río Lagarto Bridge and catch the Puntarenas–Santa Elena bus around 3:15pm. For information on getting to various beaches, see sections below.

ESSENTIALS There is a small **tourist information center** (tel. 666-1606) three blocks south of the modern white church on Liberia's central park. The center is open Monday through Saturday from 9am to 5pm.

Orientation The highway passes slightly to the west of town. At the intersection with the main road into town, there are several hotels and gas stations. If you turn east into town, you will come to the central square in less than a kilometer.

Founded in 1769, Liberia is the capital of Guanacaste province, and though it can hardly be considered a bustling city, it does have the distinction of having a more colonial atmosphere than does any other city in the country. Narrow streets are lined with charming old adobe homes, many of which have ornate stone accents on their facades.

Liberia is best looked upon as a base for exploring this region. From here it is possible to do day trips to nearby beaches and three national parks. Several moderately priced hotels are located on the outskirts of Liberia at the intersection of the Interamerican Highway and the road out to the Nicoya Peninsula and its many beaches. See "Where to Stay," later in this section, for detailed descriptions of the area's lodging options.

WHAT TO SEE & DO

To find out more about what there is to see and do in this region, first stop by the tourist information center, which is located three blocks south of the modern white church on Liberia's central park. While you're here gathering information, you can quickly tour the center's little museum of Guanacaste culture. The emphasis is on the life of the sabanero.

North of Liberia, you'll find three national parks, though only two of them currently have any facilities for visitors.

Santa Rosa National Park is about 30 kilometers north of Liberia on the Interamerican Highway. The park, which covers the Santa Elena Peninsula, has both historic and environmental significance. Santa Rosa was Costa Rica's first national park. However, it was not founded to preserve the land but to preserve a building, known as La Casona, which played an important role in Costa Rican independence.

Today, however, the park is best known for its remote, pristine beaches, which are sometimes accessible by four-wheel-drive vehicle, but usually can only be reached by hiking 13 kilometers. Playa Nancite is known for its *arribadas* (massed egg-layings) of olive Ridley sea turtles, which come ashore to nest by the tens of thousands each year in October. Nearby Playa Naranjo is best known for its perfect surfing waves, which break at Witch's Rock just offshore. On the northern side of the peninsula is the even more remote Playa Blanca, which can be reached in the dry season if you have a four-wheel-drive vehicle. This beach is reached by way of the village of Caujiniquil.

Rincón de la Vieja National Park, which has its main entrance 25 kilometers northeast of Liberia down a badly rutted dirt road, is an area of geothermal activity similar to Yellowstone National Park in the United States. Fumaroles, geysers, and hot pools cover a small area of this park, crating a bizarre, other-worldly landscape. There are several lodges around the perimeter of the park, and all offer guided hikes and horseback rides into the park. In addition to hot springs and mudpots, there are waterfalls, a lake, and a volcanic crater to be explored. The bird-watching here is excellent, and the views out across the pasturelands to the Pacific Ocean are stunning.

Leisurely raft trips (no white water) are offered by **Safaris Corobici** (tel. 669-1091) about 40 kilometers south of Liberia. They have two-hour ($35), three-hour ($43), and half-day ($60) trips that are great for families and bird-watchers. Along the way you may see many of the area's more exotic animal residents—howler monkeys, iguanas, caiman, coatimundis, otters, toucans, parrots, mot-mots, trogons, and many other species of birds.

If you are staying in Liberia and want to tour the surrounding countryside with a guide, contact **CATA Tours** (tel. 669-1026) in nearby Cañas. This company offers boat tours down the Bebedero River to Palo Verde National Park, which is south of Cañas and is best known for its migratory bird populations. They also lead a horseback trip up through the cloud forest on Miravalles Volcano, which is north of Cañas.

And of course you'll have a wide variety of beaches nearby, all easily accessible as day trips. Many of these are described in detail in the sections that follow in this chapter.

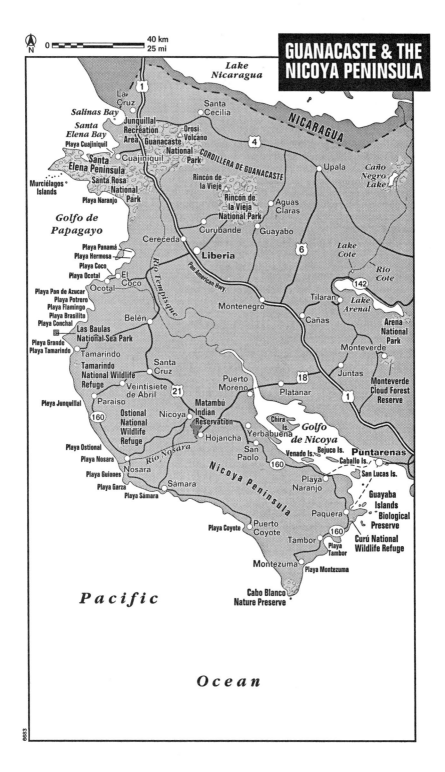

GUANACASTE & THE NICOYA PENINSULA

Lake Nicaragua

La Cruz

Santa Cecilia

NICARAGUA

Salinas Bay

Santa Elena Bay

Playa Cuajiniquil

Junquillal Recreation Area Guanacaste

Orosí Volcano

CORDILLERA DE GUANACASTE

National Park

Upala

Caño Negro Lake

Santa Elena Peninsula

Cuajiniquil

Murciélagos Islands

Santa Rosa National Park

Playa Naranjo

Rincón de la Vieja

Rincón de la Vieja National Park

Aguas Claras

Golfo de Papagayo

Cereceda

Curubande

Guayabo

Lake Cote

Río Cote

Playa Panamá
Playa Hermosa
Playa Coco
Playa Ocotal

Liberia

Tilaran

Lake Arenal

Playa Pan de Azucar
Playa Potrero
Playa Flamingo
Playa Brasilito
Playa Conchal

El Coco

Ocotal

Montenegro

Cañas

Arena National Park

Las Baulas National Sea Park

Belén

Pan American Hwy.

Río Tempisque

Monteverde

Playa Grande
Playa Tamarindo

Tamarindo

Santa Cruz

Puerto Moreno

Platanar

Juntas

Monteverde Cloud Forest Reserve

Tamarindo National Wildlife Refuge

Veintisiete de Abril

Playa Junquillal

Paraíso

Matambú Indian Reservation

Nicoya

Chira Is.

Golfo de Nicoya

Ostional National Wildlife Refuge

Hojancha

Yerbabuena

Venado Is.

Bejuco Is.

Puntarenas

Caballo Is.

Playa Ostional

Río Nosara

San Paolo

San Lucas Is.

Playa Nosara

Nosara

Nicoya Peninsula

Playa Naranjo

Guayaba Islands Biological Preserve

Playa Guiones
Playa Garza

Sámara

Paquera

Playa Sámara

Playa Coyote

Puerto Coyote

Tambor

Playa Tambor

Curú National Wildlife Refuge

Montezuma

Playa Montezuma

Pacific

Cabo Blanco Nature Preserve

Ocean

6683

WHERE TO STAY

IN TOWN

Expensive

HOTEL LAS ESPUELAS, Apdo. 88-5000, Liberia, Guanacaste. Tel. 506/666-0144, or (in the U.S.) 305/539-1630, or toll free 800/245-8420. Fax 506/225-3987 or (in the U.S) 305/539-1123. 44 rms. A/C TV TEL SAFE
$ Rates: $60 single; $80 double; $70 triple. AE, MC, V.

This hotel is located out on the Interamerican Highway, two kilometers south of Liberia. The name means "spurs" and is a reference to this being cowboy (sabanero) country, but despite the rugged epithet, this is the most luxurious hotel in Liberia. The open-air lobby and adjacent dining room and bar all have the feel of a modern hacienda. Surrounding the hotel are spacious gardens that are shaded by huge old Guanacaste trees. The trees and garden together give this hotel an oasis-like feel. The guest rooms are attractive, though a bit small, and have polished tile floors. In the bathroom, you'll find a basket of toiletries, which is a rarity in Costa Rican hotels. Overall, however, the amenities here are only slightly more upscale than at the other similar, and less expensive, hotels in Liberia.

Dining/Entertainment: There's a large and attractive dining room serving moderately priced international and Costa Rican meals. There is also a small bar adjacent to the restaurant.

Facilities: Small swimming pool, two tennis courts

Moderate

HOTEL EL SITIO, Liberia, Guanacaste. Tel. 506/666-1211. 52 rms. TV TEL
$ Rates: $31.50–$45.50 single; $45–$65 double. AE, DC, MC, V.

Located about 80 yards west of the fire station on the road to Santa Cruz and the beaches, this is the newest of Liberia's hotels, and as such, is one of the nicest. However, all the hotels here seem to follow the same basic Spanish-influenced hacienda style and offer similar amenities—gardens, swimming pool, shade trees. Throughout the hotel, there are red-tile floors and original paintings of local Guanacaste scenes on the walls. All the rooms are carpeted, and most rooms are very clean. You also have a choice of twin or double beds. Unfortunately, the air conditioners can be noisy, and some rooms are mildewed and musty. Check before agreeing to a room. You'll pay considerably more for a room with an air conditioner, so if you're on a budget, you might want to stick with a fan. The pool area is shady (a welcome relief from the strong Guanacaste sun), and there is even one of those famous pre-Columbian basalt balls in the garden. Beside the pool, there is a rancho-style bar/restaurant. Other amenities and services include horseback riding, bike rentals, a children's play area, a whirlpool tub, tour arrngements, and a car-rental desk.

NUEVO HOTEL BOYEROS, Apdo. 85, Liberia, Guanacaste. Tel. 506/666-0722 or 666-0157. Fax 506/666-2059. 60 rms. A/C
$ Rates: $27.45 single; $38.20 double; $42.90 triple. AE, MC, V.

You'll find this economical hotel just before the main Liberia intersection on the Interamerican Highway, and though it isn't as attractively landscaped as other similar hotels in town, it's all right in a pinch. Arches with turned wooden railings and a red-tile roof give this two-story motel-style building a Spanish feel. In the courtyard of the hotel are two pools—one for adults and one for children—and a rancho bar/snack bar. All the rooms have a private balcony or patio overlooking the pool and gardens. The furniture is getting old and worn, but if you're in town for just one night, you shouldn't be too uncomfortable. The small restaurant, which happens to have a few tables on a terrace under a huge "rubber" tree (actually a type of ficus or fig), serves meals ranging in price from $3.45 to $6.10.

Budget

HOTEL BRAMADERO, Carretera Interamericana, Libera, Guanacaste. Tel. 506/666-0371. Fax 506/666-0203. 25 rms (all with bath).
$ Rates: $14.05–$19.65 single; $20.25–$29.10 double; $24.05–$33.65 triple (higher prices are for A/C rooms). AE, MC, V.

There isn't much parking at this small, motel-style place, but the rates are good, and the rooms are clean though cramped and very simply furnished. Some rooms can be a bit musty, so ask to see a couple. Behind the restaurant is the hotel's small pool, which is wonderfully cooling in an area that is the hottest, driest, and dustiest in Costa Rica. Rooms around the pool can be noisy at night, especially on the weekends, when families from San José flee the cool elevations for the warmth of the lowlands. At the front of the hotel, there is a large open-air restaurant and bar, which gets a lot of traffic noise and serves very mediocre, though filling, meals.

HOTEL GUANACASTE, 25 meters west and 100 meters south of the bus station, Liberia, Guanacaste. Tel. 506/666-2287. Fax 506/666-0085. 27 rms (all with private bath).
$ Rates: $10.10 single; $14.15 double; $18.20 triple. V.

This very economical little hotel is primarily a hostel-type establishment catering to young travelers on a tight budget. In addition to the simply furnished rooms, there's a basic soda serving cheap Tico meals. The management here can help arrange trips to nearby national parks and tell you about other interesting budget accommodations, including campgrounds, in the area. You'll find this basic hotel around the corner from Hotel Bramadero.

NEAR CAÑAS

Moderate

HOTEL HACIENDA LA PACÍFICA, Apdo. 8-5700, Cañas, Guanacaste. Tel. 506/669-0266 or 669-0050. Fax 506/669-0555. 33 rms.
$ Rates: $40 single; $67 double; $83 triple. AE, MC, V.

⭐ If you want a central location for exploring the national paks of this region, there are few better choices than the Hacienda La Pacífica. Originally started as a research facility and wild-animal rehabilitation center, the hotel is now a spacious little resort hotel with attractive grounds and a large pool. The hotel is located on the banks of the pretty Corobici River, which is a good place for birdwatching. Though the hotel is 40 kilometers south of Liberia, it is still convenient for visiting Santa Rosa and Rincón de la Vieja national parks, as well as Palo Verde National Park and Lomas Barbudal Biological Reserve. Rooms vary in size, though all have tile floors and a patio of some sort. The larger rooms have private sun patios, as well as another patio. These rooms also have sliding-glass doors that make the rooms quite bright. High ceilings keep them cool. The open-air restaurant is shady and cool and serves moderately priced meals. The lodge offers a number of services, including horseback riding ($10 per hour), bike rentals ($1.70 per hour), guided walks ($10), rafting trips ($32 for two hours), and tours to the different national parks. On the grounds, you'll also find a restored 19th-century adobe house, and nearby there is a small, privately owned zoo.

NEAR RINCÓN DE LA VIEJA NATIONAL PARK

Moderate

HACIENDA LODGE GUACHEPELIN, Apdo. 636, Alajuela. Tel. 506/441-6545, 441-6994, or 666-2429. Fax 506/442-1910. 6 rms (none with private bath), 2 dorms.
$ Rates: $9 per person in dorm; $15 single; $35–$40 double. Meals are an additional $16 per person per day. No credit cards.

Located 23 kilometers northeast of Liberia on the edge of Rincón de la Vieja National Park, this rustic lodge is housed in a 112-year-old ranch house. The rooms are pretty basic, and the dorms are actually the old bunkhouse. The ranch is still in operation today, and in addition to exploring the park, you can ride horses and commune with the pigs, dairy cows, and beef cattle. It isn't easy to get to the lodge and once you arrive you'll need a few days to explore the park, so plan on taking all your meals here and going on a few guided tours. A horseback tour with bilingual guide will cost around $24 per person for a half-day ride. When you contact the lodge to make a reservation, you can arrange to be picked up in Liberia for $9 per person ($16 round-trip). If you're driving a car, you'd better have four-wheel-drive or high clearance (though in the dry season it's sometimes passable in a regular car). To reach the lodge, drive about 5 kilometers north of Liberia and turn right on the dirt road to Curubande, which you will pass through in about 12 kilometers. Continue on this road for another 6 kilomters, passing through the ranch's gate, before arriving at the lodge. This is one of the closest lodges to the thermal springs (10 kilometers) and bubbling mudpots (5 kilometers) of Rincón de la Vieja National Park. Horseback rides can be arranged to the geothermal areas, as well as to various lakes, the top of a nearby dormant volcano, and some beautiful waterfulls.

LOS INOCENTES LODGE, Apdo. 1370-3000, Heredia. Tel. 506/265-5484 or 679-9190. Fax 506/237-8282 or 265-5217. 11 rms.

$ Rates (including three meals): $51 single: $102 double. MC, V.

Set on a ranch 14 kilomters from la Cruz, near the Nicaraguan border, Los Inocentes is popular with naturalists interested in exploring the nearby forests. Horseback rides ($25 per day) through the ranch are the most popular activities, and in fact the ranch does a brisk business in tours coming up here from various Nicoya Peninsula beaches to do some riding. The rooms are comfortable though basic and have tile floors. Some have high ceilings, and all open onto large verandas with hammocks and wicker rocking chairs. Meals are simple but filling. In addition to horseback riding, there are nature trails and a swimming pool. There's a great view of Orosi Volcano from the lodge.

RINCÓN DE LA VIEJA MOUNTAIN LODGE, Apdo. 114-5000, Liberia, Guanacaste. Tel. 506/685-5422, 666-2369, or 225-1073. Fax 506/666-0473. 24 rms (17 with private bath).

$ Rates: $16 single without bath, $18–$22 single with bath; $32 double without bath, $36–$44 double with bath. MC, V.

This is the closest lodge to the Las Pailas mudpots and the Azufrale hot springs. The rustic lodge is surrounded by grasslands that conjure up images of the African savannah. This is the end of the road and feels very remote (i.e., the road here is really, really bad). The polished-wood main lodge looks like a cross between a ranch hacienda and a mountain cabin. There's a long veranda set with chairs, and inside a small lounge and dining room with long tables for communal meals. The rooms with shared baths are quite small, but those with private baths have lots of space. These latter rooms, which have cement floors, have hammocks on their verandas, and some back up to a small stream. Meals, which are simple but hearty Tico fare, will cost you $24 to $28 a day. The lodge offers numerous day-long tours either on foot or on horseback. Transportation from Liberia can be arranged at additional cost. If you are driving, follow the directions to the Hacienda Lodge Guachepelin and continue driving on this dirt road for another seven kilometers, passing the turnoff for the park entrance.

SANTA CLARA LODGE, Apdo. 17, Quebrada Grande de Liberia, Guanacaste. Tel. 506/666-0085 or 221-1000. Fax 506/666-0475. 7 rms (none with bath), 1 cabin.

$ Rates: $13–$20 single without bath; $26–$30 double without bath, $37.50 double with bath; $39–$40 triple without bath, $46 triple with bath. Meals are an additional $14 per person per day. No credit cards.

Santa Clara Lodge is located on a working dairy farm in the foothills of the mountains. With shady grounds on the banks of a small river, the setting is quite tranquil.

You can sit beneath the palapa sipping a drink and listen to the chickens clucking in the yard or go for a swim in the mineral-water pool. The lodge is well suited for exploring the region if you have your own car or want to arrange tours. Santa Rosa, Guanacaste, and Rincón de la Vieja national parks are all within an hour's drive. You can also hike through field and forest to four different waterfalls. Guided hikes ($7) and horseback rides ($10 to $20) can be arranged, and the trip to the hot springs is particularly recommendable. Rooms are simply furnished, as you might expect on a working ranch, and only the cabin has a private bath. Meals are filling Tico fare such as rice and beans, steaks, chicken and fries, salads, and fruits. It is also possible to camp here. To reach the lodge, head north from Liberia for about 23 kilometers and turn right on the road to Quebrada Grande. In Quebrada Grande, turn right at the soccer field and contine for another 4 kilometers. You can also arrange free daily transportation from Liberia to the lodge if you phone in advance.

WHERE TO DINE

You don't have too many choices for dining in Liberia, so your hotel dining room is certainly going to be the most convenient. However, the hotels serve standard fare at best. For meals a cut above what you would expect in this cow town, try the following restaurants.

RESTAURANTE POKOPI, 100 meters west of the gas station on the road to Santa Cruz. Tel. 666-1036.
    Cuisine: CONTINENTAL. **Reservations:** Not required.
$ **Prices:** Main courses $2.05–$10.15. AE, MC, V.
    Open: Sun–Thurs 10am–10pm, Fri–Sat 10am–midnight.
It doesn't look like much from the outside, but this tiny restaurant has a surprising amount of class inside. An even more pleasant surprise is the unusual (for rural Costa Rica) variety of continental dishes on the menu. Order one of their delicious daiquiris while your peruse the menu, which is on a wooden cutting board. You have your choice of dolphin (the fish, not the mammal) prepared five different ways, pizza, chicken Cordon Bleu, chicken in wine sauce, and other equally delectable dishes. However, for a real surprise, order the chateaubriand. It comes to your table with great flare, surrounded by succulent fresh vegetables and a tomato stuffed with peas. Don't miss this treat. Attached to the restaurant is a disco that swings into action at 9pm on the weekend. And you thought you were out in the sticks.

RESTAURANT RINCÓN COROBICI, Interamerican Highway, 4 kilometers north of Cañas. Tel. 669-0303.
    Cuisine: COSTA RICAN/INTERNATIONAL. **Reservations:** Not accepted.
$ **Prices:** Appetizers $1.45–$6.10; main courses $3.05–$17.60. MC, V.
    Open: Daily 8am–10pm.
⭐ The open-air dining room and deck here overlook a beautiful section of the Corobici River. The sound of rushing water tumbling over the rocks in the riverbed is soothing accompaniment to the simple-but-filling meals. The whole fried fish is the number-one choice here, though they also have steaks, lobster, shrimp, and sandwiches. This restaurant makes an ideal lunch stop if you are heading to or from Liberia or have just done a rafting trip on the Corobici River. Be sure to try the fried yuca chips. You may never go back to french fries.

2. PLAYA HERMOSA & PLAYA PANAMÁ

258 kilometers NW of San José; 40 kilometers SW of Liberia

GETTING THERE By Air The nearest airport with regularly scheduled service is in Tamarindo. There you can arrange a taxi to bring you the rest of the way.

By Bus Express buses leave San José daily at 3:30pm from Calle 12 between avenidas 5 and 7. Duration: 5 hours. Fare $8.50.

Alternatively, you can first take a bus to Liberia (see above for details) and then take a bus from Liberia to Playa Hermosa or Playa Panamá. Buses leave Liberia for these two beaches daily at 11:30am and 7pm. Duration: 45 minutes. Fare: $1.10.

By Car Follow the directions for getting to Liberia, then head west toward Santa Cruz. Just past the village of Comunidad, turn right. In about 11 kilometers you will come to a fork in the road. Take the right fork. It takes about 5 hours from San José.

DEPARTING The bus to San José leaves daily at 5am. Buses to Liberia leave Playa Panamá at 6am and 4pm, stopping in Playa Hermosa a few minutes later. Ask at your hotel where to catch the bus.

ESSENTIALS **Orientation** There are no real towns here, just a few houses and hotels on and near the beach. You will come to Playa Hermosa first, followed by Playa Panamá a few kilometers later on the same road.

Playa Hermosa means "beautiful beach," which is a very appropriate name for this crescent of sand. Surrounded by dry, rocky hills, this curving gray-sand beach is long and wide and rarely crowded, despite the presence of the Condovac La Costa condominium development on the hill at the north end of the beach. Fringing the beach is a swath of trees that stay surprisingly green right through the dry season. The shade provided by these trees is a big part of the beach's appeal. It gets hot here and some shade is always appreciated at the beach. At both ends of the beach rocky headlands jut out into the surf, and at the base of these rocks, you'll find tide pools that are fun to explore.

Beyond Playa Hermosa, you'll find the even more secluded and appealing Playa Panamá. This big bay is bordered by a shady forest and there is a rather basic cabina place. However, at the time of my last visit there were a couple of big resorts under construction. By the time you visit, they should be complete, so check with a travel agent or the I.C.T. center in San José. Depending upon your point of view, these resorts will have either completely spoiled Playa Panamá or turned it into one of the best beaches in the country. Regardless of what you think of the resort, when you visit, you might still be able to find a stretch of beach all to yourself, where you can sit back and watch the pelicans feeding just offshore.

WHAT TO SEE & DO

In the middle of Playa Hermosa, you'll find **Aqua Sport** (tel. 670-0050), the tourist information and water-sports equipment rental center for Playa Hermosa. Kayaks, sailboards, canoes, bicycles, beach umbrellas, snorkel gear, and parasails are all available for rental at fairly reasonable rates. This is also where you'll find the local post office, public phones, and a restaurant (see "Where to Dine" below). Up at the north end of the beach, you'll find the **Virgin Diving** dive shop (670-0472) where you can rent requipment ($10 for mask, snorkel, and fins; $24 for regulator, B.C., and tank), arrange dive trips ($55 for a two-tank dive), and take scuba classes ($295 for an open-water course). Either beach is usually good for swimming, though Playa Panamá is slightly more protected.

WHERE TO STAY

EXPENSIVE

LA COSTA HOTEL & VILLAS, Playa Hermosa, Guanacaste. Tel. 506/221-2264, 221-8949, or 233-1862. Fax 506/222-5637. 156 rms. A/C TV TEL

$ Rates: Dec–Apr and July, $105 single or double; May–June and Aug–Nov, $77 single or double. AE, DC, MC, V.

This is currently the area's biggest and most luxurious hotel and the only full-service resort on Playa Hermosa. Set on a steep hillside at the north end of the beach, La Costa is built with Mediterranean styling. The best rooms are those that are at the top of the hill and farthest from the beach—you'll need to be in good shape to stay here. Unfortunately the resort was not designed for walking and there are no sidewalks and little shade. Luckily, the two pools are both at the top of the hill, so if you are staying up high, you don't have to walk down to the beach to take a swim. The villas have kitchens and lots of space, but there is air conditioning in the bedrooms only. Though these rooms are the closest to the beach, there are few views. The newer hotel rooms, on the other hand, have the best views, attractive furniture, tile floors, and air conditioning throughout.

Dining/Entertainment: The hotel has numerous eating establishments. La Pampa is the hotel's most formal dining room and specializes in steaks. Frutas y Flores is more casual and is open throughout the day. El Pelícano is a snack bar by the pool. Bars include Las Lapas, which is on the beach; Chico & Pepe, by the main pool; Bayview, by the second pool; and La Carretera, an indoor lounge. There is also a discotheque that can really get packed on the weekends.

Services: Diving-equipment rentals, scuba classes, dive trips, jet-ski rentals.

Facilities: Two swimming pools, tennis court, dive shop, gift shop.

MODERATE

CABINAS PLAYA HERMOSA, Apdo. 117, Liberia, Guanacaste. Tel. 506/670-0136. Fax 506/670-0136. 20 rms (all with bath).

$ Rates: $15.55 single; $31.10 double. No credit cards.

This little hotel, tucked away under shady trees and surrounded by green lawns, is run by Italians who make sure that their guests enjoy the quiet vacation they dreamed about before leaving home. Each large room has a pair of Adirondack chairs on its front porch, and the beach is only a few steps away. Rooms, even though rather dark, are large, and have a lot of closet space and double beds. Horseback riding and boat trips can be arranged. The open-air restaurant has a rustic tropical feel to it, with unfinished tree trunks holding up the roof. Seafood and homemade pasta are the specialties heres. Menu prices range from $4.75 to $10.15. To find the hotel, turn left at the first road into Playa Hermosa. The hotel's white archway gate is just after the curve.

CABINAS SULA-SULA, Playa Panamá, Guanacaste. Tel. 506/670-0492 or 253-0728. 6 rms.

$ Rates: $60–$75 for one to six people. Campsites: $3.05 per person per night. MC, V.

By the time you visit Playa Panamá, the latest big resorts will likely have opened and this quiet beach will have changed its character completely. However, if you are looking for economical accommodations with plenty of space and lots of cool shade, Cabinas Sula-Sula is just the ticket. The problem is that the rates here aren't that great unless you have three or more people. The rooms are fairly basic, though they do have kitchenettes and fans. There are some nature trails, but very little in the way of landscaping. Because of the trees there is good bird-watching. If you have a tent you can camp out here and have access to showers and toilets.

EL VELERO HOTEL, Playa Hermosa, Guanacaste. Tel. 506/670-0330. Fax 506/670-0310. 14 rms.

$ Rates: $35–$56 single; $52–$66 double. MC, V.

This small Canadian-owned hotel is now the nicest moderately priced place on Playa Hermosa. It's located right on the beach and has its own small swimming pool which is an open-air bar. White walls and polished tile floors give El Velero a Mediterranean flavor. The guest rooms are large and most have high ceilings. The upper third of room walls are screen, so there is plenty of cross ventilation. Fans also help keep the rooms cool. Bathrooms are small and have showers only. The hotel has its own restaurant, which offers a good selection of fish and shrimp dishes in the $7.80-to-$12.20 range. Various tours, horseback riding, and fishing trips can be arranged through the hotel.

WHERE TO DINE

AQUA SPORT, on the beach. Tel. 670-0450.
  Cuisine: CONTINENTAL. **Reservations:** Not accepted.
$ Prices: Main courses $3.40–$18.95. MC, V.
  Open: Daily 9am–9pm (noon–9pm in rainy season).
Part of the Aqua Sport market and equipment-rental shop is a small open-air restaurant with tables of polished hardwood. The beach is only steps away, and the atmosphere is very casual. The food, however, is much better than what you would expect from such a place The focus is on continental—with paella for $13.50, grilled lobster for $18.90, and shrimp à la diabla for $8.15.

3. PLAYA DEL COCO & PLAYA OCOTAL

253 kilometers NW of San José; 35 kilometers W of Liberia

GETTING THERE By Air The nearest airport with regularly scheduled flights is in Tamarindo. There you can arrange a taxi the rest of the way to Playa del Coco.

By Bus An express bus leaves San José at 10am daily from Calle 14 between avenidas 1 and 3. Duration: 5 hours. Fare: $3.85. From Liberia, buses leave at 5:30 and 8:15am, and 12:30, 2, 4:30, and 6pm. Duration: 45 minutes. Fare: $1.10.

By Car Follow the directions for getting to Liberia and Playa Hermosa, but take the left fork instead. It takes about five hours from San José.

DEPARTING The bus for San José leaves daily at 9:15am. Buses for Liberia leave at 5:30 and 7am, and 2, 3, and 6pm.

ESSENTIALS Orientation Playa del Coco is a small but busy beach town with most of the hotels and restaurants right on the water. Playa Ocotal is south of Playa de Coco on a dirt road that leaves the main road just before the beach. Playa Ocotal is a collection of vacation homes and hotels, and has one bar on the beach.

Playa del Coco is one of the most easily accessible of the Guanacaste beaches, with a paved road right down to the water, and has long been a popular destination with middle-class Ticos from San José. Unfortunately, most of the hotels right in town are quite run-down, and the water doesn't look too clean (this is a busy fishing port). The crowds that come here like their music loud and constant, so if you're in search of a quiet retreat, stay away. On the other hand, if you're looking for a beach with cheap hotels and plenty of cheap food and beer close at hand, you may enjoy Playa del Coco.

The beach, which is a grayish-brown sand, is quite wide at low tide and almost nonexistent at high tide. In between high and low, it's just right. Trash is a bit of a problem right in town. However, if you walk down the long, curving beach to the north of town, you're bound to find a nice, clean spot to unfold your blanket. Better still, if you have a car, head over to Playa Ocotal, which is a couple of kilometers down a dirt road. This is a tiny pocket of a cove bordered by high bluffs, and is quite beautiful.

WHAT TO SEE & DO

There is not much to do here except lie on the sand, hang out in the sodas and bars, or go to the discos. If you're interested, you might be able to join a soccer match (the soccer field is in the middle of town). Over at nearby Playa Ocotal there are often volleyball games by the soda on the beach. It's also possible to arrange horseback rides; ask your hotel.

Mario Vargas Expeditions (tel. 670-0351) rents scuba-diving and snorkeling equipment, offers scuba classes, and leads dives. A two-tank dive will run you $55; snorkeling equipment is $8 a day; a PADI open-water course is $300. Similar rates are offered by **Rich Coast Diving** (tel. 670-0176).

WHERE TO STAY

EXPENSIVE

EL OCOTAL BEACH RESORT, Apdo. 1, Playa del Coco, Guanacaste. Tel. 506/670-0321. Fax 506/670-0083. 28 rms, 12 bungalows, 3 suites. A/C TV TEL

$ Rates: Dec 16–Aug 15, $80 single, $90 double, $105 bungalow, $130–$170 suite; Aug 16–Dec 15, $70 single, $80 double, $105 bungalow, $120–$150 suite. AE, DC, MC, V.

This is the most luxurious hotel in the Playa del Coco area, although, unfortunately, I have received complaints about the quality of service here. The guest rooms vary in age, though all are fairly spacious and attractively furnished. The older rooms are those closer to the beach, while those with the best views and greatest comfort are those atop a hill overlooking a dramatic stretch of rocky coastline. Scuba diving and sportfishing are the main draws here, though diminutive Playa Ocotal is one of the prettiest little beaches along this stretch of coast and offers good swimming.

Dining/Entertainment: El Ocotal's restaurant is one of its greatest assets. The large room is surrounded on three sides by walls of glass and has a stunning view of Playa Ocotal and miles of coastline. There is also patio dining. Seafood is the specialty and the prices are moderate.

Services: Scuba classes, rentals, and trips are sone of the hotel's most popular services. There are also boat excursions, fishing charters, surfing excursions, a car-rental desk, and a tour desk.

Facilities: The hotel's main swimming pool is quite attractive and has a little artificial waterfall. Ranchos beside the pool provide shady shelter when the sun gets too strong. There are also two other pools, tennis courts, a hot tub, and a dive shop.

MODERATE

HOTEL LA FLOR DE ITABO, Apdo. 32, Playa del Coco, Guanacaste. Tel. 506/670-0292 or 670-0011. 18 rms, 8 apts. A/C

$ Rates: $45–$60 single; $45–$65 double; $95 apartment for one to four people. AE, DC, MC, V.

This is the most luxurious of the hotels right in Playa del Coco, and though it is not on the beach, the pool is large and the grounds are lushly planted. Toucans and parrots squawk and talk amid the flowers, adding their own bright colors to an already colorful garden. Stone reproductions of pre-Columbian statues provide a touch of the mysterious at this quiet retreat. With fewer than two dozens rooms, service here is reliably good. The rooms are spacious (especially the apartments), are attractively decorated with wood carvings and Guatemalan textiles, and are found within beautiful two-story houses. Italian dishes are the specialty of the restaurant, with prices ranging from $6.10 to $10.15 for entrées. The bar is decorated with flags from all over the world and is a popular hangout with sport fishermen. There is even a small casino here. In addition to a pool, the hotel has a volleyball court, children's play area, and a small park.

HOTEL VILLA CASA BLANCA, Apdo. 176, Playa del Coco, Guanacaste. Tel. 506/670-0448. 10 rms.

$ Rates: $40–$45 single; $50–$55 double; $60–$65 triple. MC, V (add 6% surcharge).

With friendly, helpful owners, beautiful gardens, and attractive rooms, this bed-and-breakfast inn is my favorite spot in the area. The inn is located in a new development and is built in the style of a Spanish villa. All the guest rooms have their own distinct character, and though some are a bit cramped, there are others that feel quite roomy. One room has a canopy bed and a beautiful bathroom with step-up bath. A little rancho serves as an open-air bar and breakfast area, and beside this is a pretty little lap pool with a bridge over it. Villa Blanca also represents several rental houses and condos in the area, so if you plan to stay for a week or more or need lots of room, ask about these.

BUDGET

CABINAS CHALE, Playa del Coco, Guanacaste. Tel. 506/670-0036 or 235-6408. Fax 506/670-0303. 21 rms (all with bath).
$ Rates: $19.55 single; $21.10 double; $24.40 triple. No credit cards.
Located down a dirt road to the right as you are coming into town, this small hotel is quite a bit better than those directly on the beach, and is also much quieter. Your only company as you stroll down to the beach, which is only 150 feet away, may be a herd of grazing cattle. The rooms are simply furnished with double beds, overhead fans, tile floors, and refrigerators, and each comes with a Tico clothes-washing sink called a *pila*. Some larger rooms have just been added and these are a bit nicer than the older rooms. There is a Spartan, screen-walled bar that is open only during the busy season (November to April), and a small pool on a raised patio in back.

COCO PALMS HOTEL, Apdo. 188-5019, Playa del Coco, Guanacaste. Tel 506/670-0367. Fax 506/670-0117. 20 rms.
$ Rates: $17.75 single; $20.70–$23.65 double; $26.60 triple. DC, MC, V.
This hotel is, by far, the best deal in Playa del Coco. The hotel is located about a block from the beach and overlooks the soccer field. The large guest rooms have tile floors, double beds, ceiling fans, and modern bathrooms with bamboo accents. Window seats, big picture windows (unfortunately with no view), wall sconces, vanities, and pastel colors round out the decor. There's a pool in the walled garden area in the back and a rancho-style bar beside the pool. An open-air restaurant completes the picture.

WHERE TO DINE

There are dozens of cheap open-air restaurants at the traffic circle in the center of El Coco village. These restaurants serve Tico standards, with the emphasis on fried fish. Prices are quite low, and so too is the quality for the most part. For better food try the following two places. For views, you can't beat the restaurant at El Ocotal Beach Resort.

HELEN'S, 100 meters south of the ice factory. Tel. 670-0221.
   Cuisine: COSTA RICAN/SEAFOOD. **Reservations:** Not accepted.
$ Prices: Main courses $4.05–$10.15. No credit cards.
   Open: Daily 11am–11pm.
There was no sign yet for this out-of-the-way place when we were last there, but by the time you arrive in town, Helen will probably have put one up. This is a local favorite, and because Helen's husband is a fisherman, the seafood is always absolutely fresh. The ceviche comes in a big bowl and is enough for meal. Be sure to try the lobster soup if it's on the menu.

EL RANCHO DE OCOTAL, Playa Ocotal. No phone.
   Cuisine: INTERNATIONAL. **Reservations:** Not accepted.
$ Prices: Sandwiches and main courses $2.40–$7.50.
   Open: Daily 8am–10pm.
This open-air restaurant near the beach at Playa Ocotal specializes in wood-oven pizzas, but is also popular for its swimming pool. You can order a meal or just a

drink and use the pool for as long as you like. There are also steaks and seafood on the menu.

4. PLAYAS FLAMINGO, POTRERO & BRASILITO

280 kilometers NW of San José; 66 kilometers SW of Liberia

GETTING THERE   By Air   The nearest airport with regularly scheduled flights is in Tamarindo. From there you can arrange a taxi.

By Bus   Express buses leave San José daily at 8 and 10:30am from the corner of Calle 20 and Avenida 3, stopping at Playas Flamingo, Potrero, and Brasilito. Duration: 6 hours. Fare: $5.10.

Alternatively, there are buses from this same San José station to Santa Cruz at 7:30 and 10:30am and 2, 4, and 6pm. Duration: 5 hours. Fare: $3.40.

From Santa Cruz, there are buses to Playas Flamingo, Brasilito, and Potrero daily at 6:30am and 3pm. Duration: 1½ hours. Fare: $1.50.

By Car   The most direct route is by way of the Tempisque River ferry. Take the Interamerican Highway west from San José, and 47 kilometers past the turnoff for Puntarenas turn left for the ferry. After crossing the Tempisque River, follow the signs for Nicoya, continuing north to Santa Cruz. About 16 kilometers north of Santa Cruz, just before the village of Belen, take the turnoff for Playas Flamingo, Brasilito, and Potrero. After another 20 kilometers, take the right fork to reach these beaches. The drive takes about 6 hours.

On Fridays and Saturdays, when beach traffic is heavy, it is often quicker to drive all the way north to Liberia and then come back south, thus avoiding the lines of cars waiting to take the ferry. This also applies if you are heading back to San José on a Sunday.

DEPARTING   Express buses to San José leave Playa Potrero at 9am and 2pm, stopping a few minutes later in Playa Brasilito and Playa Flamingo. Ask at your hotel where the best place is for catching the bus. Buses to Santa Cruz leave at 9am and 5pm. If you are heading north toward Liberia, get off the bus at Belen and wait for a bus going north.

ESSENTIALS Orientation   These three beaches are strung out over several miles of roads. Playa Flamingo is down a side road, while the villages of Brasilito and Potrero are right on the main road.

These three beaches were among the first in Costa Rica to attract international attention, and today Playa Flamingo is the most highly developed beach on this stretch of coast. This isn't surprising when you see the blue water and narrow strand of white sand that is Playa Flamingo or the pink, crushed-shell beach of nearby Playa Conchal. The views from Playa Potrero are beautiful and, in Brasilito, budget travelers have a chance at some fun in the sun without spending a fortune. What makes this grouping of beaches so memorable are the little, rocky islands offshore and the long sweeps of beach that are separated by a rugged peninsula.

On Playa Brasilito you will find one of the only two real villages in the area. The soccer field is the center of the village, and around its edges you'll find a couple of little *pulperias* (general stores). There's a long stretch of beach, and though it is of gray sand, it still has a quiet, undiscovered feel to it (at least on weekdays). Playa Brasilito is rapidly becoming popular both with Ticos and budget travelers from abroad. There's now a disco here and on weekends it can get pretty crowded and noisy.

Only a few miles away and at the opposite end of the scale is the luxury resort beach called Playa Flamingo. This is one of Costa Rica's top resort beaches, with luxury hotels, a marina, a private airstrip, retirement and vacation homes, and, best of all, one of the only white-sand beaches in the area. In fact, the old name for this beach was Playa Blanca, which made plenty of sense. When the developers moved in, they needed a more romantic name than "White Beach," so it became Playa Flamingo, even though there are no flamingos.

You'll probably want to spend plenty of time on this beautiful beach. Playa Flamingo is on a long spit of land that forms part of Potrero Bay, or Bahia Flamingo, as the developers wish it to be known. On the ocean side of the peninsula, there is the long white-sand beach, behind which is a dusty road and then a mangrove swamp. At the end of the sand spit is a fortress-like rock outcropping upon which most of Playa Flamingo's hotels and vacation homes are built. There are great views from this rocky hill. If you are not staying on Playa Flamingo, you should know that there are parking spots all along the beach road where you can park your car for the day. There is, however, little shade on the beach, so be sure to use plenty of sunscreen and bring an umbrella if you can. The bay side of the peninsula is where the marina is located.

If you continue along the road from Brasilito without taking the turn for Playa Flamingo, you will soon come to Playa Potrero. The sand here is a brownish-gray, but the beach is long, clean, and deserted. You can see the hotels of Playa Flamingo across the bay.

WHAT TO SEE & DO

Though Playa Flamingo is the prettiest beach in this area, Playa Potrero tends to have the gentlest surf, and therefore is the best swimming beach. Playa Conchal, which is nearly legendary for its beach of crushed pink seashells, is a short walk south of Brasilito, and though it is beautiful, it is also known for its dangerous riptides. The water at Playa Brasilito is often fairly calm, which makes it another good swimming choice.

The **Bahia Flamingo Resort Hotel & Club** has a dive shop that offers open-water courses for $280 and two-tank dive trips for $60. At Marina Flamingo Yacht Club, you'll find the **Quicksilver Dive Shop** (tel. 654-4010, ext. 177), which offers scuba courses, equipment rental, and dive trips. In Playa Brasilito, there is **Costa Rica Diving** (tel. 654-4021), which offers the same services. Both dive shops offer trips out to the Catalina and Bat Islands.

At the Marina Flamingo Yacht Club you can also look into doing some sportfishing for marlin or sailfish. There are several boats here that will take you out for a half day or full day of fishing.

You can contact the **Flamingo Marina Resort Hotel & Club** (tel. 233-8056 or 257-1431), which offers full-day fishing trips for between $550 and $895 depending on the size of the boat and the number of people on the trip. **Club Villas Pacifica** (tel. 654-4137) offers half-day fishing charters for between $450 and $950 and full-day trips for between $695 and $1,250. Another option is to contact Tom Bradwell at **Blue Marlin Sport Fishing** (tel. 654-4043), who offers trips at competitive rates.

If you'd rather stay on dry land, you can arrange a horseback ride with **Jalisco Tours** (tel. 654-4106). They charge around $10 per hour for their rides. Other options include a round of minigolf at Hal's American Bar & Grill or hitting a bucket of balls at the driving range at Tio's Bar & Restaurant. Both these places are inland from Playa Flamingo, the latter on the road to Playa Flamingo and the former on the main road.

If you're staying at the Playa Flamingo area for a while, but would like to see a bit more of Costa Rica than the beach and the Pacific, contact **Turistas Amigo Flamingo** (tel. 654-4238), which offers boat tours of the Tamarindo mangroves, visits to Santa Rosa National Park, horseback rides on a nearby ranch, trips to a nearby artisan's village, and night tours to see nesting sea turtles.

WHERE TO STAY

EXPENSIVE

FLAMINGO MARINA HOTEL, Playa Flamingo (Apdo. 321-1002, Paseo de los Estudiantes, San José), Guanacaste. Tel. 506/654-4141 or (in San José) 233-8056. Fax 506/654-4035 or (in San José) 221-8093. 23 rms, 8 suites, 19 cabinas, 4 apts. TV TEL

$ Rates (including continental breakfast): $95 single or double: $120 cabina; $160 suite or apt; $240 condo. AE, DC, MC, V.

⭐ Located up the hill from the beach, the Flamingo Marina Hotel offers one of the most attractive settings here at Flamingo Beach. A big open-air lobby is done up to resemble an old village and overlooks both the swimming pool and the bay. There are a variety of room types to choose from, all of which have refrigerators. The standard rooms have tile floors and lots of wood accents, while the suites have tiled whirlpool tubs, and wet bars in the seating area. All the rooms have patios or balconies and most have bay views.

Dining/Entertainment: The restaurant serves continental dishes with an emphasis on seafood. The bar beside the pool has seating in a big, cold-water whirlpool tub.

Services: Tour desk, sportfishing charters, snorkeling and diving trips and classes.

Facilities: There are two swimming pools (one with a swim-up bar), a tennis court, and a gift shop.

HOTEL AUROLA PLAYA FLAMINGO HOLIDAY INN, Playa Flamingo (Apdo. 7802-1000, San José), Guanacaste. Tel. 506/654-4010, 654-4011, (in San José) 233-7233, or toll free (in the U.S.) 800/HOLIDAY. Fax 506/654-4060 or (in San José) 255-1036. 88 rms. A/C TV TEL

$ Rates: $105–$160 single or double. AE, DC, MC, V.

This hotel, right across the road from the beach at Playa Flamingo, has long been the favorite choice of vacationing gringos, and during 1993 the hotel underwent a total facelift that should make it even more comfortable. The reconstruction was still in progress when I visited, but you can expect a couple of restaurants and bars, a good-size pool, a tennis court, as well as rooms that meet the international standards of Holiday Inns. Though it is considered the best hotel at Playa Flamingo, the buildings are rather barracks-like from the outside and the grounds lack shade or much else in the way of landscaping.

VILLAS FLAMINGO, Playa Flamingo, Guanacaste. Tel. 506/654-4215 or (in San José) 239-0737. Fax 506/654-4215. 57 condos.

$ Rates: $100 single or double; $110 triple; $130 quad. AE, MC, V.

Ⓢ Villas Flamingo, a condominium development, is down at the south end of Playa Flamingo, which is much shadier and more attractive than the more developed north end of the beach. You're also closer to the beach than at any other hotel except the Holiday Inn. The condos here are two stories with two bedrooms, two bathrooms, full kitchens, tile floors throughout, and attractive decor. The grounds are well landscaped and cared for, and there are some big, old shade trees around. The living rooms are fronted by a wall of glass, though only the rooms closer to the beach have much of a view. White walls and red-tile roofs give this place a very Mediterranean feel.

MODERATE

BAHIA FLAMINGO BEACH RESORT, Playa Potrero (Apdo. 45-5051, Santa Cruz), Guanacaste. Tel. and Fax 506/654-4183. 14 rms (all with bath).

$ Rates: Not yet set at press time. MC, V.

This comfortable little beach hotel is on Playa Potrero and, from the beach in front, has a view of Playa Flamingo across the bay. Set in a green garden with a white wooden fence around the property, the Bahia Flamingo feels like a private home in the country. A laid-back atmosphere prevails—with hammocks for dozing, a pool, and miles of nearly deserted beach for strolling and swimming. The hotel was undergoing a complete remodeling when I last visited, so you can expect the rooms to be attractive and comfortable when you visit. Fishing and snorkeling trips can be arranged. To find this hotel, watch for the sign pointing down a road to the left a mile or so after you pass the turnoff for Playa Flamingo. The hotel's restaurant is a breezy, high-ceilinged room and has a nice view of green lawns, white fence, and blue ocean. Meals average $5 to $10.

CLUB VILLAS PACÍFICA, Playa Flamingo (Apdo. 10, Santa Cruz), Guanacaste. Tel. 506/654-4137 or 654-4139. Fax 506/654-4138. 4 rms, 4 condos. A/C TV Tel

$ Rates: Dec 15–Mar 31, $75 double, $85 triple, $105 condo single or double; Apr 1– Dec 14, $65 double, $75 triple, $95 condo single or double. Fishing packages available. AE, MC, V.

This place is primarily a sportfishing resort and is set back quite a ways from the beach just outside of Brasilito. However, the grounds are attractive and the buildings are up on a hill that is surrounded by forest. The condos are huge and can sleep up to six people. They all have tile floors, big patios, high ceilings, big bathrooms, and full kitchens.

Dining/Entertainment: The dining room here is the best restaurant in the Playa Flamingo area and is open daily from 6am to 11pm (closed on Monday in the low season). There is a sweeping view of the bay from a deck and a long, curving bar. The restaurant itself is cool and cavernous and is constructed with lots of stone. The menu changes every three days and features excellent continental fare with an emphasis on fresh fish. Prices range from $11 to $16 for entrées.

Services: Sportfishing charters.

Facilities: Swimming pool, tennis court.

HOTEL SUGAR BEACH, Playa Pan de Azucar (Apdo. 90), Guanacaste. Tel. 506/654-4242 or (in the U.S.) 307/733-4692. Fax 506/654-4329 or (in the U.S.) 307/733-1058. 26 rms.

$ Rates: Nov–Mar, $65 single or double without A/C, $90 single or double with A/C; Apr–Oct, $55 single or double without A/C, $70 single or double with A/C. AE, MC, V.

Just as the name implies, the Hotel Sugar Beach is located on a white-sand beach—one of the few in the area and therefore one of the most attractive in my opinion. The beach is on a small cove surrounded by rocky hills. Unfortunately, the hills become very brown and desolate in the dry season (which is when most tourists come to visit), so don't expect the verdant tropics if you come down here in March or April. The hotel itself is perched above the water. Nature lovers will be thrilled to find wild howler monkeys and iguanas almost on their doorsteps. Snorkelers also should be happy here; this cove has some good snorkeling in the dry season. Most of the rooms have air-conditioning, and are either recently remodeled or were just built. The newest rooms are set back amid the trees and are quite large. Tile floors, wicker furniture, beautiful carved doors, and big bathrooms all add up to first-class comfort. The rooms without air-conditioning are the oldest and most basic, though they are in an interesting circular building. Hammocks under the trees provide a great way to while away a hot afternoon. The open-air dining room is in a circular building with a panoramic vista of ocean, islands, and hills. There are daily specials with prices from $6 to $13.50 for entrées. Scuba-diving and snorkeling trips, horseback riding, and fishing boat charters can be arranged. When I last visited there were plans to add a swimming pool and bar as well as some sea kayaks.

CABINAS CONCHAL, Playa Brasilito (Apdo. 185-5150, Santa Cruz), Guanacaste. Tel. 506/654-4257. 7 rms (all with private bath).

$ Rates: Nov–Mar, $17.75–$23.65 single, $23.65 double, $29.55 triple; April–Oct, $11.85 single, $17.75 double, $23.65 triple. No credit cards.

Located on the south edge of Brasilito, Cabinas Conchal consists of several yellow buildings inside a walled compound. The stucco-and-stone construction gives the buildings a bit of character. Some rooms have just a double bed, while others have a double and a pair of bunk beds. Table fans help keep the rooms cool.

CABINAS CRISTINA, Playa Potrero (Apdo. 121, Santa Cruz), Guanacaste. Tel. 506/654-4006. 5 rms (all with bath).

$ Rates: $23.30 single; $28.60 double; $35.30 triple; $41.95 quad. No credit cards.

Ⓢ This little place is located on Playa Potrero across the bay from Playa Flamingo and a few kilometers north of Brasilito. Although Cabinas Cristina isn't right on the beach, it's still a great value in this area of high-priced hotels. The rooms are spacious and very clean (they fill up fast), with hot plates, refrigerators, dressers, bars with stools, tiled baths, and double and bunk beds. On the veranda there are large rocking chairs. The friendly owner, Daniel Boldrini, speaks some English. There is a small pool in the middle of a grassy green yard and a thatched-roof palapa. Playa Potrero is a 5-minute walk down a dirt road, and Restaurant La Perla is only 50 yards away (see "Where to Dine," below).

HOTEL BRASILITO, Playa Brasilito, Santa Cruz, Guanacaste. Tel. and Fax 506/654-4237. 15 rms (all with private bath).

$ Rates: $16.90 single; $23.65 double. No credit cards.

This hotel, right in Brasilito and just across a sand road from the beach, offers basic, small rooms that are generally quite clean. There's also a bar and big open-air restaurant serving economical meals. This is the best value in town, though the building across the street seems to be a disco, which means don't plan on going to bed early on the weekends. The hotel also rents snorkeling equipment, bicycles, body boards, and horses.

LONG-TERM STAYS & CAMPING

If you plan to be here for a while or are coming down with friends or a large family, you might want to consider renting a house. They rent for anywhere between $100 and $300 per day in the high season (slightly less in the low season). For information and reservations, contact Sea View Rentals, Apdo. 77, Santa Cruz, Guanacaste (tel. 506/654-4007; fax 654-4009).

If you're interested in camping, talk to Alvaro Chinchilla at Hal's American Bar & Grill. He was about to open up a campground nearby when I last visited and expected to charge $2 per person per night.

WHERE TO DINE

The best restaurant in the area is the dining room at Club Villas Pacífica (see above for details).

AMBERES, Playa Flamingo near the Flamingo Marina Hotel. Tel. 654-4001.

Cuisine: CONTINENTAL. **Reservations:** Recommended in high season.

$ Prices: Appetizers $5.75–$6.10; main courses $5.40–$16.90. MC, V.

Open: Daily 6:30–10pm.

This is the happening spot in Flamingo. Not only is it the most upscale restaurant outside of a hotel, but it also boasts a bar, a disco, and even a tiny casino. So, you can come for dinner and make it an evening. Fresh fish served either meuniere or provence style are two of the best dishes on the menu. One drawback is that they play their music way too loud at dinner. Luckily the open-air disco doesn't get cranking until 10pm. The bar opens at 5pm.

HAL'S AMERICAN BAR & GRILL, between the turnoff for Playa Flamingo and Playa Potrero. Tel. 654-4213.

Cuisine: INTERNATIONAL. **Reservations:** Not accepted.

$ Prices: $6.50–$10. MC.

Open: Daily 3:30–11pm.

If you've been down in Costa Rica for a while and long for a familiar meal and setting, try Hal's. Not only can you get a pizza or burger, but you can also play a round of miniature golf before or after your meal. Pasta, burgers, and steaks are the staples, but there is also a long list of side orders that includes such offerings as stuffing, french fries, roast peppers, buffalo wings, and a Greek salad. The roast chicken is the specialty of the house. A round of miniature golf costs $2.70 for adults and $1.35 for children. The restaurant operates a shuttle bus to Playa Flamingo.

MARIE'S, Playa Flamingo near the Flamingo Marina Hotel. Tel. 654-4136.
   Cuisine: INTERNATIONAL/SEAFOOD. **Reservations:** Not accepted.
$ Prices: Appetizers $1.35–$5.40; main courses $4.40–$16.90. MC, V.
   Open: Daily 7am–9pm. **Closed:** Tues May–Sept.
Right in the middle of all the luxury hotels at Playa Flamingo is a great little place for a snack or a full dinner. The menu is primarily sandwiches and other lunch foods, but on the blackboard behind the bar you'll find daily specials such as mahimahi (called dorado down here) and, from August to December, lobster and conch. You'll also find such Tico favorites as casados and ceviche. Tables in the open-air restaurant are made from slabs of tree trunks. Be sure to try the three-milks cake (a Nicaraguan speciality), which just might be the moistest cake on earth.

RESTAURANT LA PERLA, Playa Potrero, at the corner near Cabinas Cristina. No phone.
   Cuisine: AMERICAN/COSTA RICAN. **Reservations:** Not accepted.
$ Prices: All meals $1.35–$2.35. No credit cards.
   Open: Daily 6am–10pm.
La Perla, an unusual open-air restaurant with chain-link fencing for walls, is primarily the local community center, but also serves up decent breakfasts and lunches. You can chat with Perlita, the resident parrot, while you wait for your meal.

---

5. PLAYA TAMARINDO

295 kilometers NW of San José; 73 kilometers SW of Liberia

GETTING THERE   By Air   Sansa (in San José: tel. 233-0397, 233-5330, or 233-3258) files to Tamarindo daily at 9:30am from San José's Juan Santamaria International Airport (free transportation from downtown office to airport). Duration: 40 minutes. Fare: $52 each way.
   Travelair (tel. 220-3054 or 232-7883) flies to Tamarindo daily at 6am from San José's Pavas International Airport. Duration: 50 minutes. Fare: $66 one way, $114 round-trip. A second flight leaving at 9:30am stops in Tamarindo after first making three other stops en route; fare is the same. Duration: 1 hour and 40 minutes.

By Bus   An express bus leaves San José daily at 4pm from Calle 20 between avenidas 1 and 3. Duration: 6 hours. Fare: $4.65.
   Alternatively, you can catch a bus to Santa Cruz from this same station and then take a bus from Santa Cruz to Tamarindo. Buses leave San José for Santa Cruz daily at 7:30 and 10:30am and 2, 4, and 6pm. Duration: 5 hours. Fare: $3.40.
   Buses from Santa Cruz to Tamarindo leave daily at 4:30, 6:30, 8:30, and 11:30am and 1 and 8:30pm. Duration: 1½ hours. Fare: $1.60.
   Another express bus leaves San José daily at 3:30pm from Calle 14 between avenidas 3 and 5. Duration: 5½ hours. Fare: $4.65.
   If you are coming from Liberia, you can take a Santa Cruz or Nicoya bus (which run almost hourly) and get off in the village of Belen, which is south of Filadelfia and wait for the next Tamarindo-bound bus. However, since buses to Tamarindo are infrequent, you may have a long wait. It may be better to go to Santa Cruz to do your waiting.

By Car   The most direct route is by way of the Tempisque River ferry. Take the Interamerican Highway west from San José, and 47 kilometers past the turnoff for Puntarenas, turn left toward the ferry. After crossing the Tempisque River, follow the signs for Nicoya, continuing north to Santa Cruz. About 16 kilometers north of Santa Cruz, just before the village of Belen, take the turnoff for Tamarindo. In another 20 kilometers take the left fork for Playa Tamarindo. The drive takes about 6 hours.

On Fridays and Saturdays, when beach traffic is heavy, it is often quicker to drive all the way north to Liberia and then come back south, thus avoiding the lines of cars waiting to take the ferry. This also applies if you are heading back to San José on a Sunday.

DEPARTING   Sansa flights leave for San José at 10:25am daily. Travelair flights leave at 7 and 11:20am daily. Buses leave for San José daily at 5:45 and 6:45am, though this latter bus only goes to Santa Cruz where you must transfer to the San José bus.

ESSENTIALS   Orientation   The unpaved road leading into town runs parallel to the beach and dead-ends just past Cabinas Zully Mar. There are a couple of side roads off this main road where most of the new hotels are to be found.

Tamarindo is a long, wide swath of white sand that curves gently from one rocky headland to another. Behind the beach are low, dry hills that can be a very dreary brown in the dry season but instantly turn green with the first brief showers of the rainy season. Though there is only one major resort hotel in town, several smaller hotels have made Tamarindo one of the most popular beaches on this coast. Fishing boats bob at their moorings at the south end of the beach, and brown pelicans fish just outside the breakers. A sandy islet offshore makes a great destination if you are a strong swimmer; if you're not, it makes a great foreground for sunsets. Because of the strong waves here, Tamarindo is popular with surfers.

Nearby is Playa Grande, one of the last nesting sites for the giant leatherback turtle, which is the largest turtle in the world. This beach is usually too rough for swimming, but there are often great surfing waves.

WHAT TO SEE & DO

Tamarindo is a long beach and though it can be great for swimming at times, it is often too rough. You also have to be careful when and where you swim on Tamarindo Beach. There are rocks just offshore in several places, some of which are exposed only at low tide. An encounter with one of these rocks could be nasty, especially if you are bodysurfing. Also, you should avoid swimming near the estuary mouth, where the currents can carry you out away from the beach. If you want to try some surfing or other water-sports activity, drop by **Iguana Surf** (tel. 654-4019), which is up the road toward the Hotel Pasatiempo and then down a side road a bit. These folks rent snorkeling equipment ($10.15 per day), boogie boards ($6.75 per day), sea kayaks ($10 per hour), and surfboards ($20 per day). You can also rent similar equipment, as well as bicycles, beach chairs, umbrellas, and mats, at slightly lower rates from **Tamarindo Tour/Rentals** (tel. 654-4078), which is located on the right as you come into town. Both places are open daily.

The leatherback sea turtles nest between August and February on Playa Grande, and during this time there are night tours to see nesting turtles. The tours cost anywhere between $11.85 per person. Only a few guides are licensed to operate these tours and all groups are required to use only red-light flashlights. No flash photography is allowed because any sort of light can confuse the turtles and prevent them from laying their eggs. Before going on one of these tours, make sure that your guide will be following all precautions aimed at protecting the turtles.

Papagayo Excursions (tel. 680-0859 or 680-0652), which has its office at the Hotel Tamarindo Diria, offers folks a chance to go after the big ones that abound in the waters offshore. From here it takes only 20 minutes to reach the edge of the continental shelf and the waters preferred by marlin and sailfish. Although fishing is good all year, the peak season for billfish is between mid-April and August. Rates for the boat are $250 to $450 for a half day and $350 to $700 for a full day. Alternatively, you can contact **Tamarindo Sportfishing** (tel. 654-4090), which offers half-day trips for between $250 and $500 and full-day trips for between $350 and $800.

If you aren't an angler, you can arrange to go horseback riding through Papagayo Excursions. Rates for horses, with a guide, are $25 for two hours. This company also offers two-hour boat tours of the nearby estuary for $25 per person and two-tank scuba-diving trips for $60. The estuary tours, which head back into the mangrove swamp near Tamarindo, are very popular and are offered by several companies around town. Ask at your hotel, and you should be able to arrange one of these boat trips for under $13.

WHERE TO STAY

EXPENSIVE

HOTEL EL JARDÍN DEL EDEN, Playa Tamarindo (Apdo. 1094-2050, San Pedro), San José. Tel. and Fax 506/654-4111. 20 rms. A/C
$ Rates (including continental breakfast): $85–$130 single or double. AE, MC, V.

Though it isn't right on the beach, this is the most luxurious and comfortable hotel in Tamarindo. It also offers the best service and the best meals in town. There are excellent views from the guest rooms, which are in Mediterranean-style buildings on a hill 150 yards from the beach. The owners of the hotel are French and Italian and have brought to their hotel a touch of sophistication that is often lacking at beach hotels in Costa Rica. The guest rooms all have ceiling fans as well as air-conditioning, and there are balconies with views of the Pacific. The honeymoon room has a huge bathroom with a tub, while other rooms have showers only. Service here is very personal and the staff can help you arrange various tours and excursions.

Dining/Entertainment: The thatched-roof open-air dining room features excellent French and Italian meals with nightly specials.

Facilities: There are two swimming pools, one of which has a swim-up bar. There's also a whirlpool tub. The terraces surrounding the pools and tub have thatched palapas for shade, and there's even a little artificial waterfall flowing into one of the pools.

NAHUA GARDEN SUITES, Playa Tamarindo (Apdo. 63), Guanacaste. Tel. 506/680-0776. Fax 506/680-0776. 5 suites. A/C
$ Rates: Nov–Apr, $85 single or double; May–Oct, $65 single or double. No credit cards.

Located down a side road near the turnaround, Nahua Garden Suites offers unexpected comfort. The suites are actually condominiums and come complete with kitchens that have all appliances and pantries. You'll find a queen bed in the bedroom and beautiful teak doors on the bathrooms. There are also big bath towels (a rarity in Costa Rica). Vaulted ceilings give the suites the feeling of being quite large, and in the living room there is a futon couch and dining room table. Outside in the attractively landscaped garden, you'll find a small swimming pool. The owners are from Canada and can offer help on planning itineraries, and can also help anyone interested in real estate in the area. It's about 200 yards to the beach.

TAMARINDO DIRIÁ, Playa Tamarindo (Apdo. 6762-1000, San José), Guanacaste. Tel. 506/680-0652 or 289-8616. Fax 506/289-8727 or 680-0652. 70 rms. A/C TV TEL
$ Rates: Apr–Oct, $75 single $91 double; Nov–Mar, $85 single, $105 double. AE, MC, V.

This is Tamarindo's old reliable beachfront resort hotel and in 1993 it underwent a facelift that gave the hotel a slightly more modern look without affecting much modernization of the rooms. Wedged into a narrow piece of land between a dusty road and the beach, the Diriá manages to create its own little world of tropical gardens and palm trees. The remodeled rooms are done in contemporary pastel colors with red-tile floors. Some rooms have separate seating areas, and most have hairdryers, clock-radios, and a basket of toiletries in the small bathroom. However, it is the beachfront location and attractive gardens that make this hotel a worthwhile place to stay.

Dining/Entertainment: The big open-air bar-restaurant beside the pool features a different menu nightly, with prices for main dishes ranging from $5 to $10. There is also a lunch buffet in the garden most days.

Services: Tour desk, beach-equipment rentals.

Facilities: Swimming pool, gift shop, game room.

MODERATE

HOTEL EL MILAGRO, Playa Tamarindo (Apdo. 145-5150, Santa Cruz), Guanacaste. Tel. 506/654-4042 or 441-5102. Fax 506/441-8494. 32 rms. SAFE

$ Rates (including continental breakfast): $40–$50 single or double with fan; $50–$60 single or double with A/C, AE, MC, V.

This place started out as a restaurant but has expanded into an attractive little hotel on the edge of town. It's located across the road from the beach, and the rooms are lined up facing each other behind the restaurant. The front wall of each room is made of louvered doors that can be opened up to give the room plenty of air. These doors open onto small semicircular patios. Rooms are comfortable and have high ceilings. Pretty gardens and some big, old shade trees make El Milagro even more attractive. The restaurant serves excellent continental dishes, and there is a swimming pool with a swim-up bar. There's also a children's pool. Various tours and excursions can be arranged through the hotel.

HOTEL PASATIEMPO, Playa Tamarindo, Santa Cruz, Guanacaste. Tel. and Fax 506/680-0776. 10 rms.

$ Rates: Nov–Mar, $69 single or double; Apr–Oct, $49 single or double. AE, MC, V.

This newer hotel is set back from the beach a couple of hundred yards in a grove of shady trees. The guest rooms are housed in duplex buildings with thatch roofs and each room has its own patio with a hammock. There's plenty of space in every room and some even sleep five people. In the center of the five duplexes is a small pool. There is also a popular rancho-style open-air bar that has an evening happy hour and good snacks. The adjacent restaurant serves excellent pastas and fresh fish, and is one of the best restaurants in town. There is also a small boutique here.

PUEBLO DORADO HOTEL, Playa Tamarindo (Apdo. 1711-1002, San José), Guanacaste. Tel. and Fax 506/222-5741. 27 rms. A/C

$ Rates: $40 single; $50 double; $60 triple. AE, MC, V.

This two-story, blindingly white hotel has a central garden courtyard and looks a bit like a Los Angeles apartment building. There's a small pool at the back of the garden and above the pool is an open-air restaurant and a bar serving meals in the $4 to $8 range. Guest rooms are done in white tile and have big bathrooms and double beds. In the guest rooms and elsewhere around the hotel there are huge stone masks (reproductions of pre-Columbian stone carvings) mounted on the walls. Though this hotel is across the road from the beach, it still offers one of the best deals in Tamarindo if you want a place with air-conditioning and a swimming pool.

BUDGET

In addition to the hotels listed below, there is also a private campground across the road from the Tamarindo Turicentro on the outskirts of town.

CABINAS MARIELOS, Playa Tamarindo, Guanacaste. Tel. 506/654-4041.
14 rms (all with bath).

$ Rates: $12.20 single; $20.30 double; $23.65 triple. No credit cards.

This place is located down a palm-shaded driveway across the road from the beach. Rooms are clean and fairly new, though small and simply furnished. There are tile floors and wooden chairs on the patios. The bathrooms have no doors on them but are otherwise quite acceptable. There is even a kitchen that guests can use. The garden provides a bit of shade.

CABINAS ZULLY MAR, Tamarindo, Guanacaste. Tel. 506/226-4732. 27 rms (all with bath).

$ Rates: $20.30 single; $25.60–$39.75 double; $30.55–$46.25 triple. No credit cards.

The Zully Mar has long been a favorite of budget travelers staying in Tamarindo. The newer rooms, which are in a two-story white-stucco building with a wide, curving staircase on the outside, have air-conditioning and are more comfortable. The doors to these guest rooms are particularly interesting; they're hand carved with pre-Columbian motifs. There are also high ceilings with fans, tile floors, a long veranda, and large bathrooms. The older rooms, though smaller, are also clean and pleasant. Although there are mango trees out front for shade, there is little other landscaping, and the sandy grounds look a bit unkempt. Don't let this bother you: Miles of beach are just across the street, as are a restaurant and bar.

HOTEL POZO AZUL, Playa Tamarindo, Santa Cruz, Guanacaste. Tel. 506/680-0147 or 654-4280. 27 rms (all with bath).

$ Rates: $29.35–$37.10 single, double, or triple; $46.35 quad. No credit cards.

This is one of the first hotels you spot as you drive into Tamarindo. It's on the left side of the road and therefore is not on the beach. There isn't much shade on the grounds, but there are swimming pools for adults and kids. In the 17 rooms with air-conditioning, there are also hot plates, refrigerators, tables and chairs, large windows, and *pilas* (sinks) for washing clothes. Some rooms have covered parking to keep your car out of the blistering heat. There is no restaurant here, so you'll have to either cook your own meals or travel into town to one of the few restaurants. In recent years, the Pozo Azul has become a surfer hangout.

NEARBY ACCOMMODATIONS

LAS TORTUGAS HOTEL, Playa Grande, Guanacaste. Tel. and Fax 506/680-0765. 11 rms, 2 suites. A/C

$ Rates: Nov–Mar, $85 single or double, $125 suite; Apr–Oct, $58 single or double, $110 suite. No credit cards.

Playa Grande is best known for the leatherback turtles that nest here, and much of the beach is now part of Las Baulas National Park, which was created to protect the turtles. However, this beach is also popular with surfers, who make up a large percentage of the clientele at the beachfront Las Tortugas Hotel. The rooms here are all quite large and most have interesting stone floors and semicircular shower stalls. High ceilings help keep the rooms cool, but there is also air-conditioning. The upper suite has a curving staircase that leads up to its second room. The hotel's restaurant is on the second floor so that it has a view of the waves and beach. There is also a small bar and a swimming pool.

WHERE TO DINE

MODERATE

COCONUT CAFE, on the left as you come into town. No phone.
Cuisine: INTERNATIONAL. **Reservations:** Not accepted.

$ Prices: Appetizers $3.40–$6.80; main courses $6.45–$19.60. No credit cards.
Open: Daily 6–10pm.

★ This is one of Tamarindo's more atmospheric restaurants. A thatch roof, wicker furniture, and a raised deck all add up to a gringo fantasy of the tropics, but isn't that what you came down here for anyway? The Coconut Café serves some of the most imaginative food in town, including such dishes as red chicken curry, mahi-mahi macadamia, shrimp brochettes, and fondue. However, because the menu changes daily, you can expect other equally enticing dishes when you visit. Below the dining room there is a comfortable lounge. The only drawback here is that the very dusty road is only a few feet away.

EL MILAGRO, on the left as you enter town. Tel. 654-4042.
   Cuisine: CONTINENTAL/COSTA RICAN. **Reservations:** Not required.
$ **Prices:** Appetizers $1.55–$3.05; main courses $5.40–$21.65. AE, MC, V.
   Open: Daily 7am–11pm.
Lush gardens and wide terraces make this the most attractive restaurant in town, and you might even be able to go for a swim in the adjacent pool if you're so inclined. Reproductions of pre-Columbian stone statues stand in the gardens and the bar has carved-wood columns. On those rare occasions when it is raining, you can retreat to one of the indoor dining rooms. Though the emphasis here is on seafood, you'll also find such unexpected offerings as beef fondue for two, fried Camembert, banana flambé, crêpes with ice cream, and hot fruits in amaretto sauce.

BUDGET

FIESTA DEL MAR, at the end of the road. No phone.
   Cuisine: STEAK/SEAFOOD. **Reservations:** Not accepted.
$ **Prices:** Main courses $3.95–$8.80. MC, V.
   Open: Daily 11am–11pm.
Located across the circle from the beach, the Fiesta del Mar specializes in steaks and seafood cooked over a wood fire. Try the grilled steak in garlic sauce for $8.80 or the whole fried fish for $4.75. The open-air dining area is edged with greenery and has a thatch roof, so it feels very tropical. There is also live marimba music several nights a week.

RESTAURANT ZULLY MAR, at the end of the road. No phone.
   Cuisine: COSTA RICAN. **Reservations:** Not accepted.
$ **Prices:** Meals $3.40–$16.90. No credit cards.
   Open: Daily 7am–10pm.
This restaurant, opposite the hotel of the same name, is right on the beach at the end of the road that leads into Tamarindo. It's a basic Tico-style open-air restaurant, but the food is good, and the view can't be beat. Sit and watch the boats bob in the swells just offshore while you dine on fresh fish sautéed in garlic. The bar is a popular hangout with locals and tourists, and you should not miss ordering a big bowl of ceviche to accompany a few drinks. Be forewarned, this place is mobbed on weekends.

PANADERÍA JOHANN, on the road into town. No phone.
   Cuisine: BAKERY. **Reservations:** Not accepted.
$ **Prices:** $2–$9. No credit cards.
   Open: Daily 6am–8pm.
★ There are always fresh-baked goodies at this Belgian-run bakery on the outskirts of Tamarindo, although what you might find on any given day is never certain. Possibilities include croissants, pizzas, chocolate eclairs, and different types of bread. A whole pizza goes for around $9. If you are heading out to the beach for the day, be sure to stop by and pick up some bread or pastries. There are a few tables out back where you can eat your pizza. There is also a separate open-air restaurant right next door.

6. PLAYA JUNQUILLAL

30 kilometers W of Santa Cruz; 20 kilometers S of Tamarindo

GETTING THERE **By Air** The nearest airport with regularly scheduled flights is in Tamarindo. You can arrange a taxi from the airport to Playa Junquillal.

By Bus An express bus leaves San José daily at 2pm from the corner of Calle 20 and Avenida 3. Duration: 5 hours. Fare: $5.31.

Alternatively, you can take a bus to Santa Cruz (see above under "Playas Flamingo, Potrero & Brasilito" for details) and then take a bus from Santa Cruz to Playa Junquillal at 6:30 pm. Duration (Santa Cruz to Playa Junquillal): 1½ hours. Fare: $1.60.

By Car Take the Interamerican Highway from San José and 47 kilometers past the turnoff for Puntarenas, turn left toward the Tempisque ferry. After crossing the Tempisque River, continue north through Nicoya to Santa Cruz. In Santa Cruz, head west 14 kilometers to the town of 27 de Abril, which is where the pavement ends. From here it is another 18 kilometers to Playa Junquillal.

DEPARTING The express bus to San José leaves Playa Junquillal daily at 5am. There is also a bus to Santa Cruz daily at the same time.

ESSENTIALS The hotels mentioned here are all along the main road.

Playa Junquillal (pronounced hoon-key-*awl*) is a long, windswept beach that, for most of its length, is backed by grasslands. This gives it a very different feel from other beaches on this coast. There is really no village to speak of here, so if you're heading out this way, plan on getting away from it all. Once here, your options for what to do are limited to whatever is on offer at your chosen hotel. However, the long beach is good for strolling and the sunsets are superb.

WHAT TO SEE & DO

Other than walking on the beach, swimming when the surf isn't too strong, and exploring tide pools, there isn't much to do here, which is just fine with me. This beach is ideal for anyone who just wants to relax without any distractions. Bring a few good books. Actually, the larger hotels here—Antumalal, Iguanazul, and Villa Serena—all offer plenty of activities and facilities, including volleyball, swimming pools, tennis courts, and even a disco at Hotel Antumalal. Sportfishing trips can also be arranged at most hotels. At the Iguanazul, guests can rent bicycles or mopeds, which are both good ways to get up and down this beach.

WHERE TO STAY AND DINE

EXPENSIVE

HOTEL ANTUMALAL, Playa Junquillal (Apdo. 49-5150, Santa Cruz), Guanacaste. Tel. and Fax 506/680-0506. 23 rms. SAFE

$ Rates: Dec–Apr, $70 single, $80 double, $90 triple; May–Nov, $45 single, $50 double, $55 triple. AE, DC, MC, V.

Located at the end of the road into Playa Junquillal, the Antumalal is the lushest and oldest hotel on the beach. The owners are Italian, so don't be surprised if you encounter Italian tour groups. The big, old shade trees and lush gardens create a world of tropical tranquility that is perfect for romance and relaxation. Guest rooms are all in duplex buildings with stucco walls and beautiful murals on inside walls. Out front you'll find a big patio with a hammock, while inside there are brick floors, colorful Guatemalan bedspreads, and big bathrooms.

Dining/Entertainment: The dining room is housed under a huge, high-peaked rancho that has a fascinating driftwood chandelier hanging from the ceiling. The menu includes plenty of good Italian dishes. There's a bar here in the restaurant, plus another beside the pool. There is also a small discotheque.

Services: Horseback riding, boat charters for fishing and scuba diving.

Facilities: The swimming pool, with its swim-up bar, is only a few steps from the beach and is beautiful at night when the underwater lights are on. Other facilities include a tennis court, exercise room, and miniature golf course.

HOTEL VILLA SERENA, Playa Junquillal (Apdo. 17, Santa Cruz), Guanacaste. Tel. and Fax 506/680-0737. 10 rms.

$ Rates (including three meals): $120 double. MC, V.

Though the rate here is quite a bit higher than elsewhere at Playa Junquillal, keep in mind that all your meals are included. With this in mind, the actual room rates here would fall in the upper moderate range. Villa Serena is surrounded by neatly manicured lawns and gardens, and is directly across the street from the beach, which is free of rocks here and is excellent for swimming most of the time. The hotel's main building houses the second-floor dining room, which overlooks the beach. Art nouveau decorations and European art abound throughout the building, giving the hotel a very sophisticated feel for such a remote location. The rooms are all individual bungalows that are quite roomy and have ceiling fans and dressing rooms. Each has its own covered patio, and only steps away is the small pool. The German owner is very friendly and helpful.

Dining/Entertainment: The dining room serves excellent European meals with plenty of variety for those who decide to stay for a while.

Services: Horseback riding, fishing charters.

Facilities: Swimming pool, tennis court.

MODERATE

HOTEL EL CASTILLO DIVERTIDO, Playa Junquillal, Santa Cruz, Guanacaste. Tel. (in Santa Cruz) 506/680-0015. 7 rms.

$ Rates: Dec–Apr, $30.65–$35 double; May–Nov, $24.50 double. No credit cards.

Quite a few people have moved to Costa Rica from around the world in hopes of living out fantasy lives impossible in their home countries. This fanciful hotel is just such a creation. Built by a young German, the hotel is a tropical rendition of a classic medieval castle (well, sort of). Ramparts and a turret with a rooftop bar certainly grab the attention of passersby. Guest rooms here are fairly small, though rates are also some of the lowest in the area.

IGUANAZUL HOTEL, Playa Junquillal (Apdo. 130-1550, Santa Cruz), Guanacaste. Tel. and Fax 506/680-0783. 24 rms. SAFE

$ Rates: Dec–Apr, $47.50 single, $60 double, $72 triple; May–Nov, $35 single, $45 double, $52 triple. AE, MC, V.

Though the gravel road leading up to this hotel doesn't make Iguanazul seem too promising, once you step through the entry and see the resortlike pool, you may well be captivated, as my wife and I were. Set on a windswept, grassy bluff above a rocky beach, Iguanazul is far from the madding crowd. This is definitely a spot for sun worshippers who like to have a good time, and the clientele tends to be young and active. The pool is large, as is the surrounding patio area. There's a volleyball court, and the bar plays lively classic rock throughout most of the day. Don't, however, expect a tropical setting; grasslands surround the hotel, which gives the area the feel of Cape Cod or the Outer Banks. Guest rooms are beautifully decorated with basket lampshades, wicker furniture, red-tile floors, high ceilings, and blue-and-white tile bathrooms.

There are also plenty of things to do around here. You can rent horses, bicycles, mopeds, and body boards. There are board games, table tennis, and karaoke music in the evenings. There's also a well-stocked gift shop.

BUDGET

HIBISCUS HOTEL, Playa Junquillal (Apdo. 163-5150, Santa Cruz), Guanacaste. Tel. (in Alajuela) 506/441-2282. 5 rms (all with private bath).
$ Rates: Dec–Apr, $15–$30 single, $15–$40 double, $45 triple; May–Nov, $15–$28 single or double. No credit cards.

Though the accommodations here are very simple, the French owner makes sure that everything is always clean and in top shape. The grounds are pleasantly shady and the beach is just across the road. The least expensive room is quite small and has only cold water, but in this climate, you really don't need the hot water that the more expensive rooms offer.

7. PLAYA SÁMARA

35 kilometers S of Nicoya; 245 kilometers W of San José

GETTING THERE   By Air Sansa (in San José: tel. 233-0397, 233-3258, or 233-5330) flies to Carillo (15 minutes south of Sámara) daily at 9:30am from San José's Juan Santamaría International Airport. The flight makes two stops en route. Duration: 1 hour and 45 minutes. Fare: $46 each way.

Travelair (in San José: tel. 220-3054 or 232-7883) flies to Carillo daily at 9:30am from San Jose's Pavas International Airport. The flight makes one stop en route. Duration: 55 minutes. Fare: $58 one way, $100 round-trip.

By Bus An express bus leaves San José daily at noon from Calle 14 between avenidas 3 and 5. Duration: 6 hours. Fare: $5.55.

Alternatively, you can take a bus from this same San José station to Nicoya and then catch a second bus from Nicoya to Sámara. Buses leave San José for Nicoya daily at 6, 8, and 10am, noon, and 1, 2:30, 3, and 5pm. Duration: 6 hours. Fare: $4.85.

Buses leave Nicoya for Sámara and Carillo Monday through Friday at 3pm and Saturday and Sunday at 8am. Duration: 2 hours. Fare: $1.65 (Sámara) and $2.20 (Carillo).

By Car Follow the directions for Playa Junquillal above, but in Nicoya, follow the signs south on a road that is paved for a few kilometers but then turns into an unpaved road under construction (or destruction as it often seems to be).

DEPARTING The express bus to San José leaves daily at 4am. Buses for Nicoya leave Monday through Friday at 6am and Saturday and Sunday at 2pm. Buses leave Nicoya for San José daily at 4, 7:30, and 9am, noon, and 2:30 and 4pm.

ESSENTIALS Sámara is a busy little town at the bottom of a steep hill. The main road heads straight into town, passing the soccer field before coming to an end at the beach. Just on the edge of town is a road to the left that leads to several of the more expensive hotels listed below. This road also leads to Playa Carillo and the Guanamar Resort.

Playa Sámara is a pretty beach on a horseshoe-shaped bay. Because the village of Sámara is fairly easily accessible by bus or car, and because there are several cheap cabina places, sodas, and discos here, this beach is popular with Tico families out for a little weekend beach partying. In the wake of this partying, the beach can get trashed. However, the calm waters of this bay are perfect for swimming because the rocks across the mouth of the bay break the waves. A small, rocky island and steep cliffs on the far side of the bay make this a very attractive spot, and the beach is long and wide. Directly behind the main beach is a wide, flat valley that stretches inland and to the north.

WHAT TO SEE & DO

The main activities here in Playa Sámara seem to be hanging out in the sodas and dancing into the early morning hours. One disco here even has rooms right off the dance floor—or is it a hotel that has a disco right outside the guest-room doors? Whichever it is, no one there goes to sleep until the disco shuts down.

You'll find that the beach is nicer and cleaner down at the south end near Las Brisas del Pacifico hotel. For fewer crowds, head south to Playa Carillo, a long, flat beach about 15 minutes from Sámara.

Spelunkers may want to head 62 kilometers northeast of Playa Sámara on the road to the Tempisque ferry. Here, at Barra Honda National Park, there is an extensive system of caves.

WHERE TO STAY & DINE

EXPENSIVE

VILLAS PLAYA SÁMARA, Playa Sámara (200 meters north of Centro Colón, Avenida 5 and Calle 38, San José), Guanacaste. Tel. 506/233-0223 or 223-7587. Fax 506/221-7222. 35 rms. SAFE
$ Rates: $75 single; $95 double; $145 quad. AE, MC, V.

Located 5 minutes south of town, this is the newest luxury hotel in Sámara and consequently the gardens are a bit sparse. However, other than that, this beachfront resort is a great place. Built to resemble a village, the resort consists of numerous bungalows varying in size from one to three bedrooms. Attractive though not overly luxurious, the so-called villas are outfitted with bamboo furniture, and there are tiled baths (hot water is provided by rather noisy water heaters). All the villas also have kitchens and patios, and some of the nice touches include colorful bedspreads and artwork, basket lampshades, and vertical blinds on the windows. White stucco exterior walls and red-tile roofs give the villas a Mediterranean look.

Dining/Entertainment: The open-air restaurant overlooks the pool and serves good seafood. There is also a casino above the restaurant.

Services: Horse, bicycle, and moped rentals.

Facilities: The swimming pool here is beautiful at night and has a swim-up bar and adjacent cold-water whirlpool tub. Other facilities include tennis, volleyball, and badminton courts.

MODERATE

HOTEL LAS BRISAS DEL PACÍFICO, Playa Sámara (Apdo. 129-6100, Ciudad Colón), Guanacaste. Tel. 506/680-0876 or (in San José) 233-9840. Fax 506/680-0876 or (in San José) 233-9840. 27 rms.
$ Rates: Dec–Apr, $45–$80 single or double; $60–$95 triple. AE, MC, V.

Located on the same road as the Marbella, this hotel is set amid very shady grounds right on the beach and backs up to a steep hill. Most of the rooms are up a long and steep flight of stairs at the top of the hill. However, in exchange for climbing the stairs, you do get an excellent view of the bay. These hilltop rooms have large balconies and walls of glass that take in the views. However, they also can get very hot and stuffy if you don't opt for an air-conditioned room. At the base of the hill, there are rooms in stucco duplexes with steeply pitched tile roofs and red-tile patios. These rooms have cold-water showers only, but it's never cool enough here to warrant hot showers. Only a few steps from the beach, there is a small pool with a cold-water whirlpool. There is also a second pool and restaurant at the top of the hill. The main dining room is a breezy open-air restaurant surrounded by lush garden plantings. The menu changes daily but entrée prices range from $6.50 to $8.50. The management here is German as are many of the guests.

HOTEL MARBELLA, Playa Sámara, (Edificio Cristal, Avenida 1a, San José), Guanacaste. Tel. and Fax 506/233-9980. 14 rms, 6 apts.

$ Rates: Nov–Mar, $35 single, $42–$45 double, $50 triple, $60 apt; Apr–Oct, $18 single, $28 double, $35 triple, $50 apt. AE, MC, V.

Though it is a bit of a walk to the beach and the immediate surroundings are none too appealing, this small German-run hotel is properly tropical in decor. You'll find the Marbella just around the corner from the road that leads down to the soccer fields and the beach. Guest rooms are fairly large, and have red-tile floors and woven mats for ceilings. There are open closets and modern bathrooms with hot water. The apartments are a good choice for families or long-term stays. There's a small swimming pool in a gravel courtyard and a second-floor dining room with rattan chairs and a bamboo-fronted bar. All the rooms have a balcony or porch, though not necessarily any sort of a view. The dining-room menu focuses on seafood and changes daily. Prices are in the $6-to-$15 range. You'll also find a bar and snack bar here.

BUDGET

CABINAS BELVEDERE, Playa Sámara (George Salina Cortes, Galleria Musical, Second Level, San José), Guanacaste. No phone. 2 rms, 3 chalets (all with private bath).

$ Rates (including continental breakfast): $20.30 single; $27.05 double. No credit cards.

These tropical Swiss chalets are arranged on the hillside across the street from the Hotel Marbella on the inland edge of town.

The two rooms are rather small and are in the main house, adjacent to the hotel's restaurant, which has a good view of the Pacific. However, I like the miniature, thatched-roof chalets, which have porches and more space. I guess these were inspired by the Swiss Family Robinson.

NEARBY PLACES TO STAY & DINE

GUANAMAR BEACH & SPORTFISHING RESORT, Puerto Carillo, Guanacaste (Apdo. 7-1880-1000, San José; or in the U.S: Costa Sol International, 1717 North Bayshore Dr., Suite 3333, Miami, FL 33132). Tel. 506/239-2000 or toll free (in the U.S.) 800/245-8420. Fax 506/239-4839 or (in the U.S.) 305/539-1123. 42 rms. A/C TV TEL

$ Rates: $110–$120 single or double. MC, V.

About 15 minutes south of Sámara you'll find the Guanamar resort, which is set on a hillside above long, flat Playa Carillo. The location provides some spectacular views, but it is a long walk down to the beach and a hot walk back up. However, you can spend your time on the extensive hardwood decks that surround the hotel's pool. These decks give the resort's main public areas the feel of a huge treehouse. For many years this was a private sportfishing resort, and fishing for marlin and sailfish is still one of the main attractions of Guanamar. Guest rooms are spacious though not overly attractive. However, the views from the decks and patios make up for any lack in the interior decor. Try to get one of the newer bungalow rooms.

Dining/Entertainment: The dining room is housed in a large rancho at one end of the deck that passes by the swimming pool. At the other end of the deck is a second rancho that houses another bar area. In the dining room, there are trunks of palm trees growing up through the wooden floor. The menu includes international dishes, including some Japanese dishes, with prices ranging from $6.10 to $8.10 for entrées.

Services: Room service, tour arrangements, fishing-boat charters, and boat tours. Bicycle, boogie-board, horse, snorkeling-equipment, and water-ski rentals.

Facilities: The swimming pool is built up and out from the hillside and is surrounded by an attractive hardwood deck. There is also a gift shop.

WHERE TO DINE

There are numerous inexpensive sodas in Sámara, and most of the hotels have their own dining rooms. My favorite place to eat is the dining room at Las Brisas. In town, try the following:

COLOCHOS BAR, on the main street through town. Tel. 680-0445.
 Cuisine: COSTA RICAN/INTERNATIONAL. **Reservations:** Not accepted.
$ Prices: Appetizers $2.05–$3.40; main courses $3.40–$16.90. No credit cards.
 Open: Daily 11am–10pm.

This open-air rancho restaurant on the main road into town offers a great selection of seafoods. There are four different types of ceviche, lobster dishes, paella, and plenty of shrimp plates. Prices are very reasonable and portions are large. Though there's a thatch roof over your head, you'll find lace doilies on the tables.

8. PLAYA NOSARA

55 kilometers SW of Nicoya; 266 kilometers W of San José

GETTING THERE By Air Sansa (in San José: tel. 233-0397, 233-3258, or 233-5330) flies to Nosara daily at 9:30am from San José's Juan Santamaría International Airport. The flight makes one stop en route. Duration: 1 hour and 10 minutes. Fare: $46 each way.

Travelair (in San José: tel. 220-3054 or 232-7883) flies to Nosara daily at 9:30am from San José's Pavas International Airport. The flight makes two stops en route. Duration: 1 hour and 15 minutes. Fare: $58 one way, $100 round-trip.

By Bus An express bus leaves San José daily at 6:15am from Calle 14 between avenidas 3 and 5. Duration: 7 hours. Fare: $6.90.

Alternatively, you can take a bus from San José to Nicoya (see above under "Playa Sámara" for details), and then catch a second bus from Icoya to Nosara. A bus leaves Nicoya for Nosara daily at 1pm. Duration: 2 hours. Fare: $1.80.

By Car Follow the directions above for getting to Playa Sámara, but watch for a fork in the road a few kilometers before you reach that beach. The right-hand fork leads, in another 22 kilometers, to Nosara.

DEPARTING The bus to San José leaves daily at 1pm. The bus to Nicoya leaves daily at 6am. Buses leave Nicoya for San José daily at 4, 7:30, and 9am, noon, and 2:30 and 4pm.

ESSENTIALS The village of Nosara is about 5 kilometers inland from the beach, while most of the hotels listed here are on the beach itself. If you need a taxi, phone 680-0857.

Playa Nosara is actually several beaches, almost all of which are nearly deserted most of the time. Because the village of Nosara is several kilometers from the beach, and because the land near the beach has been turned into a large, spread-out resort community, Nosara has been spared the sort of ugly, uncontrolled growth characteristic of Sámara. All of the hotels are spread out and most are tucked away down side roads. There is not the hotels-on-top-of-hotels feeling that you get at Playa Flamingo. In fact, on first arriving here, it's hard to believe there are any hotels around at all. Nosara has long been popular with North American retirees, and they too have made sure that their homes are not crammed check-by-jowl in one spot. Their houses are hidden amongst all the trees that make Nosara one of the greenest spots on the Nicoya Peninsula. So, if you are looking for reliably sunny weather and a bit of tropical greenery, this is a good bet.

The best way to get to Nosara is to fly, and with only a few flights a week, you had better plan to stay put for awhile, which of course should go without saying anyway. The roads out here are in horrendous shape, and though some sections are in the process of being widened and paved, it will probably still be quite a few years before the blacktop reaches Playa Nosara.

WHAT TO SEE & DO

There are several beaches at Nosara, including the long, curving Playa Guiones, Playa Nosara, and, my personal favorite, diminutive Playa Pelada. This latter is a short, white-sand beach lined with sea grasses and mangroves. However, there isn't too much sand at high tide, so you'll want to hit the beach when the tide's out. At either end of the beach there are rocky outcroppings that contain tide pools at low tide. Surfing and bodysurfing are both good here. Because the village of Nosara is several miles inland, these beaches are very clean, secluded, and quiet.

Most of the hotels in the area can arrange fishing charters for around $250 for a half day or $400 for a full day. These rates are for one to four people. You can also contact **Pesca Bahia Garza** (tel. 680-0856) and arrange a half-day or full-day's fishing trip.

For about the same price, you can also do a night tour to nearby Playa Ostional to watch nesting olive Ridley sea turtles. These turtles come ashore by the thousands in a mass egg-laying phenomenon known as an arribada. These arribadas take place 4 to 10 times between July and November, with each arribada lasting between 3 and 10 days. Consider yourself very lucky if you should happen to be around during one of these fascinating natural phenomena. Even if it is not turtle-nesting season, you may want to look into going up to Playa Ostional. During the dry season, you can usually get there in a regular car, but during the rainy season, you'll need four-wheel-drive. This beach is part of Ostional National Wildlife Refuge. At the northwest end of the refuge is India Point, which is known for its tidepools and rocky outcrops.

Bird-watchers should get in touch with Estrella del Pacifico hotel, which offers a three-hour bird-watching trip to the mangrove swamps of the Río Nosara. The cost is $23.65 per person. It is also possible to arrange hiking and horseback-riding trips at the Rancho Suizo Lodge.

WHERE TO STAY

EXPENSIVE

CONDOMINIO DE LAS FLORES, Playa Nosara (Apdo. 3-5233, Nosara), Guanacaste. Tel. 506/680-0696. 13 condos.
$ Rates: $80 per day; $500 per week; $1,500 per month. No credit cards.
These older condominiums were some of the first accommodations in Nosara and are still the largest and most comfortable. They're located right across the road from pretty little Playa Pelada and Doña Olga's, which is a popular open-air restaurant and bar. Each of the condos has two bedrooms, two bathrooms, and a complete kitchen, so they're ideal for a family or two couples planning to stay for a while. There are ocean views from most rooms, and all the condos have large balconies.

MODERATE

ESTANCIA NOSARA, Playa Nosara (Apdo. 37, Bocas de Nosara), Guanacaste. Tel. and Fax 506/680-0378. 10 rms.
$ Rates: $40 single; $46 double; $54 triple; $62 quad. MC, V.
Although this hotel is a mile or so from the beach, it's set amid shady jungle trees and has a swimming pool and tennis court, which together make Estancia Nosara a good value. There's a manmade waterfall tumbling from a small hill of stones near the pool (though it wasn't operating last time I visited) and reproductions of pre-Columbian stone statues in the lush garden. The guest rooms

are in two buildings and have red-tile floors, kitchenettes, high ceilings, overhead fans, showers with hot water, and plenty of closet space, so you can move in for a long stay if you're so inclined. There's a large open-air restaurant serving moderately priced meals. Use of the tennis court will cost $5 an hour, and horses ($8 per hour) and bikes ($7 per day) can also be rented. A full day of fishing arranged through the hotel will cost $400 for the boat, which can take up to four people.

ESTRELLA DEL PACÍFICO, Playa Nosara (Apdo. 68-5233, Bocas de Nosara), Guanaaste. Tel. 506/680-0763. Fax 506/680-0856. 12 rms, 6 bungalows. A/C
$ Rates: $55–$65 single; $65–$85 double; $75–$95 triple.
This is one of the newer hotels in the area, and the gardens still have a few years to go before they fill in the bare spots left over from construction. There isn't much shade either, so bring plenty of sunscreen. The room decor is very simple, but quite attractive. There are white tile floors, high ceilings, overhead fans, and well-designed bathrooms. The least expensive rooms are those without air-conditioning. The dining room, with its wood ceiling and arched windows overlooking the pool, serves moderately priced meals. The swimming pool itself has a swim-up bar. There is also a tennis court here, and you can rent body boards, surfboards, tennis rackets, and snorkeling gear. Best of all, the beach is only 100 yards away.

HOTEL PLAYAS DE NOSARA, Playa Nosara (Apdo. 4, Bocas de Nosara), Guanacaste. Tel. 506/680-0495. 16 rms.
$ Rates: $50–$60 single; $65–$75 double. No credit cards.
Perched high on a hill above both Playa Pelada and Playa Guiones, this older hotel has the best views in the area, if not necessarily the best accommodations. The rooms that overlook the long sweep of sand known as Playa Guiones all have balconies so you can take in the great view. The rooms, which are rather basic, are in white buildings accented with blue, which gives them a slightly Greek appeal. There are high ceilings and jalousie windows, so the rooms catch the breezes and stay fairly cool. The gardens, though fairly lush, seem untended. It's a bit of a walk down to the beach, and all in all, prices here seem a bit high.

RANCHO SUIZO LODGE, Playa Nosara (Apdo. 14, Bocas de Nosara), Guanacaste 5233. Tel. 506/255-0011. Fax 506/255-2155. 10 rms.
$ Rates: Nov–Apr, $29 single, $40 double; May–Oct, $25 single, $30 double. No credit cards.
Though this pleasant little lodge is not located right on the beach, the waves are just a 5-minute walk down a trail. The guest rooms, which are fairly small, are in several little cabins across a footbridge from the parking area. However, despite the size, the rooms are comfortable and have double beds, bamboo furniture, porches, and big windows. Bathrooms have tiled showers with cold water only. The owner's aviaries, full of exotic birds, are between the thatched-roof dining room and the bungalows, so on your way to meals, you can talk to the birds. Only breakfast and dinner are served in the restaurant, with prices ranging from $2.50 to $3 for breakfast and around $6 to $8 for dinner. Various tours can be arranged through the hotel, and bikes ($10 per day), horses ($10 per hour), and fishing boats ($250 per half day) can all be hired. Peace and quiet are the main offerings of this hotel, and most of the people who stay here are as interested in nature as they are in getting a tan.

BUDGET

CABINAS CHOROTEGA, Nosara, Guanacaste. Tel. 506/680-0836. 10 rms (4 with private bath).
$ Rates: $6.80 single; $13.55 double. No credit cards.
Located on the outskirts of Nosara village, Cabinas Chorotega is about 5 kilometers from the beach, so you'll need to have some sort of transportation if you stay here and want to go the beach. The rooms are very basic but clean, and the rooms with private baths are a particularly good value. Some rooms have more windows and are quite a bit brighter than others, so look at a couple of rooms if you can.

A NEARBY PLACE TO STAY & DINE

VILLAGGIO LA GUARIA MORADA, Playa Garza (Apdo. 860-1007, Centro Colón, San José), Guanacaste. Tel. 506/680-0784 or (in San José) 233-2476. Fax 506/222-4073. 30 bungalows, SAFE

$ Rates: $108 single, double, or triple. MC, V.

This is the most expensive and luxurious hotel in this part of the peninsula and cultivates an exclusive, clublike ambience. Though the landscape all around is cattle pastures, once you pass through the guarded gate, you enter a tropical fantasy compound. A huge, three-story thatched-roof building serves as resaurant, bar, and casino, and surrounding this impressive building are the smaller thatched-roof bungalows. The overall impression is of a tropical Indian village. Directly in front of the resort is a ³/₄-mile curving beach, and a short walk away is a smaller beach of pink sand. Unfortunately, service at Villaggio tends to be cold and rather formal, not what you would expect at a beach resort. Also, for some reason, the entire resort smelled of mothballs when I last visited.

The guest rooms, in either individual or duplex bungalows, are simple, yet comfortable. The louvered walls open up to connect the patio with the bedroom, creating a single large living area. There are interesting bamboo ceilings and overhead fans, and in the bathroom you'll find hot water provided by showerhead heaters. The overall effect is of a tropical-Mediterranean fusion.

Dining/Entertainment: Because the hotel is Italian owned, the menu is heavy on Italian dishes, and these are some of the best meals to be had here. Prices range from $6.25 to $21.65 for entrées. In the same building, you'll find a very comfortable bar and a small open-air casino. Right on the edge of the beach, there is a small, open-air disco as well.

Services: Horse rentals, fishing charters, water-ski rentals, tour arrangements.

Facilities: The swimming pool, made with small blue tiles, is quite lovely. There are also some palapas for shade, and a gift shop.

WHERE TO DINE

DOÑA OLGA'S, on the beach at Playa Pelada. No phone.
   Cuisine: COSTA RICAN. **Reservations:** Not accepted.
$ Prices: Main courses $1.70–$16.90. No credit cards.
   Open: Daily 6:30am–10pm.

Little more than a roof with some tables under it, Olga's is still the most popular restaurant in Nosara. Gringos and Ticos alike hang out here savoring fried fish casados, sandwiches, and breakfasts that include huge plates of bacon. On the weekends the cavernous structure beside the restaurant becomes a lively disco.

---

9. PLAYA TAMBOR

150–168 kilometers W of San José (not including ferry ride);
20 kilometers S of Paquera; 38 kilometers S of Naranjo

GETTING THERE   By Air   Travelair (in San José: tel. 220-3054 or 232-7883) flies to Tambor daily at 9:30am from San José's Pavas Airport. Duration: 25 minutes. Fare: $45 one way, $80 round-trip.

By Bus and Ferry   If you are traveling from San José by public transportation, it will take you two buses and a ferry ride to get to Tambor. This can require spending a night in Puntarenas, so don't plan on heading out this way unless you have plenty of time.

Buses leave San José for Puntarenas daily every 30 minutes between 5am and 7pm from the corner of Calle 12 and Avenida 9. Duration: 2 hours. Fare: $2.60.

From Puntarenas take the *lancha* (tel. 661-2830), which leaves from the pier behind the market at 6am and 3pm (also at 11am on Monday and Friday). This passenger launch should not be confused with the two car ferries that also leave from Puntarenas, and you should always check the schedule before making plans. Duration: 1½ hours. Fare: $1.70.

The bus south to Tambor will be waiting to meet the lancha when it arrives in Paquera. Duration: 1½ hours. Fare: $2.85.

By Car Take the Interamerican highway from San José to Puntarenas and catch either the Naranjo ferry or the Paquera ferry.

The Naranjo ferry leaves daily at 4, 7, and 10:30am and 1:30 and 4pm. Duration: 1½ hours. Fare: $8.80 for cars, $1.25 for adults, and 70¢ for children.

The Naviera Tambor ferry to Paquera leaves daily at 7:45 and 11:30am and 3:15 pm. Duration: 1½ hours. Fare: $11.50 for a car; $2.05 for adults, $4.75 for adults in first class; $1.05 for children, $2.70 for children in first class.

Tambor is about an hour south of Paquera and 2½ hours south of Naranjo. These roads are almost all gravel and are in very bad shape. Be prepared for some rough riding.

DEPARTING The Paquera bus, which originates in Montezuma, passes through Tambor around 6:15am and 2:45pm (also at 10:45am on Monday and Friday) and meets the Paquera ferry, which leaves for Puntarenas at 8am and 5pm (also at 1pm Monday and Friday). Total duration: 3½ hours. Total fare: $3.95.

The car ferry from Paquera leaves at 9:45am and 1:30 and 5:15pm. The car ferry from Naranjo leaves at 5:15 and 8:30am, noon, and 3 and 6pm.

ESSENTIALS Though there is a small village of Tambor, through which the main road passes, the hotels themselves are scattered along several kilometers. You'll see signs for these hotels as the road circles around Playa Tambor.

Once a sleepy fishing village, Tambor became, in 1993, the site of Costa Rica's first all-inclusive beach resort. Though the Playa Tambor Resort currently has only 440 rooms, there are plans to build more hotels as part of this mega-development. Needless to say, these developments are forever changing the face of this quiet, protected bay. Playa Tambor is a long scimitar of beach protected on either end by rocky headlands. These headlands give the waters a certain amount of protection from Pacific swells, making this a good beach for swimming. Unfortunately, if you aren't staying at the Playa Tambor Beach Resort, there is almost no access to the beach.

WHAT TO SEE & DO

Playa Tambor Beach Resort is an all-inclusive, full-service resort, so if you are staying here, you'll have access to all manner of beach toys. If you're staying at Hotel Tango Mar, you won't have access to so many toys, but you will have the Nicoya Peninsula's only golf course on the premises. Both Playa Tambor Beach Resort and Hotel Tango Mar offer tours around this part of the peninsula. Both hotels also offer horseback riding. Playa Tambor Beach Resort also has the **Tropic World Diving Station** (tel. 661-1915 or 661-2039) dive shop that offers open-water courses ($300) and dive trips ($60 for a two-tank dive).

Curú National Wildlife Refuge, 16 kilometers north of Tambor has several pretty, secluded beaches, as well as forests and mangrove swamps. White-faced monkeys are often spotted here, as are quite a few species of birds.

WHERE TO STAY

HOTEL TANGO MAR, Tambor, Puntarenas (Apdo. 3877-1000, San José).
Tel. 506/223-1864 or 223-3429. Fax 506/255-2697. 18 rms, 4 villas. TV
$ Rates: Dec–Apr, $120 single, $131 double, $142 triple, $179–$263 villa; May–Nov

(including continental breakfast), $60.50 single, $69 double, $81.50 triple, $179–$263 villa. AE, MC, V.

Before Tambor was built, Tango Mar was the luxury resort in this neck of the woods. Today it's still a great place to get away from it all. With only 18 rooms, there are never any crowds. The water is wonderfully clear and the beach is fronted by coconut palms and luxuriant lawns. If you choose to go exploring, you'll find seaside cliffs and even a waterfall that pours into a tide pool. The guest rooms vary from rustic cabins on stilts to spacious and modern beachfront rooms with big balconies and walls of glass to soak up the ocean views. Some rooms even have their own whirlpool tubs. The villas are all different, but all are spacious and relatively secluded yet close to the restaurant.

Dining/Entertainment: The small open-air restaurant overlooks the beach and has plenty of patio space. The varied menu includes plenty of fish with prices ranging from $5.40 to $18.95 for entrées. There is also an adjacent bar.

Services: Guided horseback rides ($25 to $35), boat and snorkeling tours ($30 to $35), guided hikes ($39), fishing charters ($185 to $485 for a half day, $775 for a full day for up to six people). Limited room service, golf club and bike rentals, massages.

Facilities: The swimming pool, though small, is set in a lush, secluded garden that is reached by way of a sidewalk across a frog pond. Tango Mar's 10-hole golf course is the only golf course on the Nicoya Peninsula ($25 greens fee). There are also tennis courts.

PLAYA TAMBOR BEACH RESORT, Bahia Ballena, Puntarenas (in the U.S.: Barceló Award Hotels, 150 SE Second Ave., Miami, FL 33131). Tel. 506/661-1915, or (in the U.S.) 305/539-1167, or toll free 800/858-0606. Fax 506/661-2069 or (in the U.S.) 305/539-1160. 402 rms. A/C TV TEL SAFE

$ Rates (all inclusive): Nov–Apr, $120 per person per day; May–Oct, $85 per person per day. AE, MC, V.

The all-inclusive beach resort has become the norm in much of the Caribbean, but this is Costa Rica's first (and at this time only) such resort. The Playa Tambor development has been surrounded by controversy since its inception, and charges of violating Costa Rica's environmental laws were leveled against the Spanish developers. Further controversy has surrounded the planned size for this development, which may eventually include thousands of hotel rooms. Questions of where the water will come from, and how sewage from this new tourist city will be treated have yet to be answered.

However, when you pass through the guarded gate of this resort, you would never know there was the slightest whiff of controversy surrounding it. A huge complex of open-air buildings form the lobby, theater, restaurants, and bars. Hundreds of happy vacationers soak up the sun, splash in the pool and the waves, and quietly form lines for their buffet meals. The guest rooms are housed in attractively designed buildings that are reminiscent of banana plantation houses. However, the rooms themselves are built to international standards, and though they have not even a hint of Costa Rican character, they are quite comfortable.

Dining/Entertainment: The cost of all your meals and bar drinks is included in the room rates here, and when it comes time to eat, you can choose from a buffet at El Tucán, à la carte meals at El Rancho, or fast food from the poolside El Palenque. There are also a couple of different bars, a disco, and a large theater that stages folklórico performances.

Services: Tours, including cruises, sportfishing, sunset sailboat excursions, and scuba trips, can be arranged at additional cost. Sports equipment available for use by guests free of charge includes sailboards, sea kayaks, snorkeling gear, small sailboats (Hobie Cats and Sunfish), and boogie boards. Table tennis, croquet, and badminton are also available.

Facilities: The beautiful pool, one of the largest in the country, is surrounded by hundreds of lounge chairs, and has a swim-up bar. Other facilities include lighted tennis courts, a basketball court, an outdoor exercise facility, and whirlpool tub.

WHERE TO DINE

BAHIA BALLENA, Playa Tambor. No phone.
  Cuisine: AMERICAN. **Reservations:** Not accepted.
$ **Prices:** Appetizers $2.20–$4.95; main courses $6.55–$9.80. No credit cards.
  Open: Tues–Sun 10am–10pm.
This big, open place stands beside an aging pier at the south end of Playa Tambor and is adjacent to the Bahia Ballena Yacht Club. The menu features American dishes with an emphasis on old New Orleans favorites. You can get po-boys, shrimp creole, blackened fish, or fish served any of three other ways. Meals all come with a salad, veggies, and potatoes.

EN ROUTE TO TAMBOR & MONTEZUMA

OASIS DEL PACÍFICO, Playa Naranjo (Apdo. 200-5400), Puntarenas (in the U.S.: P.L. Wilhelm 1552, P.O. Box 025216, Miami, FL 33102-5216). Tel. and Fax 506/661-1555. 36 rms.
$ **Rates:** Nov–Apr, $39.40 single, $51.60 double, $70 triple; May–Oct, $26.25 single, $39.35 double, $48.10 triple. AE, MC, V.
Located just 3 minutes from the Playa Naranjo ferry dock, this casual little resort is a family-run operation that provides a quiet place to relax in the sun. Though the beach here isn't very good for swimming, there is a good-size pool. You'll also find a kiddie pool, a play area, and plenty of lawn for the kids to play on if you should bring the family. The friendly owners will make sure you feel right at home and introduce you to their various pets—dogs, macaws, and a deer. The guest rooms have tile floors and high ceilings, and vary considerably in size. Along the tiled veranda there are hammocks just waiting for some serious relaxing. You can also try your hand at fishing from the resort's private pier. Meals in the resort's dining room often include exotic dishes prepared by the Singaporean owner. Horseback riding and fishing trips can be arranged. The greatest attraction of this place is that it is very convenient, yet feels remote.

---

10. PLAYA MONTEZUMA

166–184 kilometers W of San José (not including the ferry ride);
36 kilometers SE of Paquera; 54 kilometers S of Naranjo

GETTING THERE **By Bus and Ferry** If you are traveling from San José by public transportation, it will take you two buses and a ferry ride to get to Montezuma. This can require spending a night in Puntarenas, so don't plan on heading out this way unless you have plenty of time.
  Buses leave San José for Puntarenas daily every 30 minutes between 5am and 7pm from the corner of Calle 12 and Avenida 9. Duration: 2 hours. Fare: $2.60.
  From Puntarenas take the lancha (tel. 661-2830), which leaves from the pier behind the market at 6am and 3pm (also at 11am on Monday and Friday). This passenger launch should not be confused with the two car ferries that also leave from Puntarenas, and you should always check the schedule before making plans. Duration: 1½ hours. Fare: $1.70.
  The bus south to Montezuma will be waiting to meet the lancha when it arrives in Paquera. Duration: 1½ hours. Fare: $2.85.
  By Car Take the Interamerican Highway from San José to Puntarenas and catch either the Naranjo ferry or the Paquera ferry, which is operated by the Barceló Company and has been surrounded with controversy since it began operating. You'll probably have to arrive the night before and put your car in line to assure a space on a ferry the next morning.

The Naranjo ferry leaves daily at 4, 7, and 10:30am and 1:30 and 4pm. Duration 1½ hours. Fare $8.80 for cars, $1.25 for adults, and 70¢ for children. The Naviera Tambor ferry to Paquera leaves daily at 7:45 and 11:30am and 3:15pm. Duration: 1½ hours. Fare: $11.50 for cars; $2.05 for adults, $4.75 for adults in first class; $1.05 for children, $2.70 for children in first class.

Montezuma is about 3 hours south of Naranjo and 1½ hours south of Paquera. These roads are mostly gravel, with a few short paved sections. Be prepared for some rough riding.

DEPARTING The Paquera bus leaves at 5:30am and 2pm (also at 10am on Monday and Friday) and meets the Paquera ferry, which leaves for Puntarenas at 8am and 5pm (also at 1pm Monday and Friday). Total duration: 3½ hours. Total fare: $4.55.

The car ferry from Paquera leaves at 9:45am and 1:30 and 5:15pm. The car ferry from Naranjo leaves at 5:15 and 8:30am, noon, and 3 and 6pm.

ESSENTIALS There is a tour and a tourist information desk in a little kiosk in the center of the village. The bus stops at the end of the road into the village. From here, hotels are scattered up and down the beach and around the village's few sand streets. Motorcycles can be rented in the center of town for $40 per day (plus a $500 deposit).

Before I came to Montezuma, I had heard different opinions about this beach at the southern tip of the Nicoya Peninsula. Some people, mostly European budget travelers, thought it was the best beach in Central America. Other people, those who prefer a few more amenities, thought it would be a great beach in a few years when it had some decent accommodations and restaurants. After spending some time here myself, I have to agree with all of them. Montezuma has its charms and its drawbacks, not least of which is a problem with untreated sewage flowing onto the village's main beach from some of the establishments in the village. Unfortunately, Montezuma has gained popularity far faster than local restaurants and hotels can cope with the growing sanitary needs. This problem is further aggravated by the large numbers of people who camp on the beach. There is a severe shortage of rooms here, despite the fact that people seem to be building hotels as fast as they can. If you don't show up with reservations, you better have a tent or a hammock. And even if you do manage to get a room in the village, don't expect to go to sleep early; a disco and a bar, side by side, blast their respective music for hours on end. Head out of town if peace and tranquility are what you're seeking.

On the other hand, the water here is a gorgeous royal blue, though the waves can occasionally be too rough for casual swimming and you need to be aware of stray rocks at your feet. Be sure you know where the rocks are before doing any bodysurfing. In either direction from Montezuma is a string of sandy coves separated by outcroppings of volcanic rock that form tide pools.

WHAT TO SEE & DO

Mostly you just hang out on the beach, hang out in a restaurant, hang out in a bar, or hang out in front of the disco. However, if you're interested in more than just hanging out, head for the waterfall just south of town. This waterfall is one of those tropical fantasies where water comes pouring down into a deep pool. It's a popular spot, but it's a bit of a hike up the stream. There are actually a couple of waterfalls up this stream, but the upper falls are by far the more spectacular. You'll find the trail to the falls just over the bridge south of the village (near Las Cascadas restaurant).

Several people around the village rent horses for around $5 an hour, though most people choose to do a 4-hour **horseback tour** for $20 to $25. These latter rides usually go to a waterfall 8 kilometers north of Montezuma. This waterfall cascades straight down into the ocean. You can also ride a horse to Cabo Blanco. Luis, whose rental place is down the road that leads out of town to the left, is a reliable source for horses, as are Armando, Ana, and José, all of whom can be contacted through El Sano Banano. In the center of the village, there is a rental center where you can rent a bicycle for $8.15 per day. This center also rents boogie boards for $4.75 per day and bicycles for $1.70 per hour.

As beautiful as the beaches around Montezuma are, the beaches at **Cabo Blanco Nature Reserve,** 11 kilometers south of the village, are, in many peoples' opinions, even more beautiful. Located at the southernmost tip of the Nicoya Peninsula, Cabo Blanco preserves a nesting site for brown pelicans, magnificent frigate birds, and brown boobies. The beaches are backed by lush tropical forest that is home to howler monkeys that are often seen (and heard!). You can hike through the preserve's lush forest right down to the deserted, pristine beach. There are usually shared taxis heading out this way in the morning. The fare is $5 per person.

If you'd like to get out on the water and visit yet another beautiful beach, ask at the information center about boat trips to **Tortuga Island.** These tours last 5 hours and cost $23.65, which is a considerable savings over similar trips offered by companies in San José, although the trips out of San José include a gourmet lunch that isn't a part of trips from Montezuma.

WHERE TO STAY

MODERATE

AMOR DE MAR, Montezuma, Cóbano de Puntarenas. Tel. 506/661-1122, ext. 262. 12 rms (8 with private bath), 1 cabin.
$ Rates: $25 single or double with shared bath; $35–$45 single or double with private bath; $50 single or double in cabin. No credit cards.

It would be difficult to imagine a more idyllic spot in this price range. With its wide expanse of neatly trimmed grass sloping down to the sea, tide pools (one of which is as big as a small swimming pool), and hammocks slung from the mango trees, this is the perfect place for anyone who wants to do some serious relaxing. The owners, who have young children, love to have other families as guests and there's always a cheerful family atmosphere. However, couples and individuals will also enjoy a stay at Amor de Mar simply for the stunning location and beautiful hotel building, which abounds in varnished hardwoods. The big porch on the second floor of the main building makes a great place to sit and read or to just gaze out to sea. Only breakfast is served here, with the specialty being homemade whole-wheat French bread.

LOS MANGOS, Montezuma, Cóbano de Puntarenas. Tel. 506/661-1122, ext. 259. 10 rms (6 with private bath), 10 bungalows.
$ Rates: Dec–Mar, $25 single, double, or triple without bath; $35 single, double, or triple with bath; $50 single, double, or triple bungalow. Apr–Nov, rates are slightly lower. V.

This is the first hotel in Montezuma to have its own swimming pool. The hotel is across the road from the water south of town near Amor de Mar and takes its name from the many mango trees under which the bungalows are built (May is mango season). The rooms are fairly basic and, in an older building close to the road, are a good value. However, it is the octagonal bungalows built of Costa Rican hardwoods that are the most attractive accommodations. Each bungalow has a small porch with rocking chairs, a thatch roof, a good amount of space, and ceiling fans for stirring up the air. The swimming pool is the only one I've seen in Costa Rica that is built to look like a natural pond. There's even an artificial waterfall flowing into it. Beside the pool is a large rancho-style restaurant and bar. Meal prices are quite reasonable.

EL SANO BANANO, Montezuma, Cóbano de Puntarenas. Tel. 506/661-1122, ext. 272. Fax 506/661-2320. 3 rms, 12 cabins (all with private bath).
$ Rates: Dec–Mar, $40–$50 single or double; Apr–Nov, $30–$40 single or double. AE, MC, V.

⭐ El Sano Banano is the sort of tropical retreat many budget travelers dream about. It is located about a 10-minute walk up the beach to the left as you enter the village. From the front porch of your cabin you can sit and listen to the waves crashing on the beach a few feet away. Please do not try to drive up the beach, even if you have a four-wheel-drive vehicle. Seclusion and quiet are the main offerings of this place and the cars would ruin the atmosphere. If you don't want to carry all your bags, you can leave some of your stuff at the Sano Banano restaurant in the village. There are two types of cabins here—octagonal hardwood Polynesian-style buildings and white ferroconcrete geodesic domes that look like igloos—as well as three more standard rooms in the main building. All the rooms are set amid a lush garden planted with lots of banana and elephant-ear plants, and there are big rocks scattered beneath the shady old trees. The rooms and cabins vary in age and style, so have a look at a couple if you can. Some have refrigerators and hot plates and some have sleeping lofts. One other thing you should know is that the showers, though private, are outside of the cabins in the trees. This is the tropics. Why not?

BUDGET

HOTEL LA AURORA, Montezuma, Cóbano de Puntarenas. Tel. and Fax 506/661-2320. 6 rms (3 with private bath).

$ Rates (including breakfast): Dec–Mar, $20 single or double without bath, $25 single or double with bath; Apr–Nov, $15 single or double without bath, $20 single or double with bath. No credit cards.

Just to the left as you enter the village of Montezuma, you'll see this large white house. Because the management is German, you're likely to hear that language more than English or Spanish here. However, no matter what your nationality, you'll find a safe and friendly environment here. The rooms are arranged around the spacious second-floor porch, which has a small library of books, some hammocks and comfortable chairs, and flowering vines growing up the walls. In fact there are vines all over La Aurora, which give it a tropical, yet Gothic feel. Guest rooms are of average size and have wood walls that don't go all the way to the ceiling, which improves air circulation but reduces privacy. There is also a kitchen available to guests, and lunch and dinner are served at reasonable prices.

HOTEL MOCTEZUMA, Montezuma, Cóbano de Puntarenas. Tel. 506/661-1122, ext 258. 22 rms (15 with private bath).

$ Rates: $5.10 single without bath, $9.15 single with bath; $9.50 double without bath, $15.55 double with bath. V.

Located right in the center of the village across the street from the disco, the Hotel Moctezuma offers basic but clean rooms with fans. Some of the rooms are upstairs from the hotel's noisy bar and restaurant. If you like to go to sleep early, try to get a room at the back of the hotel's building across the street instead. The walls here don't go all the way to the ceiling, which is great for air circulation but lousy for privacy.

WHERE TO DINE

In addition to the restaurants listed below, Montezuma also has a great little ice-cream stand called La Esquina Dulce. It's in front of the Mediterraneo Ristorante and serves its own homemade ice cream in tropical fruit flavors.

LAS CASADAS, on the road out of town toward Cabo Blanco. No phone.

Cuisine: COSTA RICAN/SEAFOOD. **Reservations:** Not accepted.

$ Prices: Main courses $3.40–$9.80. No credit cards.

Open: Daily 9am–9pm.

This little open-air restaurant is built on the banks of the stream just outside of the village and takes its name from the nearby waterfalls. The short menu sometimes includes fresh fish filets, whole red snapper, or shrimp in salsa ranchera. There are few more enjoyable places in Costa Rica to have a meal. You can sit for hours beneath the thatched roof listening to the stream rushing past.

MEDITERRANEO RISTORANTE, to the left of the disco. No phone.
Cuisine: ITALIAN. **Reservations:** Not accepted.
$ Prices: Main courses $5.10–$8.10. No credit cards.
Open: Daily 6–10:30pm.

If you're craving Italian food, this is the place to find it in Montezuma. The open-air restaurant is beneath an old house just back from the beach, and there are only a few tables. Arrive early if you want to be sure of getting a seat; this place is popular. The seafood spaghetti is one of the best dishes on the menu.

EL SANO BANANO, on the main road into the village. Tel. 661-1122, ext. 272.
Cuisine: VEGETARIAN. **Reservations:** Not accepted.
$ Prices: Main courses $2.30–$5.10. No credit cards.
Open: Daily 7am–10pm.

Delicious vegetarian meals including nightly specials, sandwiches, and salads are the specialty of this ever-popular Montezuma restaurant. You can even order a sandwich with cheese from the cheese factory in Monteverde. The day's menu specials are posted on a blackboard out front early in the day so you can be savoring the thought of dinner all day. Any time of day or night, the yogurt-fruit shakes are fabulous. El Sano Banano also doubles as the local movie house. They show nightly films on a large screen and have library of more than 300 movies. After the film, you can step across the street to the disco for a Montezuman night on the town.

CHAPTER 5

THE NORTHERN ZONE

The northern zone, roughly defined here as the area north of San José and between Guanacaste province on the west and the lowlands of the Caribbean coast on the east, is a naturalist's dream come true. There are rain forests and cloud forests, jungle rivers, and an unbelievable diversity of birds and other wildlife. In addition to its reputation for muddy hiking trails and crocodile-filled rivers, the northern zone also claims one of the best windsurfing spots in the world (on Lake Arenal, which is free of crocodiles by the way) and Costa Rica's most active volcanos. Arenal Volcano, when free of clouds, puts on spectacular nighttime light shows and by day is reflected in the waters of nearby Lake Arenal. Adding a touch of comfort to a visit to the northern zone are several hot springs that vary in their levels of luxury.

1. PUERTO VIEJO DE SARAPIQUÍ

82 kilometers N of San José; 102 kilometers E of La Fortuna

GETTING THERE **By Bus** Express buses leave San José daily at 6:30, 9, and 10am, noon, and 1, 3, 3:30, and 4pm from Avenida 11 between Calle Central and Calle 1. If you are heading to La Selva, Rara Avis, or El Gavilán lodges, be sure you are on a bus going though Las Horquetas. Duration: 3 hours. Fare: $3.75.

By Car The Guápiles Highway, which leads to the Caribbean coast, heads north out of downtown San José on Calle 3 before heading east. Turn north before reaching Guápiles on the road to Río Frio and continue north through Las Horquetas, passing Rara Avis, La Selva, and El Gavilán lodges, before reaching Puerto Viejo. An alternative route goes through Heredia, Barva, Varablanca, and San Miguel before reaching Puerto Viejo. This is a more scenic route, but the road is in very bad condition in certain stretches. If you want to take this route, head west out of San José and then turn north to Heredia and follow the signs for Varablanca.

DEPARTING Express buses for San José leave Puerto Viejo daily at 4:15, 6:15, 8, and 10am and 3, 3:40, and 4:15pm. Buses leave Las Horquetas for San José daily at 7 and 11:30am and at 3 and 5:15pm.

ESSENTIALS Puerto Viejo is a small town at the center of which is a soccer field. If you continue past the soccer field on the main road and stay on the paved road, you will come to the Río Sarapiquí and the dock where you can look into arranging a boat trip.

WHAT'S SPECIAL ABOUT THE NORTHERN ZONE

Natural Spectacles

Arenal Volcano, an active volcano with a large artificial lake at its base. The eruptions put on amazing nighttime light shows.

Resplendent quetzals, among the world's most beautiful birds, can be seen in the cloud forests.

Parks/Gardens

Caño Negro National Wildlife Refuge has one of Costa Rica's largest concentrations of wading birds.

Arenal Botanical Gardens are filled with tropical flowers, as well as butterflies and hummingbirds.

Monteverde Cloud Forest Reserve, one of the most famous natural areas in Costa Rica.

Activities

Soaking in the hot river at Tabacón, on the flanks of Arenal Volcano.

World-class sailboarding on Arenal Lake.

Fishing for rainbow bass in Arenal Lake.

Boat and kayak trips on the Río Sarapiquí.

The Sarapiquí region, named for the river that drains this area, lies at the foot of the Cordillera Central mountain range. To the west is the rain forest of Braulio Carillo National Park, and to the east are Tortuguero National Park and Barra del Colorado National Wildlife Refuge. In between these protected areas lie thousands of acres of banana, pineapple, and palm plantations. It is here that you can see the great contradiction of Costa Rica. On one hand the country is known for its national parks, which preserve some of the largest tracts of rain forest left in Central America, but on the other hand, nearly every acre of land outside of those parks has been clear cut and converted into plantations (and the cutting is still continuing).

Within the remaining rain forests, there are several lodges that attract naturalists (both amateur and professional) who are interested in learning more about the rain forest. Two of these lodges, La Selva and Rara Avis, have become well known around the world for the research that has been done on their surrounding reserves.

WHAT TO SEE & DO

For the adventurous, Puerto Viejo is a jumping-off point for trips down the Río Sarapiquí to Tortuguero and Barra del Colorado on the Caribbean coast. Boat trips can be arranged at the Hotel el Bambú. A boat for three people will cost you $100 to Oro Verde Lodge and back, $200 to Tortuguero, and $250 to Barra del Colorado. Alternatively, you can head down to the town dock on the bank of the Sarapiquí and see if you can arrange a less expensive boat trip on your own. A trip down the Sarapiquí, even if it's only for an hour or two, provides opportunities to spot crocodiles, caiman, monkeys, sloths, and dozens of species of birds.

Another option is to do a kayak trip down the Sarapiquí. These trips are offered by **Rancho Leona,** La Virgen de Sarapiquí, Heredia (tel. 761-1019), a small kayaking center and guest house on the banks of the Río Sarapiquí in the village of La Virgen. The trips are done as a package that includes two nights lodging (very basic dormitory accommodations) and an all-day kayak trip that includes some basic instruction and lunch on the river. The cost for the trip is $75 per person. No experience is necessary and the river is very calm. Other more extensive trips and trips for experienced kayakers can be arranged.

All of the lodges listed below arrange excursions throughout the region, including boat trips on the Sarapiquí, guided hikes in the rain forest, and horseback or mountain-bike rides.

WHERE TO STAY & DINE

HOTEL EL BAMBÚ, Apdo. 1518-2100, Puerto Viejo, Sarapiquí. Tel. 506/225-8860 or 766-6005. Fax 506/234-9387 or 766-6132. 11 rms. TV
$ Rates: $25 single; $40 double; $50 triple; $60 quad. AE, MC, V.
This is the most luxurious hotel right in Puerto Viejo and is surprisingly attractive. I still haven't figured out why such a hotel exists in this remote and untouristed town. The guest rooms and lobby are all up on the second floor of this modern building and to reach them you must first walk through the big open-air restaurant that overlooks the dense grove of bamboo from which the hotel takes its name. The rooms all have high ceilings, tile floors, and attractive bamboo furniture. You'll find the hotel directly across the street from the soccer field in the middle of town. The hotel can arrange tours around the region as well as boat trips down the Río Sarapiquí as far as Barra del Colorado and Tortuguero.

MI LINDO SARAPIQUÍ, Puerto Viejo, Sarapiquí. Tel. 506/766-6281 or 766-6074. 6 rms (all with private bath).
$ Rates: $10.70 single; $18.20 double; $21.25 triple. MC, V.
This little family-run hotel is in the center of town overlooking the soccer field. The comfortable and clean rooms are on the second floor, above the large restaurant and bar.

NEARBY PLACES TO STAY

EL GAVILÁN LODGE, Apdo. 445-2010, San José. Tel. 506/234-9507. Fax 506/253-6556. 16 rms.
$ Rates (including breakfast): $40 single; $60 double; $90 triple. MC, V.
Located on the banks of the Río Sarapiquí just south of Puerto Viejo on the road to Río Frio, El Gavilán is surrounded by 250 acres of forest reserve (secondary forest) and 25 acres of gardens planted with lots of flowering ginger. If you're interested in orchids, plan a visit in March when these beautiful flowers are in bloom. Guest rooms are simply furnished, but do have fans and hot water, and there are always fresh flowers. The rooms in the main building are fairly basic, but have huge bathrooms with two sinks. Other rooms are in rustic duplexes with cement floors. There is also a whirlpool spa out in the garden. Tico meals are served buffet style, and there are always plenty of fresh fruits and juices (though no alcohol is served, so bring your own). Lunch and dinner each cost $8. People with an interest in the outdoors and nature are the ones who will most enjoy a stay here. There's a kilometer-long nature trail here at the lodge and various excursions can be arranged. Guided hikes through the forest ($15 per person), horseback rides ($15 per person), and river trips ($20) are all offered.

ORO VERDE STATION, Apdo. 7043-1000, San José. Tel. 506/233-6613. Fax 506/223-7479. 14 rms (8 with private bath).
$ Rates: $24.50–$30.20 single; $40.40–$50.30 double; $51.35–$86.75 triple. AE (San José office only).
Surrounded by nearly 20,000 acres of private reserve (3,000 acres of which is virgin forest) and bordering the Barra del Colorado National Wildlife Refuge, the Oro Verde Station is primarily a facility for researchers and students but is also open to the public. The nearest road is 30 miles away, so the lodge can only be reached by boat. The lodge's several high-peaked thatched-roof buildings lend a very tropical air to the facilities. Guest rooms are fairly basic, as you might expect at a research facility, and meals are often less than memorable. Both lunch and dinner are in the $5-to-$15 range. There are plenty of hiking trails; river trips and guided hikes can be arranged at additional cost.

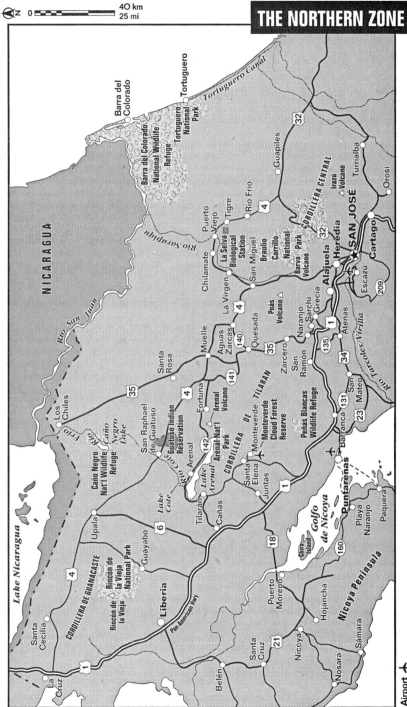

THE NORTHERN ZONE

0 — 40 km
  — 25 mi

NICARAGUA

Lake Nicaragua

Barra del Colorado

Barra del Colorado National Wildlife Refuge

Tortuguero National Park

Tortuguero National Park

Tortuguero Canal

Guapiles

CORDILLERA CENTRAL

Irazú Volcano

Turrialba

Orosi

Río San Juan

Rio Frio

Tigre

Puerto Viejo

La Selva Biological Station

San Miguel

Braulio Carrillo National Park

Barva Volcano

32

HEREDIA

SAN JOSÉ

Cartago

Chilamate

La Virgen

Alajuela

Escazú

209

Río Sarapiquí

Río San Juan

Santa Rosa

Muelle

Aguas Zarcas

Quesada

Poás Volcano

Naranjo

Sarchi

Grecia

4

35

Zarcero

San Ramón

1

Atenas

135

Río Tárcoles-Virilla

34

Los Chiles

Río Frio

San Raphael de Guatuso

Guatuso Indian Reservation

Fortuna

Arenal Volcano

Arenal Nat'l Park

CORDILLERA DE TILARAN

Monteverde

Monteverde Cloud Forest Reserve

Peñas Blancas Wildlife Refuge

San Mateo

131

23

Barranca

Caño Negro Nat'l Wildlife Refuge

Caño Negro Lake

141

142

Lake Arenal

Lake Cote

Tilarán

Cañas

Santa Elena

Juntas

1

18

Puntarenas

Chira Island

Golfo de Nicoya

Playa Naranjo

Paquera

Upala

Guayabo

6

CORDILLERA DE GUANACASTE

Rincón de la Vieja

Rincón de la Vieja National Park

Liberia

Pan American Hwy.

160

Nicoya Peninsula

Santa Cecilia

La Cruz

1

Belén

Santa Cruz

21

Nicoya

Puerto Moreno

Hojancha

Samara

Nosara

Airport ✈

6894

RARA AVIS, Apdo. 8105-1000, San José. Tel. and Fax 506/253-0844. 20 rms (10 with private bath).

$ Rates (including transportation from Horquetas, guided hikes, and three meals daily): $45 single with shared bath, $75–$85 single with private bath; $90 double with shared bath, $150 double with private bath. MC, V.

Though once the stomping grounds exclusively of scientists and students, Rara Avis was made famous by the pioneering canopy research of Dr. Donald Perry, who first erected his famous canopy cable-car system in the rain forest here at Rara Avis. Since that time, Rara Avis has become a very popular destination for people with a more casual interest in the rain forest. Though Perry's canopy cable car is no longer here, the rain forest research facility is still a fascinating place to visit. However, keep in mind that there are few lodges in Costa Rica more difficult to visit. To get to Rara Avis, you must first travel to the village of Horquetas, which is between Guápiles and Puerto Viejo de Sarapiquí. In Horquetas, you are met by a tractor that takes four hours to cover the 15 kilometers to Rara Avis's more popular lodge (there are two lodges here). The ride, over a road made of logs, is excruciatingly uncomfortable and very hard on the back, but if you've got a keen sense of adventure, go for it. The Waterfall Lodge is by far the more comfortable and has rustic rooms and a wraparound porch. The more economical El Plastico Lodge was at one time a penal colony, and though it has been renovated and converted, it is still rather Spartan. Meals are basic Tico-style dishes with lots of beans and rice. Rara Avis is adjacent to Braulio Carillo National Park and together the two have many miles of trails for you to explore. Bird-watchers take note: More than 320 species of birds have been sighted here. When making reservations, be sure to get directions on how to get to Horquetas.

LA SELVA BIOLOGICAL STATION, Apdo. 676-2050, San Pedro de Montes de Oca, San José (in the U.S.: Interlink 341, P.O. Box 02-5635, Miami, FL 33152). Tel. 506-240-6696, 240-6727, or 710-6897. Fax 506/240-6783. 15 rms.

$ Rates (including three meals daily): $88 per person. Lower rates for researchers. MC, V (add 7.53% surcharge).

If you want a rain forest experience, but are not too keen about the grueling 4-hour tractor ride to reach Rara Avis, consider this research station, which is a few kilometers south of Puerto Viejo. La Selva, like Rara Avis, caters primarily to students and researchers but also accepts visitors who are not involved in any specific scientific research. The atmosphere here is definitely that of a scientific research center. Rooms are basic, though they are large and have tiled bathrooms. High ceilings help keep them cool. The dining hall is a big bright place where students swap data over fried chicken and rice-and-beans. La Selva, which is operated by the Organization for Tropical Studies, covers 3,700 acres and is contiguous with Braulio Carillo National Park. Because scientific research is the primary objective of La Selva, researchers receive priority over casual short-term visitors. If you wish to visit La Selva, you must have a reservation, preferably made several months in advance. January through March, June, and July are the busiest months here.

SELVA VERDE LODGE, Chilamate, Sarapiquí. Tel. 506/710-6459, 220-2121, 766-6077, or (in the U.S.) toll free 800/858-0999. Fax 506/766-6011 or (in the U.S.) 904/371-3710. 40 rms.

$ Rates (including all meals): $73 single; $126 double; $159 triple. MC, V.

So, you've been hearing all about ecotourism and saving the rain forests and you want to see what it's all about, but you're accustomed to comfortable accommodations and good food. No problem. Selva Verde is just what you're looking for. Here at this beautifully designed lodge you can experience the rain forest without being uncomfortable. Located right on the main highway a few kilometers west of Puerto Viejo, Selva Verde is bounded by the Río Sarapiquí, across which is a large rain forest preserve. Rooms here are all connected by covered walkways that keep you dry even though this area receives more than 150 inches of rain each year. The lodge buildings are all built of varnished hardwoods, inside and out, and are built on pilings so that all the rooms are on the second floor. Because as few trees as possible were cut to build this lodge, you can sit on your veranda looking straight into the branches, which are often alive with birds. As you might guess, this lodge is a bird-watchers paradise, and in fact is often filled with Elderhostel tour groups that are busily working on their life lists. Meals are served in a beautiful large dining room that overlooks the river. Meals are well prepared and filling but not too creative. There are several trails on the grounds, and bicycles can be rented. Excursions that can be arranged through the lodge include river trips ($20 per person), canoe trips ($45 per person), rafting trips ($45 per person), mountain-biking trips ($25 per person), and guided walks ($5 to $8 per person).

2. ARENAL VOLCANO & LA FORTUNA

140 kilometers NW of San José; 61 kilometers E of Tilarán

GETTING THERE By Bus Buses leave San José for La Fortuna daily at 6:15, 8:40 and 11:30am from Calle 16 between avenidas 1 and 3. Duration: 4½ hours. Fare: $3.30.

Alternatively, you can take a bus to Ciudad Quesada from the same location in San José and then take a local bus from Ciudad Quesada to La Fortuna. Ciudad Quesada buses leave San José daily every hour from 5am to 7:30pm. Duration: 3 hours. Fare $2.20.

Buses leave Ciudad Quesada for La Fortuna at 5, 6, and 9:30am and 1, 3, and 6pm. Duration: 1 hour. Fare: $1.10.

By Car There are several routes to La Fortuna from San José. The most popular is to head west on the Interamerican Highway and then turn north at Naranjo, continuing north through Zarcero to Ciudad Quesada. From Ciudad Quesada one route goes through Jabillos while the other goes through Muelle. This latter route is the better road. Alternatively it is a little quicker to go first to Alajuela and then head north to Varablanca and then to San Miguel where you turn west toward Río Cuarto and Aguas Zarcas. From Aguas Zarcas, continue west through Muelle to the turnoff for La Fortuna. Travel time either way is around three hours. A new route from San Ramón (west of Naranjo) north through Tigra, though unpaved, is very scenic and passes the Villablanca and Valle Escondido lodges.

DEPARTING There are buses to San José daily at 5 and 9:30 am and 1, 3, and 6pm. Buses to Ciudad Quesada leave at 6, 7, 9:30, and 10am and 1, 2:30, and 4pm daily. From there you can catch one of the hourly buses to San José. There are also buses to Tilarán, at the northern end of Lake Arenal, daily at 7am and 4pm.

ESSENTIALS Fortuna is only a few streets wide, with almost all the hotels, restaurants, and shops clustered along the main road. There are several small information and tour-booking offices across the street from the soccer field.

Until 1937 when the mountain just west of La Fortuna was first scaled, no one ever dreamed that it might be a volcano. Gazing up at the cinder-strewn slopes of Arenal Volcano today, it is hard to believe that people could not have recognized this perfectly cone-shaped volcano for what it is. However, in July of 1968, the volcano, which had lain dormant for hundreds of years, erupted with sudden and unexpected violence. The nearby village of Tabacón was destroyed and nearly 80 of its inhabitants were killed. Since that eruption more than a quarter century ago, 5,358-foot-high Arenal has been Costa Rica's most active volcano. Frequent powerful explosions send cascades of red-hot lava rocks tumbling down the western slope of the volcano. During the day, the lava flows steam and rumble. However, it is at night that the volcano puts on its most mesmerizing show. If you should be lucky enough to be here on a clear night, you will see the night sky turned red by lava spewing from Arenal's crater. In the past few years, the forests to the south of the volcano have been declared Arenal National Park. Eventually this park should stretch all the way to Monteverde Cloud Forest Reserve.

Lying at the foot of this natural spectacle is the tiny farming community of La Fortuna. In recent years, this town has become a center for volcano watchers from around the world. There are several moderately priced hotels in and near La Fortuna, and it is here that you can arrange night tours to the best volcano-viewing spot.

WHAT TO SEE & DO

The first thing you should know is that you can't climb Arenal Volcano. It is not safe due to the constant activity; several foolish people who have ignored this warning have lost their lives. Watching Arenal's constant eruptions is the main activity in La Fortuna and is best done at night when the orange lava glows against the starry sky. Though it is possible to simply look up from the middle of town and see Arenal erupting, the view is better from the west side of the volcano, about 17 kilometers away. If you have a car, you can drive to the viewing area, but if you have arrived by bus, you will need to take a tour. These night tours are offered through every hotel in town and at several tour offices on the town's main street at a cost of $6.75.

To learn more about Arenal Volcano and volcanoes in general, try to catch the evening slide show at the **Eco-Trust Information Center** (tel. 479-9186) next to the Vaca Muca Restaurant one kilometer west of La Fortuna. These slide shows are held Tuesday, Thursday, and Saturday evenings at 6 and 8pm. This information center also includes a free museum of volcanology and has a small collection of local pre-Columbian artifacts. The center is open Tuesday through Saturday from 10am to 6pm and Sunday from 10am to 4pm.

There are also a few activities to keep you busy during the day. The first thing you might do is hike out to the **Río Fortuna waterfall.** It's about 5½ kilometers outside of town in a lush jungle setting. There is a sign in town to indicate the road that leads out to the falls, and as you hike along this road you'll probably be offered a lift. If this seems like too much exercise, you can rent a horse and guide for four hours for $13.55. You can arrange this ride through your hotel or through **Pura Vida** (tel. 479-9045). Another good ride is up to Cerro Chato, an extinct side cone on the flank of Arenal. There is a pretty little lake up here. Ask at your hotel about this trip. It should cost you around $13.50.

When you've finished your ride or hike, you'll probably want a soak in a hot spring. If so, head 12 kilometers west of La Fortuna to Tabacón, where a hot river flows down off the slopes of Arenal Volcano. At Tabacón, you can luxuriate at the **Tabacón Hot Spring Resort,** where there are several hot pools, hot waterfalls, sun decks, a restaurant and bar, and a great view of the volcano. The resort is open daily from 10am to 11pm and charges $9.50 admission. If this seems like a lot of money to pay for a soak in a hot spring, you can cross the road and walk down a gravel driveway to a less luxurious and more natural stretch of this hot river. Here you'll pay only $1.70 to soak away your aches and pains. Tabacón is about 12 kilometers west of La Fortuna on the road to Lake Arenal. A stop at the hot springs is often combined with a tour to see Arenal erupting.

You can also arrange a tour to the **Venado Caverns,** which are a 45-minute drive from La Fortuna. You'll see plenty of stalactites, stalagmites, and other limestone formations, of course, but you'll also see bats and cave fish. Tours cost $20.30 per person and are offered by Pura Vida (see above) in La Fortuna. You can also go rafting with **Rafting Safaris** (tel. 479-9076), which offers half-day raft float trips for $40 per person. Bird-watching and crocodile spotting are good on these trips.

La Fortuna is also the best place from which to make a day trip to the **Caño Negro National Wildlife Refuge.** This vast network of marshes and rivers is

100 kilometers north of La Fortuna near the town of Los Chiles. This refuge is best known for its amazing abundance of bird life, including roseate spoonbills, jabiru storks, herons, and egrets, but you can also see caiman and crocodiles. Bird-watchers should not miss this refuge, though keep in mind that the main lake dries up in the dry season, which reduces the numbers of wading birds to be seen. Pura Vida (see above) in La Fortuna offers tours to Caño Negro for $33.80 per person.

WHERE TO STAY

MODERATE

ALBERGUE BURIO, Apdo. 1234-1250, Escazú. Tel. and Fax 506/479-9076 or 228-6623. 8 rms (all with bath).

$ Rates (including continental breakfast): Dec–Apr, $20 single, $40 double; May–Nov, $15 single, $30 double. $10 for students. MC, V.

This small lodge is on the main road through La Fortuna, though it is set back from the street behind some shops and is a bit difficult to spot. There is a grassy garden, a small breakfast room, and the owners are very helpful. Guest rooms have big windows and lots of polished hardwood, and are attractively decorated with lace curtains. This hotel also operates as a youth hostel and consequently offers lower rates for students. You can arrange various tours here at the Burio, including night tours to see the volcano, trips to Tabacón hot springs, and fishing trips on Lake Arenal.

LAS CABAÑITAS RESORT, Apdo. 5-4417, La Fortuna, San Carlos. Tel. and Fax 506/479-9091. 30 cabins.

$ Rates: Dec–Apr, $60 single, $65 double; May-Nov (including breakfast and dinner), $55.75 single, $70.95 double. AE, MC, V.

⭐ Located 8 kilometers east of town, these rustic mountain cabins are the place to stay if you want the best view of Arenal Volcano. Most of the cabins face the volcano and have little porches where you can sit and enjoy the show by day or night. Each cabin is built of varnished hardwoods and has a beautiful floor, a high ceiling, louvered walls to let in the breezes, a king bed, a modern tile bathroom down a few steps from the sleeping area, and rocking chairs on the porch. There is a small swimming pool with a snack bar beside it and also a larger, full-service restaurant. Note that in the off-season, the hotel includes breakfast and dinner in the room rates. Various tours can be arranged through the hotel.

HOTEL-RANCHO EL CORCOVADO, Apdo. 25, El Tanque de La Fortuna, San Carlos. Tel. and Fax 506/479-9090. 25 rms.

$ Rates: $30 single; $40 double; $60 triple. MC, V.

Ⓢ This hotel is located 7 kilometers east of La Fortuna, and though the rooms are clean and have platform beds, they do not have views of the volcano. However, it's only a few steps outside to a spot where there are good views. About half of the rooms have air-conditioning and half have ceiling fans only. There is a small swimming pool, as well as an inexpensive restaurant serving Tico standards. This hotel isn't as attractive as Las Cabañitas just up the road, but neither is it as expensive.

BUDGET

In addition to the budget hotels listed below, there is Los Lagos campground a few minutes west of La Fortuna. This campground has forests, trails, and lakes.

HOTEL FORTUNA, La Fortuna, San Carlos. Tel. 506/479-9197. 7 rms (all with private bath).

$ Rates: $7.45 single; $14.90 double; $22.30 triple. No credit cards.

Located one block south of the gas station, this small hotel is dark and very basic, but the rooms are clean and the prices are great. Try to get a second-floor room; these are a bit brighter than those on the ground floor. There is an open-air restaurant at the front of the hotel.

HOTEL LAS COLINAS, 150 meters south of the National Bank, La Fortuna, San Carlos. Tel. and Fax 506/479-9107. 21 rms (all with private bath).
$ Rates: $13.55 single; $25.10 double; $31.20 triple. MC, V.

This modern three-story building in the center of town offers clean, modern rooms. However, you'll need to be in good shape if you stay in one of the third-floor rooms which have the best views. The stairs are very steep. There are a few rooms on the ground floor, but they don't even have windows to the outside and are very dark. My favorite room is the one with the balcony and the view of Arenal Volcano.

HOTEL SAN BOSCO, 200 meters north of the gas station, La Fortuna, San Carlos. Tel. 506/479-9050. Fax 506/479-9109. 27 rms (all with bath).
$ Rates: $12.35–$26.20 single; $21.35–$38.55 double; $25.45–$42.40 triple. V.
Located a block off La Fortuna's main street, the San Bosco has two styles of rooms. The older, cheaper rooms are small and dark and have cement floors. However, the newer rooms are much more attractive and have stone walls, tile floors, ceiling fans, reading lights, and benches on the veranda in front. Up on the top floor of the hotel, there is an observation deck for volcano viewing.

NEARBY PLACES TO STAY

NEAR THE VOLCANO

ARENAL LODGE, Apdo. 1139-1250, Escazú. Tel. 506/289-6588. Fax 506/289-6798. 15 rms.
$ Rates: $55 single; $65 double; $75 triple; $75–$95 junior suite. AE, MC V.

For stunning location and spectacular views, it's hard to beat the Arenal Lodge. Located high on a hillside a mile from Lake Arenal, this lodge has a direct, unobstructed view of Arenal Volcano's most active slope, which is six miles away on the far side of a deep valley. If you reserve one of the huge junior suites, you can actually lie in bed and gaze out at the volcano through a wall of glass. The light show on clear nights is enough to keep you awake for hours. These rooms have two queen beds, balconies, clerestory windows, two sinks in the bathroom, and lots of space. The standard rooms, though attractively decorated, have no views at all. However, if you should choose to stay in one of these more economical rooms, it is only a few steps to a large viewing deck. For the ultimate in luxury ask about the master suite, which was being renovated when I last visited. Meals, which will run you around $30 per person per day, are served in a dining room with a wall of glass, so you can ooh and ahh between bites of corvina or steak. After dinner, you can retire to the library, where there is a huge stone fireplace and a pool table. A separate lounge has a TV and VCR. The lodge can also arrange night tours ($10 per person), trips to the base of Arenal and Tabacón hot springs ($25 to $30 per person), and fishing for rainbow bass in Lake Arenal ($125 for two people for a half day). Situated on a macadamia plantation between two strips of virgin forest, the lodge has several trails that are great for bird-watching.

ARENAL OBSERVATORY LODGE, Costa Rica Sun Tours, Apdo. 1195-1250, Escazú. Tel. 506/255-2011. Fax 506/255-4410. 10 rms.
$ Rates (including breakfast and dinner): $60 single; $90 double. AE, MC.
This rustic lodge was originally built for the use of volcanologists from the Smithsonian Institution, but is today open to the public as well. The lodge is only 2½ miles from the volcano and is built on a high ridge, which gives it the best view of any of the local lodges. Lying in bed at night listening to the eruptions, it is easy to think that the lodge is in imminent danger. Some of the rooms, as well as the dining room, have superb views of the volcano. Surrounding the lodge is the Arenal National Park, which includes thousands of acres of forest and many kilometers of trails. To reach this lodge, you'll need a four-wheel-drive vehicle. There are two river crossings (including the Río Agua Caniente) to make on the 9-kilometer gravel road to the lodge.

ARENAL VISTA LODGE, Apdo. 818-1200, Pavas, San José. Tel. 506/220-2121. 25 rms.

$ Rates: $55 single; $65 double; $75 triple. AE, MC, V.

This is the newest lodge in the area. It's farther along the same road that leads to the Arenal Observatory Lodge and consequently is even more of an adventure to reach. All the modern rooms have great views of Arenal Volcano, so you can sit back and watch the volcano's fireworks displays in comfort. Meals will cost you an additional $22 per person per day.

EAST OF LA FORTUNA

HOTEL LA GARZA, Plantanar, San Carlos. Tel. 506/460-1827 or 222-7355. Fax 506/475-5015 or 222-0869. 12 rms. TEL

$ Rates: Nov–Apr, $61 single, $68 double, $82 triple; May–Oct, lower rates available. MC, V.

This is one of the newest lodges to open in the area and is set on a large working ranch just south of Muelle. *La Garza* means "the egret" in Spanish, and at the lodge you will see plenty of these birds, which roost nearby. The ranch also includes 750 acres of primary rain forest where many other species of birds can be spotted. Built on the banks of the San Carlos River, the hotel consists of six duplex bungalows, each of which has a deck overlooking the river. Large trees provide shade and the sound of the river lulls you to sleep at night. High ceilings and overhead fans help keep the rooms cool, and there are plans to add air conditioners. All the rooms are attractively decorated and have views of Arenal Volcano in the distance. When I visited, the restaurant and bar were on the far side of the river, which was crossed by a suspension footbridge. However, there were plans to build a new dining room on the same side of the river as the rooms. Tours of the region can be arranged and you can wander around the ranch observing the day-to-day activity. However, the ranch's rain forest, with all its birds and other wildlife, is the primary attraction here.

TILAJARI HOTEL RESORT, Muelle, San Carlos. Tel. 506/460-1083. Fax 506/460-1083 or 460-0979. 60 rms, 4 suites. A/C

$ Rates: Nov–Apr, $60 single, $75 double, $95 suite double; May–Oct, discounts available. AE, MC, V.

This sprawling resort just outside the farming community of Muelle (28 kilometers from La Fortuna) is a sort of country club for wealthy Costa Ricans. However, it also makes a good base for exploring this region. Covering 30 acres (unfortunately mostly shadeless lawns) and built on the banks of the San Carlos River, the Tilajari Hotel offers the most luxurious accommodations in the region. The modern buildings are painted a blinding white and have red tile roofs. About half of the rooms have views of the river, while the other face Arenal Volcano. These latter rooms are slightly larger, though the former have balconies, which makes them a bit more appealing. Large iguanas are frequently sighted on the grounds, as are crocodiles, which live in the San Carlos River.

Dining/Entertainment: There's a large open-air dining room that has both formal and informal sections. The menu consists primarily of moderately priced Tico and international dishes. There is also a bar and disco to round out the entertainment offerings.

Services: The lodge arranges tours around the region including trips to Caño Negro ($87 per person), Arenal Volcano ($40 per person), Venado Caves ($45 per person), and Fortuna Falls ($45 per person). Trips into the nearby rain forest, either on foot, on horseback, or by tractor, can also be arranged.

Facilities: Swimming pool, tennis courts, racquetball court, soccer field, sauna, game room with pool and table tennis, gift shop.

EL TUCANO RESORT & SPA, Apdo. 114-1017, San José 2000. Tel. 506/460-1822 or 233-8936. Fax 506/460-1692 or 221-9095. 90 rms, 2 junior suites, 7 suites.

$ Rates: $55 single; $66 double; $77 triple; $88 junior suite; $99–$175 suite. AE, MC, V.

⭐ Located a few kilometers north of Ciudad Quesada (San Carlos) on the road to Aguas Zarcas, El Tucano is Costa Rica's only true spa resort, and though you won't find the sort of services you'd get in Palm Springs, there are natural hot springs and natural steam rooms. Though the resort is down in a steep-walled valley and faces a lush rain forest, it is more popular with vacationing Tico families than with gringos. The rooms are set into the steep hillside and are connected by narrow, winding alleys and stairways. Most rooms are carpeted and very comfortable, with attractive decorations and tubs in the bathrooms. If you want extra space, ask for one of the suites or junior suites. This is a great place to just kick back and relax for a day or two. Don't miss the natural hot springs that flow into the stream at the back of the property.

Dining/Entertainment: The dining room here is large and formal, with excellent service and a continental menu that includes such dishes as chicken à l'orange and pasta with shrimp. A bar and casino keep adult guests happy after dark.

Services: Room service, shuttle service to San José ($20 per person one way), horseback riding ($5 per person per hour).

Facilities: Swimming pool, two tennis courts, whirlpool tubs with natural hot-spring waters, natural steam rooms, miniature golf course, gift shop, hiking trails, natural hot springs, small zoo.

SOUTH OF LA FORTUNA

VALLE ESCONDIDO LODGE, Apdo. 452-1150, La Uruca. Tel. 506/231-0906. Fax 506/232-9591. 19 rms.

$ Rates: $45 single; $55 double; $65 triple. AE, MC, V.

South of La Fortuna, on an as-yet-to-be-paved road between San Ramón and La Fortuna, is a modest hotel that provides access to some of the region's rain forests. Valle Escondido (Hidden Valley) is situated on a 990-acre farm that includes primary and secondary forest as well as fields of ornamental plants that are grown for export. Guest rooms here are spacious and comfortable, and all are carpeted. In front of the rooms run long verandas where you can sit and enjoy the tranquility of the surroundings. The lodge restaurant serves Tico and Italian meals, which will cost you $25 per person per day. There is also a small bar. Hiking, horseback riding ($5 per hour), mountain biking ($3.50 per hour), and bird-watching are the primary activities here, and tours are an additional charge.

VILLABLANCA HOTEL, Apdo. 247-1250, San Rafael de Escazú. Tel. 506/228-4603. Fax 506/228-4004. 31 cabins.

$ Rates: $65 single; $85 double; $100 triple. AE, MC, V.

⭐ Set at the end of a long dirt road, Villablanca is certainly out of the way, and perched as it is, high in the cloud forest, it isn't the sort of place people come to when they want to work on their tans. However, if you are interested in bird-watching or exploring the cloud forest, there is no better place in the country. Owned and operated by a former president of Costa Rica, this lodge consists of 31 Tico-style *casitas*, "little houses," surrounded by 2,000 acres of farm and forest. Each casita is built of adobe and has traditional tile floors and whitewashed walls with deep blue trim. This is the classic color scheme of 19th-century adobe homes throughout the country. Inside your casita, you'll find a rounded fireplace in one corner, window seats, comfortable hardwood chairs, colorful curtains, and twin beds covered with attractive bedspreads. Rooms also have electric teapots and small refrigerators. Bathrooms are done in beautiful tiles and have tubs that look out through a wall of windows. In the hacienda-like main lodge, you'll find the dining room, where simple-but-filling buffet meals are served. Also in this building are an unusual atrium garden, library, lounge, gift shop, and small bar. Adjacent to the lodge there are 11 kilometers of trails through the Los Angeles Cloud Forest Reserve. Admission to the reserve is $14 per person, and a guided hike will cost $7 per person. You can also rent horses ($9 per hour) and mountain bikes ($15 for 3 hours). Transportation to and from the lodge is $30 each way. Alternatively, you can take a public bus from San José to San Ramón and then take a taxi for around $11. If you are driving, head west out of San José to San Ramón and then head north, following the signs to Villablanca.

3. TILARÁN & LAKE ARENAL

200 kilometers NW of San José; 20 kilometers NW of Monteverde; 70 kilometers SE of Liberia

GETTING THERE By Bus Express buses leave San José for Tilarán daily at 7:30am and 12:45, 3:45, and 6:30pm from Calle 14 between avenidas 9 and 11. Duration: 4 hours. Fare: $3.10.

There are also morning and afternoon buses from Puntarenas to Tilarán. Duration: 3 hours. Fare: $1.75.

From Monteverde (Santa Elena), there is a bus daily at 7am. Duration: 3 hours. Fare $1.10.

By Car From San José, take the Interamerican Highway west toward Puntarenas and then continue north on this road to Cañas. In Cañas, turn east toward Tilarán. The drive takes 4 hours. If you are thinking of heading up this way from La Fortuna, be aware that the road is unpaved, in very bad shape, and entails several stream crossings. The road should not be tried in a regular car except during the dry season.

DEPARTING Direct buses to San José leave at 7 and 7:45am and 2 and 4:55pm. Buses to Puntarenas leave at 6am and 1pm. The bus to Santa Elena (Monteverde) leaves daily at 12:30pm. Buses to the town of Nuevo Arenal, on the far side of the lake, leave daily at 10am, and 4 and 10pm. Buses to Cañas, from where you can catch buses north or south along the Interamerican Highway, leave at 5, 6:20, 7, 7:45, and 10am and 3:30pm. Buses for La Fortuna, at the south end of Lake Arenal, leave daily at 7am and 12:30pm.

ESSENTIALS Tilarán is about 5 kilometers from Lake Arenal. All roads into town lead to the central park, which is Tilarán's main point of reference for addresses. If you need to change money, check at one of the hotels listed here. If you need a taxi to get to a lodge on Lake Arenal, phone 695-5324.

Lake Arenal, a man-made lake with an area of 33 square miles, is the largest lake in Costa Rica and is surrounded by rolling hills that are partly pastured and partly forested. At the opposite (south) end of the lake from Tilarán lies the perfect cone of Arenal Volcano. The volcano's barren slopes are a stunning sight from here, especially when reflected in the waters of the lake. The north side of Lake Arenal is a dry region of rolling hills and pastures, distinctly different from the lusher landscape near La Fortuna at the south end.

People around here used to curse the winds, which often come blasting across this end of the lake at 60 knots or greater. However, since the first sailboarders caught wind of Lake Arenal's combination of warm fresh water, high winds, and a spectacular view, things have been changing quickly. Though the town of Tilarán is still little more than a quiet farm community; out along the shores of the lake, hotels are proliferating. Even if you aren't a rabid boardhead (fanatical sailboarder), you still might enjoy hanging out by the lake in hopes of catching a glimpse of Arenal Volcano.

The lake's other claim to fame is its rainbow bass fishing. These fighting fish are known in their native South America as *guapote* and are large members of the cichlid family. Their sharp teeth and fighting nature make them a real challenge.

WHAT TO SEE & DO

If you want to try windsurfing, you can rent equipment from **Tilawa Windsurfing Center** (tel. 695-5050 or 695-5666), which has its facilities on one of the lake's few accessible beaches about five miles from Tilarán on the road around the west end of the lake. Windsurfers rent for $35 to $45 per day and lessons are also available. Over on the other side of the lake you'll find the new **Tico Wind** (fax: 695-5387), which rents equipment for $45 per day or $250 per week between November and April.

If you'd rather stay on dry land, the folks at Tilawa can arrange for you to rent a horse for $10 per hour. Up above Lake Arenal on the far side of the lake from Tilarán you'll find the beautiful little heart-shaped **Coter Lake**. This lake is surrounded by forest and has good swimming, picnicking, and some trails. A taxi to Coter Lake will cost around $12. Continuing south on the road around the lake will bring you to the town of Nuevo Arenal, where the pavement ends. If you continue another four kilometers on this road, you will come to the **Arenal Botanical Gardens** (tel. 695-5266, ext. 273), which is open Wednesday through Sunday from 9am to 5pm and charges $3.40 admission. This private garden was only started in 1991 but is already quite beautiful. Not only are there many tropical plants and flowers to be seen, but there are always butterflies and hummingbirds in the gardens.

If you want to try your hand at fishing for rainbow bass, contact **J.J.'s Fishing Tours** (tel. 695-5825). A half-day fishing trip will cost between $30 and $100 per person depending on the number of people in your party. If you'd just like to go for a boat ride on the lake, check at **Xiloe Lodge** (tel. 259-9192 or 229-0161).

WHERE TO STAY

MODERATE

BAHÍA AZUL LAKE RESORT, Laguna de Arenal, Tilarán, Guanacaste. Tel. 506/695-5750 or 695-5950. Fax 506/695-5750 or 695-5387. 15 rms. TV
$ Rates: $30 single; $54 double; $64 triple. MC, V.
Located 5 kilometers from Tilarán on a small bay of Lake Arenal, Bahía Azul is popular both with windsurfers and vacationing Ticos. Most of the rooms are in a two-story white building that sits on a grassy slope overlooking the lake and green hills beyond. However, my favorite rooms are those down closer to the water. The setting is very tranquil during the week, though on weekends it can get a bit noisy with speedboats racing around the lake. The rooms here are a bit run-down, but all have small refrigerators, ceiling fans, and large windows. There is a bar and restaurant where the meal prices range from $4 to $8. The hotel also has fishing gear and water skis for rent and offers boat trips and trips to the foot of Arenal Volcano. A taxi from Tilarán to Bahía Azul will cost you a little more than $3.

CHALET NICHOLAS, Apdo. 72-5710, Tilarán, Guanacaste. No phone. Fax 506/695-5387. 3 rms.
$ Rates (including full breakfast): $39 double. No credit cards.
S This friendly, American-owned bed-and-breakfast is located 2 kilometers west of the town of Nuevo Arenal and sits on a hill above the road. There are great views from the garden, and one of the three rooms has a view of Arenal Volcano out the window. The modern home is set on three acres and has pretty flower gardens, an organic vegetable garden, an aviary full of toucans and other colorful birds, and behind the property acres of forest through which you can hike in search of birds, orchids, butterflies, and other tropical beauties. If you don't mind the lack of privacy, the upstairs loft room is the largest. It even has its own private deck. Owners John and Catherine Nichols go out of their way to make their guests feel at home.

HOTEL TILAWA, Apdo. 92, Tilarán, Guanacaste. Tel. 506/695-5050, 695-5666, or (in the U.S.) toll free 800/851-8929. Fax 695-5766. 28 rms.

$ Rates: $47.25 single; $62.10 double; $76.10 triple. AE, MC, V.

⭐ Built to resemble the Palace of Knossos on the island of Crete, the Hotel Tilawa is an avid windsurfer's dream brought to reality. The American owners, who for years have run a windsurfing center on Lake Arenal, opened this hotel to provide wealthier windsurfers with a comfortable place to stay. The hotel sits high on the slopes above the lake and has a sweeping vista down the lake. Unusual colors and an antique paint effect make the hotel look as though it has been weathered by the ages (though it is actually only a few years old). Inside there are wall murals and other artistic paint treatments throughout the hotel. Guest rooms have dyed cement floors, Guatemalan bedspreads, and big windows. Some have kitchenettes. Hotel amenities include a swimming pool and tennis court. There is a bar beside the pool, as well as a moderately priced restaurant in the main building. The Tilawa can arrange not only windsurfing but mountain biking, horseback riding, fishing trips, and excursions around the lake.

LAKE COTER ECO-LODGE, Apdo. 6398-1000, San José. Tel. 506/221-4209. Fax 506/221-0794. 37 rms (12 with private bath).

$ Rates: $46 single without bath, $56 single with bath; $55 double without bath, $75 double with bath; $75 triple without bath, $85 triple with bath. AE, DC, MC, V.

Tucked into the forested hills above Lake Arenal is the much smaller, but natural, Coter Lake. Near this pretty little lake (down a very bad gravel road), you'll find this rustic lodge. Though the older rooms in the main lodge are overpriced and do not have private bathrooms, there are 12 much nicer comfortable cabins on a hill, a short walk from the main lodge. These cabins all have porches and great views, and if you are interested in staying here, you should be sure to request one of these rooms. Surrounding the lodge are more than 1,300 acres that include clouded forests and 10 miles of hiking trails. Within a short hike is Lake Coter, where you can swim, canoe, fish, and even windsurf.

Meals are served family style in the rustic dining room in the main lodge. Tico standards and some international dishes are the fare here, and meals will run you $21 per person per day. Transportation to and from the lodge can be arranged at additional cost. Activities available include horseback riding, mountain biking, windsurfing, canoeing, and hiking. Excursions to Arenal Volcano and Venado Caves can also be arranged.

ROCK RIVER LODGE, Apdo. 2907-1000, San José. Tel. 506/235-9348 or 222-4547. Fax 506/297-1364 or 221-3011. 6 rms.

$ Rates: $35 single or double. No credit cards.

Set high on a grassy hill above the lake, this small lodge looks as if it might have been transported from Hawaii. The guest rooms are housed in a long, low lodge set on stilts. Walls and floors are made of hardwood and there are bamboo railings along the veranda. Wind chimes let you know when the winds are up, and there are sling chairs on the porch. Rooms are of medium size and have double beds (with mosquito nets) and bunk beds, as well as modern tiled bathrooms. Though fairly simple in style, this is one of the most attractive lodges in the area. However, it's a long walk down to the lake (not to mention the walk back up). Meals will cost you around $25 per person per day, with American and Tico meals served in the spacious open-air restaurant where there's a large stone fireplace. Basically it's a very mellow scene.

VILLAS ALPINO, Apdo. 7-5710, Tilarán, Guanacaste. No phone. Fax 506/695-5387. 5 cabins.

$ Rates: Dec–Apr, $50 single, double, or triple; May–Nov, $40 single, double, or triple. No credit cards.

⭐ Built by a Dutch windsurfer, these cozy cabins have great views and all the conveniences of apartments. The refrigerator in the kitchen even comes stocked with four beers and some coffee. The kitchens also have two walls of windows that make the cabins fairly cheery. There are also picture windows beside the beds, and small porches out front to let you maximize your vista viewing time. There are Guatemalan bedspreads, and in the bathroom you'll find a river-rock wall and window seat and a brick-tile floor. Keep in mind that it's a long way down to the lake, so you'll need to have your own car if you plan to stay here. You'll find Villas Alpino on the east side of the lake.

BUDGET

CABINAS MARY, south side of the park, Tilarán, Guanacaste. Tel. 506/ 695-5479. 16 rms (11 with private bath).

$ Rates: $4.40 single with shared bath, $6.10 single with private bath; $8.80 double with shared bath, $10.85 double with private bath. No credit cards.

Located right on Tilarán's large and sunny central park, Cabinas Mary is a very basic, but fairly clean hotel. It's upstairs from the restaurant of the same name and has parking in back. Rooms are large and have plenty of windows. You even get hot water here, which is a surprise at this price. The restaurant downstairs is a gringo hangout. It's open daily from 7am to 10pm; meals cost between $3 and $6.

CABINAS EL SUEÑO, Tilarán, Guanacaste. Tel. 506/695-5347. 12 rms (all with private bath).

$ Rates: $14.15 single; $23.55 double; $27.45 triple. MC, V.

Right in the middle of this small town, Cabinas El Sueño is a simple two-story hotel, but it is clean and bright, and the management is friendly. There is parking in back of the hotel and a small courtyard complete with fountain on the second floor of the building. Downstairs there's a restaurant and bar.

WHERE TO DINE

If you are staying in Tilarán, there are numerous inexpensive eateries, including restaurants at Cabinas Mary and Cabinas El Sueño, both of which are mentioned above. Also, around the corner from Cabinas Mary, is **El Lugar,** a popular restaurant and bar that is definitely worth checking out. If you are staying outside of town, you'll likely be eating in your hotel's dining room since there are few restaurants around the shores of the lake. Worth mentioning is **Equus BBQ,** a small open-air restaurant in front of Xiloe Lodge. This restaurant specializes in roast chicken and steaks. If you are staying down near Nuevo Arenal, try the following restaurant.

RESTAURANT LAJAS, on the main street through town. Tel. 695-5266.

Cuisine: COSTA RICAN. **Reservations:** Not accepted.

$ Prices: Main courses $2.05–$3.75. No credit cards.

Open: Daily 5am-10pm.

This surprisingly fancy little restaurant is one of the best values in Costa Rica. There are red tablecloths on every table, waiters in bow ties, and a wall of mirrors to make the tiny dining room look larger than it really is, but these are only the incidentals. The real reason to eat here is for good Tico cooking at rock-bottom prices. The deal of the day is always the casado. You won't walk away hungry or poor.

4. MONTEVERDE

167 kilometers NW of San José; 82 kilometers NW of Puntarenas

GETTING THERE By Bus Express buses leave San José Monday through Thursday at 2:30pm, and Saturday (December through April) and Sunday at 6:30am from Calle 14 between avenidas 9 and 11. Duration: 3½ hours. Fare: $5.85.

There is also a daily bus at 2:15pm from Puntarenas to Santa Elena, which is only a few kilometers from Monteverde. The bus stop in Puntarenas is across the street from the main bus station. Duration: 2½ hours. Fare: $2.40.

There is a daily bus from Tilarán (Lake Arenal) at 1pm. Duration: 3 hours (40 kilometers!). Fare: $1.10.

One other option is to take Costa Rica Expeditions' van (tel. 257-0766) from San José. You must have a reservation. Fare: $35 each way.

By Car   Take the Interamerican Highway toward Puntarenas and follow the signs for Nicaragua. About 31 kilometers past the turnoff for Puntarenas, watch for the Río Lagarto Bridge. It takes about 2¼ hours to this point. Take the dirt road to the right just before the bridge. From this turnoff, it's another 38 kilometers (1½ to 2 hours) to Monteverde. The going is very slow because the road is so bad. Many people are told that this road is not passable without four-wheel-drive, but I have been driving it for years, albeit in the dry season, in regular cars. Just don't try it in the rainy season unless you have four-wheel drive. Be sure you have plenty of gas in the car before starting up to Monteverde. This grueling road eats up fuel, and the one gas station in Monteverde doesn't always have gas.

DEPARTING   The express bus to San José leaves Tuesday, Wednesday and Thursday at 6:30am, Friday, Saturday (December through April), and Sunday at 3pm. The bus from Santa Elena to Puntarenas leaves daily at 6am. If you should be heading to Manuel Antonio, take the 6am Santa Elena–Puntarenas bus and transfer in Puntarenas. To reach Liberia, take the 6am. If you should be heading to Manuel Antonio, take the 6am Santa Elena–Puntarenas bus and get off at the Río Lagarto Bridge, where the bus reaches the paved road. You can then flag down a bus bound for Liberia (almost any bus heading north). The Santa Elena–Tilarán bus leaves daily at 7am.

ESSENTIALS   As you approach Santa Elena, take the right fork in the road if you are heading directly to Monteverde. If you continue straight, you will come into the village of Santa Elena, which has a bus stop, health clinic, bank, general store, and a few simple restaurants and budget hotels.

Monteverde, on the other hand, is not a village in the traditional sense of the word. There is no center of town, only dirt lanes leading off from the main road to various farms. This main road has signs for all the hotels and restaurants mentioned here and dead-ends at the reserve entrance.

In Santa Elena, you'll find the Puntarenas bus stop, a general store, a bank, and a little health clinic. There is also a small information center (tel. 645-5137). It's located across the street from the Hotel El Tucan and is open Monday through Saturday from 9am to noon and from 1 to 6pm.

A taxi (tel. 645-5071) between Santa Elena and either the Monteverde Cloud Forest Reserve or the Santa Elena Rainforest Reserve will cost around $7. Count on $4 to $6 from Santa Elena to the lodge in Monteverde.

It is not surprising that the name Monteverde (Spanish for "Green Mountain") was chosen for this area. That is exactly what you find up here at the end of a long, rutted dirt road that passes through mile after mile of often dry, brown pasture lands. All of those pastures you pass through were once covered with dense forest, but now only small pieces of that original forest remain.

The village of Monteverde was founded in the 1950s by Quakers from the United States who wished to leave behind the constant fear of war and the obligation to support continued militarism through U.S. taxes. They chose Costa Rica because it was committed to a nonmilitaristic economic path. Although Monteverde's founders came here to farm the land, they recognized the need to preserve the rare cloud forest that covered the mountain slopes above their fields, and to that end they dedicated the largest adjacent tract of cloud forest as the Monteverde Cloud Forest Biological Reserve.

If you have an interest in the environment and are planning a trip to Costa Rica, you have no doubt already heard of Monteverde. Perched on a high mountain ridge, this tiny, scattered village and cloud forest reserve are well known both among scientific researchers and ecotravelers. Cloud forests are a mountain-top phenomenon. Moist, warm air sweeping in off the nearby ocean is forced upward by mountain slopes, and as the moist air rises it cools, forming clouds. The mountain tops of Costa Rica are almost daily blanketed in dense clouds, and as these clouds cling to the slopes, moisture condenses on forest trees. This constant level of moisture has given rise to an incredible diversity of life forms and a forest in which every square inch of space has some sort of plant growing on it. Within the cloud forest, the branches of huge trees are draped with epiphytic plants—orchids, ferns, bromeliads. This intense botanic competition has created an almost equally diverse poulation of insects, birds, and other wildlife. Monteverde Cloud Forest Biological Reserve covers 26,000 acres of forest, including several different life zones that are characterized by different types of plants and animals. Within this small area are more than 2,000 species of plants, 320 birds species, and 100 different species of mammals. It is no wonder that the reserve has been the site of constant scientific investigations since its founding.

The reserve was originally known only to the handful of researchers who came here to study different aspects of life in the cloud forest. However, as the beauty and biological diversity of the area became known outside of university circles, casual visitors began arriving. For many, the primary goal was a chance to glimpse the rare and elusive resplendent quetzal, a bird once revered by the pre-Columbian peoples of the Americas. As the numbers of visitors began to grow, lodges began opening, word spread, more lodges opened, and so on. Today Monteverde is a prime example of too many people chasing after the same little piece of nature. On a much smaller scale, Monteverde is akin to the Yosemite Valley—a place of great and fragile beauty whose very beauty is threatened by its popularity. However, despite the hordes of ecotourists traipsing the trails of Monteverde, it is still a beautiful place and offers a glimpse into the life of one of the world's most threatened ecosystems. I urge you, though, to seriously consider visiting another cloud forest area in an effort to lessen the impact of tourism on Monteverde. Other places you could visit include Villablanca and the Los Angeles Cloud Forest Reserve or the Tapantí National Wildlife Refuge, which has several nearby lodges. At either end of these places you will find far fewer crowds and usually better chances of seeing the famed resplendent quetzal.

WHAT TO SEE & DO

Don't expect to see all those plants and animals during your visit because many of them are quite rare or elusive. However, with a guide hired through your hotel or on one of the reserve's official guided 2- to 3-hour hikes, you can see far more than you could on your own. At $15.20 per person, the reserve's tours are expensive, especially after you pay the $8.10 reserve entrance fee, but I strongly recommend that you go with a guide. I went into the reserve twice in the same morning—once on my own and once with a guide—and with the guide I saw much more and learned much more about cloud forests and their inhabitants. On the other hand, while alone I saw a rare bird, a guan, that I didn't see when walking the trails with a dozen or more other interested but rather noisy visitors. There is much to be said for walking quietly through the forest on your own.

The preserve is open daily from 7am to 4pm. Because only 100 people are allowed into the preserve at any one time, you may be forced to wait for a while before being allowed in. However, if you go the afternoon before you want to visit, you can usually get tickets for early the next morning. Rubber boots are available at the reserve entrance and rent for less than $1. The trails here are very muddy, so these boots are a good idea.

Before venturing into the forest, have a look around the information center. There are several guidebooks available, as well as posters and postcards of some of the reserve's more famous animal inhabitants. Perhaps the most famous resident of the cloud forests of Costa Rica is the quetzal, a robin-sized bird with iridescent-green wings and a ruby-red breast, which has become extremely rare due to habitat destruction. The male quetzal also has two long tail feathers that make it one of the most spectacular birds on earth. The best time to see quetzals is early to midmorning, with February through April (mating season) being the easiest months to spot these magnificent birds.

Other animals that have been seen in Monteverde include jaguars, ocelots, and tapirs. After the quetzal, Monteverde's most beautiful resident was the golden toad (sapo dorado). However, due to several years of low precipitation, the golden toads seems to have disappeared from the forest, which was its only known home in the entire world. There has been speculation that the toad was adversely affected by a natural drought cycle, the disappearing ozone layer, or acid rain. Photos of the golden toad abound in Monteverde, and I'm sure you'll be as saddened as I was by the disappearance of such a beautiful creature.

Hiking opportunities can also be found outside the reserve boundaries. You can avoid the crowds at Monteverde by heading 5 kilometers north from the village of Santa Elena to the **Santa Elena Forest Reserve.** This 900-acre cloud forest is at an elevation of 5,600 feet, which makes it the highest cloud forest in the Monteverde area. There are eight kilometers of hiking trails as well as an information center. Entry fees at this reserve go directly to support local schools.

The Bajo Tigre Trail is a 2-mile-long trail that's home to several different bird species that are not usually found within the reserve. The trail starts a little past the CASEM artisans' shop and is open daily from 8am to 4pm. There is a $2.70 charge to hike this privately owned and maintained trail.

You can also go on guided three-hour hikes at the **Reserva Sendero Tranquilo** (tel. 645-6032), which has 200 acres of land, two-thirds of which is in virgin forest. This reserve is located up the hill from the cheese factory, charges $11.50 for its tours, and is open daily from 5am to 2pm seasonally.

At **Finca de Aves,** which is open daily from 7am to 5pm, there are hiking trails through primary and secondary forest on 43 acres. More than 100 species of birds have been seen here, and there are also good views. Admission is $5.

Guided night tours are another fascinating way to experience the world of the cloud forest. These tours are offered by most area hotels or can be arranged by phoning 645-5118. Glowworms, walking sticks, and luminescent fungi are among the flora and fauna to be seen at night.

When you feel like you've had enough hiking, you might want to try exploring the area on horseback. Most of the hotels here can arrange horseback rides with a guide for between $7 and $10 per person per hour. Alternatively, you can contact **Meg's Riding Stables** (tel. 645-5052), which offers three-hour guided rides for around $34.

To learn more about Monteverde, stop in at the **Monteverde Conservation League** (tel. 645-5003) office, which is located across the street from the gas station. This office is open Monday through Friday from 8am to noon and from 1 to 5pm. They also sell T-shirts and cards here, and proceeds go to help purchase more land for the Bosque Eterno de Los Niños (Children's Eternal Forest).

You can also glimpse part of the area's history at **El Trapiche,** an old-fashioned sugar mill where an ox-driven mill can be demonstrated if you make prior arrangements. El Trapiche is open daily from 10am to 7pm, and admission is $2. You'll find El Trapiche 1½ kilometers north of Santa Elena on the road to Tilarán.

Because the vegetation in the cloud forest is so dense, most of the forest's animal residents are rather difficult to spot. If you were unsatisfied with your sightings, even with a naturalist guide leading you, you might want to consider attending a slide show of photographs taken in the reserve. These slide shows are presented by the **Hummingbird Gallery** (tel. 645-5030) daily at 9:30am and 4:30pm. Admission is $3.40. There are also similar slide shows at the Monteverde Lodge several nights a week.

You'll find the Hummingbird Gallery just outside the reserve entrance. Hanging from trees around the gallery are several hummingbird feeders that attract more than seven species of these avian jewels. At any given moment, there might be several dozen hummingbirds buzzing and chattering around the building. Inside you will, of course, find a lot of beautiful mounted and unmounted color prints of humming-birds. There are also many other beautiful photos from Monteverde available in prints or postcards. The gallery is open daily from 8:30am to 4:30pm.

Birds are not the only colorful fauna in the Monteverde cloud forest. Butterflies abound here, and the **Butterfly Garden,** located near the Pensión Monteverde Inn, displays many of Costa Rica's most beautiful species. Besides the hundreds of pre-served and mounted butterflies, there are also gardens and a greenhouse where you can watch live butterflies. The garden is open daily from 9:30am to 4pm, and the admission is $5 for adults and $2.45 for children, which includes a guided tour. The best time to visit is between 11am and 1pm, when the butterflies are most active.

If you're in the mood to do some shopping, stop in at **CASEM**, which is on the right just past Restaurant El Bosque. This crafts cooperative sells embroidered cloth-ing, T-shirts, posters and postcards with photos of the local flora and fauna, their own Monteverde coffee, and many other items to remind you of your visit to Monteverde. CASEM is open Monday through Saturday from 8am to 5pm, and on Sunday from 10am to 4pm (closed Sundays May through October). Between No-vember and April, you can also visit the Sarah Dowell Watercolor Gallery, which is up the hill from the cheese factory and sells paintings by this local artist.

WHERE TO STAY

When choosing a place to stay in Monteverde, be sure to check whether the rates include meals or not. In the past all the lodges operated on the American plan (all three meals included). This practice is on the wane, though, so rates can be mislead-ing if you don't read carefully.

EXPENSIVE

MONTEVERDE LODGE, Calle Central and Avenida 1 (Apdo. 6941), San José. Tel. 506/257-0766. Fax 506/257-1665. 27 rms.

$ Rates: Dec 15–Apr 30, $67 single, $78 double, $90 triple; May 1–Dec 14, $58 single, $68 double, $78 triple. AE, MC, V.

Operated by Costa Rica Expeditions, the Monteverde is the most upscale of all the Monteverde hotels. The hotel is 5 kilometers from the reserve entrance in a secluded setting near Santa Elena. Guest rooms are large and comfortable and have angled walls of glass, in front of which are set chairs and a table, so avid bird-watchers need not even leave their room to do a bit of birding in the morning. However, the gardens and secondary forest surrounding the lodge are also home to quite a few species of birds.

Dining/Entertainment: The hotel's dining room offers excellent formal service (waiters in bow ties), great views out a wall of glass, and good Tico and interna-tional food. Meals will cost an additional $26.75 (plus tax and tip) per person per day. The big bar adjacent to the dining room is a very popular gathering spot, espe-cially with the many groups that use this lodge. There are regular evening slide shows focusing on the cloud forest.

Services: Bus service to and from San José ($35 each way), shuttle to the re-serve ($4 each way), horseback riding, various optional tours.

Facilities: This lodge's most outstanding feature is a large hot tub in a big atrium garden just off the lobby. After hiking all day, you can soak your bones un-der the stars.

MODERATE

EL ESTABLO, Apdo. 549-2050, San Pedro. Tel. 506/645-5110, 645-5033, or (in San José) 225-0569. Fax 506/645-5041. 20 rms.

$ Rates: $32 single; $40 double; $45 triple; $50 quad. AE, MC, V.

Horses are an integral part of Costa Rican culture and are a common sight in Monteverde. El Establo, as its name implies, makes use of a stable theme in its architectural design. Though the hotel is next to the road, there are 120 acres of farm behind it, and half of this area is in primary forest. Most of the rooms are situated off a large enclosed porch that contains plenty of comfortable chairs and a fireplace. Guest-room doors look as if they were salvaged from a stable, but inside, the rooms are carpeted and have orthopedic mattresses and modern bathrooms, though with showers only. The end rooms have a bit more light than others. There are even two rooms in a renovated real stable. Of course the hotel also has plenty of horses for rent at $5 per hour with a guide ($7 for nonguests). Meals will run you between $17.50 and $20 per person per day.

HOTEL BELMAR, Apdo. 17-5565, Monteverde, Puntarenas. Tel. 506/645-5201. Fax 506/645-5135. 32 rms.

$ Rates: $40 single; $50 double. Discounts sometimes available in low season. No credit cards.

You'll think that you're in the Alps when you stay at this beautiful Swiss chalet-style hotel. Set at the top of a grassy hill, the Belmar has stunning views all the way to the Nicoya Gulf and the Pacific Ocean. Afternoons in the dining room or lounge are idyllic, with bright sunlight streaming in through a west-facing wall of glass that provides a grandstand seat for spectacular sunsets. Most of the guest rooms come with wood paneling, French doors, and little balconies that open onto spendid views. Meals usually live up to the surroundings and run between $18 and $21 per person per day. The Belmar is up a road to the left of the gas station as you come into the village of Monteverde.

HOTEL DE MONTAÑA MONTEVERDE, Apdo. 70, Plaza G. Víquez, San José. Tel. 506/224-3050. Fax 506/222-6184. 22 rms, 8 suites.

$ Rates: Dec–Apr, $40 single, $60 double, $72 triple, $72–$110 suite; May–Nov, $28 single, $42 double, $50.40 triple, $50.40–$77 suite. AE, MC, V.

This long, low, motel-style building is one of the oldest hotels in Monteverde and is frequently filled with tour groups. The hotel is surrounded by 15 acres of farm and woods and there are horses available for rent. Older rooms are rustic and have wood paneling and hardwood floors. Newer rooms have queen-size beds and carpeting. There are also several spacious suites, including one with its own whirlpool tub, all of which have great views. However, my personal favorites are the four little cabins across the lawn from the main lodge. The rustic glass-walled dining room offers excellent views. Attached to the restaurant is a small bar that is always busy in the evening, when people sit around swapping stories of their day's adventures and wildlife sightings. Meals will run you around $30 per person per day. On cold nights, you can warm up in the sauna or hot tub.

HOTEL FONDA VELA, Apdo. 10165-1000, San José. Tel. 506/645-5125, 645-5119, or 257-1413. Fax 506/257-1416. 29 rms (13 with bath), 8 suites. SAFE

$ Rates: $46 single; $55 double; $63 triple; $52–$58 suite single, $62–$70 suite double, $72–$82 suite triple. AE, MC, V.

Located on the right after the sign for the Pensíon Flor Mar, the Fonda Vela is one of the more luxurious lodges in Monteverde. Guest rooms are housed in several buildings scattered among the forests and pastures of this former farm, and most have views out to the Nicoya Gulf. Lots of hardwood has been used throughout and there are flagstone floors in some rooms. About half of the rooms have bathtubs, a rarity in Costa Rica. Several large suites—two of which have sleeping lofts—are the most spacious accommodations available, but unfortunately they do not have any views. On the other hand, the dining room does have great sunset views, though the food is often fairly lackluster. Meals will run you around $20 per person per day. You'll also find a bar and a gift shop here, and laundry service and horse rentals ($8 per hour) are available.

HOTEL HELICONIA, Apdo. 10921-1000, San José. Tel. 506/645-5109. Fax 506/645-5007. 22 rms.

$ Rates: $38 single; $45 double; $55 triple. AE, MC, V.

The Heliconia, named after one of the tropics' most fascinating flowers, is one of the most comfortable and luxurious hotels in Monteverde. The main lodge building has varnished wood walls and a hardwood-floored balcony that runs the length of the second floor. Guest rooms in the main building are also done in floor-to-ceiling hardwoods that give the rooms a rustic, mountain-resort feel. Behind the main lodge there are paths that lead through attractive gardens to rooms with more space. These latter rooms also have carpeting and bathtubs in the bathrooms. There is a hot tub in a large room with a wall of glass that overlooks a bit of forest. Unfortunately, the window quickly gets steamed up, causing you to lose your view. The hotel's restaurant serves a nightly fixed menu with the emphasis on Tico standards. There is also a small bar. There are trails that lead from the hotel up to an area of virgin forest and a viewpoint.

EL SAPO DORADO, Apdo. 10165-1000, San José. Tel. and Fax 506/645/5010. 20 rms (all with bath).

$ Rates: $49.50 single; $60.50 double; $71.50 triple. No credit cards.

⭐ Located up on a steep hill from the main road between Santa Elena and the preserve, El Sapo Dorado (named for Monteverde's famous "golden toad") offers attractive cabins with good views. The cabins are built of hardwoods both inside and out and are surrounded by a grassy lawn. Big windows let in lots of light, and high ceilings keep the rooms cool during the day. The older cabins also have fireplaces, which are a welcome feature on chilly nights. The hotel's restaurant is open to the public and serves three meals daily (breakfast 7 to 10am; lunch noon to 3pm; dinner 6 to 9pm). The dinner menu changes nightly, but among the regular offerings are chicken with olive sauce, sailfish niçoise, and filet mignon with pepper cream sauce. Prices range from $5 to $8.90. There is a large patio terrace from which you can watch the sunset while listening to classical music. The bar here stays open until 11pm and is usually fairly quiet. To find the hotel and restaurant, watch for the sign on the main road to the preserve.

BUDGET

EL BOSQUE, Apdo. 1165-1000, San José. Tel. 506/645-5129 or 645-5158. Fax 506/645-5129. 20 rms.

$ Rates: $17.50 single; $24.50 double; $29.75 triple; $33.25 quad. V.

Hidden down the hill behind El Bosque restaurant (on the main road to the preserve), is one of Monteverde's best values. Though the rooms are very basic, they are clean, fairly large, and have high ceilings, picture windows, and double beds. The cement floors and simple furnishings are what help keep the rates down. The rooms are arranged in a semicircle around a minimally landscaped garden. The setting may not be spectacular, but if you're going to spend all day in the reserve, this shouldn't bother you too much. The hotel also has a camping area ($2.70 per person per night).

The hotel's restaurant is a hundred yards up a dirt road and down a path that crosses a jungly ravine on a footbridge, which turns going for breakfast into a morning bird-watching trip. Tico standards and international dishes are served here, with prices ranging from $3.05 to $12.20.

CABINAS EL GRAN MIRADOR DE SAN GERARDO, Monteverde, Puntarenas. Tel. 506/661-3750 (leave message). Fax 506/661-3505. 5 cabins (none with private bath), 12 dorm beds.

$ Rates: $8 per person in the dorm; $18 single; $25 double. No credit cards.

If you're looking for a bit more adventure and rusticity than is offered at any of the lodges in Monteverde or Santa Elena, give these friendly folks a call. The rustic wooden cabins and dormitory building are all very simply furnished, though the cabins do have great views of Arenal Volcano (when it's clear). Here's the catch: for the most part of the year you'll have to spend three hours on horseback to reach these cabins. Only during the driest months from February to May is it possible to drive a car to the cabins. The cabins are a long way from the Monteverde Cloud Forest Reserve, but they are close to the Santa Elena Rainforest Reserve.

HOTEL EL TUCAN, Santa Elena, Puntarenas. Tel. 506/645-5017. 14 rms (7 with bath).

$ Rates: $6.75 single without bath, $10.15 single with bath; $13.50 double without bath, $20.30 double with bath. No credit cards.

This very basic hotel is located on the edge of Santa Elena (on the back road from the village's main street to the road to Monteverde) and consequently does not have the rural feel of many of the area's other accommodations. Though the rooms without bath are only slightly larger than closets, they are fairly clean. Rooms with private bathrooms are in a separate building and are slightly larger. Costa Rican–style meals are served in a very basic dining room on the ground floor. Keep in mind that this hotel is 5 kilometers from the reserve. If you don't have a car, transportation to and from the reserve by taxi is going to add a bit to the cost of the room.

PENSIÓN EL PINO, Monteverde, Puntarenas. Tel. 506/645-5130. 5 rms (all with shared bath).

$ Rates: $5 single; $10 double; $15 triple. No credit cards.

These rooms are as basic as they come. They are slightly larger than those at the Pensión Manakin next door and have red-tile floors. Some rooms have double beds and others have bunk beds. No meals are available here, so you'll have to walk down the road a little ways to the nearest restaurant. You'll find the pensión just off the main road about a third of the way from Santa Elena to the reserve.

PENSIÓN FLOR MAR, Apdo. 10165-1000, San José. Tel. 506/645-5009. Fax 506/645-5011. 13 rms (3 with bath).

$ Rates (including three meals): $22 single without bath, $25 single with bath; $44 double without bath, $50 double with bath. No credit cards.

The Flor Mar was one of the first lodges to open in Monteverde and initially catered almost exclusively to professors and students doing scientific research in the reserve. Study groups are still the bulk of the Flor Mar's business, but casual visitors are also welcome, though the accommodations are very basic (scientists and students don't seem overly concerned with their accommodations). The rooms are very simply furnished, which means bunk beds in some rooms. One room is so small that it reminds me of a monk's cell. There are also no views to speak of here. However, this lodge is close to the park entrance, which is a definite plus if you don't have a car. The dining room is large and rather dark, but there is a much more appealing lounge in the lower of the lodge's two main buildings. Note that the rates here include all your meals.

PENSIÓN MONTEVERDE INN, Apdo 10165-1000, San José. Tel. 506/ 645-5156. 10 rms (all with bath).

$ Rates: $8 single; $16 double. No credit cards.

Of the numerous budget lodgings in the area, this one has the most pleasant surroundings. Located next to the Monteverde Butterfly Garden, the Monteverde Inn is a couple of hundred yards off the main road on a small farm. Owner David Savage and his family have operated this simple, rustic lodge for years. The rooms are small and come with two twin beds or a double bed. Hardwood floors keep the rooms from seeming too Spartan. It's a bit of a walk up to the park entrance, but once you reach the main road, you can try hitching a ride. Horse rentals here are $5 per hour. This is a good choice for those who have to watch their colónes. Economical meals are available.

WHERE TO DINE

Most lodges in Monteverde have their own dining rooms, and these are the most convenient places to eat. Because most visitors to Monteverde want to get an early start, they usually grab a quick breakfast at their hotel. It is also common for people to have their lodge pack them a bag lunch to take with them to the reserve. However, there are now several inexpensive restaurants scattered along the road between Santa Elena and Monteverde. Two inexpensive places worth mentioning are the Pizzeria de Johnny near the Hotel Heliconia and the Soda Cerro Verde across from the gas station. If your lodge doesn't offer meals or you've tried the food there and aren't impressed, there are a couple of options. However, keep in mind that since the lodges are scattered across more than three miles of road, it can be a long hike to eat a meal if you don't have your own vehicle.

When it comes to lunch, you can get a bag lunch from your hotel as I already mentioned, or you can piece together your own on the way to the reserve. Stop in at Stella's Bakery (across the road from the CASEM gift shop) for some fresh bread and maybe a piece of cake or some cookies. Stella's is open daily from 6am to 6pm and also has a small café where you can get pizzas, eggplant parmigiana, and salads. Next, stop by the Monteverde Cheese Factory and pick up some of the best cheese in Costa Rica (you can even see it being made). The cheese factory is open Monday through Saturday from 7:30 am to 4pm and on Sunday from 7:30am to 12:30 pm. There you have it, the ingredients for a great picnic lunch.

LA CASCADA, off the main road just past the gas station. Tel. 645-5128.
   Cuisine: INTERNATIONAL/COSTA RICAN. **Reservations:** Not accepted.
$ Prices: Complete meals $6.10–$13.20. V.
   Open: Tues–Sun 6–10pm.

This unusual restaurant is set back a bit from the main road and looks out on a waterfall, though it also looks out on what appears to have once been a rock quarry. There is even a small waterfall inside the large open-air restaurant. This has recently become the hangout for Monteverde and, as unlikely as it sounds, offers dancing to recorded music after 9pm each night. Meals are decent though comparable to what is served at most lodges in the area.

EL SAPO DORADO, road to the left as you leave Santa Elena. Tel. 645-5010.
   Cuisine: INTERNATIONAL. **Reservations:** Not accepted.
$ Prices: Appetizers $1.35–$4.60; main courses $6.60–$12.20. No credit cards.
   Open: Daily 1–10am, noon–3pm, 6–9pm.

Located high on a hill above the main road, El Sapo Dorado provides great sunsets and good food for accompaniment. The menu here is a little bit more imaginative than at most restaurants in Monteverde, which makes it well worth a visit even if you miss the sunset. A recent menu included such dishes as grilled corvina, fettuccini in peanut-squid sauce, and filet mignon in pepper-cream sauce. In addition to a large, formal dining room, there is a patio that's a great spot for lunch or an early dinner. Rounding out the entire scene is taped classical music in the evenings.

CHAPTER 6

THE CENTRAL PACIFIC COAST

The central Pacific coast offers several of the most easily accessible beaches in Costa Rica. These vary in character from the Miami-style beach-front promenade of Puntarenas to the cut-rate, fun-in-the-sun, Canadian-charter-flight hotels of Jacó to the jungle-clad hillsides of Manuel Antonio and Dominical. For the most part, this coast is not as spectacular as that of the more rugged Nicoya Peninsula, but neither is it as brown and desolate-looking in the dry season. The climate here is considerably more humid than farther north, but not nearly as steamy as along the south Pacific or Caribbean coasts. Jacó and Manuel Antonio are Costa Rica's two most developed beaches, while Puntarenas, a former seaport, offers the most urban beach setting in the country. If you are looking to get away from it all and spend as little money as possible, Dominical should be your top choice on this coast.

1. PUNTARENAS

130 kilometers W of San José; 113 kilometers S of Liberia; 60 kilometers N of Playa de Jacó

GETTING THERE **By Bus** Express buses leave San José daily every 30 minutes between 5am and 7pm from the corner of Calle 12 and Avenida 9. Duration: 2 hours. Fare: $2.60.

By Car Head west out of San José on the Interamerican Highway, passing the airport and Alajuela, and follow the signs to Puntarenas. The drive takes about 1½ hours.

By Ferry See the "Playa Tambor" or "Playa Montezuma" sections of Chapter 4 for information on crossing to Puntarenas from Paquera or Naranjo on the Nicoya Peninsula.

DEPARTING The main Puntarenas bus station is a block east of the Hotel Imperial, which is in front of the old main dock on the Paseo de los Turistas. Buses to San José leave daily every 30 minutes between 5am and 7pm. The bus to Santa Elena leaves daily at 2:15pm from a stop across the railroad tracks from the main bus station. Buses to Quepos (Manuel Antonio) leave daily at 5am and 2:30pm. A bus leaves for Liberia daily at 5:30pm.

See the "Playa Tambor" or "Playa Montezuma" sections of Chapter 4 for information on taking ferries to Paquera or Naranjo on the Nicoya Peninsula.

ESSENTIALS **Orientation** Puntarenas is built on a long, narrow sand spit that stretches 3 miles out into the Gulf of Nicoya, and marked by only five streets at its widest. The ferry docks for the Nicoya Peninsula are near the far end of town,

WHAT'S SPECIAL ABOUT THE CENTRAL PACIFIC COAST

Beaches

Manuel Antonio National Park, three idyllic beaches set amid jungle-clad hills.

Playa de Jacó, an inexpensive resort area with many deserted beaches nearby.

Dominical, great surfing, and not far away, pretty beaches and tide-pool area.

Natural Spectacles

The views of mountains, jungle,and sea from the hills of Manuel Antonio.

Waterfalls, reached by horse from Dominical.

Activities

Sportfishing out of Quepos.

A day-long cruise around the Gulf of Nicoya.

Sea-kayak trips near Quepos and Manuel Antonio.

Hiking up Mount Chirripó.

Surfing at Playa de Jacó and Playa Hermosa.

Parks

Carara Biological Reserve, a transitional forest between wet and dry regions.

---

as are the bus station and market. The north side of town faces an estuary, while the south side faces the mouth of the gulf. The Paseo de los Turistas is on the south side of town, beginning at the pier and extending out to the point. If you need a taxi, phone 661-0053 or 663-0250. Car rentals are available from Discovery Rent-a-Car (tel. 661-0328).

Puntarenas, a 10-mile-long spit of sand jutting into the Gulf of Nicoya, was once Costa Rica's busiest port, but a while back it was replaced by nearby Puerto Caldera, a modern container port facility. Since losing its port, the city has been struggling to attract more tourists. To that end the city built a sewage treatment plant to clean up the water, and Puntarenas now has the only beach-cleaning machine in Costa Rica. With a good highway leading all the way from San José, Puntarenas can be reached in an hour and a half, which makes it the closest beach to San José, at least in elapsed time if not in actual mileage.

Because Puntarenas is a city, this beach has a very different character from any other beach in Costa Rica. The beach itself, a long straight stretch of sand with gentle surf, is backed for most of its length by the Paseo de los Turistas, a promenade that is ideal for strolling. Across a wide boulevard from the paseo are hotels, restaurants, bars, discos, and shops. It's all very civilized, though the preponderance of cement gives it too much of an urban feel for my tastes. The views across the Gulf of Nicoya and the sunsets are quite beautiful, and there is almost always a cooling breeze blowing in off the water. All around town you'll find unusual old buildings, reminders of the important role Puntarenas once played in Costa Rican history. It was from here that much of the Central Valley's coffee crop was once shipped, and while the coffee barons in the highlands were getting rich, so too were the merchants of Puntarenas.

If you're in Costa Rica for only a short time and want to get in some time on the beach, Puntarenas is a good option. You can even do it in a day trip from San José. Likewise, if you are looking for a base from which to visit national parks up and down the Pacific coast, Puntarenas is one of your best bets. From here you can head north to the national parks in Guanacaste or south to Carara Biological Reserve. Also, if you are heading out to any of the beaches at the southern end of the Nicoya Peninsula, you'll be passing through Puntarenas to catch one of the three ferries. Puntarenas is most popular as a weekend holiday spot for Ticos from San José and is at its liveliest on the weekends.

WHAT TO SEE & DO

Take a walk along the **Paseo de los Turistas** and notice how similar this side of town is to a few Florida towns 50 years ago. If you want to go swimming, the ocean waters are now said to be perfectly safe. Alternatively, you can head out to the end of the peninsula to the **Balneario Municipal,** the public pool. It is huge, has a great view (albeit through a chain-link fence), and is surrounded by lawns and gardens. Entrance is only 85¢ for adults and 50¢ for children. The pool is open Tuesday through Sunday from 9am to 4pm. If the beach right here in the city doesn't appeal to you, head back down the spit to the **Playa Dona Aña,** a popular beach park with picnic tables and a restaurant.

Puntarenas isn't known as one of Costa Rica's prime sportfishing ports, but there are usually a few charter boats available. Check at your hotel or at the Hotel Colonial. Rates are usually between $300 and $400 for a half day and between $500 and $600 for a full day. These rates are for up to four people.

The most popular water excursions from Puntarenas are **yacht cruises** among the tiny uninhabited islands of the Guayabo, Negritos, and Pajaros Islands Biological Reserve. These cruises include a gourmet seafood buffet and a stop at beautiful and undeveloped Tortuga Island, where you can swim, snorkel, and sun. The water is a clear blue, and the sand is bright white. Several San José–based companies offer these excursions, with round-trip transportation from San José, but if you are already in Puntarenas, you may be able to get a discount. Calypso Tours (tel. 233-3617), Costa Sol Tropical Cruises (tel. 239-2000), and Fantasy Fun Cruises (tel. 255-0791) are just three of the companies that offer similar tours and will pick you up at your hotel in San José. The price for one of these trips is $70 (or slightly less if leaving from Puntarenas). These companies also offer sunset cruises with live music, snacks, and a bar. Calypso also offers sailing excursions on the catamaran *Star Chaser.*

WHERE TO STAY

EXPENSIVE

HOTEL FIESTA, Apdo. 171-5400, Puntarenas. Tel. 506/663-0185, 663-0808, or toll free (in the U.S.) 800/662-2990 or 800/228-5050. Fax 506/663-1516. 174 rms, 10 suites. A/C TV TEL
$ Rates: Dec 16–Apr 15, $99–$109 single or double, $109–$250 suite; Apr 16–Dec 15, $69–$100 single or double, $100–$242 suite. AE, MC, V.
There are only a handful of full-service beach resorts in Costa Rica, and only those in Jacó are closer to San José than the Fiesta. So if you're looking for a place in the sun, and you don't want to waste time getting there, this place is worth consideration. As the name implies, the Fiesta is meant for partying, or at least keeping active. It is also a convention hotel, so expect crowds. Though the resort is right on the beach, it isn't a good swimming beach, so you'll have to confine your water activities to the giant swimming pool.

The hotel is only a few years old, but many of the guest rooms are already showing their age. Though there are large TVs in all the rooms, the bathrooms in the standard rooms are small and have showers only. However, if you opt for a deluxe room or suite, you'll get more comfortable and spacious accommodations.

Dining/Entertainment: A giant rancho at the back of the hotel serves as a restaurant and bar. The latter is done up to resemble a sailboat, complete with sails and rigging. Prices in the restaurant range from $5.10 to $8.10 for entrées, though there are also set-price buffets at most meals. A second bar is on an island in the middle of the main pool, and there is also a casino in a large atrium.

Services: Rentals of snorkeling equipment, jet skis, water skis, and sailboards. Tour arrangements and excursions, including scuba trips, sportfishing charters, national-park visits, and day cruises.

Facilities: The free-form main swimming pool is huge, has an island in the middle, and is surrounded by hundreds of lounge chairs. Artificial boulders give it a more natural look. In addition, you'll find a second pool, whirlpool tub, volleyball court, two tennis courts, exercise room, game room, gift shop, and jewelry shop.

YADRAN HOTEL, At the end of the Paseo de los Turistas (Apdo. 14-5000), Puntarenas. Tel. 506/661-2662. Fax 506/661-1944. 43 rms, 1 suite. A/C TEL SAFE

$ Rates: Dec–Apr, $70–$96 single or double, $133 suite; May–Nov, $63–$82 single or double, $133 suite. AE, DC, MC, V.

This is the most luxurious in-town choice and is located at the far end of Puntarenas at the tip of the spit. Because it is in town, you'll have access to other restaurants and can stroll the Paseo de los Turistas. Also, the car-ferry dock is only a few blocks away. There are three basic types of rooms. The most expensive are those with carpeting, TV, and a view of the water. For slightly less, you can get a room with either a view or a TV. Least expensive, though largest, are the rooms with no view and no TV. These rooms are also not very attractively furnished. I like the upper-floor view rooms the best.

Dining/Entertainment: The hotel has two small restaurants, both of which overlook the pool and the beach. One is a patio restaurant, and the other is a slightly more formal indoor dining room. The seafood here is good, if a bit pricey. Entrée prices range from $6.60 to $18.95.

Services: Bicycle rentals, tour and sportfishing arrangements.

Facilities: The pool is small, but it has an attractive patio surrounding it. Gift shop.

MODERATE

HOTEL LA PUNTA, 100 meters south of the ferry terminal, Barrio El Carmel (Apdo. 228), Puntarenas. Tel. 506/661-0696. 13 rms.

$ Rates: $23.65 single; $30.40 double; $37.85 triple; $44.60 quad ($6.75 extra for A/C). AE, DC, MC, V.

This modest hotel is located out at the far end of the Puntarenas peninsula near the car-ferry dock, which makes it a great choice for anyone heading over to the Nicoya Peninsula with a car. A covered sidewalk leads from the street to the open-air bar/restaurant that also serves as a reception area. If you can overlook the mismatched sheets on the beds and the occasional stuffiness, the rooms here are generally acceptable. They all have fans, and a couple also have air-conditioning. The rooms vary in size quite a bit; the four- and five-bedrooms are huge. Try to get a room with a balcony. Out in back of the two-story hotel, there's a small but very clean and attractive swimming pool.

HOTEL LAS BRISAS, Paseo de los Turistas (Apdo. 83-5400), Puntarenas. Tel. 506/661-4040. Fax 506/661-1487. 19 rms (all with bath). A/C

$ Rates: $30 single; $50 double; $60 triple (discounts in the off-season). AE, MC, V.

Out near the end of the Paseo de los Turistas, you'll find a very clean hotel with large air-conditioned rooms, a small pool out front, and the beach right across the street. All the rooms have tile floors, double or twin beds, and small tables. Large picture windows keep the rooms sunny and bright during the day. The hotel's small open-air dining room serves some of the best food in town with the emphasis on continental dishes. The bouillabaise is excellent, and if you're lucky you might happen on a Greek-style fish special. It's worth staying here just to enjoy the food.

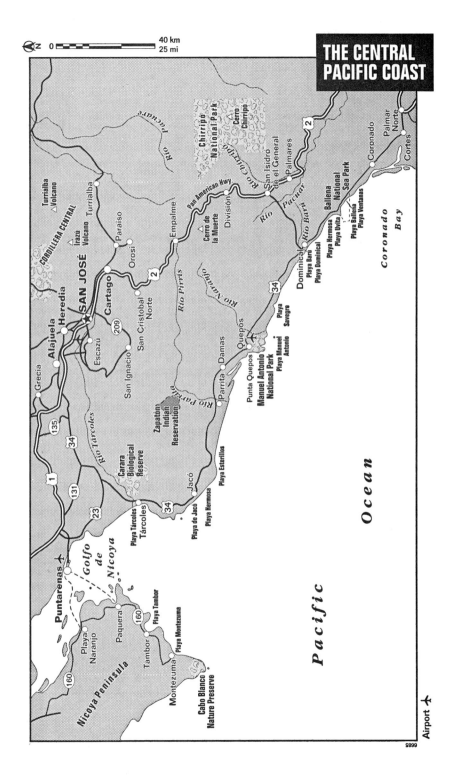

HOTEL PORTO BELLO, Apdo. 108, Puntarenas. Tel. 506/661-1322 or 661-2122. Fax 506/661-0036. 34 rms. A/C TEL
$ Rates: Dec–Apr, $45 single, $60 double, $70 triple; May–Nov, $32 single, $41 double, $60 triple. AE, MC, V.

Located right next door to the Colonial (above), the Porto Bello is a slightly more luxurious, although similar, weekend escape for wealthy Ticos. The stucco walls of the hotel are almost blindingly white, tempered by the lush overgrown garden that surrounds the buildings. Most of the rooms have high ceilings, red-tile floors, attractive teak-and-cloth headboards, and balconies or patios that are often hidden by the shrubbery. There are pools for adults and kids, with a poolside bar, and even a small beach. You can hire a water taxi for a spin around the bay or book an all-day cruise to some of the remote and picturesque islands out in the gulf. The open-air restaurant is breezy and cool, with a high ceiling and stucco walls. Grilled meats and seafood are the specialties here—with entrées ranging in price from $6 to $20.25.

HOTEL TIOGA, Paseo de los Turistas (Apdo. 96-5400), Puntarenas. Tel. 506/661-0271 or (in San José) 255-3115. Fax 506/661-0127 or (in San José) 255-1006. 46 rms (all with bath). A/C
$ Rates (including breakfast): $29.75–$44.50 single; $37.15–$55.70 double (slightly lower rates in off season). AE, MC, V.

This 1950s modern-style hotel is Puntarenas's old standard on the Paseo de los Turistas. The beach is right across the street and there are plenty of restaurants within a short walk. When you walk through the front door, you enter a courtyard with a pool that has been painted a brilliant shade of blue. In the middle of the pool, there is even a little island with a tree growing on it. The four-story hotel is built around this pleasant setting. Rooms vary in size, and some come with cold-water showers only, so if you must have hot water (not really necessary in these hot regions), be sure to request it. The larger rooms are very attractive—with huge closets and modern bathrooms. The smaller, less expensive rooms have louvered, frosted-glass windows to let in lots of light and air while maintaining some privacy. There is a cafeteria and bar on the second floor and a breakfast room and lounge on the fourth floor. You'll be able to look out across the water as you enjoy your complimentary breakfast.

BUDGET

HOTEL AYI CON, 50 meters south of the market (Apdo. 358), Puntarenas. Tel. 506/661-0164 or 661-1477. 44 rms (22 with private bath).
$ Rates: $4.60 single without bath, $6.35 single with bath; $8.80 double without bath, $12.65 double with bath. No credit cards.

Centrally located near the market and the ferry-boat docks, the Ayi Con is your basic low-budget Tico hotel. It's above a row of shops in a very busy shopping district of Puntarenas and is frequented primarily by Costa Ricans. Backpackers will find that this is probably the best and the cleanest of the cheap hotels in Puntarenas. If you're just passing through and have to spend a night in town, this place is convenient and acceptable.

WHERE TO DINE

Your hotel restaurant is likely going to be the best place to eat. At the **Porto Bello,** the grilled steaks are particularly good. Since you are in a seaport, you should be sure to try corvina—the national fish dish of Costa Rica—at least once. Another option is to pull up a table at one of the half-dozen open-air **snack bars** along the Paseo de los Turistas. They have names like Soda Rio de Janeiro and Soda Acapulco and serve sandwiches, drinks, ice cream, and other snacks. Sandwiches are priced at around a dollar.

LA CARAVELLE, Paseo de los Turistas between calles 21 and 23, Paseo de los Turistas. Tel. 661-2262.
  Cuisine: FRENCH. **Reservations:** Suggested in high season and on weekends.
$ Prices: Appetizers $2.40–$3.05; main courses $5.30–$15.20. DC, MC, V.
  Open: Wed–Sat noon–3:30pm and 6–10pm, Sun noon–10pm.
For more than 15 years, La Caravelle has been serving fine French dinners amid an eclectic café atmosphere. The restaurant's walls are decorated with a curious assortment of paintings, as well as a carousel horse, that together give La Caravelle a very playful feel. The menu, however, is strictly traditional French, with such flavorful and well-prepared dishes as tenderloin with bourguignonne sauce or a tarragon béarnaise. There are quite a few good seafood dishes, as well as a salade niçoise. There's a good assortment of both French and Chilean wines to accompany your meal, though prices are rather high (as they are all over Costa Rica).

READERS RECOMMEND

La Ostra, four blocks west of the Hotel Porto Bello. Tel. 661-0272. ". . . the best restaurant in Costa Rica is in Puntarenas—La Ostra—splendid service, fine food, and the best fresh coconut custard I've ever had."—John Sinning, Jr.

---

2. PLAYA DE JACÓ

108 kilometers W of San José; 60 kilometers S of Puntarenas

GETTING THERE By Bus Express buses leave San José daily at 7:15am and 3:30pm from Calle 16 between avenidas 1 and 3. Duration: 2½ hours. Fare: $2.30.
  From Puntarenas, you can catch Quepos-bound buses daily at 5am and 2:30pm and get off in Jacó. Duration: 1 hour. Fare: $1.60.
  Buses returning from Quepos to San José also stop in Jacó. These buses leave Quepos daily at 5 and 8am and 2 and 4pm. Duration: 2½ hours. Fare: $1.65.

By Car There are two main routes to Jacó. The easier though longer route is to take the Interamerican Highway west out of San José and get off at the Puntarenas exit. From here, head south on the Costanera, the coast road. Alternatively, you can take the narrow and winding, though more scenic, old highway, which turns off the Interamerican Highway just west of Alajuela near the town of Atenas. This highway meets the Cosanera a few kilometers west of Orotina.

DEPARTING The Jacó bus station is at the north end of town about 50 yards off the main road near the Hotel El Jardin. Buses for San José leave daily at 5am and 3pm. Buses bound for Quepos stop in Jacó around 6 and 8am and 2, 2:30, and 8pm. Since schedules can change it is best to ask at your hotel about current times of departures.

ESSENTIALS Orientation Playa de Jacó is a short distance off the southern highway. One main road runs parallel to the beach and it is off these roads that you will find most of the hotels and restaurants. You'll find a coin-operated laundry, open daily from 8am to noon and 1 to 8pm, opposite the I.C.E. building on the main drag. You can rent a car from Elegante (tel. 643-3224) for about $50 per day. There's a bank in the middle of town on the main road. Botiquín Garabito, the town's pharmacy, is down the street from the bank. There is a gas station out by El Bosque restaurant at the south end of town. The health center and post office are at the Municipal Center at the south end of town, across from El Naranjal restaurant. A public phone office, from which you can make international calls, is located in the

I.C.E. building on the main road. This office is open Monday through Saturday from 8am to noon and from 1 to 5pm.

If you're looking for a cheap place to spend a week in the sun, Playa de Jacó is currently the top choice in Costa Rica. Charter flights arrive weekly from Montréal and Toronto and consequently many of the hotels here are owned by Canadians, some of whom speak French and Spanish but little English. Jacó is also now gaining popularity with Germans, so if English is your native tongue, you may find yourself in a distinct minority here. This is the most touristy beach in Costa Rica and is a prime example of what happens when rapid growth hits a beach town. With no master plan and few building codes in effect, Jacó is now a hodge-podge of big and small hotels, cheap eateries, souvenir shops, and lots of cinderblock walls. However, on the outskirts of town and close to the beach there is still plenty of greenery to offset the excess of cement along the town's main street. In fact, this is the first beach on the Pacific coast that actually has a tropical feel to it. The humidity is palpable and the lushness of the tropical forest is visible on the hillsides surrounding town. In hotel gardens, flowers bloom profusely throughout the year.

WHAT TO SEE & DO

Unfortunately, the water here has a nasty reputation for riptides, as does most of the water of Costa Rica's Pacific coast. Even strong swimmers have been know to drown in the power rips. Storms far offshore often cause huge waves to pound on the beach, making it impossible to go in the water at all. You'll have to be content with the hotel pool (if your hotel has one) most of the time.

After you've spent some time on Playa de Jacó, you might want to visit some of the other nearby beaches, of which there are several. **Playa Esterillos,** 22 kilometers southwest of Jacó, is long and wide and almost always nearly deserted. **Playa Hermosa,** 10 kilometers southeast of Jacó, where sea turtles lay eggs from July to December, is also well know for its great surfing waves. **Playa Herradura,** about 6½ kilometers northwest of Jacó, is ringed by lush hillsides and has a campground and a few very basic cabinas. All of these beaches are beautiful and easily reached by car or bicycle (if you've got plenty of energy).

The same waves that often make Playa de Jacó unsafe for swimming make this beach the most popular in the country with gringo surfers. In addition, there are a couple of other excellent surfing beaches nearby—Playa Hermosa and **Playa Escondida.** Those who want to challenge the waves can rent surfboards for $2.50 an hour and boogie boards for $1.50 an hour. If you'd rather do a bit of sailing on a Sunfish, check with Cross Cruises at the Hotel Copacabana down near the beach in the center of town. This company charges $15 an hour or $50 for half a day. They also offer sailing lessons and beach chair and umbrella rentals.

If you would rather stay out of the surf but still want to get some exercise, you can rent a bike for $6.75 per day or $1.35 per hour. Both bikes and boards are available from several places along the main road.

If you're interested in doing some **sportfishing,** contact Viajes Jaguar (tel. 643-3242), which has its office in an older house next door to the phone office on the main road through town. A half-day fishing trip for four people will cost $300 and a full day will cost $450.

Scuba divers can arrange **dive trips** through Viajes Jaguar where a two-tank drive is a pricey $80 ($100 with equipment rental). They also rent snorkeling gear for $10 a day.

For nature lovers, the **Carara Biological Reserve,** 15 kilometers north of Jacó, has several miles of trails. There is a loop trail that takes about an hour and another trail that is open only to tour groups. Among the wildlife you might see here are caimans, coatimundis, armadillo, pacas, peccaries, river otters, kinkajous, and, of course, hundreds of species of birds. The reserve is open daily from 8am to noon and from 1 to 4:30pm. Admission is $1.35. There are several companies offering tours to Carara Biological Reserve for around $30. Check at your hotel or contact Fantasy Tours (tel. 643-3231 or 643-3383) or San José Travel (tel. 643-3258).

Horseback-riding tours are also very popular. These trips give you a chance to get away from all the development in Jacó and see a bit of nature. Contact Fantasy Tours, Unicornio Ranch (tel. 643-3019); Sanchez Madrigal Bros. (tel. 643-3203); or AFA Tours (tel. 643-3215 or 643-3248) to make a reservation. Tours lasting 3 to 4 hours cost around $25 to $30.

If you will be spending your entire Costa Rican visit in Jacó but would like to see some other parts of the country, you can arrange tours through the local office of San José Tours (tel. 643-3258). This company offers day tours to Poás and Irazú volcanoes, white-water rafting trips, cruises to Tortuga Island, trips to Brauli Carillo and Manuel Antonio national parks, and other places. They also offer overnight trips. Another local tour company, Explorica (tel. 643-3586), offers similar tours. Rates range from $50 to $70 for day trips.

WHERE TO STAY

EXPENSIVE

HOTEL HACIENDA LILIPOZA, Apdo. 15-4023, Playa de Jacó, Puntarenas. Tel. 506/643-3062. Fax 506/643-3158. 20 rms. A/C TV TEL
$ Rates (including full breakfast): $120 single or double; $146 triple; $172 quad. AE, MC, V.

Though the Lilipoza is about a mile from the beach, it is still the most elegant, luxurious, and expensive hotel in Jacó. You'll find the Lilipoza down a 600-meter gravel road off the main highway near El Bosque restaurant. What the Lilipoza has to offer is a tranquil tropical setting and huge, suite-like rooms. The gardens are attractive, and the location away from the crowds and noise along the beach assure a peaceful vacation should you choose to stay here.

Guest rooms have high ceilings, tile floors, and wicker furniture. There are also lots of windows, beautiful carved wood doors, and columned verandas. The bathrooms are some of the largest in the country. They're done in blue-and-white tiles and have two sinks, bathtubs, and bidets.

Dining/Entertainment: The dining room, which is the best restaurant in Jacó, is at the upper end of the hotel grounds and looks out over the gardens. The menu focuses on continental dishes and seafoods, with prices ranging from $6.45 to $16.90 for entrées. Adjacent to the restaurant is an open-air bar and casual restaurant that overlooks the pool.

Services: Room service, shuttle service, tour desk, car-rental desk.

Facilities: Small swimming pool, tennis court, boutique.

HOTEL JACÓFIESTA, Apdo. 38, Playa de Jacó, Puntarenas. Tel. 506/643-3147, 643-3243, or 643-3244. Fax 506/643-3148. 85 rms. A/C/ TV TEL SAFE
$ Rates: $50–$90 single, $55–$100 double. AE, MC, V.

If you are not coming down to Jacó on a Canadian charter, it is often next to impossible to find a room in the high season. This is one place to try, since they don't seem to book up completely with tour groups. Located at the east end of the beach, the Jacófiesta has rooms of various types and ages. I like the large cabina rooms, which have kitchenettes and are located near both the pool and the beach. The older buildings have smaller rooms that are adequate but that face a barren-looking garden. These rooms have small refrigerators.

Dining/Entertainment: The open-air restaurant serves international dishes with an emphasis on seafood. Entrée prices range from $6 to $15. The hotel has recently added a very modern-looking building to house its casino and disco.

Service: Tour desk, car-rental desk.

Facilities: Two adult pools, two kids' pools, tennis court, gift shop.

JACÓ BEACH HOTEL, Playa de Jacó (Apdo. 962-1000, San José), Puntarenas. Tel. 506/220-1441, or toll free (in the U.S.) 800/272-6654 or (in Canada) 800/463-6654. Fax 506/232-3154. 130 rms. A/C TEL SAFE

$ Rates: Nov–Apr, $77 single, $88 double; May–Oct (including continental breakfast), $42 single, $52 double. AE, DC, MC, V.

This is Jacó's main Canadian charter flight hotel and is packed throughout the high season with crowds fleeing the cold in Ontario and Quebec. Situated right on the beach, this five-story hotel is just what you would expect of a tropical beach resort. The open-air lobby is surrounded by lush gardens, and there are covered walkways connecting the hotel's buildings. The hotel underwent some remodeling in 1993 and now has a more modern look about it. Rooms are adequate, and have tile floors and walls of glass facing onto the balconies. However, not all rooms have good views (some face another building). Ask for a view room on a higher floor if possible. Bathrooms tend to be a bit battered, but they do have bathtubs. If you'd like more space and a kitchen, ask about the Villas Jacó Princess across the road.

Dining/Entertainment: El Muelle, the hotel's open-air restaurant, overlooks the pool and serves familiar dishes in the $4.40-to-$18.95 price range. Out by the beach, there is the Bar Guipipías, which overlooks the water and doubles as a disco. There is also a small casino.

Services: Room service, tour desk, car-rental desk, laundry service, and bicycle, motorcycle, and surfboard rentals.

Facilities: The round swimming pool seems rather small by today's resort standards and can get crowded. Tennis court, volleyball court, gift shop.

MODERATE

APARTAMENTOS EL MAR, Playa de Jacó, Puntarenas. Tel. and Fax 506/ 643-3165. 12 apts.

$ Rates: Dec–Apr, $48 single, $52 double; May–Nov, $30 single or double. MC, V.

At the east end of town, not far from the beach, is a modest apartment hotel built around a small pool and colorful garden. The apartments are clean and spacious, and each comes with a kitchen, two couches, and a double and single bed. Overhead fans and high ceilings keep the rooms cool. There is no restaurant since most guests do their own cooking. If you feel like going bicycling, they have a few bikes for rent. In the high season, El Mar also offers in-room massages and beauty-salon service.

APARTOTEL GAVIOTAS, Playa de Jacó, Puntarenas. Tel. 506/643-3092. Fax 506/643-3054. 12 apts.

$ Rates: Dec–Apr, $52.50 one to six people; May–Nov, $28 double, $34 triple, $38 quad. AE, DC, MC, V.

Although it's on the inland side of the main road and is a bit of a walk from the beach, this is one of the nicest places in town. These cheerful little apartments are intended for families or groups who plan to stay for a week or more but in the off-season are a great bargain even for two people. Each apartment has a front wall of windows looking onto the little pool, a cathedral ceiling with clerestory windows, and a fan. Floors are tile, as are the kitchen counters. The living rooms have built-in couches, and in the bedrooms you'll find a double bed and a bunk bed. In each bathroom you'll find an elegant scalloped sink. Though there is no restaurant here, there is a little bar beside the pool.

FLAMBOYANT HOTEL, Apdo. 18, Playa de Jacó, Puntarenas. Tel. 506/ 643-3146. 8 rms.

$ Rates: $30–$40 single; $35–$40 double. No credit cards.

The Flamboyant doesn't quite live up to its name, but it is still a good value. The rooms are arranged around a small swimming pool, and you are only a few steps from the beach. All the rooms are spacious and have kitchenettes, though otherwise the furnishings are quite simple. You'll find the Flamboyant down a narrow lane from the Flamboyant Restaurant, which is on the main road in the middle of Jacó.

HOTEL CLUB DEL MAR, Apdo. 107-4023, Playa de Jacó, Puntarenas. Tel. 506/643-3194. 16 rms.

$ Rates: Nov–Apr, $68–$87 single or double; May–Oct, $30–$55 single or double. MC, V.

✪ Because of its location, friendly owners, and attractively designed new rooms, this is my favorite Playa de Jacó hotel. The Club del Mar is at the far eastern end of the beach where the rocky hills meet the beach. The addition to the hotel is a two-story shell-pink building that houses four very comfortable rooms. Each has a green-tile floor, pastel bedspreads, fascinating custom-made lampshades, and tile bathroom counters. These rooms also have French doors that open onto private patios. Older rooms are almost as attractive and have Guatemalan throw rugs, bamboo furniture, kitchens, and front walls of glass. A small swimming pool is right by the beach and there is a first-class restaurant on the premises. Owner Philip Edwardes is the chef and prepares such dishes as lemon chicken and chateaubriand. However, it is the conviviality and helpfulness of Edwardes and his wife, Marilyn, that make a stay here so enjoyable. The Edwardeses also arrange horseback rides, raft trips, and various other tours.

HOTEL COCAL, Apdo. 54, Playa de Jacó, Puntarenas. Tel. 506/643-3067 or (in the U.S.) 313/732-8066. Fax 506/643-3082. 29 rms. SAFE

$ Rates: $40 single; $55 double; $70 triple. Lower rates in off-season. AE, MC, V.

No children are allowed at this hotel right on the beach, so the atmosphere is usually very peaceful. The building is done in colonial style, with arched porticos surrounding a courtyard that contains two medium-size pools, a few palapas for shade, and a thatched-roof bar. Each guest room is well proportioned with a tile floor, a double and a single bed, a desk, and a porch or balcony. However, the furniture is a bit old and has seen better days. The rooms with ocean views get the best breezes. The Cocal is on one of the nameless streets leading down to the beach from the main road through Jacó. Watch for their sign in about the middle of town. There are two dining rooms here (one on each floor) serving three meals a day. It's the upstairs dining room that has the best view of the beach. Service is generally quite good, and so is the food. Prices range from $5.75 to $17.25 for entrées.

HOTEL EL JARDIN, Playa de Jacó, Puntarenas. Tel. and Fax 506/643-3050. 7 rms.

$ Rates (including continental breakfast): Dec–Apr, $38 single or double; May–Nov, $30 single or double. MC, V.

Ⓢ Though this hotel's namesake garden is nothing to write home about, the hotel does offer economical rates, comfortable rooms, and friendly French-speaking management. This combination seems to have made El Jardin one of the more popular small hotels in Jacó. The guest rooms are large and clean, and have big bathrooms as well. There is a small pool in the center of the garden. You'll find this hotel at the far west end of the beach near the San José bus stop.

HOTEL ZABAMAR, Playa de Jacó, Puntarenas. Tel. 506/643-3174. 20 rms.

$ Rates: $20.30–$27.05 single; $23.65–$30.40 double; $33.80–$47.30 triple. Discounts for week stays. V.

The Zabamar is set back a little from the beach in an attractively planted compound. The older rooms have red-tile floors, small refrigerators, ceiling fans, hammocks on their front porches, and showers in enclosed, private patios. There are also 10 newer rooms with air-conditioning. There are even pilas (laundry sinks) in little gravel-and-palm gardens behind the older rooms. Some rooms have rustic wooden benches and chairs. The shallow swimming pool stays quite warm. Surfers get a 10% discount and will appreciate the size of the older, less expensive rooms. Prices for everyone are lower from April 15 to December 15. A little open-air bar/restaurant serves inexpensive seafood and burgers.

POCHOTE GRANDE, Apdo. 42, Playa de Jacó, Puntarenas. Tel. **506/643-3236.** Fax 506/220-4979. 24 rms.
$ Rates: Dec–Apr, $55 single or double; May–Nov, $40–$45 single or double. MC, V.

⭐ Named for a huge, old *pochote* tree on the grounds, this very attractive hotel is located right on the beach at the west end of Jacó. The grounds are shady and lush, and there's a small pool. Guest rooms are large enough to sleep four comfortably and have kitchenettes. Though all the rooms have white-tile floors and a balcony or patio, the second-floor rooms also have high ceilings. The restaurant and snack bar serve a mixture of Tico, German, and American meals (the owners are German by way of Africa). Prices for meals range from $3 to $9. There is also a gift shop. This place stays full with charter groups in the high season.

VILLAS ESTRELLAMAR, Apdo. 3, Playa de Jacó, Puntarenas. Tel. **506/643-3102.** Fax 506/643-3453. 20 rms.
$ Rates: Dec–Apr, $50–$60 single or double; May–Nov, $35–$42 single or double. MC, V.

This hotel is located on the landward side of Jacó's main road and so is a 200-yard walk to the beach. However, what you give up in proximity to the beach, you make up in attractive gardens. Estrellamar, which caters primarily to a French-speaking clientele, consists of bungalows and apartments, most of which have kitchenettes. The rooms also have tile floors and patios. Try to get a room facing the hotel's attractive pool. In addition to seating around the pool, there is a shady rancho where you can sit out of the sun. A quiet atmosphere and a pretty garden are the main attractions here.

VILLAS MIRAMAR, Playa de Jacó, Puntarenas. Tel. **506/643-3003.** 10 rms.
$ Rates: Dec–Apr, $47.30 single or double, $57.45 triple; May–Nov, $33.80 single, double, or triple, MC, V.

Located down a narrow lane off the main road through town, the Miramar is about 100 feet from the beach, though it also has its own small pool surrounded by a terrace. There is a snack bar by the pool and barbecues in the gardens in case you'd like to grill some fish or steaks. Guest rooms sport a Spanish architectural style with arched doorways, wrought-iron wall lamps, and red-tile floors throughout. There are large patios and all the rooms have kitchenettes. The apartments vary in size; the largest can sleep up to six people.

BUDGET

CABINAS ALICE, 100 meters south of the Red Cross, Playa de Jacó, Puntarenas. Tel. **506/643-3061** or 237-1412. 22 rms (all with bath).
$ Rates: $27.05 single or double; $33.80–$43.95 triple. MC, V.

Cabinas Alice, though a small and modest Tico-run place, is one of the best values in Jacó. The rooms are in the shade of large, old mango trees, and the beach is right outside the gate. Rooms here vary in age, so have a look at a couple if you can. The largest rooms are those with a kitchen, and those also happen to be the closest to the small pool and the beach. The rooms in back also come with a carved wooden headboard and matching nightstand, a tile floor, a large shower, and even potted plants. The other rooms are pretty basic, with nothing but a double and a single bed in the room. The road down to Cabinas Alice is across from the Red Cross center. Meals are served in a little dining room where you can get a fish filet fried in garlic and butter for under $5.

CABINAS LAS PALMAS, Playa de Jacó, Puntarenas. Tel. and Fax **506/643-3005.** 23 rms (all with bath).
$ Rates: $17.90–$41.90 single; $20.85–$41.90 double; $25.80–$52.40 triple. No credit cards.

Although all the rooms here are acceptable, the newer ones are a bit nicer. Some rooms come with refrigerators, hot plates, kitchen sinks, laundry sinks, and tables with four chairs, so you can set up housekeeping and stay a while. All the rooms have tile floors and very clean bathrooms, and most have two double beds. There are lots of flowers in the garden, and the location down a narrow lane off the main road makes Las Palmas a quiet place. The owner, Leonid Kudriakowsky, is from Canada and speaks English, Russian, German, and Spanish. If you're coming from San José, take the Jacó exit from the Costanera and go straight through the first (and only) intersection you come to. Take a right on the narrow lane just past Cabinas Antonio.

CHALET SANTA ANA, Playa de Jacó, Puntarenas. Tel. 506/643-3233.
8 rms (all with bath).
$ Rates: $13.55 single; $23.65 double or triple. No credit cards.
Located at the quiet east end of the beach across from Hotel Jacófiesta, Chalet Santa Ana is a small two-story building. Though it is rather basic, the guest rooms sleep up to five people and half of them have kitchenettes. There's even carpeting in the rooms, and walls are of varnished wood. The second-floor rooms have the added advantage of high ceilings and a large veranda with chairs. Though the surroundings are not too attractive, this is a good deal for Jacó.

CAMPING

There are several campgrounds in or near Playa de Jacó. **Madrigal,** at the south end of town at the foot of some jungly cliffs, is my favorite. The campground is right on the beach and has a bar/restaurant that is open from 7am to midnight. **El Hicaco,** in town and close to the beach, is right next door to an open-air disco, so don't expect much sleep if you stay here. Campsites are around $1.50 per night.

NEARBY PLACES TO STAY & DINE

PUNTA LEONA

PUNTA LEONA HOTEL & CLUB, Apdo. 8592-1000, San José. Tel. 506/ 231-3131 or 661-1414. Fax 506/232-0791. 92 rms, 73 apts.
$ Rates: $45.30 single; $54.05–$67.60 double; $64.90–$141.90 for four to eight people. AE, DC, MC, V.

This gated resort and residential community 10 kilometers north of Jacó boasts the most impressive grounds of any easily accessible hotel in Costa Rica. Rain forest, white-sand beaches (two of them), and a rocky promontory jutting out into the Pacific all add up to drama rarely encountered in Costa Rican resorts. After passing through the resort's guarded gate, you drive more than a mile down a gravel road that passes through dense primary rain forest before arriving at the grassy lawns that sprawl beneath huge trees that were spared during the construction of the buildings here. The main guest rooms are not as luxurious as one would hope, but that is the small price you must pay for such a setting. The standard hotel rooms are housed in Spanish-style buildings with red-tile roofs and white stucco walls. Inside, you'll find that the beds and bedspreads are a bit dated, but otherwise the rooms are comfortable. In addition to these rooms, there are a variety of different apartment types, including some unusual little chalets.

Dining/Entertainment: Restaurant Léon Marino serves a variety of Costa Rican and international dishes. Prices are moderate. There are also two bars, both of which serve meals, along Playa Blanca and a third on Playa Manatas that doubles as a disco.

Services: There is regular daily bus service between the guest accommodations and Playa Blanca. Scuba lessons and rental equipment are available (there is good diving at Playa Blanca).

Facilities: Two swimming pools, 4 miles of beach, boutique, supermarket.

PLAYA HERMOSA

CABINAS VISTAS HERMOSA, Playa Hermosa de Jacó, Jacó, Puntarenas. Tel. 506/224-3687. 6 rms.

$ Rates: $13.55 single; $20.30 double; $30.40 quad. No credit cards.

This little cabina place was recently taken over by new Italian owners and changes are under way. Though the rooms are pretty basic, they're right on Playa Hermosa. Because this beach is popular with surfers, that's who you'll often find staying here. All the rooms have kitchens, and those on the second floor have a nice view of the waves from the front veranda. There is even a little above-ground pool here, and a rancho contains a table-tennis table. Right next door is a hip little restaurant under separate management. Big old trees provide some welcome shade.

TERRAZA DEL PACIFICO, Playa Hermosa de Jacó (Apdo. 168), Jacó, Puntarenas. Tel. 506/643-3222, 643-3444, 643-3424, or (in the U.S.) 212/213-2399 or 213-1838. 43 rms. A/C TV TEL SAFE

$ Rates: $45 single; $50 double. AE, MC, V.

It may be a bit out of town, but the Terraza del Pacifico is the best beachfront hotel in the Jacó area. Located just over the hill at the start of Playa Hermosa, this hotel seems to have done everything right. Rooms are built so that they all have ocean views, and in the middle of the hotel complex is a circular pool with a swim-up bar. Red-tile roofs and white walls give the buildings a very Mediterranean look (the management is Italian), while hardwood balcony railings add a touch of the tropics. The guest rooms all have either a patio or balcony, and the curtains in the room have all been hand painted with colorful bird and flower images. The hotel's restaurant is located within a few feet of the high-tide mark and serves good Italian food.

READERS RECOMMEND

Hotel Copacabana, Apdo. 150, Playa de Jacó, Puntarenas. Tel. 506/643-3131.
"The Hotel Copacabana is an attractive and clean hotel situated right on the beach. . . . The hotel has a beautiful swimming pool in its central courtyard as well as a sports bar equipped with satellite TV and live music; a boutique specializing in Guatemalan and local handicrafts, clothing and souvenirs; and a restaurant serving local and Western cuisine." —Lisa J. Robertson

WHERE TO DINE

Many of the accommodations in Jacó come with kitchenettes, and if you want to save money on meals, I advise shopping at the local supermercado and fixing your own. Those hotels that don't have kitchenettes in the rooms usually have small restaurants. One of the best restaurants in town is the dining room at the Hotel Cocal. The menu includes such dishes as chateaubriand for two, wienerschnitzel, and pepper steak. The dining room at the Hotel Hacienda Lilipoza serves similar dishes and is equally highly recommended.

EL BOSQUE, 27 yards south of the gas station. Tel. 643-3009.
Cuisine: INTERNATIONAL. **Reservations:** Suggested on weekends.
$ Prices: Appetizers $2.55–$12.50; main courses $4.05–$13.20. MC, V.
Open: Tues–Sun 10:30am–9:30pm.

★ Located on the highway leading south to Manuel Antonio, El Bosque (The Forest) is set amid shady mango trees. The dining room itself is a small open-air building with hanging fern baskets and nests of oropendula birds used as decorations. The furnishings are heavy colonial reproductions. Shrimp or lobster is a pricey $13.20, but you can get a delicious corvina filet for only $4.05. If you are not in the mood for seafood, you can order steak or chicken. There is also a long list of fresh juices and fruit shakes from which to choose. El Bosque makes a great meal stop if you are on your way back from Manuel Antonio.

FLAMBOYANT RESTAURANT, on the main road east of the telephone office. Tel. 643-3023.
    Cuisine: COSTA RICAN/INTERNATIONAL. **Reservations:** Not accepted.
$ Prices: Appetizers $2.40–$11.50; main courses $3.75–$14.90. MC, V.
    Open: Lunch, Thurs–Tues 11am–5pm; dinner, Thurs–Tues 6–10:30pm.
Though it is located right on Jacó's busy main road and can be rather noisy, the Flamboyant is still one of the better restaurants in town. Seafood is the specialty here, of course, and you can get jumbo shrimp in garlic butter or a whole red snapper. However, if you are absolutely crazy about seafood, try the bounteous seafood platter. If you're not in the mood for fish, try the pepper steak or some meaty pork chops.

RESTAURANT GRAN PALENQUE, next to the Jacó Beach Hotel. Tel. 643-3419.
    Cuisine: COSTA RICAN/SEAFOOD. **Reservations:** Not necessary.
$ Prices: Appetizers $3.40–$5.10; main courses $5.75–$8.15. MC, V.
    Open: Tues–Sun 11am–10:30pm.
When I last visited Gran Palenque, the owners were in the midst of remodeling the open-air restaurant, but planned to keep the same menu. Hopefully when you visit, this restaurant will still be just a restaurant and not a full-fledged resort. Gran Palenque is set amid spacious and shady grounds where palm trees rustle in the breeze. The large restaurant is a huge thatch-roofed, open-air structure, and there is a smaller but similar building housing the restaurant's bar. This latter is right on the edge of the beach, which is only steps away. Both have unobstructed views of the ocean. With the inclusion of such Spanish specialties as paella and zarzuela, the menu is a bit more than the standard seafood-and-steaks Tico menu, but you can still get a filet mignon. All the dishes are well prepared and the prices are quite reasonable. There are also daily specials.

RESTAURANT OCEANO PACÍFICO, west of the Hotel Jacó Beach. Tel. 643-3116.
    Cuisine: COSTA RICAN/INTERNATIONAL. **Reservations:** Not accepted.
$ Prices: Main courses $3.05–$10.85. No credit cards.
    Open: Mon–Fri 10am–10pm, Sat 6am–10pm, Sun 6am–3pm.
If you follow the main road through town all the way west (past the San José bus stop), you'll come to this little open-air restaurant. Come during the day and you'll have a view of a steep, jungly hillside across an estuary. Weekends can be a bit noisy here because there is a pool right beside the restaurant. However, the view is great and the food is good and inexpensive. Try the palmito (hearts of palm) appetizer—it's a Tico treat that you don't often find up north. If you like submarine sandwiches, try the Costa Rican version, which called a *lapiz* (pencil). The dinner menu is primarily seafood.

EVENING ENTERTAINMENT

There are several discos in Jacó that stay busy on weekend nights. My favorite is the **Disco La Central** (tel. 643-3067), which is right on the beach near the east end of town. The disco is complete with flashing lights and a mirrored ball in a huge open-air hall. A garden bar in a thatched-roof building provides a slightly quieter place to have a drink. **Upe!** (tel. 643-3002), out on the road to the airport, is another favorite. Both are open Thursday through Sunday with a very low admission and reasonably priced drinks. **Los Tucanes Disco Club** is another big place and is located one street over from Disco La Central.

---

3. MANUEL ANTONIO

140 kilometers SW of San José; 69 kilometers S of Playa de Jacó

GETTING THERE   By Air   Sansa (in San José: tel. 233-0397, 233-3258, or 233-5330) flies to Quepos at 8am and 3pm daily, also at 12:15pm on Sunday and at 9:15am on Monday, Wednesday, and Friday. All flights leave from San José's Juan Santamaria International Airport. Duration: 20 minutes. Fare: $27 each way.

Travelair (tel. 220-3054 or 232-7883) flies to Quepos daily at 8:40am from San José's Pavas International Airport. Duration: 20 minutes. Fare: $35 one way, $60 round-trip. Travelair also has flights to Quepos from Golfito and Palmar Sur.

By Bus   Express buses to Manuel Antonio leave San José daily at 6am, noon, and 6pm from Calle 16 between avenidas 1 and 3. Duration: 3½ hours. Fare $5.60.

Regular buses to Quepos leave San José daily at 7 and 10am and 2 and 4pm. Duration: 5 hours. Fare: $3.40.

Buses leave Puntarenas for Quepos daily at 5am and 2:30pm. Duration: 3½ hours. Fare: $3.10.

Buses leave Jacó for Quepos daily at 6 and 8am and 2, 2:30, and 8pm. Duration: 2½ hours. Fare $1.65.

By Car   From San José, take the Interamerican Highway west to the Puntarenas turnoff and head south on the Costanera, the coastal road through Jacó. This is an excellent road until south of Puerto Caldera. From there until south of Jacó, the potholes are killers. Some are so old they've sprouted grass. At Parrita, 44 kilometers past Jacó, the pavement gives out completely and you spend the next 25 kilometers bumping along on potholed, washboarded, muddy gravel road (although this is better than the potholed paved road). Needless to say, the driving is slow.

An alternative is to take the narrow and winding old highway, which turns off the Interamerican Highway just west of Alajuela near the town of Atenas and joins the Costanera near Orotina, just in time to catch the worst of the potholes. You'll still have to drive that rutted road between Jacó and Quepos.

DEPARTING   Sansa (in Quepos: tel. 777-1170) flights to San José leave at 8:35am daily, 3:35pm Monday through Saturday, and at 12:50pm on Sunday. Sansa also has flights to Palmar Sur and Puerto Jiménez. Travelair flights leave for San José daily at 11:05am. Travelair also has flights to Palmar Sur and Golfito.

The Quepos bus station is in the market, which is two blocks east of the water and one block north of the road to Manuel Antonio. Express buses leave at 6am, noon, and 5pm (also at 3pm on Sunday). Local buses that take 5 hours leave at 5 and 8am and 2 and 4pm. In the busy winter months, get your ticket several days in advance.

Buses for Puntarenas leave daily at 4:30 and 10:30am and 3pm. Any bus headed for San José or Puntarenas will let you off in Playa de Jacó.

ESSENTIALS   Orientation   Quepos is a dusty little port town at the mouth of the Boca Vieja Estuary. After crossing the bridge into town, take the lower road (to the left of the high road). In two blocks, turn left and you will be on the road to Manuel Antonio. This road winds through town a bit before starting over the hill to all the hotels and the national park.

Getting Around   A taxi between Manuel Antonio and Quepos, or vice versa, costs anywhere from around $3. You'll always get a better price if you have your hotel call the taxi; that way the taxi driver has to charge the "official" rate. If you flag down a taxi, you're on your own. Also, if you do have the hotel call you a cab, remember only to take the taxi you've been told is coming for you. You'll be given the license plate number to watch for.

The bus from Quepos to Manuel Antonio takes 15 minutes and departs daily at 5:40, 7, 8, 9:30, 10:30, and 11:30am and 12:30, 2, 3, 4, 5, 7, and 10pm. The bus returns 20 minutes later. Fare: 30¢.

You can also rent a car from Elegante Rent A Car (tel. 777-0115) for around $50 a day. If you should be driving a car, never leave anything of value in it unless you intend to stay within sight of the car at all times. Car break-ins are commonplace here. There are now children who offer to watch your car for a small price when you leave it outside the park entrance. Take them up on the offer if you want to avoid damage to your car by thieves trying to find out what's in your trunk.

Fast Facts   You'll find Julieanne's Laundry Service around the corner from the Restaurant Isabel. It's open Monday through Friday from 7:30 to 11:30am and from 2 to 6pm. They charge $2.05 per kilo with a 2-kilo minimum. There's a pharmacy called Botíca Quepos on the corner of the main street where you make the turn for Manuel Antonio (tel. 777-0038). Open daily from 7am to 6pm.

No other beach in Costa Rica has received more international attention than Manuel Antonio. If you're planning a trip to Costa Rica, in all probability it is because you have heard of this beach. What is it about Manuel Antonio that has given it such an international reputation? Simply that it is one of the most beautiful locations in the entire country. Gazing down on the blue Pacific from high on the mountainsides of Manuel Antonio, it is almost impossible to hold back a gasp of delight. Offshore rocky islands dot the vast expanse of blue. In the foreground the rich deep green of the rain forest sweeps down to the water. It is this superb view that hotels at Manuel Antonio sell, and this view that keeps people transfixed on decks, patios, and balconies along the seven kilometers of road between Quepos and the national park entrance. It is these views that enchant both those who have only seen photos and those who have been here for a visit.

Of course there is also the national park itself, which, though it covers fewer than 1,700 acres, is one of the most popular national parks in the country and is the site of three nearly perfect little beaches. These beaches are connected by a trail that meanders through the rain forest between the beach and the mountains that rise quickly as you head inland from the water. However, Manuel Antonio National Park was created not because it had beautiful beaches but because its forests are home to the endangered squirrel monkey, three-toed sloths, purple-and-orange crabs, and hundreds of other species of birds, mammals, and plants. This stretch of coast has been almost entirely transformed into plantations, so this little rocky outcrop of forests is the region's last stronghold of nature.

However, in the past few years rampant development and ever-growing crowds of beach-goers have turned what was once a peaceful and pristine spot into an area of hastily built, overpriced hotels, packed parking areas, and noisy crowds that make seeing any wildlife almost an impossibility. This is not to say that the park is not still beautiful, nor does it mean that there are not good hotel values here. However, Manuel Antonio has become completely overburdened with adoring throngs. The stream that forms the boundary of the park and through which park visitors must wade has become polluted with garbage and human waste. On weekends the beaches are packed with people and the discos blare their music until early morning, drowning out the sounds of crickets and frogs that once lulled visitors to sleep here. A shanty town of snack shacks lines the road just outside the park, which makes this area look more like a slum than a national park. Supposedly the environs on the edge of the park are soon going to be improved, but as yet nothing has happened. Those views that are so bewitching also have their drawback. If you want a great view, you aren't going to be staying on the beach, and, in fact, you may not even be able to walk easily to the beach. This means that you'll either be driving to and from the beach, taking a lot of taxis, or riding the public bus a lot. Also keep in mind that it's hot and humid here and tends to rain a lot (even in the dry season). However, the rain is what keeps Manuel Antonio lush and green, and this wouldn't be the tropics if things were otherwise.

If you're traveling on a budget, you'll likely end up staying in the nearby town of Quepos, which was once a quiet banana port. The land to the north was used by Chiquita to grow its bananas. However, a disease wiped out the banana plantations, and now the land is planted with oil-palm trees. To reach Quepos by road, you must pass through miles and miles of these oil-palm plantations. Today Quepos is changing its image from that of shipping port to that of cluttered and dirty tourist boom town.

Despite these caveats, Manuel Antonio is still a beautiful spot, and if you plan your visit, you can avoid many of the problems that detract from its appeal. If you avoid the peak months from December to March, you will avoid the crowds. If you must come during the peak months, try to avoid weekends, when the beach is packed with families from San José. If you stay at a hotel part way up the hill from the park entrance, you will have relatively easy access to the beach, you may get a view, and best of all, you'll be out of earshot of the discos. If you visit the park early in the morning, you can leave when the crowds begin to show up at midday. In the afternoon, you can lounge by your pool or on your own patio.

WHAT TO SEE & DO

The road from Quepos dead-ends at the long **Playa Espadilla** (Espadilla Beach), which is just outside the park. This beach is often too rough for casual swimming but can be perfect for board surfing and bodysurfing. To reach the park itself, you must cross a small, polluted stream that is little more than ankle deep at low tide but can be knee or even waist deep at high tide. Just after crossing the stream, you will have to pay the park entrance fee of $1.35. Playa Espadilla Sur is the first beach you come to within the park boundaries. You can walk along this soft sand beach or follow a trail through the forest behind the beach. At the far end there is a short connecting trail to **Playa Manuel Antonio,** which is sometimes clear enough to offer good snorkeling. A branch trail from this beach leads up and around **Punta Catedral** (Cathedral Point), where there are some spectacular views. If you take this trail, wear good shoes. Cathedral Point is one of the best places to spot monkeys, though you are more likely to see the white-faced monkey than the rare squirrel monkey. From Playa Manuel Antonio (the second beach) there is another, slightly longer, trail to the third beach, **Puerto Escondido.** There is a blowhole on this beach that sends up plumes of spray at high tide. Beyond here, at Punta Surrucho, there are some sea caves. Two other trails wind their way inland from the trail between Playa Manuel Antonio and Puerto Escondido. It's great to spend hours exploring the steamy jungle and then take a refreshing dip in the ocean. The park is open daily from 7am to 4pm.

On Playa Espadilla, just a short distance outside the park, there is a little shop on the water that rents boogie boards, beach chairs, and beach umbrellas.

If you're staying in Quepos and don't want to go all the way over the hill to the park, you can swim and lounge at **Nahomi,** Quepos's public swimming pool. You'll find this pool on a tiny peninsula at the end of the road that parallels the water. Admission is $1.05 and the pool is open daily from 9am to 7pm. The rocky promontory on which the pool is built feels like an island and is surrounded by the turquoise waters of a small cove.

If your tropical fantasy is to ride a horse down a beach between jungle and ocean, contact **Stable Equus** (tel. 777-0001), which charges $30 for a 2-hour ride. This stable treats its animals more humanely than other stables in the area, and is also concerned with keeping horse droppings off the beach. If you want to combine a bit of horseback riding with a boat trip around the Isla Damas estuary, contact Planes Turisticos Nahomi (tel. 777-0161). Their all-day tour costs $65.

If you'd like a guide to take you through the national park, contact **Alberto** (tel. 777-0413), who charges $25 for a 3-hour hike.

If you're interested in **kayaking** among the rocky islets of Manuel Antonio National Park or up the nearby Isla Damas estuary, contact Rios Tropicales (tel. 777-0574). They charge $65 for a full-day paddle around the estuary (includes lunch at La Tortuga restaurant) or through the national park (with a picnic on the beach). They also offer half-day trips for $35, and white-water rafting trips on the nearby Río Naranjo ($65 to $70 full day or $45 half day). **Rafting** trips are usually only offered between June and November when the water level in the river is high enough. Ríos Tropicales also rents sea kayaks on Playa Espadilla about 200 yards north of the park entrance. Rainforest Expeditions & School (tel. 777-1170) also offers rafting trips on both the Río Naranjo and the Río Savegre and charges $65 to $75 for a full-day trip. This company also offers dive trips for $70 and guided all-day hikes for $45.

Quepos is one of Costa Rica's billfish centers, and sailfish and marlin, as well as tuna, are all common in these waters. If you're into **sportfishing** and happen to be here between December and April, contact La Buena Nota (tel. 777-0345), where you can arrange a fishing charter for around $300 per day. Other companies to try include JP Tours (tel. 777-1613); Tours Cambute (tel. 777-0082); Sportfishing Costa Rica (tel. 777-0505); and Sportfishing Karahé (tel. 777-0170).

If you'd just like to go for a cruise around the area and maybe do a bit of snorkeling or fishing, see if the *Byblos I* (tel. 777-0411) will be going out while you're around. This boat charges $80 for a 7-1/2-hour cruise that includes lunch and fishing and snorkeling gear.

If you're looking for souvenirs, try **La Buena Nota,** which is on the left just over the bridge as you enter Quepos (tel. 777-0345). This little shop is jam-packed with all sorts of beach wear, souvenirs, and U.S. magazines and newspapers, and also acts as an informal information center for the area. If you'd like to find out about renting a house, this is a good place to ask.

The market (two blocks in from the main road into town) sells lots of delicious fruit. If you're doing your own cooking, this is the place to shop. Super Quepos is a general store on the main street near the corner where you turn to head out to Manuel Antonio.

WHERE TO STAY

There are very few beachfront hotels in Manuel Antonio, so consequently, if you want to be able to walk out of your room and be on the beach without taking to the road, you're going to have to pay for the privilege. Prices at the Hotel Arboleda are steep for what you get, but if you want a nicer room for the same amount of money, you won't be on the beach.

If you're traveling on a rock-bottom budget, you'll get more for your money by staying in Quepos and taking the bus to the beaches at Manuel Antonio every day. The rooms here in Quepos may be small, but they are much cleaner and more appealing than those available in this price category on the other side of the hill.

VERY EXPENSIVE

EL BYBLOS, Apdo. 112, Quepos. Tel. 506/777-0411 or 777-0217. Fax 506/777-0009. 17 rms. TV TEL

$ Rates: Dec–Apr (including breakfast and dinner), $196 double; May–Nov, $90 double. AE, MC, V.

Though service here can be rather unprofessional at times, El Byblos is still one of the best hotels in Manuel Antonio. Keep in mind that the room rate during the high season includes breakfast and dinner in the hotel's widely acclaimed dining room. Also consider that the hotel is quite a ways uphill from the park.

Guest rooms vary in age and setting. The older rooms are set among the forest trees toward the back of the hotel grounds and, though they have neither views nor air-conditioning, they are tranquil. The newer rooms are quite luxuriously large and have air-conditioning and partial ocean views. These rooms have tile floors, wicker furniture, seating areas by the windows, and attractively designed bathrooms. The main drawback of these rooms is that the road, which gets a lot of noisy traffic, is just outside the window. Be aware that there is a telephone charge even if you use a calling card number.

Dining/Entertainment: The dining room is on a large covered deck that looks out to the forest trees. The open-beamed hardwood construction is evocative of the tropics and sets an exotic mood for the gourmet French dinners that are seved here nightly. There's a decent wine selection (French and Chilean), and a small bar to the side where you can have a cocktail before or after dinner. Meal prices, if you aren't staying here, range from $7.70 to $23 for entrées.

Services: Room service, laundry service, beach and airport shuttles, sportfishing charters, diving trips, day cruises.

Facilities: The small swimming pool is set on the edge of the forest.

LA MARIPOSA, Playa Manuel Antonio, Quepos. Tel. 506/777-0355, 777-0456, or (in New York) 212/932-2277, or toll free (in the U.S.) 800/223-6510 or (in Canada) 800/268-0424. Fax 506/777-0050. 10 villas. SAFE

$ Rates (including full breakfast and gourmet dinner): $132 single; $200 double. No credit cards.

This is Manuel Antonio's premier accommodation and offers spacious, attractively designed and decorated rooms, and the most breathtaking view in Manuel Antonio. Perched on a ridge at the top of the hill between Quepos and Manuel Antonio, La Mariposa (The Butterfly), commands a mountains-to-the-sea vista of more than 270 degrees. Needless to say, the sunsets here are knockouts. La Mariposa is for those people who truly want to get away from it all (i.e., telephones, TVs, fax machines) and sit back doing nothing at all for a while. Keep in mind, however, that should you decide to abandon the view and the pool, you're a long way from the beach (either a steep hike or a short drive). The rooms here are all bilevel villas that meld the best of the tropics and the Mediterranean. The villas are divided into a large bedroom and bathroom on the upper floor and a spacious living room and deck on the lower floor. There are stucco walls and painted tiles, bamboo ceilings, and hardwood floors. Behind the two queen beds in the bedroom, there is a huge tropical mural. The bathrooms are absolutely huge and have small atrium gardens. They also have high ceilings, skylights, blue-and-white tile counters, and shelves of plants. You just won't want to leave your villa.

Dining/Entertainment: Both breakfast and dinner are included in the rates at La Mariposa. The four-course continental dinners are among the best in Manuel Antonio, and are also available to nonguests for $20.30 per person (a great deal). The emphasis is on seafood. The open-air restaurant is set on a red-tiled terrace that takes in all the views. There is also a small bar.

Facilities: The small swimming pool is set on its own terrace.

EXPENSIVE

HOTEL ARBOLEDA, Apdo. 211, Quepos. Tel. 506/777-0092. Fax 506/777-0414. 40 rms.

$ Rates: Dec–Apr, $85–$95 double; May–Nov, $40–$60 double. AE. MC, V.

The Arboleda is one of the few beachfront hotels in Manuel Antonio, and it is, unfortunately, overpriced for what you get. Rooms are divided between those on the hillside and those down closer to the beach (though none are actually right on the beach). The grounds are rather unkempt and there is an excess of whitewashed concrete that further detracts from the surroundings. This is one of the few hotels I've ever visited in which the cheaper rooms are closer to the water. These rooms are fairly small and have fans only, but they are definitely the better choice here. The more expensive rooms have air-conditioning, but they're rather dark and have small bathrooms.

Dining/Entertainment: There are two restaurants here. One is by the pool near the top of the hill, and the other is down by the beach. Both serve similar, moderately priced meals. The restaurant by the beach also has a bar with a pool table.

Services: Airport shuttle, horse rentals, sportfishing charters.

Facilities: Swimming pool.

KARAHÉ, Apdo. 100-6350, Quepos. Tel. 506/777-0170. Fax 506/777-0152. 32 rms.

$ Rates (including breakfast): $70–$100 single or double; $90–$125 triple. AE, DC, MC, V.

★ Of the few beachfront hotels in Manuel Antonio, this is the nicest, although if you opt for the cheapest (and oldest) rooms in the hotel, you'll be a steep uphill climb from the beach. On the other hand, if you should decide to go for the top end, you'll find a room of international standards that should please even the most finicky traveler (unless, of course, you need a telephone and TV). The cheapest rooms have the best views, but do not have air-conditioning, while the medium-priced and top-end rooms have air-conditioning and less spectacular views. These latter rooms also have balconies. The gardens of the upper half of the hotel are quite lush and are planted with flowering ginger that often attracts hummingbirds. However, down in the lower part of the hotel grounds, the gardens are not nearly as attractive. The hotel is located on both sides of the road about 500 yards before you reach the end of the road at Manuel Antonio.

Dining/Entertainment: The hotel's restaurant is built at treetop level midway between the highest and lowest rooms. Entrée prices range from $4.75 to $12.50, and the specialty of the house is shish kebabs cooked over an indoor barbecue. There is also a snack bar near the pool, which is where you'll find the hotel's bar.

Services: Sportfishing charters, laundry service.

Facilities: Swimming pool, whirlpool tub.

EL LIRIO, Apdo. 123, Quepos. Tel. 506/777-0403. 9 rms. SAFE

$ Rates: Dec–Apr, $80 single, double, or triple; May–Nov, $35 single, double, or triple. No credit cards.

Though most of the rooms here overlook the road and consequently can be a bit noisy, there are some quieter rooms at the back of the grounds near the swimming pool. A Mediterranean style prevails here, with arches, stucco walls, and red-tile floors and roofs. Rooms have high ceilings, mosquito nets over the beds, southwestern-motif, pastel bedspreads, and tiled bathrooms. The grounds are quiet, lush and are planted with many tropical flowers. There are also some big trees that provide shade. You'll find El Lirio on the left near the top of the hill as you drive from Quepos to Manuel Antonio. All in all this is a very attractive place and is a particularly good deal in the low season.

Dining/Entertainment: Only breakfast is available.

Facilities: The swimming pool, though small, is surrounded by a pretty deck.

MODERATE

APARTOTEL EL COLIBRI, Apdo. 94, Manuel Antonio, Quepos. Tel. 506/777-0432. 10 rms.

$ Rates: Dec–Apr, $49 single, $59.50 double, $69.10 triple, $78.75 quad; May–Nov, $26.25 single, $35 double, $43.75 triple, $52.50 quad. V.

★ If you have dreams of a secluded tranquil retreat where you can laze in a hammock and watch hummingbirds sipping nectar from crimson flowers, this hotel is for you. The eight elegant rooms are set amid a garden that would have kept Monet or Gaugin happy for years. Narrow paths wind up a hill through lush vegetation that completely hides the rooms from the street. You'll feel as though you have the whole place to yourself in these cozy duplex rooms, each of which has a king-size bed with a Guatemalan bedspread, high ceilings with overhead fans, screen-and-cinderblock walls that make the most of the prevailing breezes, red-tile floors, framed posters of Costa Rican wildlife, and French doors that lead to a patio. The spacious patios make the rooms seem much larger than they are and come with hammocks, tables and chairs, and barbecues for grilling any fish you might catch. There are even rooms with beautiful kitchenettes with blue-and-white-tile counters and espresso coffee makers. True tropical elegance. There are a couple of older rooms close to the road that are not nearly as nice as the others.

CABINAS ESPADILLA, Manuel Antonio, Quepos. Tel. and Fax 506/777-0416. 31 rms.

$ Rates: $47.30–$60 single, double, or triple. No credit cards.

There isn't much shade around these cabinas, but they are clean and close to the beach. The rooms are spacious and most have kitchenettes. Though there isn't much in the way of decor or closet space in any of them, there are beds for up to four people with a double bed and a bunk bed. High ceilings and fans keep the older rooms cool, and in the newer, more expensive rooms there is air-conditioning. Bars on the windows ensure security. The older rooms here are way overpriced, but the newer rooms are fairly reasonable.

LA COLINA, Apdo. 191, Quepos. Tel. 506/777-0231. 5 rms.

$ Rates (with continental breakfast): Dec–Apr, $29 single, $40 double; May–Nov, $18 single, $25 double. V.

⑤ This casual little bed-and-breakfast is operated by two men from Quebec who moved down to Manuel Antonio a few years ago and converted this house into a B&B. Though the rooms are fairly small, they are very stylishly decorated. There are black-and-white-tile floors, louvered French doors, and despite the small size of the rooms, a good writing desk. Outside each room there are some chairs on the patio. Breakfast is served in your room or on the patio and might consist of a crêpe or pancake and coffee.

COSTA VERDE, Apdo. 106-6350, Quepos. Tel. 506/777-0584 or 777-0187. Fax 506/777-0506. 30 rms.

$ Rates: Dec–Apr, $60–$90 single or double; May–Nov, $40–$70 single or double. AE, DC, MC, V.

⑤ The guest rooms at Costa Verde have long been some of my favorite in the area. With their screen walls they seem to sum up the sensual climate of the tropics. No need for walls when they only keep out the breezes. Over the years Costa Verde has continued to add new rooms, and today the original rooms are some of the least expensive, but are still quite pleasant. All the rooms, old and new, have ocean views, kitchenettes, and balconies, and the more expensive rooms have loads of space. There's a very pretty little pool set into the hillside and up above the pool is an open-air restaurant that looks into the forest trees, where sloths are sometimes seen. To one side of the dining room is a long bar. If you want to be close to the pool and restaurant, you'll have to spring for one of the more expensive studio apartments. Costa Verde is about half way down the hill to Manuel Antonio and has good views.

EL DORADO MOJADO, Apdo. 238-6350, Quepos. Tel. 506/777-0368. Fax 506/777-1248. 4 rms, 4 villas. A/C SAFE

$ Rates: Dec–Apr, $52.50 single, $65.60–$109.35 double, $118.10 triple; May–Nov, $35–$65.60 single, $43.75–$65.60 double, $65.60 triple. MC, V.

★ The architectural uniqueness of the buildings at this small hotel make it one of the most interesting places to stay in Manuel Antonio. Unfortunately, the hotel stays booked for much of the year with sportfishing tours. There are both "villas," with full kitchens, and smaller standard rooms that are very luxurious. The buildings are set back in the forest and are connected by a raised walkway below which are unusual tropical plants. The buildings resemble modernized banana plantation houses and have walls of glass that extend up for two stories and then angle into the wall to form an atrium effect. Standard rooms are either upstairs (hardwood floors and more light) or downstairs (red and painted tile floors). Other interesting and attractive touches include cane-sided cupboards, open-air showers with walls of glass block, and Guatemalan bedspreads. The villas also have TVs, carved, antique headboards, and Murphy beds. Some people might find the forest shade a bit dark, but it is still a beautiful setting.

HOTEL CASITAS ECLIPSE, Apdo. 11-6350, Quepos. Tel. 506/777-0408 or (in the U.S.) 619/753-6827. Fax 506/777-0408. 10 casitas, 10 rms. A/C

$ Rates: Nov 15–Apr 15, $65 single or double, $85–$100 one-bedroom casita, $150 two-bedroom casita; Apr 16–Nov 14, $40 single or double, $50–$60 one-bedroom casita, $90 two-bedroom casita. V.

⭐ Located close to the top of the hill between Quepos and Manuel Antonio, these beautiful *casitas* (little houses) are some of the most boldly styled structures in Manuel Antonio. Each casita is basically a miniature Mediterranean villa. Their styling makes them seem much larger than they actually are, though they are certainly plenty roomy as well. All are painted a blinding white, which is contrasted by red roof tiles. Unfortunately the casitas are a bit close to the road, and there is as yet no buffer against traffic noises. The casitas, though simply furnished, are very comfortable and attractive inside. There are tile floors, built-in banquettes, high ceilings, and full kitchens. Each sleeps up to five people and has a big patio. You can rent either the entire casita, just the downstairs, or, if you don't need all the space, just the upstairs bedroom, which has a separate entrance and private patio of its own. Considering what you get in this price range down closer to the beach, this is a great deal. There are no ocean views here, but directly behind the hotel grounds is the park itself.

Dining/Entertainment: The poolside snack bar serves breakfast as well as bar drinks.

Facilities: Swimming pool.

HOTEL MIRADOR DEL PACÍFICO, Apdo. 164, Quepos. Tel. and Fax 506/ 777-0119. 20 rms, 3 villas.

$ Rates (including continental breakfast): Dec–Apr, $55–$75 single or double, $100 villa double, $130 villa quad (villa rates do not include breakfast). AE, MC, V (add 6% surcharge).

Located 200 yards up the road from the Hotel Plinio, this new, tastefully designed and decorated lodge is set amid shady trees on a steep hillside. From the hotel's verandas you can look out over the forest to the ocean far below. Guest rooms have a Central American touch, with Guatemalan rugs and placemats on the walls, and a few rooms have fake stuffed parrots hanging from their ceilings. The smaller, less expensive rooms have twin beds, while the larger, more expensive rooms have doubles. The newest rooms overlook the pool. If you want the convenience of a kitchen and a bit more space, try one of the unusual little villas. The German owner has had a fascination with funiculars (cable cars) for years, and has built one of his own. It carries guests to a tiny restaurant/bar at the top of the property. From here there is a magnificent view of the mountains, forests, and ocean. There is also a snack bar by the pool, and the hotel provides transportation to the park twice a day.

HOTEL PLINIO, Apdo. 71, Quepos. Tel. 506/777-0055. Fax 506/777-0558. 6 rms, 6 suites.

$ Rates (including full breakfast): Dec–Apr, $35–$40 single, $50–$55 double, $65–$80 suite; May–Nov, lower rates available. AE, MC, V.

⭐ The Plinio was for many years a favorite of budget travelers visiting Manuel Antonio, and though its room rates have crept up over the years, it's still a great value. The hotel is built into a steep hillside, so it's a bit of a climb from the parking lot up to the guest rooms and restaurant (about the equivalent of three flights of stairs). Once you are up top, though, you'll think you're in a treehouse. Floors and walls are polished hardwood, and there are even rooms with tree-trunk pillars. The hotel's suites are the best value. These are built on either two or three levels. Both types have sleeping lofts, while the three-story rooms also have rooftop decks. My favorite room is known as the jungle house and is set back in the forest. The restaurant, which is the most popular in Manuel Antonio, serves a variety of good Italian food in a price range of $5.40 to

$9.50 for entrées. Behind the hotel there's a forest with 5 kilometers of trails, and, at the top of the hill, a 50-foot-tall observation tower with an incredible view. There's also a snack bar near the pool for lunch meals. A lap pool, kid's pool, and recreation room with library round out the amenities here.

HOTEL SULA BYA BA, Apdo. 203, Quepos. Tel. 506/777-0547. 9 rms. SAFE

$ Rates: Dec–Apr, $28 single, $35 double, $45 triple; May–Nov, slightly lower rates. AE, MC, V.

You're still a long way from the beach when you stay at the Sula Bya Ba, but the artistic decor and atmosphere make this one of the most interesting hotels at Manuel Antonio. Lower rates further add to the hotel's appeal. Rooms are large and uncluttered, and seem to be a hybrid of pueblo and Japanese motifs. The doors are reminiscent of shoji screens, and there are opaque windows around the showers, which make the bathrooms quite bright. Color schemes are very soothing and there are works of art on display in all the rooms. Breakfast is available and is usually served on a patio in the garden.

BUDGET

CABINAS PEDRO MIGUEL, Manuel Antonio, Quepos. Tel. 506/777-0035. 14 rms. (all with bath).

$ Rates: $20.30 single; $27.05 double; $54.05 triple. No credit cards.

Located a kilometer out of Quepos on the road to Manuel Antonio (across from Hotel Plinio), these cabinas are very basic (cement floors and cinderblock walls), but at least they're out of town and surrounded by forest. The second-floor rooms are newer and cleaner, and there's even a glimpse of the water from the veranda. One of the rooms is huge and has an entire wall of screen that looks out into the trees. This room also has a kitchen. During the high season there is a restaurant serving barbecued steaks and various salads. There's a tiny swimming pool that sometimes has water in it. The management here is very friendly.

CABINAS PISCIS, Apdo. 219, Quepos. Tel. 506/777-0046. 6 rms (all with bath).

$ Rates: Dec–Apr, $20.30 single or double, $23.65 triple or quad; May–Nov, $16.90 single or double, $20.30 triple or quad. No credit cards.

If you want to be within walking distance of the park but out of earshot of the discos' booming speakers, and you don't want to spend a lot of money, this is one of the only choices you have left. The rooms are basic but clean, and the management is very friendly. The beach is just a hundred yards or so down a forest trail. You find Cabinas Piscis on the beach side of the road just before you reach the bottom of the hill and Manuel Antonio.

CABINAS VELA-BAR, Apdo. 13, Manuel Antonio, Quepos. Tel. 506/777-0413. Fax 506/777-1071. 9 rms (all with bath), 1 apt, 1 house.

$ Rates: $11–$29 single; $20–$63 double; $43–$71 triple; $64 quad. AE, MC, V.

You'll find this unusual little hotel up the dirt road that leads off to the left just before the end of the road to Manuel Antonio National Park. There's a wide variety of room choices in various price ranges at Vela-Bar. If you're on a budget, you can stay in a tiny room, or, if you have more money to spend, you can opt for a spacious one-bedroom house that has tile floors and arched windows. There are double beds and tiled bathrooms in the rooms. The open-air restaurant/bar is deservedly very popular. Check the chalkboard for the day's special. Prices range from $5.10 to $11.50 for entrées.

HOTEL MALINCHE, Quepos. Tel. and Fax 505/777-0093. 28 rms (all with bath).

$ Rates: $8–$30 single; $15–$35 double. V.

A good choice for backpackers, the Hotel Malinche is located on the first street to your left as you come into Quepos. You can't miss the hotel's arched brick entrance. Inside you'll find bright rooms with louvered windows but no screens, so be sure to buy some mosquito coils (mosquito-repelling incense coils are available in drugstores and general stores) before night falls. The rooms are small but have hardwood floors and clean bathrooms. The more expensive rooms are new and have air-conditioning and carpets.

HOTEL QUEPOS, Apdo. 79, Quepos. Tel. 506/777-0274. 29 rms (9 with bath).
$ Rates: $8.45 single without bath, $10.15 single with bath; $16.90 double without bath, $20.30 double with bath. No credit cards.
This little budget hotel is both comfortable and clean. There are hardwood floors, ceiling fans, a large sunny TV lounge, even a parking lot and laundry service. The management is very friendly, and downstairs from the second-floor hotel is an interesting souvenir shop and a charter fishing office. This hotel is across from the soccer field on the way out of town toward Manuel Antonio.

WHERE TO DINE

The most expensive meals around are at El Byblos and La Mariposa, though their dinners are rather inconsistent. For the cheapest meals around, head to one of the dozen or so open-air shacks near the side of the road just before the circle at the entrance to the park. The standard Tico menu prevails with prices in the $2.70-to-$8.10 range. Though these little places lack atmosphere, they do have a view of the ocean and the service is often better than in more formal restaurants.

MODERATE

BARBA ROJA, Quepos–Manuel Antonio Road. Tel. 777-0331.
  Cuisine: SEAFOOD/CONTINENTAL. **Reservations:** Suggested in high season.
$ Prices: Appetizers $2.35–$5.10, main courses $5.50–$15.60; sandwiches $2.35–$3.05. No credit cards.
  Open: Tues–Sun 7:30am–10:30pm.
Perched high on a hill with stunning views over jungle and ocean, the Barba Roja is the kind of restaurant that people discover on the last day of their vacation and wish they had known about the day they arrived. The rustic interior is done with local hardwoods that give the dining room a warm glow. Take a seat at the counter, and you can sit for hours gazing out at the view. If you tire of the view, glance around at some of the original art by local artists. There is even a gallery attached to the restaurant. Best of all, however, is the food. On the blackboard, there are daily specials such as grilled fish steak served with a salad and baked potato. The restaurant is open for breakfast and serves delicious whole-wheat french toast. For lunch, there are a number of different sandwiches, all served on whole-wheat bread. If you are in the mood to hang out and meet interesting people from all over the world, spend some time at the bar sipping piña coladas or margaritas.

KAROLA'S, Quepos–Manuel Antonio Road. Tel. 777-0424.
  Cuisine: SEAFOOD/CONTINENTAL. **Reservations:** Not accepted.
$ Prices: Appetizers $2.55–$3.75; main courses $4.75–$14.20. No credit cards.
  Open: Thurs–Tues 7am–10pm.
★ The steep driveway leading down to this open-air restaurant is within a few feet of the Barba Roja parking lot but is easily overlooked. Watch closely when you're up at the top of the hill. The restaurant is across a footbridge from its parking lot and is set against a jungle-covered hillside. Far below you can see the ocean if you are here during the day. Grilled seafoods are the specialty, but they also do peel-and-eat shrimp with a great house sauce. Desserts, such as lemon chiffon pie, are good, and you can order margaritas by the pitcher.

PLINIO RESTAURANT, 1 kilometer out of Quepos toward Manuel Antonio. Tel. 777-0055.
  Cuisine: ITALIAN/GERMAN. **Reservations:** Recommended in high season.

$ Prices: Appetizers $2.70–$6.45; main courses $5.45–$9.50. MC, V.
Open: Daily 7–10am and 5–10pm.

⭐ This is the most popular restaurant in Manuel Antonio and is part of one of my favorite hotels also. The open-air restaurant is a sort of covered deck about three stores above the parking lot, so be prepared to climb some steps before you get to eat. It's worth it, though. The basket of bread that arrives at your table shortly after you sit down is filled with delicious treats, and the menu is also full of tempting dishes. Italian is the primary cuisine here, but you may also encounter some German specials. Some of my favorite dishes include the spaghetti with pesto and the broccoli-and-cauliflower parmigiana. There's also a great antipasto platter that includes prosciutto, salami, and cheese.

RESTAURANT VELA-BAR, 100 meters down side road near the park entrance. Tel. 777-0413.
Cuisine: INTERNATIONAL. **Reservations:** Not accepted.
$ Prices: Appetizers $2.05–$6.10; main courses $5.10–$11.50. AE, MC, V.
Open: Daily 7–10am, 11:30am–2:30pm, 5:30–11pm (closed at lunch June–Nov).
The Vela-Bar is a small and casual place the serves some of the more creative cookery in Manuel Antonio. Seafood and vegetarian meals are the specialties here, and the most interesting dishes are almost always the specials posted on the blackboard. A typical day's choices might include fish in sherry or wine sauce. As the name implies, this is also a bar, which seems to be Manuel Antonio's gay hangout.

BUDGET

GEORGE'S AMERICAN BAR, on road to Manuel Antonio, 100 meters from the dike. No phone.
Cuisine: MEXICAN/AMERICAN. **Reservations:** Not accepted.
$ Prices: All dishes $2.05–$4.05. No credit cards.
Open: Mon–Sat 8am–10pm.
If you are in Quepos and want a cheap and familiar meal, drop in at George's. Just watch for the sign with the stars and stripes and the eagle. This gringo hangout serves such comfort foods as hamburgers, brownies, burritos, guacamole, and even a mahi-mahi burger con queso. There's also a full bar and occasional live music.

LA TORTUGA, Isla Damas. No phone.
Cuisine: SEAFOOD. **Reservations:** Not accepted.
$ Prices: Main dishes $3.40–$10.80. V.
Open: Daily 9am–8pm.
This is one of the most unusual restaurants in Costa Rica and though it is just a basic Tico hangout, it is an experience that should not be missed. To reach it, you must first drive north out of town toward Playa de Jacó. Watch for the COMPLEJO TURISTICO sign and turn west for another mile or so. When you reach the water, you'll find a boatman waiting to take you out to the restaurant on a large converted boat. If there is no boatman around, flash your lights and beep your horn; someone will soon come for you. The menu is primarily fish, and the owner seems to always have the very best catches of the day. The great seafood, exhilarating boat ride, and the view across the estuary to the forested mountains beyond make this place well worth the effort. If the TV is blaring, ask them to turn it down; they'll oblige.

EVENING ENTERTAINMENT

The main evening entertainment at Manuel Antonio is the disco that appears after dark at Restaurant Mar y Sombra. If this one is too crowded, there is the one next door. You can also hang out at the Vela-Bar, which is up the road to the left just before you reach Manuel Antonio and seems to be popular with gay men. The bar at the Barba Roja restaurant, across from Hotel Divisamar, is another good place to hang out and meet people in the evenings. If you are staying in Quepos, check out the Disco Arco Iris, which is across the bridge from town and is built over the water.

EN ROUTE TO DOMINICAL

Playa Matapalo is a long strand of flat beach that is about midway between Quepos and Dominical. Though it is not as spectacular as either of those other two beaches, it does have its charms. Unfortunately, the surf is often too rough to allow much swimming here, though boogie boarding can be good. Foremost among this beach's charms are peace and quiet. With only three places to stay, there are no crowds here, and Matapalo is still basically a little village. The beach itself is about a kilometer from the village, and the hotels listed here are right on the beach. In addition to these two places, there is an Italian restaurant that serves economical meals and a Tico cabina place with a disco.

EL COQUITO DEL PACÍFICO, Playa Matapalo (Apdo. 6763-1000, San José). Tel. 506/233-1731 or 222-4103. Fax 506/222-8849. 6 cabinas.
$ Rates: $36 double; $42 triple; $48 quad. No credit cards.
This little collection of cabinas is operated by the same people who run the Hotel Ritz/Pension Continental, a budget-travelers' standard in San José. The cabinas are all quite large and have white-tile floors, high ceilings, colorful sheets on the beds, and overhead fans. There is a small restaurant/bar, and you can rent mountain bikes and boogie boards. Horseback rides can also be arranged. There are plans to add a swimming pool. This is one of the first places you come to when you hit the beach.

TERRAZA DEL SOL, Playa Matapalo. Tel. 506/771-0711. 4 cabinas.
$ Rates: Dec–Apr, $45 single or double; May–Nov, $18–$25 single or double. No credit cards.
Operated by French Canadians, the Terraza del Sol is a few hundred yards beyond El Coquito on the same road. Rooms here are quite similar, though they have yet to have their cement floors tiled. There are shuttered doors and windows, and little patios in front of each cabina. The rooms are quite comfortable, but it is the food served at the hotel that makes this a truly memorable place. Imagine driving down a gravel road in the middle of nowhere and finding a gourmet French dinner, complete with champagne, awaiting your arrival! A complete dinner will cost you around $15 and might include boeuf bourguignon, tomato salad, a cream soup of one sort or another, and a flambéed crêpe filled with fruit and chocolate sauce for dessert.

---

4. DOMINICAL

29 kilometers SW of San Isidro; 42 kilometers S of Quepos;
160 kilometers S of San José

GETTING THERE By Air The nearest airport with regular service is in Quepos. From there you can hire a taxi, rent a car, or take the bus.

By Bus To reach Dominical, you must first go to San Isidro del El General or Quepos. Buses for San Isidro de El General leave San José daily every hour from 5:30am to 5pm from Calle 16 between avenidas 1 and 3. Leave no later than 9:30am if you want to catch the 1:30pm bus to Dominical. Duration: 3 hours. Fare: $3.25.
From San Isidro de El General, buses leave for Dominical at 7am and 1:30 and 3pm. The bus station for Dominical is one block south of the main bus station and two blocks west of the church. Duration: 1½ hours. Fare: $1.85.

From Quepos, buses leave daily at 5:30am and 1:30pm. Duration: 2 hours. Fare: $2.10.

By Car From San José, head south (toward Cartago) on the Interamerican Highway. Continue on this road all the way to San Isidro de El General, where you turn right and head down toward the coast. The entire drive takes about 5 hours.

DEPARTING Buses leave Dominical for San Isidro de El General daily at 7:30am and 3pm, but you'll have to catch the morning bus if you want to get to San José that same day. Buses to Quepos leave around 8:30am and 3pm. Buses leave San Isidro for San José every hour from 5:30am to 5pm.

ESSENTIALS Dominical is a small village on the banks of Río Baru. The village is to the right after you cross the bridge and centers around the soccer field and general store, where there is a public telephone.

_____

As the prices and crowds at Manual Antonio have steadily increased over the years, people have begun heading south down the coast to find other less expensive and less crowded beaches. Some have landed at the above-mentioned Playa Matapalo (see "En Route to Dominical," above), but most make it to Dominical and drop their bags. The road south leads through mile after mile of oil-palm plantations, but here, 60 kilometers south of Manuel Antonio, the mountains once again meet the sea. From Dominical south the coastline is dotted with tide pools and tiny coves. Dominical is the largest village in the area and has several small lodges both in town and along the beach to the south. The village enjoys an enviable location on the banks of Río Baru, which at this point, just before emptying into the ocean, becomes a wide lagoon. There is good bird-watching along the banks of the river. Life is still slow in Dominical, though in the past few years the village has become something of a surfers' hangout. However, for the time being, soccer games are still the biggest events in town.

WHAT TO SEE & DO

Because the beach right in the village of Dominical is unprotected and at the mouth of a river, it is often much too rough for swimming. However, you can go for a swim in the lagoon at the mouth of the Río Baru, or head down the beach a few kilometers to the little sheltered cove at Roca Verde. If you have a car, you can continue driving south, exploring beaches as you go. At the village of Uvita, 16 kilometers south of Dominical, you'll reach the northern end of the **Ballena Marine National Park,** which protects a coral reef that stretches from Uvita south to Playa Piñuela and includes the little Isla Ballena, which is just offshore. This park is named for the whales that are often sighted close to shore in the winter months.

Although the beaches stretching south from Dominical should be beautiful enough to keep most people content, there are lots of other things to do. Several local farms offer **horseback tours** through forests and orchards, and at some of these farms you can even spend the night. **Hacienda Baru** (tel. 771-1903), leave message) offers several different hikes and tours, including a walk through mangroves and along the river bank (good bird-watching, a rain-forest hike through 200 acres of virgin jungle, an all-day trek from beach to mangrove to jungle that includes a visit to some Indian petroglyphs, an overnight camping trip, and a combination horseback-and-hiking tour. Tour prices range from $12.50 to $60 if there is only one person. The more people there are in your group, the lower the per-person rate (maximum six people per tour). Hacienda Baru can also help you arrange various hikes and horseback rides on other nearby farms.

Finca Brian y Milena, Apdo. 2-8000, San Isidro de El General (tel. 771-1903, leave message), offers day and overnight trips to their farm in the hills outside of Dominical. Here you can bird-watch, explore the tropical rain forest, and visit a working farm where tropical fruits, nuts, and spices are grown. If you stay for several nights, you can visit the Santo Cristo or Diamante waterfalls by horseback or on foot. Rates range from $30 for a day trip for one person ($40 for two) to $190 for two people for five days and nights. Horse rentals are additional.

Down near Uvita there are several beautiful waterfalls that make wonderful destinations for hikes or horseback rides. Ask at Uvita's Soda Cocotico for Jorge Diaz, who leads people to the Emerald Pools Falls, which are a great place to go for a swim.

Reel & Release (tel. 771-1903, leave message) offers fishing charters. A full-day fishing trip for four will cost $425, for two people the cost is $375. Half-day trips are $250 for two people and $280 for four people.

WHERE TO STAY

MODERATE

CABAÑAS ESCONDIDAS, Apdo. 364, San Isidro de El General (in the U.S.: c/o Selva Mar, AAA Express, 1641 NW 79th Ave., Miami, FL 33126). Tel. 506/771-1903. 6 rms (all with private bath).
$ Rates (including breakfast): $35 single or double; $45 triple. No credit cards.

⭐ Travelers with a New Age outlook will want to make Cabañas Escondidas their first choice in Dominical. The spiritual folks who operate this casual bed-and-breakfast prefer guests with a similar outlook on life. Most mornings will find guests meditating on the porch of their cabiñas or doing tai chi chuan in the garden. You really need to have your own car if you plan to stay here, because meals other than breakfast are not always available. The six cabañas are situated high on a hill overlooking the Pacific Ocean and are all spread out so that they feel very secluded. Two of the cabañas have sleeping lofts, and the three newer ones are all done in a beautiful Japanese style with shoji screen and stone walls. Some of the cabañas are quite a hike from the parking area, so travel light. Down below is a beautiful little cover with tide pools and safe swimming. There are plans to add some more cabañas and a restaurant down here. Surrounding the lodge are 80 acres of farmland and virgin rain forest. Tours of the forest can be arranged for $10 to $15 per person, and there are bicycles available for rent. You'll find Cabañas Escondidas about 6 kilometers south of Dominical.

HOTEL RÍO LINDO, Dominical. Tel. 506/771-2009. Fax 506/771-1725. 10 rms (all with private bath).
$ Rates: Dec–Apr, $20.30 single, $33.80 double, $40.55 triple; May–Nov, slightly lower rates. No credit cards.

This is one of the newest hotels in Dominical and is located just across the bridge where the road turns into the village. Rooms here are simple but clean and all have ceiling fans. The upstairs rooms are definitely the better choice here. These rooms are larger, have nicer furnishings, and better ventilation. Adjacent to the hotel is the Restaurant Maui, a moderately priced place that seems to keep the stereo blaring all day long.

PUNTA DOMINICAL, Apdo. 196-8000, San Isidro de El General. Tel. and Fax 506/771-1903. 4 cabins.
$ Rates: $35 single; $45 double; $55 triple; $60 quad; $75 one to six people in large cabin. No credit cards.

⭐ Located about 5 kilometers south of Dominical on a rocky point, this place has a stony cove on one side and a sandy beach on the other. The cabins and restaurant are set among shady old trees high above the surf, and have excellent views of both coves. The best views are to be had from the cabins higher up the hill, but all have good views. The cabins, built on stilts and constructed of dark polished hardwood, all have big porches with chairs and hammocks. Screened and louvered walls are designed to catch the breezes. The bathrooms are large and have separate changing areas. The hotel's open-air restaurant, which specializes in seafood, is the best in Dominical. Entrée prices range from $3.75 to $14.90.

BUDGET

In addition to the places listed here, if you continue south another 16 kilometers, you'll find a campground on Playa Ballena and a couple of basic cabina places in Uvita.

ALBERGUE WILLDALE, Dominical. Tel. 506/771-1903 (leave message). 7 rms (all with private bath).
$ Rates: $20 single; $25 double; $30 triple. No credit cards.

⭐ The Albergue Willdale is located directly across from the soccer field and is by far the friendliest place in Dominical. Directly behind the lodge is the river, where you can go swimming, fishing, or paddling around. The owners of this lodge are from Virginia, and they'll gladly fill you in on all there is to do in the area. The rooms are large and have big windows and patios. There are reading lights, fans, hot water, and attractive Mexican bedspreads. If you are interested in staying for a while, the Dales also rent a very comfortable house up in the hills for $120 a night. The house even has its own swimming pool.

BELLA VISTA, Dominical (c/o Selva Mar, Apdo. 215-8000, San Isidro de El General). Tel. 506/771-1903. Fax 506/771-0060. 4 cabins.
$ Rates (including breakfast): $15–$20 single; $30–$40 double. No credit cards.

⭐ "Bella Vista" means "beautiful view" and that is exactly what you get when you stay at one of these rustic little cabins high in the hills south of Dominical. This is a very basic sort of place, but the owners are very friendly and the location is superb. Transportation between Dominical and Bella Vista is $10 per person each way. Simple meals are served ($3 for lunch, $5 for dinner), though one of the cabins has its own kitchen. The favorite activity here is an all-day horseback ride through the rain forest to a beautiful waterfall. The price of $40 per person includes your horse, guide, and a lunch.

CABINAS NAYARIT, 200 meters west of Rancho Coco, Dominical. Tel. 506/771-1878. 13 rms (all with private bath).
$ Rates: Dec–Apr, $20.27–$40.54 single or double; May–Nov, $13.55–$27.05 single or double. No credit cards.
Wedged between the mouth of the Río Baru and the beach, there are several sandy lanes lined with simple houses and some cabina places, of which the Cabinas Nayarit are the best. There are several styles of room here including older ones with fans and lots of beds (crowded), older rooms with air-conditioning, and (most expensive) newer rooms with air-conditioning, skylights, carved wooden headboards, and jalousie windows.

ROCA VERDE, Dominical. Tel. 506/771-2490. 12 rms (7 with private bath).
$ Rates: $6.75 single, double, or triple without bath; $16.90 single or double with bath; $20.30 triple with bath. No credit cards.
This is the best of the basic hotels in Dominical, and though it is a couple of miles out of town, they do have a restaurant where you can get equally inexpensive meals. The setting is superb—on a little cove with rocks and tide pools at the near end. If you're driving, you'll only be able to take the back road from town at low tide, since the road actually crosses a section of the beach. The cheaper rooms are very basic, with wooden walls, a fan, one small window, and a couple of beds. The shared toilets and showers are comparable to what you might find at a campground. The more expensive cabins have private baths and a decidedly tropical feel. There's a disco every Saturday night at Roca Verde's open-air restaurant/bar. Be prepared.

WHERE TO DINE

Right in town, there's the **Soda Laura,** which serves basic Tico meals and has a nice view of the river mouth. Prices range from $1.70 to $6.75. Other options right in Dominical include **Jungle Jim's,** a gringo hangout and sports bar, and the **Bar Maui.** These latter two places have meals for between $3.50 and $15. However, if you want the best food in the area, head south of town to **Punta Dominical** where there is a little open-air restaurant affiliated with a small hotel (see above for details).

5. SAN ISIDRO DE EL GENERAL

120 kilometers SE of San José; 123 kilometers NW of Palmar Norte; 29 kilometers NE of Dominical

GETTING THERE By Bus Express buses leave San José daily at 5:30am and 5pm from Calle 16 between avenidas 1 and 3. Duration: 3 hours. Fare: $3.25.

There are also buses from Puerto Jiménez to San Isidro daily at 3:30am and 11am. Duration: 5 hours. Fare: $4.50.

There are also buses from Golfito to San José that stop in San Isidro. These buses leave daily at 5am and 1pm. Duration: 5 hours. Fare $6.15.

By Car It is a long and winding road from San José to San Isidro; this section of the Interamerican Highway is one of the most difficult sections of road in the country. Not only are there the usual car-eating potholes, but you must also contend with driving over the 11,000-foot-high Cerro de la Muerte (Mountain of Death), which the I.C.T. (Costa Rican Tourism Board) would like to rename Buenavista (Beautiful View). This aptly named mountain (in either case) is legendary for its dense afternoon fogs, blindingly torrential downpours, steep drop-offs, constant switchbacks, and breathtaking views. In other words, drive with care. And bring a sweater; it's cold up at the top. It'll take you about 3 hours to get to San Isidro.

DEPARTING Buses for San José leave daily every hour between 5:30am and 5pm. Buses to Dominical leave daily at 7am and 1:30 and 3pm. Buses to Golfito leave around 10am and 2 and 6pm. Buses to Puerto Jiménez leave daily at 5:30am and noon.

ESSENTIALS Downtown San Isidro is just off the Interamerican Highway. The main bus station is two blocks west of the north end of the central park.

San Isidro de El General is the largest town in this region and is located on the Interamerican Highway in the foothills of the Talamanca Mountains. Though there isn't much of anything to do right in town, this is the jumping-off point for trips to Chirripó National Park. This is also the transfer point if you are coming from or going to Dominical, and all buses traveling the Interamerican Highway stop here.

WHAT TO SEE & DO

At 12,412 feet in elevation, Mount Chirripó is the tallest mountain in Costa Rica, and because of the great elevations within **Chirripó National Park,** temperatures often go well below freezing. If you are headed up this way, come prepared for chilly weather. The elevation and low temperatures have produced a very different sort of environment for Costa Rica. Above about 10,000 feet only stunted trees and shrubs can survive in regions known as *paramos*. If you are driving the Interamerican Highway between San Isidro and San José, you will pass through the paramo on the Cerro de la Muerte (Mountain of Death).

Hiking up to the top of **Mount Chirripó** is one of Costa Rica's great adventures. On a clear day (usually in the morning), you can see both the Pacific Ocean and the Caribbean Sea from the summit. You can do this trip fairly easily on your own if you have brought gear and are an experienced backpacker. It will take you around four days to hike from the park entrance to the peak and back down again. For much of the way you'll be hiking through cloud forests that are home to the resplendent quetzal, Costa Rica's most beautiful bird. These cloud forests are cold and damp, though, so come prepared for rain and fog. To reach Chirripó National Park from San Isidro, catch a bus to San Gerardo de Rivas at 5am or 2pm. Buses return to San Isidro at 7am and 4pm. Park admission is $1.35. If you'd like to do the trip with a guide, contact Chirripó Trekking Adventures (tel. 254-4811 or 254-6096).

WHERE TO STAY & DINE

HOTEL CHIRRIPÓ, south side of church, San Isidro de El General. Tel. 506/771-0529. 46 rms (20 with private bath).
$ Rates: $5.25 single without bath, $8.45 single with bath; $9 double without bath, $13.90 double with bath; $20.80 triple with bath. V.
This budget hotel is about the best you'll find right in San Isidro and is located on the central square within a couple of blocks of all the town's bus stations. Rooms vary considerably. Some have windows (and street noise), and some have no windows or street noise. Stay away from the rooms in front, since these are the noisiest. There's a large restaurant at the front of the lobby.

EN ROUTE TO SAN JOSÉ

Between San Isidro de El General and San José, the Interamerican Highway climbs to its highest point in Costa Rica and crosses over the Cerro de la Muerte. This area has recently acquired a newfound importance as one of the best places in Costa Rica to see resplendent quetzals in the wild. March, April, and May are nesting season for the quetzals, and this is usually the best time to seem them. However, in this area, it is usually possible to seem them year round.

ALBERGUE DE MONTAÑA SAVEGRE, (Apdo. 482, Cartago) kilometer 80 Carretera Interamericana Sur, San Gerardo de Dota. Tel. 506/771-1732. 14 cabins.
$ Rates (including three meals): $50 per person. No credit cards.
⭐ This working apple and pear farm has recently acquired quite a reputation for itself as one of the best places in the country to see quetzals. The farm has long been popular as a weekend vacation and picnicking spot for Ticos, but now people from all over the world are searching out the rustic lodge. The rooms here are quite basic, but if you're serious about bird-watching this shouldn't matter. Hearty Tico meals are served, and if you want to try your hand at trout fishing, you might luck into a fish dinner. You'll find this lodge 9 kilometers down a dirt road off the Interamerican Highway.

ALBERGUE DE MONTAÑA TAPANTÍ, kilometer 62 Carreter Interamericana Sur, Macho Gaff, Cartago (Apdo. 1237-1000, Pavas). Tel. 506/232-0436. 10 rms.
$ Rates: $50 single or double; $60 triple; $70 quad. MC, V.
If you want to hike around in the cloud forest, see quetzals, and then return to a large, comfortable room with a private bath, then this deluxe lodge is what you're looking for in this area. The buildings at Tapantí are built to resemble Swiss chalets. You may think you're in Switzerland when you feel how cold it gets here at night. The lodge is at 10,000 feet and frost is not uncommon. However, there is a

fireplace in the lounge. Most of the guest rooms are actually suites with separate bedrooms and living rooms. Luckily, they also have heaters. The lodge's dining room serves such Swiss specialties as beef fondue and raclette, as well as other continental dishes. Guided hikes, horseback rides, and bird-watching walks are all available through the lodge.

FINCA DE EDDIE SERRANO-MIRADOR DE QUETZALES, kilometer 70 Carretera Interamericana Sur, Tres Junio de Dota. No phone. 8 rms (all with shared bath).
$ Rates (including three meals): $20 per person. No credit cards.

S This very rustic lodge hadn't yet opened when I last visited, but was very close. The small lodge sits on a terrace above the farm's old homestead and overlooks a beautiful valley. Construction is of slab boards and most of the rooms are tiny cubicles with bunk beds, although there are a couple of rooms that have a double bed as well as a bunk bed. Meals are served in the building's central lounge area where there is a woodstove to take the chill off the high-altitude nights (the lodge is at 8,450 feet). This place is definitely for younger bird watchers who don't mind very basic accommodations. Despite the rusticity here, the Serrano family is very helpful and friendly, though little English is spoken. They offer guided hikes and night tours ($6.80 per person for two to three hours), though you can often see quetzals right from the lodge itself.

READERS RECOMMEND

GENESIS II, Cañon, Cerro de la Muerte (tel. 506/288-0739, fax 506/551-0070).
"We thoroughly enjoyed our visit here. The owners are very friendly and informative. They took us on a great walk through their rain forest. . . . Birders will enjoy this place, as they have 4 or 5 kilometers of great trails. This place isn't overrun like Monteverde. I can only give the rooms a C-. Yes, they are dank and the kerosene heaters aren't my favorite. However, the plant and animal life make this a worthwhile stopover if you are in the vicinity of the Interamerican Highway." — Frampton Simons, Atlanta, Georgia

THE SOUTHERN ZONE

The heat and humidity are more than many people can handle, but this remote southern region of Costa Rica is one of the country's most beautiful and wild areas. Lush forested mountains tumble into the sea, streams still run clear and clean, and scarlet macaws squawk raucously in the treetops. However, this beauty does not come easy; you must have plenty of time (and/or money) and a desire for a bit of adventure if you want to explore this region. Because there are few roads, most of the most fascinating spots can be reached only by small plane or boat, though hiking and four-wheeling will also get you into some memorable surroundings as well.

Because the south is such a long drive from San José (about 8 hours), it has been the last area of Costa Rica to open up to tourism. There are still relatively few places to stay down here, but that is, of course, changing almost weekly. With the opening of a duty-free port at Golfito, even Ticos are discovering this region.

1. DRAKE BAY

145 kilometers S of San José; 32 kilometers SW of Palmar

GETTING THERE   By Plane   The closest airport to Drake Bay is in Palmar Sur, a taxi and boat ride away. Sansa (tel. 233-0397, 233-3258, or 233-5330) has flights to Palmar Sur on Tuesday, Thursday, and Saturday at 7:45am and Monday, Wednesday, and Friday at 9:15am from San José's Juan Santamaría International Airport. The former flight stops at Coto 47 en route, and the latter stops at Quepos en route. Duration: 1½ hours. Fare: $46 each way.

Travelair (tel. 220-3054 or 232-7883) has flights to Palmar Sur daily at 8:40am from San José's Pavas International Airport. This flight stops at Quepos en route. Duration: 55 minutes. Fare: $58 one way, $100 round-trip.

By Bus   Express buses leave San José daily at 5, 6:30, 8:30 and 10am and 2:30 and 6pm from Avenida 18 between calles 2 and 4. Duration: 5 hours. Fare: $4.30.

You can also catch a Golfito-bound bus from this same station and get off in Palmar Norte.

Once in Palmar Norte, ask around about when the next bus goes out to Sierpe. If it doesn't leave for a while (and they aren't frequent) consider taking a taxi.

By Taxi and Boat   Once you arrive at either the Palmar Norte bus station or the Palmar Sur airstrip, you'll need to take a taxi to the village of Sierpe. The fare should be between $10 and $15. A seat on a boat from Sierpe down river to Drake Bay will cost you another $15.

WHAT'S SPECIAL ABOUT THE SOUTHERN ZONE

Beaches

Drake Bay, where there are miles of small deserted beaches backed by rain forest.

Playa Zancudo, a budget traveler's dream come true, and good swimming, too.

Playa Pavones, with what may be the longest surfable wave in the world.

Great Towns/Villages

Golfito, an old banana-shipping port complete with company housing and jungle-covered hills on the edge of town.

Natural Spectacles

The largest population of scarlet macaws in Costa Rica is to be found on the Osa Peninsula.

Parks/Gardens

Corcovado National Park on the Osa Peninsula, one of Costa Rica's most remote national parks.

The Wilson Botanical Gardens, which are planted with an amazing variety of tropical plants from around the world. Caño Island Biological Reserve, with pre-Columbian archaeological sites and great diving.

Activities

Hiking the beaches and rain forests of Corcovado National Park.

Bird-watching at Drake Bay.

Sportfishing out of Drake Bay and in the Sierpe River.

DEPARTING Have your lodge arrange your boat trip back up river to Sierpe. Also be sure to have the lodge arrange a taxi to meet you in Sierpe for the trip to Palmar Sur or Palmar Norte. If you're on a budget, you can take the late morning public bus from Sierpe to Palmar Norte. In the two Palmars you can make onward plane and bus connections. Almost any bus headed north will take you to San José, and almost any bus heading south will take you to Golfito.

ESSENTIALS Because Drake Bay is so remote and only accessible by water or chartered plane, it is almost imperative that you have a reservation before arrival. The lodges listed here are scattered along several kilometers of coastline.

D rake Bay, named for Sir Francis Drake, who is believed to have anchored here in 1579, is a small bay on the northern coast of the Osa Peninsula. Little more than a collection of lodges catering to naturalists, anglers, scuba divers, and assorted vacationers, the bay can only be reached by boat or chartered plane, which makes it one of the more remote destinations in Costa Rica. Because of the bay's remoteness, there has been little development here. Accommodations vary from tents on wooden platforms and cement-walled cabinas to very comfortable lodges. However, you won't find any luxury hotels here, so if those are your accustomed standards, skip Drake Bay. There are no phone or power lines to Drake Bay (though there are radio phones and electrical generators). The village of Drake Bay has its own water system, but it is infamous for its unreliability. If you're headed out this way you may occasionally find yourself without water for a shower, but the problem rarely lasts long.

Emptying into the bay is the tiny Río Agujitas, which acts as a protected harbor for small boats and is a great place to do a bit of canoeing or swimming. It is here in the Río Agujitas that many of the local lodges dock their boats. Stretching south from Drake Bay are miles and miles of deserted beaches. Adventurous explorers will find tide pools, spring-fed rivers, waterfalls, forests trails, and some of the best bird-watching in all of Costa Rica. If a paradise such as this appeals to you, Drake Bay makes a good base for exploring the peninsula.

South of Drake Bay lay the wilds of the Osa Peninsula and Corcovado National Park. This is one of Costa Rica's most beautiful regions, yet it is also one of its least accessible. Corcovado National Park covers about half of the peninsula and contains the largest virgin lowland rain forest in Central America. For this reason, Corcovado is well known among naturalists and researchers studying rain-forest ecology. Take note of the operative words here—rain forest. It does, indeed, rain here. In fact, some parts of the peninsula receive more than 250 inches per year. In addition to producing lush forests, this massive amount of rain also produces more than a few disgruntled visitors. If you're of the opinion that rain ruins a vacation, you might want to consider elsewhere in Costa Rica.

WHAT TO SEE & DO

Beaches, forests, and solitude are the main attractions of Drake Bay, with Corcovado National Park being the area's star attraction. The Osa Peninsula is home to an unbelievable variety of plants and animals: more than 140 species of mammals, 267 species of birds, and 117 species of amphibians and reptiles. Though you aren't likely to see a high percentage of these animals, you can expect to see quite a few, including several species of monkeys, coatimundis, scarlet macaws, parrots, and hummingbirds. The tallest tree in Costa Rica, a 230-foot-tall silk-cotton tree, is located within the park, as is Costa Rica's largest population of scarlet macaws. Other inhabitants here include jaguars, tapirs, sloths, and crocodiles. If you're lucky, you might even see one of the region's *osas*. Though the word means "bear" in English, in this case it refers to the giant anteaters that live on the peninsula.

Around Drake Bay and within the national park there are many miles of trails through rain forests and swamps, down beaches, and around rock headlands. All of the lodges listed below offer guided excursions into the park. It is also possible to begin a hike around the peninsula from Drake Bay. Within the park camping is allowed and there are several ranger stations where you can get a dorm bed and a meal. To find out more about hiking and camping in Corcovado National Park, contact the park headquarters in Puerto Jiménez (see below for details) or the national parks' headquarters in San José at Avenida 9 between calles 17 and 19 (tel. 233-6701).

One of the most popular excursions from Drake Bay is a trip out to Caño Island and the Caño Island Biological Reserve for a bit of exploring and snorkeling or scuba diving. The island is located about 12 miles offshore from Drake Bay and was once home to a pre-Columbian culture about which little is known. A trip to the island will include a visit to one of this culture's cemeteries, and you'll also be able to see some of the stone spheres that are commonly believed to have been carved by the people who once lived in this area. The island is most unique for its geological isolation: Due to plate tectonics, the island has remained separate from the rest of Central America for more than 40 million years. The dominant tree species is the huge cow or milk tree, which produces a milky sap that can be drunk. Few animals or birds live on the island, but the coral reefs just offshore teem with life and are the main reason most people come here. Most of the lodges listed below offer trips to Caño Island. You can also do some sportfishing while you're in the area. Almost any of the lodges can arrange a charter boat for you.

WHERE TO STAY & DINE

I have chosen to list nightly room rates at the following lodges. However, all but the least expensive couple of places do most of their business as package trips that include several nights lodging, all meals, transportation, and tours. If you intend to do several tours while you are here, be sure to ask about these packages.

0 | 38 km / 24 mi.

N

Tapanti National Wildlife Refuge

Chirripó Indian Reservation

Bribri

Cerro de la Muerte

CORDILLERA DE TALAMANCA

Talamanca Indian Reservation

Bribri Indian Reservation

Cerro Chirripó

Costa Rica/Panama International Friendship Park

San Isidro de El General

Cerro Kamuk

PANAMA

Peñas Blancas

Pan American Hwy.

Dominical

Río Pacuare

Buenos Aires

Salitre Indian Reservation

Playa Ballena

Brujo

Coronado

Palmar Norte Airport

Boca Brava

Cortés

Curré Indian Reservation

Coronado Bay

Palmar Norte

Sierpe

Río Sierpe

Sabanilla

Piedras Blancas

San Vito

Sabalito

Río Chocuaco

2

Las Cruces Botanical Garden

Caño Island

Playa Colorado

Drake

Chocuaco Lake

Rincón

Golfo Dulce

Golfito Airport

Río Claro

Caño Island Biological Preserve

Corcovado Lake

Osa Indian Reservation

Golfito

Osa Peninsula

Playa Zancudo

Corcovado National Park

Jiménez

Zancudo

Playa Sirena

Playa Tamale

Playa Carate

Pavonnes

Punta Banco

PANAMA

Pacific

Ocean

Airport

EXPENSIVE

AGUILA DE OSA INN, Apdo. 10486-1000, San José (in the U.S.: P.O. Box 025312, Miami, FL 33102-5312, Cuenta no. 250). Tel. 506/296-2190 or 232-7722. Fax 506/232-7722. 14 rms.

$ Rates (including three meals): $95 single; $160 double; $210 triple. MC, V.

The rates and the comfort level here are the highest in Drake Bay, and though the views are some of the best around, I'm not convinced the prices here are warranted. Situated high on a hill overlooking Drake Bay and the Pacific Ocean, the Aguila de Osa Inn offers attractively decorated, comfortable rooms. There is a bar built atop the rocks on the bank of the Río Agujitas, and a dining room with a good view of the bay. Meals are simply prepared but tasty and filling. All the guest rooms have hardwood floors, ceiling fans, and excellent views. Excursions available through the lodge include hikes in Corcovado National Park ($55), trips to Caño Island ($55 for snorkelers, $110 for scuba divers), horseback rides ($55), and sportfishing ($450 to $850 for a full day).

COCALITO LODGE, Apdo. 63, Palmar Norte, Osa Peninsula. No phone in Costa Rica. Tel. (in Canada) 519/782-4592. Fax (in Costa Rica) 506/786-6150 or 786-6335. 6 rms (all with private bath).

$ Rates (including three meals): May–Nov, $38.50–$50 single, $77–$100 double; Dec–Apr, $50–$65 single, $100–$130 double. No credit cards.

The owners of this little place right on the beach south of La Paloma Lodge are gringos who have been living here for years. Their choice of this remote alternative lifestyle has translated into a rustic and casual beachfront lodge that attracts primarily a younger crowd. Some of the rooms are a bit cramped and dark, but there are also larger and more expensive cabinas that offer plenty of room. In my opinion, Cocalito's greatest attraction is that it is right on a beautiful little cove bordered on both ends by rocky outcrops. At all of the more expensive lodges here in Drake Bay, you have to do a bit of walking (often down muddy trails) to get to a swimmable beach. So, if having the beach right outside your door is more important than having a large luxurious room, Cocalito might be for you. The lodge's dining room also offers excellent meals, with many ingredients from the owners' organic garden. In fact, a small cruise ship stops here every week for a big beach buffet dinner (be prepared for the crowds). A variety of tours are offered including trips to Caño Island ($50 for snorkelers, $110 for scuba divers), guided hikes ($15 to $50), horseback rides ($35), deep-sea fishing ($350 per day for three people), and boat tours of the nearby mangrove swamp ($50).

DRAKE BAY WILDERNESS CAMP, Apdo. 98-8150, Palmar Norte, Osa. Tel. and Fax 506/771-2436. 4 tents (all with shared bath), 21 rms.

$ Rates (including three meals): Tents, $44 single, $88 double; rooms, $66 single, $132 double, $198 triple. MC, V.

This is one of the most convenient and best located of the lodges at Drake Bay. It backs onto the Río Agujitas and fronts onto the Pacific, but because it's on a rocky spit, there isn't a good swimming beach right here. The lodge offers a variety of accommodations of different ages and styles. Budget travelers can opt for a large tent, while those seeking more comfort can ask for one of the new rooms. These newer rooms have ceiling fans, verandas, and good mattresses on the beds, The older rooms, though smaller, are also comfortable. The family-style meals are filling, with an emphasis on fresh seafood and fresh fruits. Tours offered by Drake Bay Wilderness Camp include hikes within the national park ($40), trips to Caño Island ($40 for snorkelers, $100 for scuba divers), and sportfishing charters for $240 per day.

MARENCO BIOLOGICAL RESERVE, Centro Comercial El Pueblo, Local No. 49-50, (Apdo. 4025-1000), San José. Tel. 506/221-1594 or 233-9101. Fax 506/255-1340. 25 rms.

$ Rates (including three meals): $75 single; $150 double; $225 triple. No credit cards.

Marenco is located a few kilometers south of Drake Bay, and is consequently the closest lodge to the national park. The lodge, which is set on a hillside overlooking the ocean, is surrounded by 1,235 acres of private reserve. There are more than 4 kilometers of trails through the reserve and the bird-watching here is often excellent. Accommodations are comfortable though fairly simple. All the rooms have ocean views and porches so you can enjoy the sunsets and bird-watch right from your room. The newer rooms are larger and more comfortable, though even the older rooms have a lot of style. Rooms are mostly in duplex cabins around the landscaped grounds, and if you get one of the larger rooms, you can lie in bed and gaze out at the forest through walls of screen. The thatch roofs give the compound the feel of a small village. Meals are served family-style in an open-air dining room that has a great view down the hill to the Pacific. Marenco offers the same sorts of tours available at other lodges and charges similar rates.

LA PALOMA LODGE, Apdo. 97-4005, San Antonio de Belen, Heredia. Tel. and Fax 506/239-0954 or 239-2801 (radio phone at the lodge). 5 rms, 5 cabins.
$ Rates (including three meals): Rooms, $75 single, $120 double, $180 triple; cabins, $150 double, $225 triple. May–Nov 15, rates are 10% lower. Packages available. No credit cards.

Bird-watchers will find no better place to stay in Drake Bay. Situated on a hill that can leave the out-of-shape a bit winded, La Paloma offers expansive ocean views. The main lodge building is a huge open-air, thatched structure with a long veranda. Over in one corner is a sitting area that makes for a pleasant place to meet other lodge guests. Unfortunately, the beach is down at the bottom of the hill, and the trail can be very muddy. However, for my money, the cabins here at La Paloma are the best buys in the area. The two older cabins are my favorites simply for their spaciousness and seclusion. Four screen walls keep you in touch with nature and let the ocean breezes blow through. There is electricity in the evenings for those who like to stay up late reading. However, if you're like me, you'll want to get up at dawn to watch the early-morning birds. These cabins, as well as the newer ones, are built on stilts and have large verandas that look into the trees and shrubs, which are all alive with beautiful birds. The rooms, though much smaller, are still very attractive and have good views from their verandas, which, like cabins, have hammocks. Excursions available include hikes in the park ($55), trips to Caño Island ($65), horseback rides ($55), half-day hikes ($25), and sportfishing charters ($285 half day, $400 full day). There are also canoes, kayaks, and snorkeling equipment for rent.

MODERATE

ALBERGUE JINETES DE OSA, Drake Bay, Osa Peninsula. No phone. 5 rms (all with shared bath).
$ Rates (including three meals): $30 single; $60 double; $90 triple. No credit cards.
Though the rooms here are small and dark, this is still one of the nicer budget places at Drake Bay. The wooden construction of the building and the long veranda almost directly above the beach are what give this lodge the edge over others in its class. It is also the closest budget place to the nearly deserted beaches south of the Río Agujitas. Basic Tico-style meals are served in a small open-air dining room.

CABINAS CECILIA, Drake Bay, Osa Peninsula. No phone. 5 cabins (2 with private bath).
$ Rates (including three meals): $25 single; $50 double.
This is about as cheap as it gets at Drake Bay. Though Cecilia's cabinas, housed in a cinder-block bunker, are rather stark, there is a long veranda and a nice view of the bay. Rooms vary in size and some have bunk beds, while others have twin or double beds. Other than the beds, there is no furniture in the rooms. Meals are served in a separate open-air dining room a short distance from the cabinas.

CORCOVADO ADVENTURE TENT CAMP, Drake Bay, Osa Peninsula. Tel. 506/238-2726. Fax 506/260-4434. 10 tents (all with shared bathrooms).
$ Rates (including three meals): $60 double. No credit cards.

If you don't mind camping, this place, midway between the lodges at Drake Bay and Marenco Biological Reserve, is a good moderate choice. The tents are quite large and are set on wooden decks, and a nice swimming beach is only a few yards away. There are plenty of modern showers and toilets. The large dining room serves simple meals with an emphasis on fresh seafood. Various tours are available and there are kayaks and snorkeling gear available for rent. With rates comparable to those of the cheapest places in the village and tents as large as some of the village's cheapest rooms, this makes a good choice for anyone who prefers a bit more seclusion and more of an adventurous setting. Excursions you can arrange here include guided hikes ($55), trips to Caño Island ($55), horseback rides ($55), and sportfishing charters ($375 to $450 for a full day for up to four people).

NEARBY PLACES TO STAY

HOTEL PARGO, Sierpe. Tel. 506/788-8111. 10 rms (all with private bath).
$ Rates: $13.50–$17.55 single $18.95–$23 double. No credit cards.
This modern two-story hotel is the only hotel right in Sierpe, and is located right at the dock from which boats leave to head down river to Drake Bay. So, if you are on your way to Drake Bay and expect to arrive in Sierpe late in the day (when no boats are heading down river), this is where you should spend the night. Rooms are fairly large, though simply furnished, and are clean. The higher prices are for rooms with air-conditioning, however there are also ceiling fans in all the rooms. There is an inexpensive open-air restaurant adjacent to the hotel.

RIO SIERPE LODGE, Apdo. 818-1200, Pavas. Tel. 506/220-1712 or 220-2121. Fax 506/232-3321. 11 rms.
$ Rates (including three meals and transportation to and from Palmar): $65 single; $130 double; $195 triple. No credit cards.
This lodge is located on the south bank of the Río Sierpe near the river mouth. You won't have direct access to any beaches if you stay here, but all the same excursions are available at comparable prices. This lodge is best known as a fishing lodge and offers various fishing packages. The lodge is surrounded by forests and there are hiking trails on the property. Meals in the dining room feature international cuisine with an emphasis on fresh fruits, fish, and chicken. Naturalists, anglers, and scuba divers are all catered to here. Adventurous types can do a two-day horseback trek that includes camping in the rain forest. Note that taxi and river transfers between Palmar and the lodge are included in the rates, which makes this place slightly more economical than the other lodges I've listed.

2. PUERTO JIMÉNEZ

35 kilometers W of Golfito by water (90 kilometers by road);
85 kilometers S of Palmar Norte.

GETTING THERE By Air Sansa (tel. 233-0397, 233-3258, or 233-5330) has flights Monday, Wednesday, and Friday at 9:15am to Puerto Jiménez from San José's Juan Santamaría International Airport. The flight stops at Quepos and Palmar Sur en route. Duration: 1 hour and 25 minutes. Fare: $52 each way.

By Bus Express buses leave San José daily at 6am and noon from Calle 12 between avenidas 7 and 9. Duration: 8 hours. Fare: $7.70.

Buses from San Isidro to Puerto Jiménez leave daily at 5:30am and noon. These buses leave from next to the church in San Isidro. Duration: 5 hours. Fare: $4.50.

By Boat There is daily passenger launch service from Golfito to Puerto Jiménez at noon. The boat leaves from the minicipal dock. Duration: 1½ hours. Fare: $2.70.

It is also possible to charter a water taxi in Golfito for the trip across to Puerto Jiménez. You'll have to pay around $30 for two people.

By Car Take the Interamerican Highway east out of San José (through San Pedro and Cartago) and continue south on this road. In three hours or so, you'll pass through San Isidro de El General. In another three hours or so, take the turnoff for La Palma and Puerto Jiménez. This road is paved for a ways but at Rincon turns to gravel. The last 35 kilometers are slow and rough, and, if it's the rainy season, too muddy for anything but a four-wheel-drive vehicle.

DEPARTING Buses to San José leave Puerto Jiménez daily at 5 and 11am. Buses to San Isidro leave at 3:30am and 11am. The launch to Golfito leaves from the public dock at 6am.

ESSENTIALS Puerto Jiménez is a dirt-laned town on the southern coast of the Osa Peninsula. The public dock is down the road at the north end of the soccer field. The bus stop is in the center of town. There are several general stores here.

Puerto Jiménez, located on the east side of the Osa Peninsula is about as sleepy a little town as you'll find in Costa Rica—a couple of gravel streets, the ubiquitous soccer field, and a block of general stores, sodas, butcher shops, and bars. On first glance it is hard to imagine anything ever happening here, but looks are often deceiving. Signs in English on walls around town advertise a variety of tours, with most of the excursions being to nearby Corcovado National Park. The national park has its headquarters here, and this town makes an excellent base or starting point for exploring this vast wilderness. Puerto Jiménez is also somewhat of a boom town in the style of the United States' wild west. There's gold in them thar hills! Gold miners use Puerto Jiménez as an outpost, stocking up on staples before heading out to work their claims and cashing in their finds every time they come to town.

WHAT TO SEE & DO

Though a few gringos have, over the years, come to Puerto Jiménez to try their luck at gold panning, the primary reason for coming here these days is to arrange a visit to **Corcovado National Park.** Within a couple of hours by four-wheel-drive vehicle, there are several entrances to the park. However, there are no roads into the park, so once you reach any of the entrances, you'll have to start hiking. Exploring Corcovado National Park is not something to be undertaken lightly, but neither is it the expedition that some people make it out to be. The biggest problems of overnight backpacking trips through the park are the heat and humidity. Frequent rain storms cause the trails to be quite muddy, and should you choose the alternative of hiking on the beach, you will have to plan your hiking around the tides. Often there is no beach at all at high tide. Be sure to pick up a tide table at the park headquarters' office in Puerto Jiménez. You'll find the headquarters one block over from the main street (toward the water) at the end of town near the soccer field (tel. 735-5036).

Coming around from the south, you can enter the park at the La Leona ranger station, which has a campground, some very basic dormitory accommodations, and a cantina. It is 3 kilometers to La Leona from Carate, which is the end of the dirt road from Puerto Jiménez. Alternatively, you can travel to **El Tigre,** about 14 kilometers by dirt road from Puerto Jiménez, where there is another ranger station, campground, and cantina. Trails from El Tigre go only a short distance into the park. From the Los Patos ranger station, which is reached from the town of La Palma north of Puerto Jiménez, there is a 19-kilometer trail through the park. This latter trail leads to Sirena, a ranger station and research facility. Frequented primarily by scientists studying the rain forest, Sirena has basic accommodations, a cantina, a campground, and a land strip used by charter flights. From Sirena it is 16 kilometers along the beach to La Leona and 25 kilometers along the beach to San Pedrillo, the northern entrance ranger station, which also has a campground and cantina. From San Pedrillo it is another 9 kilometers to Marenco Biological Reserve and about 14 kilometers to Drake Bay. Park admission is $1.35 per person. Campsites in the park are $2.10 per person per night. A dorm bed will run you $2.70, and meals are around $13.50 per day.

If you're not into hiking in the heat, you can charter a plane in Puerto Jiménez to take you to Carate, Sirena, Drake Bay, or even Tiskita Lodge, which is across the gulf. Contact Saeta (735-5060).

If you're interested in doing some billfishing or deep-sea fishing, check around the public dock for notices of people with charter boats. Rates are usually around $400 for a full day or $300 for a half day.

WHERE TO STAY
IN TOWN
Budget

AGUA LUNA, in front of the public dock, Puerto Jiménez. Tel. 506/735-5033, 735-5034, or 735-5108. 3 rms (all with private bath). A/C TV TEL
$ Rates: $33.80 single, double, or triple. V.
Though there are only three rooms here, they offer the most luxury of any of the intown lodgings in Puerto Jiménez. Agua Luna is located right at the foot of the town's public dock and backs up to a mangrove forest. The most surprising feature in each of these rooms is the huge bathroom, which includes both a shower and a tub facing a picture window that looks into the mangroves. There are double and twin beds in the rooms, and on the tiled veranda out front, you'll find hammocks for lounging. The only drawback here is that there isn't much landscaping, just a gravel parking area.

CABINAS MARCELINA, Puerto Jiménez. Tel. 506/735-5007. 6 rms (all with private bath).
$ Rates: $5.40–$6.75 single; $9.45–$12.15 double; $12.15–$14.20 triple. No credit cards.
Located a block off Puerto Jiménez's main street, these basic rooms are a good choice for anyone on a shoestring budget. The owner keeps the tile-floored rooms clean and there is surprisingly little mildew (always a problem in cinderblock buildings). Bathrooms are basic but adequate.

CABINAS PUERTO JIMÉNEZ, 50 meters north of Bar y Restaurant El Rancho, Puerto Jiménez. Tel. 506/735-5090 or 735-5152. 6 rms (all with private bath).
$ Rates: $6.75 single; $13.50 double; $20.25 triple. No credit cards.
This basic little place is located right on the waterfront at the north end of the soccer field. The exterior of the building, with its varnished wood, is much more appealing than the rooms themselves. Though large, the guest rooms have cement floors and are very basic. However, they are generally clean and are the best choice in town for budget travelers.

HOTEL MANGLARES, Apdo. 55-8203, Puerto Jiménez de Golfito. Tel. 506/735-5002. Fax 506/735-5121. 10 rms.
$ Rates: $25 single; $30 double. MC, V.
Bird-watchers will want to make this their base in Puerto Jiménez. The hotel is on the edge of the mangrove forest, and some of the rooms can be reached only by an elevated walkway through the mangroves. The trees, and several bird feeders, assure good bird-watching. Though the rooms in front are a bit small and can be musty, the rooms in back are very attractive, and surprisingly don't cost any extra. These latter rooms are surrounded by an attractive garden as well as mangroves. All the rooms have fans to keep you cool, and there is a restaurant serving inexpensive Tico standards.

AROUND THE OSA PENINSULA
Expensive

LAPA RIOS, Apdo. 100, Puerto Jiménez, Osa Peninsula. Tel. and Fax 506/735-5130. 14 bungalows.

$ Rates (including three meals and transfers between Puerto Jiménez and the lodge): Mid-Apr to mid-Nov, $126.50 single, $192 double, $84 per extra person; mid-Nov to mid-Apr, $145 single, $203 double, $88 per extra person. Discounts for children up to 10 years old. AE, MC, V (add 6% surcharge).

Though there are hotels in Costa Rica with more amenities, there is no place more luxurious or private. If you are looking for the ultimate luxury getaway this may be the place for you. However, keep in mind that there are no TVs, no telephones, no air-conditioning, no discos, no shopping, no paved roads, no other nearby hotels to visit, and no crowds. In fact, other than a beautiful little pool and a tropically exotic bar, there is nothing around to distract your attentions from the stupendous views of the forest and ocean far below. Lapa Rios is surrounded by its own 1,000-acre private rain forest reserve, which is home to toucans, parrots, hummingbirds, monkeys, and myriad other wildlife. To give you a closer look at the rain forest, there are several miles of trails, and the resident naturalist can be hired for guided walks. However, if bird-watching is your thing, you need go no farther than the lodge's parking lot, which seems to be a popular spot with numerous avian species.

The hotel consists of seven duplex buildings perched along three ridges. Each spacious room is totally private and oriented toward the view. Walls have open screening and the ceiling is a high-peaked thatch roof. In true Arabian-nights fashion, mosquito nets drape languidly over the queen-size beds. A large deck and tiny tropical garden complete with outdoor shower more than double the living space of each room. The buildings are constructed of local materials such as palm thatch, bamboo, mangrove wood, and other hardwoods. Perhaps the most surprising aspect of each room is the screen-walled shower that lets you drink in the views while you bathe.

Dining/Entertainment: The centerpiece of the open-air dining room is a 50-foot-tall spiral staircase that leads to an observation deck tucked beneath the peak of the building's thatch roof. In one corner of the dining room is the tropical bar. Each evening there is a choice of three meals, which though well prepared frequently lack creativity. Breakfasts, on the other hand, are large and delicious.

Services: Guided walks; horseback riding; boat trips; sportfishing; jungle camping trips; day trips to Corcovado National Park, Caño Island, and Wilson Botanical Gardens; snorkeling equipment; body board and surfboard rentals. Tours range from $15 to $40 per person.

Facilities: Swimming pool, hiking trails.

Moderate

BOSQUE DEL CABO WILDERNESS LODGE, Apdo. 2907-1000, San José. Tel. 506/222-4547 or 222-7738. Fax 506/221-3011. 4 cabins.

$ Rates (including three meals): $75 singe; $110 double; $150 triple. No credit cards.

This simple yet tasteful lodge is located 500 feet above the water at the southern tip of the Osa Peninsula. The lodge is surrounded by 300 acres of land that the owners purchased in order to preserve a piece of the rain forest. The thatched-roof cabins are attractively furnished and are set amid beautiful gardens. Meals are well prepared and filling and usually feature fruits grown on the premises. There's a trail down to a secluded beach that has some tide pools. Surfing is a popular activity here, as are hiking and horseback riding. Trips to the national park or out fishing can be arranged. It will cost you around $14 for a taxi out here.

Budget

CORCOVADO LODGE TENT CAMP, Costa Rica Expeditions, Apdo. 6941-1000, San José. Tel. 506/257-0766 or 222-0333. Fax 506/257-1665. 20 tents.

$ Rates (including three meals): $42.30 single; $69.60 double. AE, MC, V.

At the opposite end of the luxury scale from Lapa Rios, though no less enjoyable for anyone accustomed to camping, is Costa Rica Expeditions, Corcovado Lodge Tent Camp, which is built on a low bluff right above the

(S) beach. Behind the tent camp, forested mountains rise up, and just a few minutes' walk away is the entrance to Corcovado National Park. To reach this lodge is an adventure in itself. You can either take a five-seater chartered plane to the gravel landing strip at Carate and then walk for 45 minutes to the lodge, or take the lodge's specially designed pontoon boat from Golfito or Puerto Jiménez. If you have a four-wheel-drive vehicle, you can get as far as the landing strip and then walk the remaining 1.5 kilometers. Once you're here, you have a real sense of being away from it all.

Accommodations are in large tents pitched on wooden decks. Each tent has two twin beds, a table, and a couple of folding chairs on the front deck. Toilets and showers are a short walk away, and there are enough so that there is usually no waiting. Meals are served in a large screen-walled dining room furnished with picnic tables. A separate but similar building is furnished with hammocks, a small bar, and a few board games. Services at the lodge include guided walks and boat excursions both into the national park and out to Caño Island. Package rates that include transportation and tours are also available, and are actually the way most people come here.

WHERE TO DINE

BAR RESTAURANT AGUA LUNA, 25 meters north of the public pier. Tel. 735-5034.
  Cuisine: COSTA RICAN. **Reservations:** Not accepted.
$ **Prices:** Main courses $3.40–$10.15. No credit cards.
  Open: Daily 9am–11pm.
The first restaurant you come to after arriving in Puerto Jiménez by boat is also the best restaurant in town. Little more than a collection of thatch ranchos (the equivalent of Mexican palapas), set amid shady gardens, Agua Luna has a nice view of the water. The bar is popular and the music is always loud so don't expect a quiet, romantic dinner for two. Seafood is plentiful and prices for fish dinners are low even for Costa Rica, so enjoy.

SODITA CAROLINA, on the main street. No phone.
  Cuisine: COSTA RICAN. **Reservations:** Not accepted.
$ **Prices:** All items $2.35–$6.75. No credit cards.
  Open: Daily 6am–10 or 11pm.
This is Puerto Jiménez's budget travelers' hangout and also serves as an unofficial information center. The walls are plastered with notices for tours to the national park and information on hiring taxis, guides, and planes. The restaurant is opposite the bus stop, so it makes a good place to hang out while waiting to leave town. Once again, seafood is the way to go. They've got good fried fish as well as a variety of ceviches. The black bean soup is usually good, and the casados are filling and cost less than $3. If you need a place to stay, ask here. When I last visited, they were building some cabinas behind the restaurant. The rate was expected to be under $15 for a double room.

3. GOLFITO

87 kilometers S of Palmar Norte; 337 kilometers S of San José

GETTING THERE   By Air   Sansa (tel. 233-0397, 233-3258, or 233-5330) has flights to Golfito Monday through Saturday at 6am and Wednesday through Friday at 1pm from San José's Juan Santamaría International Airport. Duration: 45 minutes. Fare: $52 each way.

Travelair (tel. 220-3054 or 232-7883) has flights to Golfito daily at 8:40am from San José's Pavas International Airport. The flight stops in Quepos and Palmar Sur en route. Duration: 1 hours and 25 minutes. Fare: $66 one way, $114 round-trip.

By Bus Express buses leave San José daily at 7 and 11am and 3pm from Avenida 18 between calles 2 and 4. Duration: 8 hours. Fare: $6.15.

By Boat A passenger launch leaves Puerto Jiménez, on the Osa Peninsula, daily at 6am. Duration: 1½ hours. Fare: $2.70.

You may also be able to hire a boat to take you across the Golfo Dulce to Golfito. However, there are not very many available to Puerto Jiménez, so you're likely to have to pay quite bit ($50 to $75) for such a service.

By Car It is a straight shot down the Interamerican Highway south from San José to Golfito. However, it is a long and arduous road. In the 8 hours it takes to drive the 337 kilometers from San José, you'll pass over the Cerro de la Muerte (Mountain of Death), which is infamous for its dense fog and torrential downpours. Also for almost the entire length of this road, you will have to contend with potholes of gargantuan proportions. Just remember if the road is suddenly smooth and in great shape, you can bet that around the next bend there will be a bottomless pothole that you can't swerve around. Take it easy.

DEPARTING Sansa flies to San José Monday through Saturday at 7am and Wednesday through Friday at 2pm. Travelair flies to San José daily at 9:45am with a stop at Quepos en route. Buses leave for San José daily at 5am and 1pm from the bus station near the municipal dock. The passenger launch to Puerto Jiménez leaves daily at noon.

ESSENTIALS You can rent a car or four-wheel-drive Isuzu Trooper from Golfito Rent A Car, Avenida 6 between calles 7 and 9 (tel. 257-3747, 257-3727, or, after 6pm, 257-3707). If you need to change money, you can do so at the gas station in the middle of town. Golfito Centro (tel. 775-0449, fax 775-0506), on the upper main street in Golfito, is a combination informal information center and real estate office. Drop by to find out about new lodges in the area, horseback-riding trips, jungle tours, fishing trips, and boat rentals and tours.

This old banana port is set on the north side of the Golfo Dulce and is at the foot of lush green mountains. The setting alone is beautiful enough to make this one of the most attractive cities in the country, but Golfito also has an undeniable charm all its own. Sure, the area around the municipal park is kind of seedy, but if you go a little bit farther along the bay, you come to the old United Fruit Company housing. Here you'll find well-maintained wooden houses painted bright colors and surrounded by neatly manicured gardens. It's all very lush and green and clean, an altogether different picture than is painted by most port towns in this country. These old homes are experiencing a sort of renaissance as they become small hotels catering to shoppers visiting the adjacent duty-free shopping center.

WHAT TO SEE & DO

There isn't a whole lot to do in Golfito other than make connections to other places. You can walk or drive through town admiring the United Fruit Company buildings, drop in at one of the souvenir shops, and have a drink overlooking the gulf. However, because this area is gaining in popularity, more tourist-oriented activities are becoming available here in town. Check the bulletin boards in restaurants around town to see what sort of **tours or activities** are available when you arrive. When I was last in town, the folks who run El Jardín Restaurant (tel. 775-0235) were renting open-deck sea kayaks for $35 per day. However, they had plans to move their rental operation across the gulf to Puerto Jiménez.

To arrange jungle tours, horseback rides, boat rentals, and fishing trips, check with Golfito Centro (tel. 775-0449), which has its office on the upper road through downtown Golfito.

The waters off Golfito offer some of the best sportfishing in Costa Rica, and if you'd like to try hooking into a possible world record marlin or sailfish, contact Steve Lino at Golfito Sportfishing (tel. 288-5083). A full day's fishing trip will cost between $350 and $550. This company operates out of nearby Zancudo Beach and also offers multiday packages. Another company to check with is Leomar Sportfishing & Diving (tel. 775-0230), which offers trips at similar prices.

About 30 minutes by boat out of Golfito, you'll find **Casa Orchidia,** a private botanical garden. Two-hour tours of the gardens cost $5 per person with a minimum of four people. You'll also have to hire a boat to get there, which should cost you around $75 for the trip and waiting time.

If you have a serious interest in botanical gardens, consider an excursion to **Wilson Botanical Gardens** (tel. 773-3278), which is located in the town of San Vito, which is about 65 kilometers to the northeast. The gardens are owned by the Organization for Tropical Studies and include more than 2,000 species of tropical plants from around the world. Among the plants grown here are many endangered species, which makes the gardens of interest to botanical researchers. Despite the scientific aspects of the gardens, there are also many beautiful and unusual flowers amid the manicured grounds. If you'd like to stay the night here, there are rustic rooms and cabins. Rates, including three meals, are $55 per person in the rooms and $75 per person in the cabins. You'll find the gardens about 6 kilometers before San Vito. To get here from Golfito, drive back out to the Interamerican Highway and continue south toward Panama. In Cuidad Neily, turn north.

WHERE TO STAY
IN TOWN
Moderate

HOTEL SIERRA, Apdo. 37, Golfito (Apdo. 5304-1000, San José). Tel. 506/ 775-0666 or (in San José) 506/233-9693 or 224-3300. Fax 506/775-0087 or 224-3399. 72 rms. TV TEL A/C

$ Rates: $39 single; $46.80 double; $53.30 triple. AE, DC, MC, V.

Located right beside the airstrip, the Hotel Sierra has become the hotel of choice of people flying in and out of Golfito. It offers the most luxurious accommodations in town, with a courtyard swimming pool, aviaries full of squawking macaws, and a big dining room and bar. The building is constructed to be as open and breezy as possible, though the guest rooms also have modern air conditioners. Covered walkways connect the hotel's various buildings and lots of tropical plants and cages full of birds lend an exotic flavor to the surroundings. The rooms also have pale-blue tile floors, and windows on two sides to let in plenty of light. Bathrooms are very large, and there are also safes in all the rooms. The swimming pool is fairly large and even has a swim-up bar. For light meals and snacks, there is a casual restaurant on the far side of the pool. Prices in the main dining room are also fairly moderate, and there are several lobster dishes for around $15. A casino and tour operator round out the facilities at the hotel. All in all this place offers very good value.

Budget

CASA BLANCA LODGE, 300 meters south of the Depósito Libre, Golfito. Tel. 506/775-0124. 7 rms (all with private bath).

$ Rates: $4.75 single; $9.50–$14.20 double; $23.65 triple or quad. No credit cards.

In the old United Fruit Company neighborhood near the airport, there are many pretty, old houses surrounded by attractive, neatly manicured gardens. Several of these old homes have been turned into inexpensive hotels catering to shoppers visiting the free port. This is one of the nicer of the small family-run hotels. The rooms upstairs are more attractive and more comfortable than the rooms on the ground floor, which tend to be dark and musty.

LAS GAVIOTAS HOTEL, Apdo. 12-8201, Golfito. Tel. 506/775-0062. Fax 506/ 775-0544. 18 rms, 3 cabañas.

$ Rates: $26.70–$38.20 single or double; $34.30–$44.30 triple; $46.65 cabaña. AE, MC, V.

If you want to be right on the water, this is your best (and only) choice in Golfito. Situated a short taxi ride out of town on the road that leads out to the Interamerican Highway, Las Gaviotas has long been the hotel of choice on the Golfo Dulce. There is a long pier which attracts the sailboat and sportfishing crowd. For landlubbers, there's a small pool built out over the water. Guest rooms, which are set amid attractive gardens, all face the ocean, and though they are quite large, they're a bit Spartan. There are little tiled patios in front of all the rooms, and the cabañas have little kitchens. The more expensive rooms have air-conditioning. A large open-air restaurant looks over the pool to the gulf, while around the corner there is a large open-air bar. In addition, there's a small gift shop. The waterfront location is this hotel's greatest asset.

GOLFO AZUL, Barrio Alameda, 300 meters south of the Depósito Libre, Golfito. Tel. 506/775-0871. Fax 506/775-0832. 24 rms.

$ Rates: $23.90 single or double, $26.50 triple; $46.20 single to quad with air-conditioning. MC, V.

Azul offers a quiet location amid the most attractive part of Golfito. Many of the people who stay here are Ticos in town to shop at the nearby Depósito Libre (Free Port). However, anyone will appreciate the clean rooms. The smallest rooms are cramped, but there are larger rooms, some with high ceilings that make them feel even more spacious. Bathrooms are tiled and have hot water, and rooms have either fans or air-conditioning. The hotel's restaurant is housed in an older building and is brilliantly white inside and out. Meals are quite reasonably priced. The hotel also has a few rental cars available.

OUTSIDE OF TOWN
Expensive

PUNTA ENCANTO, Golfito (in the U.S.: Dick or Jackie Knowles, P.O. Box 481, Chautauqua, NY 14722). Tel. (in the U.S.) toll free 800/543-0397. Fax 506/775-0373 box 28. 9 rms.

$ Rates (including three meals): $95 single; $130 double; $165 triple. No credit cards.

This small lodge is located a 30-minute boat ride up the bay from Golfito and if you stay for a minimum of three nights, there is no charge for the transfers to and from Golfito. The star attraction here is the lodge's deserted beach, which is great for swimming. Surrounding the lodge are acres and acres of rain forest. Guided tours into the forest are available for $6 per person. The guest rooms are simply furnished, though comfortable, and have views of the water. Meals, a combination of Tico and American favorites, are served family style. The lodge can also arrange tours of the nearby Casa Orchidia Botanical Gardens for $12 per person. A trip up the Esquinas River to go bird- and monkey-watching will cost $160 for a boat that can hold eight people. For many years, this was a sportfishing camp, and fishing trips are still offered. It will cost you $35 per hour to fish in the bay and $450 for a full day of deep-sea fishing. Fishing packages are also available. This charmingly casual lodge offers a tranquil getaway for anyone who is looking for tropical solitude.

RAINBOW ADVENTURES, Apdo. 63, Golfito (in the U.S. contact: Michael Medill, 5875 N. Kaiser Rd., Portland, OR 97229). Tel. 506/775-0220 or (in the U.S.) 503/690-7750. Fax (in the U.S.) 503/690-7735. 4 rms, 3 cabins.

$ Rates (including three meals): $130–$150 single; $160–$180 double. No credit cards.

If your vision of the perfect tropical hideaway is a luxurious little open-walled cabin overlooking a secluded beach that is backed by tropical jungle, then Rainbow Adventures may just be your pot of gold. This isolated lodge is surrounded by 1,000 acres of rain forest that abuts Corcovado National Park. The grounds immediately surrounding the lodge are neatly manicured gardens planted with exotic fruit trees, flowering shrubs, and palms from around the world. Your adventure begins in Golfito, where the lodge's speedboat picks you up for the 45-minute boat ride to the lodge. Days are spent lounging in hammocks, swimming, sunning, and exploring the jungle, reading, bird and wild animal watching, and maybe a bit of fishing. But mostly you get to just do nothing, and not feel guilty about it. Be warned, however, that if you need TV, telephone, crowds, shopping, or discos, you should stay away from Rainbow Adventures.

Rooms in the main lodge, which is made almost completely of polished tropical hardwoods, are all decorated with antiques, stained glass, and Oriental carpets. The second-floor rooms are the least expensive and smallest rooms available. However, they still have plenty of room. For only $5 more, you can have the penthouse, a large third-floor room with four open walls and tree-top views of the gulf. Only slightly more expensive are the spacious cabinas, which are built on stilts and have open living rooms and large bedrooms that can be divided into small rooms.

Meals are generally served buffet style with a set menu each evening. However, the creativity of the chef and the quantities of food guarantee that everyone leaves the table satisfied. Many of the ingredients come from the lodge's own garden, as do many of the delicious juices that are served throughout the day. Though beer is available, you should bring your own liquor. Fishing trips (barracuda, roosterfish, snook, and red snapper are plentiful), boat charters ($35 per hour for a boat that can carry four passengers), and guided hikes can all be arranged. A private beach provides protected swimming and, in the dry season, some good snorkeling (equipment available at no charge). The best section of the mile-long beach is a few hundred yards from the lodge.

WHERE TO DINE

JARDIN CERVECERO ALAMEDAS, 100 meters south of the Depósito Libre. Tel. 775-0126.
   Cuisine: COSTA RICAN/SEAFOOD. **Reservations:** Not required.
$ Prices: Appetizers $2.05–$8.80; main courses $2.40–$8.80. MC, V.
   Open: Tues–Sat 7am–midnight (Dec–Mar open daily).
If you are staying at the Hotel Sierra, Golfo Azul, or any of the other hotels up near the Depósito Libre, this should be your first choice of where to eat. The restaurant is located underneath an old house that is built on stilts. White chairs and dark green tablecloths provide a sort of fern-bar feel, while outside real tropical gardens surround the house. There are great deals on seafood here, including a long list of ceviches. The only drawback is that they tend to play the stereo too loud.

POLLO FRITO RANCHERO, 30 meters north of the public dock. No phone.
   Cuisine: COSTA RICAN/INTERNATIONAL. **Reservations:** Not accepted.
$ Prices: All dishes 85¢–$6.75. No credit cards.
   Open: Daily 11am–10pm.
If you like the atmosphere at the Samoa, but are on a rock-bottom budget, try this smaller rancho almost next door. You get a view of the water from the small tables, and you can fill up on burgers or fried chicken.

SAMOA DEL SUR, 100 meters north of the public dock. Tel. 775-0233.
   Cuisine: CONTINENTAL. **Reservations:** Not required.
$ Prices: Appetizers $2.70–$10.15; main courses $4.05–$16.90. AE, MC, V.
   Open: Daily 8am–2am.
It's hard to miss the Samoa del Sur. It's that huge circular rancho just north of the public dock. This oversized jungle structure seems out of place in a town where cinder blocks are the preferred construction material, but its tropical atmosphere is certainly well appreciated. The restaurant's biggest surprise, however, is its extensive menu of familiar continental and French dishes such as onion soup, salade niçoise, filet of fish meuniere and paella. There are also pizzas and spaghetti. There's a good view of the gulf, which makes this great spot for a sunset drink or dinner. Later in the night, you can work up a sweat at the adjacent Disco Loco.

4. PLAYA ZANCUDO

19 kilometers S of Golfito (by boat); 35 kilometers S of Golfito (by road)

GETTING THERE By Air The nearest airport is in Golfito. See above for details.

By Boat Water taxis can be hired in Golfito to make the trip out to Playa Zancudo. However, trips depend on the tides and weather conditions. You're more likely to get a boat early in the morning before the winds pick up and make the waters choppy. Currently it costs $6.75 per person for a water taxi, with a minimum charge of $20.30.

Alternatively, there is a passenger launch from the municipal dock in Golfito Monday, Wednesday, and Friday at 8am. Beacause the schedule sometimes changes, be sure to ask in town for the current schedule. Duration: 45 minutes. Fare: $1.35.

By Bus There is no regularly scheduled bus service to Zancudo.

By Car If you've got a four-wheel-drive vehicle, you should be able to make it out to Zancudo even in the rainy season, but be sure to ask in Golfito before leaving the paved road. A four-wheel-drive taxi will cost around $20 from Golfito. It takes about 2 hours when the road is in good condition.

DEPARTING The public launch to Golfito leaves at 6am Monday, Wednesday, and Friday from the dock near the school in the center of Zancudo. If you're heading to Pavones or the Osa Peninsula next, contact Zancudo Boat Tours, which is sometimes willing to make the trips to these two places. They charge $10.15 per person with a minimum charge of $30.40 for either trip.

ESSENTIALS Zancudo is a long narrow peninsula (sometimes only 100 yards or so wide) at the mouth of the Río Colorado. On one side is the beach, and on the other is a mangrove swamp. There is only one road that runs the length of the beach, and it is along this road, spread out over several kilometers of long, flat beach, that you will find the hotels mentioned here. It's about a 30-minute walk from the public dock near the school to the popular Cabinas Sol y Mar.

Playa Zancudo is one of Costa Rica's main backpacker hangouts, which means basically that there are plenty of cheap rooms, some cheap places to eat, and lots of young gringos around. These factors alone are enough to keep Zancudo jumping through the winter months. The beach itself is long and flat, and because it is protected from the full force of Pacific waves, is relatively good for swimming. However, it is certainly not one of the most beautiful beaches in the country. Behind the beach, which disappears at high tide, are piles of driftwood and plastic flotsam and jetsam that have washed up on the shore. There is a splendid view across the Golfo Dulce, though, and the sunsets are hard to beat. Because there is a mangrove swamp directly behind the beach, mosquitoes here can be a problem. Be sure to bring insect repellent.

WHAT TO SEE & DO

The main activity at Zancudo is relaxing, and folks take it seriously. There are hammocks at almost every lodge, and if you bring a few good books, you can spend quite a few hours swinging slowly in the tropical breezes. Sure there's a bar that doubles as a disco, but people are more likely to spend their time just hanging out in restaurants meeting like-minded folks or playing board games.

If you're feeling more energetic, consider a boat tour. Susan and Andrew Robertson, who rent out two small houses here in Zancudo also operate **Zancudo Boat Tours** (tel. 775-0353, leave a message). Excursions they offer include a trip up the Río Coto to bird- and wildlife-watch, snorkeling trips, and trips to the Casa Orchidia botanical garden. Tour prices are $15 per hour for two people, $20 per hour for three people, and $25 per hour for four people.

WHERE TO STAY

BUDGET

CABINAS SOL Y MAR, Apdo. 87, Playa Zancudo, Golfito. Tel. 506/775-0353. Fax 506/775-0373. 4 rms (all with private bath).
$ Rates: Dec 1–Apr 30, $30–$35 single or double; May 1–Nov 30, $25–$30 single or double. No credit cards.

Though owners Bob and Monika Hara have only four rooms, they have for several years have been the most popular lodging in Zancudo. Two of the rooms are modified geodesic domes with tile floors, verandas, and tin roofs. The bathrooms have unusual showers that consist of a tiled platform surrounded by smooth river rocks. The bathrooms also have translucent roofs that flood the rooms with light. The other two rooms are larger and newer, but aren't as architecturally interesting. You'll have to decide between space and character. There is an adjacent open-air restaurant that is the best and most popular place to eat in Zancudo. Seafood dishes are the specialty here (the whole fried fish is good) and prices are very reasonable.

CABINAS ZANCUDO, Playa Zancudo, Golfito. Tel. 506/773-3006 or 773-3027. 20 rms (all with private bath).
$ Rates: $10.15–$13.50 single or double. No credit cards.

This is your basic Tico weekend beach getaway. The rooms are small, dark, and musty. There's no cross ventilation, and half of the rooms are in a building facing the back wall of another building. Weekends are crowded and can be noisy, especially in the dry season. However, if you don't have much money to spend, this is a good choice. There is a *pulperia* (general store) on the premises, as well as a restaurant and bar.

LOS COCOS, Apdo. 88, Golfito. Tel. 506/775-0353 (leave a message). 2 cabins.
$ Rates: $30 per night; $500–$600 per month. No credit cards.

Though owners Susan and Andrew Robertson prefer to rent their two small houses by the month, in a pinch they'll rent by the night. Set under the trees near Cabinas Sol y Mar (which is the contact for Los Cocos), these two houses are old banana plantation housing that the Robertsons salvaged and rebuilt here. The houses have big verandas, bedrooms, and large eat-in kitchens. Bathrooms are down a few steps in back and have hot water. If you plan to stay in Zancudo for a while, you'll certainly appreciate the refrigerator and hot plate.

HOTEL LOS ALMENDROS, Apdo. 41, Playa Zancudo, Golfito. Tel. 506/775-0515. 10 rms (all with private bath).
$ Rates: $20 single; $30 double; $40 triple. V.

Though this simple lodging up at the north end of Zancudo is primarily a fishing lodge, it is also one of the more comfortable and attractive places in town. The rooms all look out onto a bright green lawn of soft grass, with the waves crashing on the beach a few steps beyond. The rooms have hardwood floors, small clean bathrooms, ceiling and floor fans, and small verandas. There is a small restaurant that, of course, specializes in fresh fish. The lodge offers many different types of fishing excursions.

WHERE TO DINE

The best restaurant in Zancudo is at Cabinas Sol y Mar. The small open-air spot is also a popular hangout for resident gringos as well as travelers.

5. PLAYA PAVONES

40 kilometers S of Golfito

GETTING THERE **By Air** The nearest airport is in Golfito. See above for details.

By Bus There is a bus to Pavones from Golfito daily at 2pm. Duration: 3½ hours. Fare: $1.80.

By Car If you have a four-wheel-drive vehicle, you should be able to get to Pavones even in the rainy season, but be sure to ask in Golfito before leaving the paved road. A four-wheel-drive taxi from Golfito to Pavones will cost between $30 and $40. It takes around three hours from Golfito.

DEPARTING The bus to Golfito leaves daily. Ask in the village for the current departure time.

ESSENTIALS Pavones is a tiny village with few amenities and no electricity.

I f you are a serious surfer, you have already heard about Playa Pavones. The wave here is reputed to be the longest rideable wave in the world. It takes around six feet of swell to get this wave cranking, but when the surf's up, you're in for a long, long ride. So long, in fact, that it's easier to walk back up the beach to where the wave is breaking than it is to paddle back. Other than surfing, nothing much goes on here. However, the beach is quite nice, with some rocky areas that give Pavones a bit more visual appeal than Zancudo has. As of yet, accommodations here are very basic except for Tiskita Lodge, actually several kilometers south of Pavones.

WHAT TO SEE & DO

Other than surfing when the surf is up and swimming when its not, there isn't a whole lot to do. You can walk the beach, swing in your hammock, or if you feel energetic, go for a horse ride.

WHERE TO STAY & DINE

Right in Pavones, there are several very basic lodges renting rooms for between $10 and $20 per night for a double. There are also a couple of sodas where you can get Tico meals. South of Pavones, you'll find the following lodge.

TISKITA JUNGLE LODGE, Costa Rica Sun Tours, Apdo. 1195-1250, Escazú. Tel. 506/255-3418. Fax 506/255-4410. 3 rms, 10 cabins.

$ Rates (including three meals): $65 single: $130 double; $195 triple. Packages (including transportation from San José and two guided walks) per person: four days/three nights $495; five days/four nights $560. AE, MC, V.

This small lodge is nearly on the Panamanian border, with the beach on one side and rain forest covered hills behind. Though primarily an experimental fruit farm growing exotic tropical fruits from around the world, Tiskita is also a great place to get away from it all. There's a dark-sand swimming beach, tide pools, farm, and forest to explore, and great bird-watching (230 species have been sighted). Of the 400 acres here, 250 are in primary rain forest, while the rest is in orchards and pastures. The lodge itself is set on a hill a few hundred yards from the beach and commands a superb view of the ocean.

Accommodations are in deluxe rustic cabins with screen walls and verandas. Constructed of local hardwoods, the cabins have a very tropical feel, and if you're a bird-watcher, you'll be happy to know that you can just sit on the veranda and add to your life list. Accommodations are also available in the older main lodge. Meals are served family style and though not fancy, are certainly tasty and filling.

CHAPTER 8

THE CARIBBEAN COAST

1. **TORTUGUERO NATIONAL PARK**
• **WHAT'S SPECIAL ABOUT THE CARIBBEAN COAST**
2. **LIMÓN**
3. **CAHUITA**
4. **PUERTO VIEJO**

Though this was the coast that Christopher Columbus discovered in 1502 and christened Costa Rica ("Rich Coast"), it has until recently remained *terra incognita*. It was not until 1987 that the Guápiles Highway opened between San José and Limón. Prior to that the only routes down to this region were the famous jungle train (which is no longer in operation), and the narrow winding road from Turrialba to Siquerres. More than half of this coastline is still inaccessible except by boat or small plane. This inaccessibility has helped preserve large tracts of virgin lowland rain forest, which are now set aside as Tortuguero National Park and Barra del Colorado National Wildlife Refuge. These two parks, on the northern reaches of this coast, together form one of Costa Rica's most popular destinations with ecotravelers. Of particular interest are the sea turtles that nest along this stretch of coast.

So remote was the Caribbean coast from Costa Rica's population center in the Central Valley that it developed a culture all its own. Until the 1870s, there were few non-Indians in this area. However, when Minor Keith built the railroad to San José and began planting bananas, he brought in black laborers from Jamaica to lay the track and work the plantations. These people were well adapted to the hot, humid conditions of these lowlands and established fishing and farming communities up and down the coast. Today dreadlocked Rastafarians, reggae music, Créole cooking, and the English-based patois of this Afro-Caribbean culture give this region a distinctly Jamaican flavor. Many visitors find fascinating this striking contrast with the Spanish-derived Costa Rican culture. However, in beach towns such as Cahuita and Puerto Viejo, some visitors see only a drug-and-surf culture, and there is no denying that surfing and partying are a way of life for many people, local and visitor alike, in these two towns. Though you need not participate in such activities, if this lifestyle is offensive to you, consider heading to one of the many beaches on the Pacific coast.

1. TORTUGUERO NATIONAL PARK

250 kilometers NE of San José

GETTING THERE By Air Sansa (tel. 233-0397, 233-3258, or 233-5330) has flights Tuesday, Thursday, and Saturday at 6am that fly first to Barra del Colorado and then to Tortuguero from San José's Juan Santamaría International Airport. Duration: 65 minutes (Tortuguero). Fare: $41 one way.

Travelair (tel. 220-3054 and 232-7883) has flights daily at 6am to Barra del Colorado and Tortuguero from San José's Pavas International Airport. Duration: 55 minutes (Tortuguero). Fare: $51 one way, $88 round-trip.

WHAT'S SPECIAL ABOUT THE CARIBBEAN COAST

Beaches
Long, nearly deserted beaches both north and south of the village of Cahuita. There's also a coral reef here.

Miles of beaches and blue water south of Puerto Viejo.

Natural Spectacles
The Tortuguero canals, which will make you feel like you're exploring deep in the Amazon.

Parks
Tortuguero National Park, known for the turtles that lay their eggs on the beaches.

Cahuita National Park, with forest trails, deserted beaches, and a coral reef.

Activities
Surfing the Salsa Brava in Puerto Viejo.

Snorkeling among the coral and clear water south of Puerto Viejo.

Guided walks through the Bribri Indian Reservation and elsewhere around Puerto Viejo.

Fishing for tarpon and snook in Tortuguero and Barra del Colorado.

Regional Food and Drink
Run-down soup, a coconut-based favorite of the Caribbean coast's Créole residents.

Homemade fresh cocoa candies from the cacao trees around Puerto Viejo.

Many lodges in this area operate charter flights as part of their package trips.

By Boat   Though flying to Tortuguero is convenient if you have only a limited amount of time, the boat trip through the canals and rivers of this region is the highlight of any visit to Tortuguero. All of the more expensive lodges listed below operate boats, and will make arrangements for your trip through the canals. However, if you are coming on the cheap and plan to stay at one of the less expensive lodges or at a budget cabina place in Tortuguero, you will have to arrange transportation yourself. In this, you have a couple of options.

In Cahuita, a small beach town south of Limón, Cahuita Tours (tel. 758-1515, ext. 252) will arrange round-trip boat transportation for around $60. This price also includes transportation from Cahuita to the dock in Moin, which is the port just outside of Limón. Alternatively, you can go directly to Moin yourself and try to find a boat on your own. You should be able to negotiate a fare of between $40 and $60 depending on how many people you can round up to go with you. One boat captain to check with is Modesto Wilson (tel. 226-0986), who owns a boat named *Francesca*. Wilson offers economical overnight packages to Tortuguero. The trip from Moin to Tortuguero takes between three and four hours. Laura's Tropical Tours (tel. 758-2410) also offers boat tours to Tortuguero from Moin.

It is also possible to travel to Tortuguero by boat from Puerto Viejo de Sarapiquí (see Chapter 5, "The Northern Zone"). From this town, expect to pay $200 to $250 for a boat to either destination. Check at the public dock in Sarapiquí or ask at the Hotel El Bambú.

DEPARTING   Sansa flights to San José leave Tortuguero at 7:20am and then leave Barra del Colorado at 7:50am. Travelair flights leave Tortuguero at 7:05am and fly directly to San José.

ESSENTIALS   Tortuguero National Park is one of the most remote locations in Costa Rica. There are no roads into this area, so all transportaion is by boat or plane. Most of the lodges are spread out over several kilometers to the north of the village of Tortuguero. The Tortuguero National Park entrance and ranger station is at the south end of Tortuguero Village. In the center of the village is an information kiosk that outlines the cultural and national history of this region. Turtle-nesting season is mid-June through mid-September, and this is the most popular time to visit Tortuguero.

The name "Tortuguero" is a reference to the giant Atlantic green sea turtles (*tortugas*) that nest on the beaches of this region every year between July and September. The chance to see nesting sea turtles is what attracts many people to this remote region, but the trip here is equally interesting. This stretch of coast is connected to Limón, the Caribbean coast's only port city, by way of a series of rivers and canals that parallel the sea, often only 100 yards or so from the beach. This aquatic highway is lined for most of its length with dense rain forest that is home to howler monkeys, three-toed sloths, toucans, and great green macaws. A trip up the canals is akin to cruising the Amazon, though on a much smaller scale.

North of Tortuguero is Barra del Colorado National Wildlife Refuge. This area is better known among anglers than naturalists. The waters at the mouth of the Río Colorado offer some of the best tarpon and snook fishing in the world. See the "Alternative/Adventure Travel" section of Chapter 2 for details on fishing lodges in this area.

WHAT TO SEE & DO

First of all, let me say up front that you don't come to this area for the beaches. Though they are long and deserted, the surf is usually very rough and the river mouths have a nasty habit of attracting sharks that feed on the many fish that live there. What you can do here is explore the rain forest, both on foot and by boat, and if you're here between July and September, watch sea turtles nesting at night. All of the lodges listed below, with the exception of the Cabinas Ribersai in Tortuguero Village, offer various hikes, night tours, and boat trips through the canals. See the individual lodge listings for rates on these tours. If you are coming up here on a package trip, you will likely have already arranged your excursions before arriving. All of the lodges along this coast offer fishing trips and fishing packages. If you want to try your hand at reeling in a monster tarpon, it will generally cost you between $30 and $35 per hour, including a boat, guide, and tackle.

Tortuguero Village is a tiny collection of houses connected by footpaths. In the center of the village you'll find a kiosk that has information on the cultural and natural history of this area. On the south side of the village, you'll find the headquarters for **Tortuguero National Park.** Within this section of the park there are several trails. Admission to the park is $1.35, and camping is allowed here at the ranger station for a small fee.

In the village, you can rent dugout canoes, known here in Costa Rica as *cayucos*. You can also find people with boats who will take you on tours through the canals. There are a couple of souvenir shops in the village—the Jungle Shop (which donates 10% of its profits to local schools) and Paraiso Tropical Gift Shop.

WHERE TO STAY & DINE

Though the room rates below appear quite high, keep in mind that they include round-trip transportation (which amounts to around $100 per person) and all meals. When broken down into nightly room rates, most of the lodges charge between $40 and $60 for a double per night.

EXPENSIVE

TORTUGA LODGE, Avenida 3 and Calle Central (Apdo. 6941-1000), San José. Tel. 506/257-0766 or 222-0333. Fax 506/257-1665. 25 rms.
$ Rates (including transportation and all meals): $323–$382 single, two days/one night;

$598–$780 double, two days/one night. $413–$429 single, three days/two nights; $730–$858 double, three days/two nights. AE, MC, V.

Just a quick glance at the rates above will tell you that Tortuga Lodge is quite a bit more expensive than other lodges in the area. However, keep in mind that these rates all include airfare in at least one direction. The higher rates also include deluxe accommodations, which are the largest and most comfortable in the area. On the other hand, the standard rooms are small and dark, so I recommend paying the extra for a deluxe room. In general, what you are paying for are all the years of experience that Costa Rica Expeditions, the lodge's owner, brings to Tortuguero. Service here is generally quite good, as are the meals served in the screen-walled dining room. There are several acres of forest behind the lodge, and a few kilometers of trails wind their way through the trees. This is a great place to look for colorful poison-arrow frogs. Most packages include a couple of different tours, including boat trips through the canals, visits to Tortuguero Village, and trips to see the turtles laying eggs. There are also several optional tour° including fishing trips, hikes to Tortuguero Hill, and night hikes.

MODERATE

HOTEL ILAN-ILAN, Apdo. 91-1150, San José. Tel. 506/255-2262 or 255-2031. Fax 506/255-1946. 20 rms.

$ Rates (including transportation and all meals): $344–$454 double, two days/one night; $454–$686 double, three days/two nights. AE, MC, V.

Named after a fragrant tropical flower that grows on the hotel grounds, the Ilan-Ilan is on the opposite side of the canal from the beach. Guest rooms are fairly basic, though large, and are all angled toward the canal so they each get a bit of a breeze. Screened windows in front and back and overhead fans also help keep the rooms cool. Be sure to ask for one of the rooms with a double bed if that's what you prefer; some rooms have only twin beds. Tico meals are served in the small screen-walled dining room, and there is a bar where you can chat with other guests. If you come in by bus and boat, your bus will make a brief stop at Braulio Carillo National Park so you can have a look at the rain-forested mountains before descending into the lowlands. There are bilingual guides to point out wildlife and answer questions both during the boat trip to the lodge and during outings through the nearby canals and (in season) to the beach at night to watch sea turtles laying their eggs. The lodge also has several acres of forest land through which there are several kilometers of trails. The higher room rates include travel one way by air.

JUNGLE LODGE, Apdo. 1818-1002, San José. Tel. 506/233-0133 or 233-0155. Fax 506/222-0778. 34 rms.

$ Rates (including transportation and all meals): $284 single, three days/two nights; $436 double, three days/two nights; $552 triple, three days/two nights. AE, DC, MC, V.

Located just south of Ilan-Ilan on the same side of the river and about a kilometer from Tortuguero National Park, the Jungle Lodge offers rooms in wooden buildings raised up above the ground on pilings. There are long verandas set with chairs where you can sit and bird-watch or just relax and listen to the forest. Most rooms have windows on two sides to let the breezes through, plus ceiling fans. Wooden floors and walls give these rooms an attractive, tropical look. Simple-but-filling meals such as fried chicken or fish with rice and beans are served buffet-style at long tables in a screen-walled dining hall. Tours, led by bilingual guides, include boat tours through the canals to look for wildlife, a visit to Tortuguero Village, a hike through the forest, and (in season) trips over to the beach to watch the sea turtles lay their eggs. Optional canoe tours and night tours are also available for $10 and $15 respectively. Fishing trips cost $35 per hour for two people. This is a big place and can seem crowded and impersonal at times.

LAGUNA LODGE, Apdo. 344, San Pedro, San José. Tel. and Fax 506/225-3740. 14 rms.

$ Rates (including transportation and all meals): $438 double, three days/two nights. MC, V.

This is one of the newest and smallest lodges in the area and is located 2 kilometers north of Tortuguero Village on the beach side of the canal. Because this lodge is fairly new, the gardens are not yet very developed and so the grounds look a bit barren. However, the rooms are all very attractive, with wood walls, waxed hardwood floors, and tiled bathrooms with screened upper walls to let in air and light. Each room also has a little veranda. There's a small screen-walled dining room that serves tasty meals. A little covered deck has also been built over the water, and there is even a tiny beach area on the river. When I visited, the lodge was planning to build a barbecue and a rancho for hammocks. The lodge owners live here year-round, which makes Laguna Lodge a bit more personal than other Tortuguero lodges. Several different optional tours are available.

MAWAMBA LODGE, Apdo. 10050-1000, San José. Tel. 506/223-7490, 223-2421, or 222-5463. Fax 506/255-4039. 36 rms.

$ Rates (including transportation and all meals): $438–$538 double, three days/two nights. AE, MC, V.

Located about 500 meters north of Tortuguero Village on the beach side of the canal, Mawamba is a good choice for anyone who would like to be able to wander this isolated stretch of beach at will. This place is a bit more rustic than the lodges on the opposite side of the canal. Rooms have unvarnished wood floors, twin beds, cold-water showers, and table fans only. However, there are wide verandas and plenty of hammocks around for anyone who wants to kick back. Meals are above average for Tortuguero and might include pasta and lobster or chicken in béchamel sauce. Plus there is usually good, fresh bread. You can dine either in the screened-in dining room or out on the patio. Tours included in the rates include a four-hour boat ride through the canals and a guided forest hike. There are also slide shows every other night that focus on the natural history of this area. Optional tours include a night hike ($15) and fishing trips ($30 per hour for two people).

BUDGET

CABINAS RIBERSAI, Barra Tortuguero, Limón. Tel. 506/710-6716. 4 rms.
$ Rates: $15 single; $25 double. MC, V.

Though these rooms are tiny and cramped, they're the best in town. They sit off by themselves near the soccer field on the south side of the village and are very close to the beach. Two of the rooms have double beds and two have bunk beds. Luckily, they all have fans. You can find out about the rooms at the Abastecador Riversan, a general store that is just south of the national park information kiosk.

EL MANATEE LODGE, Tortuguero, Limón. Tel. 506/288-1828. 5 cabins.
$ Rates: $40 double. No credit cards.

⑤ If you'd like to have a Tortuguero jungle lodge experience, but don't have the bucks to spend on the above places, this is your next best choice. This lodge is located across the canal and about a kilometer north of Tortuguero Village. The young owners live here and have slowly built the lodge themselves over the years. The rooms are fairly basic, with cement floors and floor fans, but they have attractive curtains and new fixtures in the bathrooms. There's even warm water. Some rooms have two separate rooms, one of which has bunk beds. Breakfast ($4) and dinner ($6) are available. Canal tours and turtle-watching walks are $10 per person for two hours, and there are canoes that can be rented for $5. Transportation up here and back can be arranged in Moin near Limón for $50 to $60 round-trip. Piece it all together and you come up with a three-day, two-night trip with tours, meals, and transportation from Limón for around $250 for two people!

NEARBY LODGE

PARISMINA TARPON RANCHO, Apdo. 10560-1000, San José. Tel. 506/257-3553 or 771-2583, or toll free (in the U.S.) 800/862-1003. Fax 506/222-1760. 20 rms.

THE CARIBBEAN COAST

Caribbean

Sea

38 km
24 mi.

NICARAGUA

Río San Juan

Barra de Colorado Airport
Barra del Colorado
*Boca del
Río Colorado*

Río
Chirripó

Río Colorado

Barra del Colorado
National Wildlife Refuge

Boca del Río Tortuguero
Tortuguero
Tortuguero Airport

Tortuguero
National Park

Cariari

Río Frío

Tortuguero
Canal

Río Reventazón

Río Pacuare

Boca del Río Pacuare

32

Guapiles

Braulio Carrillo
National Park

CORDILLERA CENTRAL

Turrialba
Volcano

Guayabo
National
Monument

Siquirres

Limón

Limón Airport

Irazú
Volcano

Turrialba

Paraiso

Tapantí
National
Wildlife
Refuge

Río Chirripó Atlántico

Chirripó
Indian
Reservation

Cahuita
National
Park

36

Playa Cahuita

Cahuita

Playa Chiquita
Playa Uva

Cerro de
la Muerte

Cerro
Chirripó

CORDILLERA DE TALAMANCA

Talamanca
Indian
Reservation

Bribri
Indian
Reservation

BriBri

Puerto
Viejo

Gandoca-
Manzanillo
National
Wildlife Refuge

San Isidro
de el General

PANAMA

$ Rates: $330 double, two days/one night; $430 double, three days/two nights. V.
This lodge is located about midway between Limón and Tortuguero at the mouth of the Río Parismina. For more than 30 years the American owners have been catering to fishermen and other visitors, and today the lodge offers great service, comfortable accommodations, filling meals, and attractive gardens. The rooms all have ceiling fans and good mattresses to assure you a good night's sleep. Outside your door, you'll find a pleasant veranda overlooking the garden. Tortuguero National Park begins a few kilometers to the north of the lodge, and, on an all-day boat tour, you'll get to explore the park's waterways. Other tours included in the price of packages are a visit to nearby Parismina Village and a night walk to spot nesting turtles or crocodiles. Fishing for tarpon and snook is still a primary attraction here at Parismina and for an extra $100 per person you can do two half-day fishing trips.

2. LIMÓN

160 kilometers E of San José

GETTING THERE By Bus Express buses leave San José daily every hour on the hour between 5am and 7pm from the corner of Avenida 3 between calles 19 and 21. Duration: 2½ hours. Fare: $2.70 to $3.25 (deluxe).

By Car The Guápiles Highway heads north out of San José on Calle 3 before turning east and passing close to Barva Volcano and through Braulio Carillo National Park en route to Limón. The drive takes about 2½ hours. Alternatively, you can take the old highway, which is equally scenic, though slower. This highway heads east out of San José on Avenida Central, and passes through San Pedro before reaching Cartago. From Cartago on, the road is narrow and winding, and passes through Paraiso and Turrialba before descending out of the mountains to Siquirres where the old highway meets the new. This route will take you 4 hours or more to Limón.

DEPARTING Express buses leave for San José almost hourly between 6am and 8pm. The bus stop is one block east and half a block south of the municipal market. Buses to Cahuita and Puerto Viejo leave daily at 5 and 10am and 1 and 4pm. The Cahuita bus stop is at Radio Casino, which is one block north of the municipal market. Buses to Punta Uva and Manzanillo, both of which are south of Puerto Viejo, leave Limón daily at 9am and 4:30pm.

ESSENTIALS Orientation Nearly all addresses in Limón are measured from the market or from Parque Vargas, which is at the east end of town. The bus stop for buses out to Playa Bonita is just around the corner to the north of the Cahuita bus stop.

It was just offshore from present-day Limón that Christopher Columbus is believed to have anchored in 1502, on his fourth and last voyage to the New World. Though he felt this was potentially a very rich land and named it Costa Rica, it never quite lived up to his expectations. However, the spot where he anchored has proved over the centuries to be the best port on the Caribbean coast. It was from here that the first shipments of bananas headed to North America in the late 19th century. Today, Limón is a busy port city that ships millions of pounds of bananas northward every year.

WHAT TO SEE & DO

There is little to see or do here in Limón. You can take a seat in Parque Vargas downtown along the sea wall and watch the city's citizens go about their business. There are even supposed to be some sloths living in trees here. Maybe you'll spot them. Take a walk around town if you're interested in architecture. When banana shipments built this port, many local merchants erected elaborately decorated buildings, several of which have survived the city's many earthquakes. If you want to get in some beach time while you're here in Limón, hop in a taxi or a local bus and head north to **Playa Bonita,** a small public beach park. Although the water isn't very clean and I don't recommend swimming, the setting is much more attractive than downtown. This beach is very popular with surfers.

The biggest event of the year in Limón, and one of the most fascinating festivals in Costa Rica, is the annual **Carnival,** which is held for a week around Columbus Day (October 12). For one week of the year, languid Limón shifts into high gear for a nonstop bacchanal orchestrated to the beat of reggae, soca, and calypso music. During the revelries, residents of the city don costumes and take to the streets in a dazzling parade of color. If you want to experience this carnival, make hotel reservations early.

If you are planning on heading up to Tortuguero on your own, see "Tortuguero National Park," above, for details on how to get there from Limón.

WHERE TO STAY & DINE

MODERATE

CABINAS COCORI, Playa Bonita (Apdo. 1093), Limón. Tel. 506/758-2930. 6 apts.
$ Rates: $40–$50 one to five people. MC, V.
Located on the water just before you reach Playa Bonita, these apartments command a fine view of the cove and crashing surf. The grounds are in need of landscaping, but the rooms are quite nice. A two-story white building houses the apartments, each of which has a kitchenette with hot plate and refrigerator, two bedrooms, and a bathroom. A long veranda runs along both floors. Staying at this location is far preferable to staying in town. You can get here by bus or taxi. When I was last in town, the Cocori was undergoing a major expansion, so expect more rooms when you visit.

HOTEL MARIBU CARIBE, Apdo. 13062050, San Pedro. Tel. 506/758-4543, 758-4010, 758-3541, or (in San José) 253-1838. Fax 506/758-3541 or (in San José) 234-0193. 52 rms. A/C TEL SAFE
$ Rates: $65.60 single; $75.25 double; $106.75 triple. AE, MC, V.
Located on top of a hill overlooking the Caribbean and built to resemble an Indian village, the Maribu Caribe is a pleasant, if not overly luxurious, choice if you are looking to spend some time in the sun. The hotel is popular with Tico families from San José because it is easy to get to for weekend trips. The guest rooms are in circular bungalows with white-tile floors and varnished wood ceilings. The furnishings are a bit old but are still comfortable.

The hotel's Restaurant Quiribri has the best view in Limón, or on the entire Atlantic coast for that matter. It's built out over the edge of a steep hill with tide pools and the ocean almost directly below. In addition to the formal dining room, there are also tables outside on a curving veranda that makes the most of the view. Entrée prices range from $6.45 to $18.25 and the emphasis is on seafood prepared in the continental style. There is a bar here, as well as a bar/snack bar by the pool. The Maribu Caribe can help you with tour arrangements, and has a gift shop.

HOTEL MATAMA, Apdo. 686, Limón. Tel. 506/758-1123 or 758-4409. Fax 506/ 758-4499. 16 rms. A/C
$ Rates: $62 single; $74 double; $91 triple; $108 quad. AE, MC, V.
Almost directly across the street from Cabinas Cocori, the Matama is in a class by itself. The hotel consists of several multiplex buildings set amid dense tropical vegetation across the road from the ocean. The strikingly modern design of the buildings, both inside and out, is a welcome surprise in an area of generally unmemorable accommodations. Each room is decorated with attractive matching drapes and bedspreads and has comfortable wicker furniture and, best of all, large bathrooms with solarium gardens that bring the jungle right

into your bath. There are even some units with lofts. Splashing around in the small pool, you'll be surrounded by the sounds of the jungle, and if you want to explore nearby jungles further, you can arrange trips here at the hotel. Seafood is the specialty of the large open-air restaurant, with prices ranging from $4.05 to $16.90. The meals are well prepared and elegantly served, but the service can be a bit slow. Room service is also available.

BUDGET

HOTEL ACON, Avenida 3 and Calle 3 (Apdo. 528), Limón. Tel. 506/758-1010. Fax 506/758-2924. 39 rms (all with bath). A/C TEL
$ Rates: $21.80 single; $28.45 double; $33.65 triple. AE, MC, V.

This older in-town choice is the best you can do in Limón. The rooms, all of which are air-conditioned (almost a necessity in this muggy climate), are clean and have two twin beds and a large bathroom. The restaurant on the first floor just off the lobby is a cool, dark haven on steamy afternoons, highly recommended for lunch or as a place to beat the heat. Prices range from $2.85 to $11.50. The second-floor disco stays open late on weekends, so don't count on a quiet night.

PARK HOTEL, Avenida 3 between calles 1 and 3, Limón. Tel. 506/758-3476 or 758-2400. Fax 506/758-4364. 31 rms (all with bath).
$ Rates: $9.70–$15.10 single; $16.85–$20.50 double. V.

You can't miss this pink, yellow, and turquoise building across the street from the fire station. It's certainly seen better years, but in Limón there aren't too many choices. What makes this place memorable is it's aging tropical ambience, so don't expect clean and new. Be sure to ask for a room on the ocean side of the hotel because these are brighter, quieter, and cooler than those on the side of the hotel that faces the fire station. The large, sunny dining room off the lobby serves standard Tico fare at very reasonable prices.

---

3. CAHUITA

200 kilometers E of San José; 42 kilometers S of Limón

GETTING THERE By Bus Express buses leave San José daily at 5am and 2 and 4pm from Avenida 11 between Calle Central and Calle 1. Duration: 4 hours. Fare: $6.35.

Alternatively, you can take a bus to Limón (see above for details) and then take a Cahuita-bound bus from Limón. These latter buses leave Limón daily at 5 and 10am and 1 and 4pm from Radio Casino, which is one block north of the municipal market. Duration: 1 hour. Fare: 85¢ to $1.30.

By Car Follow the directions above for getting to Limón, and, as you enter the outskirts of Limón, watch for a paved road to the right (it's just before the railroad tracks). Take this road south to Cahuita, passing the airstrip and the beach as you leave Limón.

DEPARTING Express buses from Sixaola (on the Panama border) stop in Cahuita around 7 and 10am and 4pm en route to San José. However, these buses are almost always full. To avoid standing in the aisle all the way to San José, take a bus first to Limón, and then catch one of the hourly Limón–San José buses. Buses to Limón leave daily at 6:30 and 10am, noon, 1:30, and 5pm. Buses headed from Limón to Puerto Viejo stop in Cahuita around 6 and 11am and 2 and 5pm.

ESSENTIALS Orientation There are only eight sand streets in Cahuita, so you shouldn't get lost. Three roads lead into town from the highway. Buses usually take the road that leads into the heart of town and drop their passengers at the Salon Vaz bar. An alternate route bypasses town and heads toward Playa Negra, which is just north of town. As you're coming from the north, the first road leads to the north end of Playa Negra. If you come in on the bus and are staying at a lodge on Playa Negra, head out of town on the street that runs between Salon Vaz and the small park. This road will curve to the left and continue a mile or so out to Playa Negra. The village's main street dead-ends at the entrance to the national park (a footbridge over a small stream).

You can arrange to have laundry done at Moray's, which is one of the two tour companies in town. The police station is located where the road from Playa Negra turns into town. The post office, next door to the police station, is open Monday through Friday from 8am to 5pm. You can change money at Cahuita Tours.

Keep an eye out for poisonous snakes around here. I was almost bitten by one on a path on Playa Negra. If you aren't a herpetologist, assume that all snakes here are poisonous.

Cahuita is one of the most laid-back villages you'll find anywhere in Costa Rica, and if you spend any time here, you'll likely find yourself slipping into a heat-induced torpor that affects anyone who ends up here. The gravel streets are almost always deserted, and the social heart of the village is the front porch of the Salon Vaz, Cahuita's main bar and disco. The village traces its roots to Afro-Caribbean fishermen and laborers who settled in this region in the mid-1800s, and today the population is still primarily English-speaking blacks whose culture and language set them apart from other Costa Ricans.

The main reason people come to Cahuita, other than its laid-back atmosphere, are its miles of pristine beaches that stretch both north and south from town. The beaches to the south, as well as the forest behind them and one of Costa Rica's few coral reefs beneath the waters offshore, are all part of Cahuita National Park. However, silt and pesticides washing down from nearby banana plantations are taking a heavy toll on the coral reefs, so don't expect the snorkeling to be fantastic.

WHAT TO SEE & DO

You'll immediately feel the call of the long scimitar of beach that stretches south from the edge of town. This beach is glimpsed through the trees from Cahuita's sun-baked main street, and extends a promise of relief from the heat. You can walk on the beach itself or follow the trail that runs through the forest just behind the beach. The best place to swim is beyond the Peresoso (Lazy River), a few hundred yards inside **Cahuita National Park.** The trail behind the beach is great for bird-watching, and if you're lucky, you might see some monkeys or a sloth. The loud whooping sounds you hear off in the distance are the calls of howler monkeys, which can be heard from more than a mile away. Nearer at hand, you are likely to hear crabs scuttling about amid the dry leaves on the forest floor. There are half a dozen or so species of land crabs living in this region. My favorites are the bright orange-and-purple ones. The trail behind the beach stretches a little more than four miles to the southern end of the park at **Puerto Vargas,** where you will find a beautiful white-sand beach, the park headquarters, and a primitive campground with drinking water and outhouses. The reef is off the point just north of Puerto Vargas. The national park is open daily from dawn to dusk. Admission is $1.35 and the camping fee is $2.05 per person per day.

Outside the park, the best place for swimming is **Playa Negra.** If you want to find out where the best diving spots are (there is even a sunken ship you can visit), I suggest a snorkeling trip by boat. There are two companies running boats out to the reef. **Morays** (tel. 758-1515, ext. 216), on the road to Playa Negra near the police station and post office, charges $16.90 with gear. If you just want to rent snorkeling gear, it will cost you $4.05 per day. Moray's also rents bicycles ($1.05 per hour, $4.75 per day) and binoculars, and arranges boat trips to Tortuguero ($60). **Cahuita Tours & Rentals** (tel. 758-1515, ext. 216), around the corner on the village's main street, charges the same price for boat trips. Snorkeling gear rents for $5.10 per day). You can also rent surf boards ($6.75 per day), boogie boards ($5.40 per day), and bicycles ($1.35 per hour, $6.75 per day). Cahuita Tours arranges various tours including trips to Tortuguero ($60) and to the Bribri Indian Reservation ($20.30).

Brigitte (watch for the sign on Playa Negra) rents horses for $5.10 per hour and also offers 4-hour guided horseback rides (you must have prior experience) for $25.70. This same trip is also offered by Moray's and Cahuita Tours.

Bird-watchers who have a car should head north 9 kilometers to the Aviaros de Caribe bed-and-breakfast lodge where canoe tours of **Estrella Estuary** are available. Nearly 300 species of birds have been sighted in the immediate area. The canoe trips cost $25 per person.

At Restaurant Vaz and a couple of other places around the village, you can pick up a copy of Paula Palmer's *What Happen, A Folk-History of Costa Rica's Talamanca Coast* (Publications in English, 1993). The book is a history of the region based on interviews with many of the area's oldest residents. Much of it is in the traditional Créole language, from which the title is taken. It makes fun and interesting reading, and you just might bump into someone mentioned in the book.

For **evening entertainment,** the Salon Vaz, a classic Caribbean bar, is the place to spend your nights (or days for that matter) if you like cold beer and very loud reggae and soca music. Located right across the street from Cahuita's central park, Salon Vaz doubles as the bus stop and community meeting point. There are always folks hanging out on the front porch or steps while a five-foot-tall speaker blares at their backs. At night the back room of this bar becomes a very lively disco.

WHERE TO STAY

MODERATE

CABINAS ATLANTIDA, Cahuita, Limón. Tel. 506/758-1515, ext. 213. 30 rms.
$ Rates (including continental breakfast): $45.50 single; 49.90 double; $56 triple. AE, MC, V.
Set amid lush gardens and wide green lawns and run by French Canadians, the Atlantida is one of my favorite hotels in Cahuita. You'll find it beside the soccer field out by Playa Negra, about a mile out of town. The guest rooms are done in a a style reminiscent of local Indian architecture, with thatched roofs and pale yellow stucco walls. All rooms have a patio with bamboo screen divider for privacy, and when you sit there, you'll be gazing into a flourishing garden. A large aviary on the grounds is home to several toucans that were rescued after an earthquake several years ago. Although only breakfast is included in the rates above, you can also order dinner for under $10. The meals are served in a rancho dining room. Breakfasts include fresh fruit and fresh juice, rolls and homemade marmalade, and there is free coffee all day long. Continental-style dinners are some of the best in town, though they are only available to hotel guests. A couple of different tours can be arranged using the hotel's Land Rover. The beach is right across the street and the hotel also has a small pool.

CHALET HIBISCUS, Apdo. 943, Limón. No phone. Fax 506/758-1543 or 758-0652. 1 house, 2 cabins (all with bath).
$ Rates: Dec–Apr, $45 cabin (single or double), $90 house (one to six people); May–Nov, $40 cabin, $75 house. No credit cards.
If you're planning a long stay in Cahuita, I advise checking into this beautiful chalet. Although it is about 2 kilometers from town on the road along Playa Negra, it is well worth the journey. The house has two bedrooms and sleeps up to six people. There is hardwood paneling all around, a full kitchen, hot water, red-tile floors, a pila for doing your laundry, and even a garage. A spiral staircase leads to the second floor, where you'll find hammocks on a balcony that looks over a green lawn to the ocean. The attractive little cabinas have wicker furniture and walls of stone and wood. If you ever wanted to be marooned on the Mosquito Coast, this is the place to live out your fantasy. There's even a swimming pool. The chalet is both simple and elegant; the setting, serene and beautiful. Be sure to ring the bell outside the gate—there are guard dogs on the grounds.

HOTEL JAGUAR CAHUITA, Cahuita, Limón (Apdo. 7046-1000, San José).
Tel. 506/226-3775 or 758-1515, ext. 238. Fax 506/226-4693. 45 rms.

$ Rates (including breakfast): $21–$35 single; $48.10–$61.25 double. MC, V.

Located directly across the sandy road from Playa Negra, the Jaguar is Cahuita's largest and most ambitious hotel to date. However, despite the fact that the rooms are the biggest in town and are close to the water, they leave a lot to be desired. Rooms were designed with solar principles in mind to stay cool and make the most of prevailing breezes. Unfortunately, sometimes the breezes aren't enough, and small table-top fans have had to be added to the rooms. Though half the rooms have views of the water, the rest face only the front rank of rooms. Surrounding the hotel are 17 acres of forest and brush through which a short nature trail has been cut. You're almost certain to see at least one sloth on a morning walk here. There's an open-air dining room that serves very good, moderately priced meals. Many of the ingredients used in the meals come from trees on the hotel property.

MAGELLAN INN, Plaza Víquez, Cahuita. No phone. Fax 506/758-0652. 6 rms.

$ Rates (including continental breakfast): $45 single; $55 double; $65 triple. DC, MC, V.

This small inn is out at the far end of Playa Negra (about 2 kilometers north of Cahuita) and is the most luxurious hotel in the area. The six large rooms are all carpeted and have French doors, vertical blinds, big tiled bathrooms with hardwood counters, and king-size beds with attractive bedspreads. Each rooms has its own tiled veranda with an overhead fan and bamboo chairs. Though there are no TVs, phones, or air-conditioning in the rooms right now, there seem to be plans to add these amenities in the future. There is a casually sophisticated combination bar/lounge and breakfast room that has Oriental-style rugs and wicker furniture. However, most memorable are the hotel's sunken pool and garden, both of which are built into a crevice in the ancient coral reef that underlies this entire region. There is often good bird-watching here in the hotel gardens. The owners, Jean-Paul Feuillatre and Elizabeth Newton are from France and Canada respectively.

BUDGET

ALBY LODGE, Apdo. 840, Limón. No phone. 4 cabins (all with bath).

$ Rates: $30 single, double, or triple. No credit cards.

Located about 150 yards down the lane to the right just before you reach the park entrance, the Alby Lodge is a fascinating little place hand-built by German owners Yvonne and Alfons Baumgartner. Though these four small cabins are close to the center of the village, they are surrounded by a large lawn and feel secluded. The cabins are all quintessentially tropical with thatch roofs, mosquito nets, hardwood floors and beams, big shuttered windows, tile bathrooms, and a hammock slung on the front porch. You won't find more appealing rooms in this price range.

CABINAS ATLANTIC SURF, Cahuita, Limón. No phone. 6 rms.

$ Rates: $10.15 single; $13.55 double; $16.90 triple.

These small but attractive rooms are a great choice for budget travelers. In a town where all the newer hotels seem to be built of cement, the rustic, varnished wood walls, floors, and small porches of these rooms are a welcome sight. There are fans and tiled showers within, and Adirondack chairs on the porches. The upstairs rooms have high ceilings but still get pretty warm. The Atlantic Surf is down the lane beside the Cabinas Sol y Mar only 100 yards from the park entrance.

CABINAS RHODE ISLAND, Cahuita, Limón. Tel. 506/758-1515, ext. 264. 11 rms (all with private bath).

$ Rates: $6.50–$9 single $10–$15 double. No credit cards.

These newer cinder-block rooms are down the lane beside the Cabinas Sol y Mar. The rooms are on the left, but the owners live in the house across the street. The rooms are very basic, but they're clean and have a tiled veranda. You're within 100 yards of the park entrance if you stay here.

CABINAS TITO, 250 meters southeast of G.A.R., Cahuita, Limón. Tel. 506/758-1515, ext. 286. 6 cabins (all with bath).

$ Rates: Dec–Apr, $30 double; May–Nov, $15–$20 double. No credit cards.

Located down a grassy path off of the road to Playa Negra, these little cabins are quiet and comfortable. They're surrounded by a shady yard, and the owner's old Caribbean wood-frame house is to one side. The cabins are made of cement block with tin roofs, but they have tile floors and front porches with a couple of chairs. Two of the cabins have little refrigerators, and at least one has a tiled wall and wicker headboard for the bed. The good value and pleasant surroundings have made this place an instant hit with budget travelers.

SEASIDE JENNY'S, Cahuita, Limón. Tel. 506/758-1515, ext. 256. 9 rms (all with bath).

$ Rates: Dec–Apr, $23.65–$27.05 single or double, $28.40–$31.80 triple; May–Nov, $16.90–$20.30 single or double, $18.25–$21.62 triple. No credit cards.

Located 200 yards straight ahead (toward the water) from the bus stop, Jenny's place has been popular for years, and her newer rooms are some of the best in town in this price range. Best of all they're right on the water, so you can go to sleep to the sound of the waves. All of the rooms have shuttered windows, and on their porches there are sling chairs and hammocks. The more expensive rooms are on the second floor and have a better view and high ceilings. There are a couple of rooms in an older building, which, though it has a big porch and plenty of Caribbean atmosphere, is not quite as nice as the newer building.

SURF SIDE CABINS, Apdo. 360, Limón. Tel. 506/758-1515, ext. 246. 23 rms (all with bath).

$ Rates: $13.50–$20.30 single or double. No credit cards.

Despite its name, this hotel is not right on the water; however, it is one of the nicer places in Cahuita. All the rooms are clean and have jalousie windows that let in a lot of light and air. There are rooms with double beds, twin beds, and bunk beds. The hotel does actually have a few rooms close to the water, but these rooms are always in high demand. The restaurant is popular with locals, who sit and play dominoes for hours, and it can get noisy at times. Prices for Tico meals range from $2.70 to $12.15. While I was eating here one night, a large sloth crawled into the open-air restaurant from an adjacent tree. With entertainment like that, it's hard not to recommend this place, although the hotel management can be rather unfriendly.

NEARBY PLACES TO STAY

AVIARIOS DEL CARIBE, Apdo. 569-7300, Limón. No phone. Fax 506/758-4459. 5 rms.

$ Rates (including full breakfast): $60 double. No credit cards.

If you prefer bird-watching to beaching, this is the place to stay on this section of the Atlantic coast. As the name implies, birds are important here. The B&B is located on the edge of a small river delta, and within the immediate area, the lodge's owners have spotted nearly 300 species of birds. You can work on your life list either from the lawns; from the second-floor, open-air dining room and lounge; or from a canoe paddling around the nearby canals. This house is built up on stilts and is surrounded by a private wildlife sanctuary that also includes forests with trails. The guest rooms here are all large and comfortable and have fans, tile floors, potted plants, fresh flowers, and modern bathroom fixtures. Some rooms also have king beds. In the lounge area you'll find a fabulous mounted insect collection, as well as terrariums that house live snakes and poison-arrow frogs. Lunch and dinner are also available here.

WHERE TO DINE

If you'd like to try some of the local foods, check out the little shack just before the bridge leading into the national park. The folks here sell meat and vegetable turnovers (called patties) for about 75¢, as well as delicious coconut tarts, various stews with coconut rice, and a refreshing tamarind drink that's a bit like lemonade. Also, local women cook up pots of various local specialties and sell them from the front porch of Salon Vaz (the disco) on Friday and Saturday nights. A full meal will cost you about $2.50. For snacks, there is a tiny bakery on the left side of the main road as you head toward Playa Negra. The coconut pie, brownies, ginger snaps, banana bread, and corn pudding are all delicious. Prices range from 55¢ to 75¢.

BUDGET

BRIGITTE'S RESTAURANTE, Playa Negra Road, north of Cabinas Atlantida. No phone.
 Cuisine: SWISS/CREOLE. **Reservations:** Not accepted.
$ Prices: Main courses $3.75–$7.45. No credit cards.
 Open: Thurs–Tues 8am–10pm.
Brigitte is from Switzerland but she's been in Cahuita for quite a few years, so her menu includes an eclectic blend of cuisines. You can get a good Créole soup with cow's tail and cow's feet, but you can also get a steak with mushroom sauce. There are good salads and home-baked breads as well. You never know what might show up as the daily special. The restaurant is located at the back of a house just off the Playa Negra Road. Just follow the signs.

MARGARITAVILLE, Playa Negra Road, 2 kilometers north of Cahuita near Cabinas Cocal. No phone.
 Cuisine: INTERNATIONAL. **Reservations:** Not accepted.
$ Prices: Complete meals $4.05–$4.75. No credit cards.
 Open: Daily 7–10am, noon–2pm, and 6–9pm.
There's only one dish served each night at this little restaurant, but if you drop by ahead of time and make a special request, the friendly owner may try to accommodate you. However, if you're an adventurous eater, I'm sure you'll enjoy whatever is coming from the kitchen, which might be a local Créole dish made with coconut milk or roasted chicken or eggplant lasagne. All the breads are home-baked, and there are great sandwiches at lunch. The tables here are set up on the porch of an old house and they all have a view of the ocean through the trees. It's all very mellow, definitely not to be missed.

PIZZERIA EL CACTUS, on the road from the south end of Playa Negra to the highway. No phone.
 Cuisine: ITALIAN. **Reservations:** Not accepted.
$ Prices: Pizza or spaghetti $3.35–$6.10. No credit cards.
 Open: Tues–Sun 4–9pm.
There are only a few tables at this small open-air restaurant, so be sure to arrive early if you have your heart set on pizza. Try the pizza Cahuita, which is made with tomatoes, mozzarella, salami, red peppers, olives, and oregano. There's also one made with hearts of palm. The pizzas are just the right size for one hungry person. Also on the menu are seven types of spaghetti, salads, and ice cream.

RESTAURANT EDITH, by the police station. Tel. 758-1515, ext 248.
 Cuisine: SEAFOOD. **Reservations:** Not accepted.
$ Prices: Main courses $3.40–$11.50. No credit cards.
 Open: Mon–Sat 7am–noon, 3–6pm, and 7–10pm; Sun 4–10pm.
It's a mystery to me why this place is so popular, but is is and has been for several years. Though the Créole cooking is great, if you don't get here very early (before 6pm), you may have to wait an hour for your meal. Miss Edith is a local lady who decided to start serving up home-cooked meals to all the hungry tourists hanging around. While Miss Edith's daughters take the orders, Mom cooks up a storm out back. The menu, when you can get ahold of it, is long, with lots of local seafood dishes and Créole combinations such as yuca in coconut milk with meat or vegetables. After you've ordered, it is usually no more than 45 minutes until your meal arrives. It's always crowded here, so don't be bashful about sitting down with total strangers at the big table. Miss Edith's place is at the opposite end of town from the park entrance and is just around the corner from the main street.

4. PUERTO VIEJO

200 kilometers E of San José; 55 kilometers S of Limón

GETTING THERE   By Bus   Express buses to Puerto Viejo leave San José daily at 3pm (also at 8am on Saturday and Sunday) from Avenida 11 between Calle Central and Calle 1. Duration: 5 hours. Fare $6.10.

Alternatively, you can catch a bus to Limón (see above for details), and then transfer to a Puerto Viejo–bound bus in Limón. These latter buses leave daily at 5 and 10am and 1 and 4pm from Radio Casino, which is one block north of the municipal market. Duration: 1½ hours. Fare: 85¢ to $1.30.

By Car   To reach Puerto Viejo, continue south from Cahuita for another 16 kilometers. Watch for a gravel road that forks to the left from the paved highway. This road will take you into the village after another 5 kilometers.

DEPARTING   Express buses leave Puerto Viejo for San José daily at 7am (also at 3:30pm on Saturday and Sunday). Buses for Limón leave daily at 6am and 1 (except Sunday) and 4:30pm. Buses to Punta Uva and Manzanillo leave Puerto Viejo daily around 8am and 4:30pm. These buses return from Manzanillo at 9am and 4:30pm. There are also northbound buses that stop in Home Creek, out on the highway 5 kilometers from Puerto Viejo, at 6:30 and 9:30am and 4pm. If you can arrange transportation to Home Creek, you could also catch one of these buses.

ESSENTIALS   Orientation   The gravel road in from the highway runs parallel to Playa Negra just before entering the village of Puerto Viejo, which has all of about six dirt streets. The sea will be on your left and forested hills on your right as you come into town. Public phones are located at Hotel Maritza and Pulpería Manuel Leon. The nearest bank is in Bribri, about 10 kilometers away. There is a Guardia Rural police post near the park on the beach. It's another 15 kilometers or so on a bad gravel road south to Punta Uva.

Though Puerto Viejo is even smaller than Cahuita, it has an even more lively atmosphere due to the many surfers who come here from around the country and around the world to ride the village's famous Salsa Brava wave. For nonsurfers, there are also some good swimming beaches, and if you head still farther south, you will come to the most beautiful beaches on this coast. The waters down in this region are some of the clearest anywhere in the country and there is good snorkeling among the coral reefs.

You may notice, as you make your way into town from the highway, that there are cacao trees planted along the road. These trees are all suffering from a blight that has greatly reduced the cocoa-bean harvest in the area. However, you can still get delicious cocoa candies here in Puerto Viejo. Don't miss them.

WHAT TO SEE & DO

Most people who show up in this remote village have only on thing on their mind—**surfing.** Just offshore from the village park is a shallow reef where powerful storm-generated waves sometimes reach 20 feet. These waves are the biggest and most powerful on the Atlantic coast. Even when the waves are small, this spot is recommended only for very experienced surfers because of the danger of the reef. For swimming, head out to Playa Negra, along the road into town, or to the beaches south of town where the surf is much more manageable.

If you aren't a surfer, there isn't much else for you to do here. The same activities that prevail in Cahuita are the norm here as well. Read a book, take a nap, or walk on the beach. However, if you have more energy, you can rent a bicycle or a horse (watch for signs) and head down the beach toward Punta Uva, which is a little less than 8 kilometers down a potholed gravel road.

You should be sure to stop in at the **Association Talamanqueña de Eco-**

turismo y Conservacion (ATEC) office across the street from the Soda Tamara. This local organization is concerned with preserving both the environment and the cultural heritage of this area and promoting ecologically sound development in the region. They publish and sell *Coastal Talamanca, A Cultural and Ecological Guide*, a small booklet packed with information about this area. They also offer quite a few different tours. There are half-day walks that focus on nature and either the local African-Caribbean culture or the indigenous Bribri culture. These walks pass through farms and forests and along the way you'll learn about local history, customs, medicinal plants, and Indian mythology as well as have an opportunity to see sloths, monkeys, iguanas, keel-billed toucans, and other wildlife. There are four different walks through the nearby Bribri Indians' **Kekoldi Reserve.** There are also more strenuous hikes through the primary rain forest. ATEC also offers snorkeling trips to the nearby coral reefs and snorkeling and fishing trips in dugout canoes. Bird walks and night walks will help you spot more of the area wildlife. There are even overnight treks. The local guides who lead these tours are a wealth of information and make a hike through the forest a truly educational experience. Don't miss an opportunity to do a tour with ATEC. Half-day walks (and night walks) are $11.70 and full-day walks are $19.45. A half day of snorkeling or fishing is $15.55. The ATEC office is open Tuesday through Saturday from noon to 6pm and Sunday from 8am to noon.

If you continue south on the coast road from Puerto Viejo, you will come to a couple of even smaller villages. Punta Uva is 8 kilometers away, and Manzanillo is about 15 kilometers away. There is a trail along the beach from Barra Cocles to Manzanillo, a distance of about 10 kilometers. Another enjoyable hike is from Monkey Point to Manzanillo (about 5½ kilometers). There is a reef offshore from Manzanillo that is good for snorkeling. Still farther south is the **Manzanillo-Gandoca Wildlife Refuge,** which extends all the way to the Panamanian border. Within the boundaries of the reserve live manatees, crocodiles, and more than 350 species of birds. The reserve also includes the coral reef offshore. On one 5½-mile-long beach within the reserve, four species of sea turtles nest between March and July.

Souvenirs Denise, across the street from Soda Tamara, sells, hand-painted T-shirts and coconut-shell jewelry. There are also a couple of pulperías (general stores) in the village.

If you'd like to learn more about the culture of the local Bribri Indians, look for a copy of *Taking Care of Sibö's Gifts*, which was written by Paula Palmer, Juanita Sánchez, and Gloria Mayorga.

WHERE TO STAY

MODERATE

EL PIZOTE, Apdo. 230-2200, Coronado. Tel. 506/758-1938 or 229-1428. Fax 506/229-1428. 8 rms (none with bath), 6 bungalows, 1 casita.
$ Rates: $31 single without bath, $75 single with bath; $46 double without bath, $75 double with bath; $60 triple without bath, $89 triple with bath; $69 quad without bath, $99 quad with bath; $100 casita single, double, or triple, $110 casita quad. MC, V.

Although it bills itself as a surf resort, this comfortably rustic little lodge would be ideal for anyone who simply wants to get away from it all. Located about 500 meters outside of town, El Pizote is set back across the road from a long black-sand beach. The rooms are in two beautiful, unpainted wooden buildings that are completely hidden from the road or even from the parking lot. You have to walk through a dense grove of dracaena plants, which you might recognize as a common houseplant. The rooms are cool—with polished wood walls, double beds, and absolutely beautiful bathrooms that have wood slat floors in the showers and huge screen windows looking out on dense jungle. There are unusual burlap-and-bamboo window shades, as well as ceiling fans and reading lamps. For activity, there are hiking trails in the adjacent forest and a volleyball court. You can also rent snorkeling and scuba equipment as well as sea kayaks. There is also good bird-watching here. The restaurant serves only breakfast ($8) and dinner ($14.50), but drinks are available all day. There is a set menu each evening, which might be lobster with broccoli or an equally delectable fish plate. If arriving by bus, ask the bus driver to let you off at the entrance to the lodge. It's on the stretch of road that runs along the beach just before entering town. If you're looking for someplace more rustic, ask the lodge owner about his new jungle lodge.

BUDGET

CABINAS BLACK SANDS, Puerto Viejo, Limón. Tel. 506/758-3844 (leave message). 3 rms (none with bath).
$ Rates: $16.90 single or double; $50 for six people. No credit cards.

The owners of this rustic, beachside thatch house are refugees from chilly Wisconsin. They offer basic accommodations in a secluded spot on a long black-sand beach. The three rooms are all in a single rustic, thatched-roof building, which has a communal kitchen and dining-room table. If there are six of you, you can rent the entire house. If you don't have the whole place to yourself, re-member that the folks next door can hear everything you say because the walls don't go all the way to the ceiling. It's wonderfully tranquil out here, and though it's a long walk to the nearest restaurant, there is a general store nearby where you can buy groceries for doing your own cooking. If arriving by bus, be sure to get off at the Pulpería Violeta before the road reaches the beach. Otherwise it's a long walk back out from the bus stop in town.

CABINAS CHIMURI, Puerto Viejo, Limón. Tel. 506/758-3844 (leave message). 4 cabins (none with bath).
$ Rates: $22–$33 single, double, or triple; $33 quad. No credit cards.

If you don't mind being a 15-minute walk from the beach and are an inveterate camper, I'm sure that you'll enjoy this rustic lodge. It's built in traditional Bribri Indian-style with thatched-roof A-frame cabins in a forest setting. In fact, it's a short stroll down a trail from the parking lot to the lodge buildings, and there are other trails on the property as well. This lodge is definitely for nature lovers who are used to roughing it: Accommodations are very basic, but there is a kitchen for guests to use. The lodge also runs several different hiking trips into the rain forest and the ad-jacent Bribri Indian Kekoldi Reserve. If arriving by bus, be sure to get off at the trail to Cabinas Chimuri before the road reaches the beach.

CABINAS JACARANDA, Puerto Viejo, Limón. No phone. 4 rms (1 with bath).
$ Rates: $10.15 single without bath; $12.20 double without bath, $16.90 double with bath; $20.30 triple with bath. No credit cards.

This basic backpackers' special has a few nice touches that sets it apart from the others. The floors are cement, but there are mats. Japanese paper lanterns cover the lights and mosquito nets hang over the beds. The Guatemalan bedspreads add a dash of color and tropical flavor, as do the tables made from sliced tree trunks. If you are traveling in a group, you'll enjoy the space and atmosphere of the big room. The Garden Restaurant, adjacent to the rooms, serves the best food in town.

CASA VERDE, Puerto Viejo, Limón. Tel. 506/758-0854 or 758-3844 (leave mes-sage). 8 rms (4 with private bath).
$ Rates: $11.50 single without bath, $25 single with bath; $16.90 double without bath, $25 double with bath. No credit cards.

This little hotel is located on a side street on the south side of town. The older rooms, with shared bath, are in an interesting building with a wide, covered breezeway between the rooms and the showers and toilets out in back. The front and back porches of this building are hung with hammocks. The newer rooms are behind the house next door and are a bit larger than the older rooms. These new rooms have high ceilings, tile floors, and a veranda.

ESCAPE CARIBEÑO, Puerto Viejo, Limón. Tel. 506/758-3844. 12 rms, 1 apt.
$ Rates: $26.25 single; $30.65 double; $33.25 triple; $35–$48.10 quad; $52.50 apartment (one to three people). MC, V.

★ Located just outside of Puerto Viejo on the road to Punta Uva, Escape Caribeño consists of 12 little white cabins with brick pillars and tiled patios. Clerestory windows, vertical blinds, and rather fancy hardwood furniture give these cabins the aesthetic edge over many area places in this price range. There are reading lamps by the beds and small refrigerators in every room. The attractive gardens have been planted with bananas and palms. It's a 5 minute walk into town or out to a beautiful beach that has a small island just offshore.

NEARBY PLACES TO STAY

EXPENSIVE

PUNTA COCLES, Puerto Viejo, Limón (Apdo. 11020-1000, San José). Tel. 506/234-8055, 234-8051, or (in the U.S.) toll free 800/325-6927. Fax 506/234-8033. 60 rms. A/C
$ Rates: $70–$150 single; $80–$150 double; $90–$150 triple. AE, MC, V.
Though this is the most expensive and largest hotel in the area, it is certainly not the best. The two biggest complaints I have are that no consideration was put into preserving the property's rain forest when the hotel was built, and it is a long, hot walk to the beach. Situated several hundred yards from the beach, the hotel is in a huge clearing in the jungle and offers virtually no shade and hardly any landscaping. Rooms do not get any sea breezes and consequently must be air-conditioned. Though the rooms are for the most part large and modern, they lack character.
   Dining/Entertainment: There's a large open-air restaurant that serves overpriced meals, and a bar by the pool
   Services: Laundry service, sports-equipment rentals.
   Facilities: Swimming pool.

MODERATE

LAS PALMAS RESORT, Edificio Cristal, Fifth floor, Avenida 1 between calles 1 and 3 (Apdo. 6942-1000), San José. Tel. 506/255-3939. Fax 506/255-3737. 40 rms.
$ Rates (including breakfast): $39.40 single; $49 double; $70.85 triple. AE, DC, MC, V.
Located 5 miles south of Puerto Viejo in the village of Punta Uva, Las Palmas Resort is one of the only true beachfront hotels in the area. The only drawback is that on the weekends throngs of people flock to the beach right in front of the hotel and the peace and quiet disappear. The beach here stretches for miles, and when the water is calm, snorkeling is good among the coral just offshore. There isn't much shade here, though, so bring plenty of sunscreen. Guest rooms are clean and comfortable, but not very attractive. Basically what you're paying for is the location, not the atmosphere or decor. The open-air restaurant serves moderately priced Tico and continental meals, with an emphasis on lobster and seafood. There is also a bar/snack bar near the entrance to the hotel. Additional amenities include a small swimming pool and a tennis court. Various tours and horseback rides can be arranged through the hotel. There's also a dive shop that gives lessons, leads trips, and rents equipment.

VILLAS DEL CARIBE, Puerto Viejo, Limón (Apdo. 8080-1000, San José). Tel. 506/233-2200. Fax 506/221-2801. 12 apts.
$ Rates: $70 single or double; $80 triple; $90 quad. AE, MC, V.
★ If you want to be right on the beach and have spacious comfortable accommodations, there is not better choice in this area. Villas del Caribe, built in a sort of contemporary Mediterranean style and set on a 100-acre nature reserve, offers two-story town-house apartments with full kitchens and a choice of one or two bedrooms. The living rooms have built-in sofa beds, and just outside there is a large terrace complete with barbecue grill. The kitchens are attractively designed with blue tile counters. Bathrooms are tropical fantasies with wooden-slat shower doors, potted plants on a platform by the window, louvered and screened walls that let in light and air, and more blue tile counters. Upstairs

you'll find either a single huge bedroom with a king bed, or two smaller bedrooms (one with bunk beds). There's a balcony, with hammock, off the main bedroom. The water, which is usually fairly calm, is only steps away through the coconut palms and there is some coral just offshore that makes for good snorkeling. The hotel can arrange horseback rides, fishing trips, snorkeling and diving, even oxcart rides.

BUDGET

MIRAFLORES LODGE, Playa Chiquita, Puerto Viejo, Limón (in the U.S.: P.O. Box 432434, Miami, FL 33243). Tel. 506/233-5127 or (in the U.S.) 305/663-0257. Fax 506/233-5390. 5 rms (2 with bath).

$ Rates (including breakfast): $20 single without bath, $35 single with bath; $25 double without bath, $35 double with bath; $35 triple without bath, $52.50 triple with bath. No credit cards.

Located a few miles south of Puerto Viejo on the road to Punta Uva, Miraflores Lodge is basically a private home with a few rooms available. Because it is a private home, the decor is far more attractive than at other lodges in the area. The large second-floor porch, which is virtually an open-air living room, is decorated with wood carvings, masks, and Panamanian and Guatemalan textiles. Huge vases hold fresh flowers and there is a free-form table made from a slice of tree trunk. Surrounding the lodge is a flower farm where heliconias, ginger, banana, anthurium, and orchids are grown. The guest rooms with private bath are very large and can sleep up to six people in two sleeping areas. Walls and doors are faced with cane, and there are hardwood floors in the second-floor rooms. Full payment is required on making reservations during the December-to-April busy season (40% deposit the rest of the year); these deposits are nonrefundable. The operation of this lodge seems very spotty; be absolutely certain that there will be someone there to check you in before committing to a stay here. I met a couple who were never able to find anyone to check them into the lodge and had to stay elsewhere.

PLAYA CHIQUITA LODGE, Avenida 2 between calles 17 and 19 (Apdo. 7043-1000), San José. Tel. 506/233-6613. Fax 506/223-7479. 11 rms (all with bath).

$ Rates: $25 single; $35 double; $45 triple. AE, V (accepted only at the San José office).

This place just oozes jungle atmosphere and is sure to please anyone searching for a steamy retreat on the beach. Set amid the shade of large old trees a few miles south of Puerto Viejo toward Punta Uva (watch for the sign), the lodge consists of unpainted wooden buildings set on stilts and connected by wooden walkways. There are wide verandas with rocking chairs and seashell mobiles hanging everywhere. Rooms are dark and cool with wide-board floors and paintings by local Indian artists. The top of the bathroom wall is screened so you can gaze out into the jungle as you shower. There is a short trail that leads down to a private little swimming beach with beautiful turquoise water, as well as tide pools. Meals here cost from $2 to $12 and choices range from spaghetti to lobster; since the management is German you can expect a few German dishes as well. Throughout the day there are free bananas and coffee.

WHERE TO DINE

To really sample the local cuisine, you need to look up a few local ladies. Ask around for Miss Dolly and see if she has anything cooking. Her specialties are bread (especially banana) and ginger biscuits, but she will also fix a special Caribbean meal for you if you ask a day in advance and she has time. Miss Sam makes pineapple rolls, plantain tarts, and bread. Miss Daisy makes pan bon, ginger cakes, patties (meat-filled turnovers), and coconut oil (for tanning). Just ask around for these folks and someone will direct you to them. If you have an opportunity, be sure to try rundown soup, which is a spicy coconut-milk soup made with anything the cook can run down.

CAFE PIZZERIA CORAL, on the road to the soccer field. No phone.

Cuisine: PIZZA. **Reservations:** Not accepted.
$ Prices: Pizza $3.65–$6.80; pasta $4.05–$4.75. No credit cards.
Open: Tues–Sun 7–11am and 6–9:30pm.

Though the owner here is from El Salvador, she cooks a great pizza. She also bakes great chocolate cake! Some of the goodies not to be missed are the pumpkin soup, the tomato and green peppercorn pizza (the peppercorns are grown locally), the summer wine (a bit like sangría), and of course the chocolate cake (though the key lime pie and cheesecake are good too). The open-air dining room is up a few steps from the street and has hardwood floors and wood railings. You'll find the Cafe Pizzeria Coral about two blocks from the water in the center of the village.

GARDEN RESTAURANT, Cabinas Jacaranda. No phone.
Cuisine: CARIBBEAN/ASIAN. **Reservations:** Not accepted.
$ Prices: Appetizers $2.20–$2.70; main courses $4.40–$5.75. No credit cards.
Open: Thurs–Mon 5:30–9pm.

Located a couple of blocks from the water (near the soccer field), this restaurant serves the best food in Puerto Viejo and some of the best in all of Costa Rica. The co-owner and chef is from Trinidad by way of Toronto and has created an eclectic menu that is guaranteed to please. You'll find such surprising offerings as chicken saté (a Thai dish), yakitori (Japanese), Jamaican jerk chicken, calypso curry chicken, and chicken Bangkok. There are also daily specials and lots of delicious fresh juices. Many of the ambrosial desserts are made with local fruits, and there are also such delights as ginger spice cake and macadamia chocolate torte. Every dish is beautifully presented, usually with edible flowers for garnish.

SODA TAMARA, on the main road through the village. No phone.
Cuisine: COSTA RICAN. **Reservations:** Not accepted.
$ Prices: Main courses $2.40–$5.45. No credit cards.
Open: Wed–Mon 7am–9pm.

This little Tico-style restaurant has long been popular with budget-conscious travelers and has an attractive setting for such an economical place. There's a small patio dining area in addition to the main dining room, which is a bit dark. The white picket fence in front gives the restaurant a very homey feel. At the counter inside, you'll find homemade cocoa candies and unsweetened cocoa biscuits. These are made by several ladies in town, but unfortunately, for several years, the cocoa trees in this area have been dying from some type of blight.

NEARBY PLACES TO DINE

EL DUENDE FELIZ, on the main road, Punta Uva. No phone.
Cuisine: ITALIAN. **Reservations:** Not accepted.
$ Prices: Appetizers $2.75–$6.45; main courses $5.10–$12.20. No credit cards.
Open: Sat–Wed 11am–2pm and 6–9pm, Thurs–Fri 6–9pm.

Isn't it reassuring to know that even in the middle of nowhere, you can get a plate of spaghetti or a pizza? El Duende Feliz is on the outskirts of Punta Uva Village and serves a wide selection of authentic Italian dishes. Seafood shows up quite a bit, of course. Depending on the day's catch, you can get seafood spaghetti and pizza with clams among other dishes. There are also steaks and plenty of pasta dishes. You can even finish off your meal with a scoop of gelati and an espresso.

NATURALES, on the main road, Punta Uva. No phone.
Cuisine: SWISS/CONTINENTAL. **Reservations:** Not accepted.
$ Prices: Main courses $3.75–$12.50. No credit cards.
Open: Fri–Wed 4–10pm.

Located south of Playa Chiquita on the road to Punta Uva, Naturales is built into a hillside at the top of a steep flight of 48 steps. From this tree house–like vantage point there is a great view of the water and the surrounding forests. Every day there is a different menu with four entrée choices, and though you won't find any seafood on the menu, you may find the likes of beef fondue or homemade pastas. If you order a day in advance, you can have special meals prepared.

APPENDIX

METRIC MEASURES

Length

1 millimeter (mm)	=	.04 inches (*or* less than ¹⁄₁₆ in.)
1 centimeter (cm)	=	.39 inches (*or* just under ½ in.)
1 meter (m)	=	39 inches (*or* about 1.1 yards)
1 kilometer (km)	=	.62 miles (*or* about ⅔ of a mile)

To convert kilometers to miles, multiply the number kilometers by .62. Also use to convert kilometers per hour (kmph) to miles per hour (m.p.h.).

To convert miles to kilometers, multiply the number of miles by 1.61. Also use to convert speeds from m.p.h. to kmph.

Capacity

1 liter (l)	=	33.92 fluid ounces =	2.1 pints	=	1.06 quarts
	=	.26 U.S. gallons			
1 Imperial gallon	=	1.2 U.S. gallons			

To convert liters to U.S. gallons, multiply the number of liters by .26.

To convert U.S. gallons to liters, multiply the number of gallons by 3.79.

To convert Imperial gallons to U.S. gallons, multiply the number of Imperial gallons by 1.2.

To convert U.S. gallons to Imperial gallons, multiply the number of U.S. gallons by .83.

Weight

1 gram (g)	=	.035 ounces (*or* about a paperclip's weight)
1 kilogram (kg)	=	35.2 ounces = 2.2 pounds
1 metric ton	=	2,205 pounds = 1.1 short ton

To convert kilograms to pounds, multiply the number kilograms by 2.2.

To convert pounds to kilograms, multiply the number of pounds by .45.

Area

1 hectare (ha)	=	2.47 acres		
1 square kilometer (km²)	=	247 acres	=	.39 square miles

To convert hectares to acres, multiply the number of hectares by 2.47.

To convert acres to hectares, multiply the number of acres by .41.

To convert square kilometers to square miles, multiply the number of square kilometers by .39.

To convert square miles to square kilometers, multiply the number square miles by 2.6.

Temperature

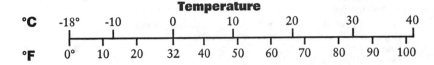

°C	-18°	-10		0		10		20		30		40
°F	0°	10	20	32	40	50	60	70	80	90	100	

To convert degrees Celsius to degrees Fahrenheit, multiply °C by 9, divide by 5 and add 32 (example: 20°C × 9/5 + 32 = 68°F).

To convert degrees Fahrenheit to degrees Celsius, subtract 32 from °F, multiply by 5, then divide by 9 (example: 85°F - 32 × 5/9 = 29.4°C).

INDEX

Now Save Money on All Your Travels by Joining
FROMMER'S ™ TRAVEL BOOK CLUB
The World's Best Travel Guides at Membership Prices

FROMMER'S TRAVEL BOOK CLUB is your ticket to successful travel! Open up a world of travel information and simplify your travel planning when you join ranks with thousands of value-conscious travelers who are members of the FROMMER'S TRAVEL BOOK CLUB. Join today and you'll be entitled to all the privileges that come from belonging to the club that offers you travel guides for less to more than 100 destinations worldwide. Annual membership is only $25 (U.S.) or $35 (Canada and foreign).

The Advantages of Membership

1. Your choice of *three* free FROMMER'S TRAVEL GUIDES (any *two* FROM-MER'S COMPREHENSIVE GUIDES, FROMMER'S $-A-DAY GUIDES, FROMMER'S WALKING TOURS *or* FROMMER'S FAMILY GUIDES—plus *one* FROMMER'S CITY GUIDE, FROMMER'S CITY $-A-DAY GUIDE *or* FROMMER'S TOURING GUIDE).
2. Your own subscription to **TRIPS AND TRAVEL** quarterly newsletter.
3. You're entitled to a **30% discount** on your order of any additional books offered by FROMMER'S TRAVEL BOOK CLUB.
4. You're offered (at a small additional fee) our **Domestic Trip-Routing Kits.**

Our quarterly newsletter **TRIPS AND TRAVEL** offers practical information on the best buys in travel, the "hottest" vacation spots, the latest travel trends, world-class events and much, much more.

Our **Domestic Trip-Routing Kits** are available for any North American destination. We'll send you a detailed map highlighting the best route to take to your destination—you can request direct or scenic routes.

Here's all you have to do to join:

Send in your membership fee of $25 ($35 Canada and foreign) with your name and address on the form below along with your selections as part of your membership package to **FROMMER'S TRAVEL BOOK CLUB, P.O. Box 473, Mt. Morris, IL 61054-0473.** Remember to check off your *three* free books.

If you would like to order additional books, please select the books you would like and send a check for the total amount (please add sales tax in the states noted below), plus $2 per book for shipping and handling ($3 per book for foreign orders) to:

FROMMER'S TRAVEL BOOK CLUB
P.O. Box 473
Mt. Morris, IL 61054-0473
(815) 734-1104

[ ] **YES.** I want to take advantage of this opportunity to join FROMMER'S TRAVEL BOOK CLUB.

[ ] **My check is enclosed.** Dollar amount enclosed_____*
(all payments in U.S. funds only)

Name_____

Address_____

City_____ State_____ Zip_____
All orders must be prepaid.

To ensure that all orders are processed efficiently, please apply sales tax in the following areas: CA, CT, FL, IL, NJ, NY, TN, WA and CANADA.

*With membership, shipping and handling will be paid by FROMMER'S TRAVEL BOOK CLUB for the three free books you select as part of your membership. Please add $2 per book for shipping and handling for any additional books purchased ($3 per book for foreign orders).

Allow 4–6 weeks for delivery. Prices of books, membership fee, and publication dates are subject to change without notice. Prices are subject to acceptance and availability.

Please Send Me the Books Checked Below:

FROMMER'S COMPREHENSIVE GUIDES
(Guides listing facilities from budget to deluxe,
with emphasis on the medium-priced)

	Retail Price	Code		Retail Price	Code
☐ Acapulco/Ixtapa/Taxco 1993–94	$15.00	C120	☐ Japan 1994–95 (Avail. 3/94)	$19.00	C144
☐ Alaska 1994–95	$17.00	C131	☐ Morocco 1992–93	$18.00	C021
☐ Arizona 1993–94	$18.00	C101	☐ Nepal 1994–95	$18.00	C126
☐ Australia 1992–93	$18.00	C002	☐ New England 1994 (Avail. 1/94)	$16.00	C137
☐ Austria 1993–94	$19.00	C119	☐ New Mexico 1993–94	$15.00	C117
☐ Bahamas 1994–95	$17.00	C121	☐ New York State 1994–95	$19.00	C133
☐ Belgium/Holland/ Luxembourg 1993–94	$18.00	C106	☐ Northwest 1994–95 (Avail. 2/94)	$17.00	C140
☐ Bermuda 1994–95	$15.00	C122	☐ Portugal 1994–95 (Avail. 2/94)	$17.00	C141
☐ Brazil 1993–94	$20.00	C111	☐ Puerto Rico 1993–94	$15.00	C103
☐ California 1994	$15.00	C134	☐ Puerto Vallarta/Manzanillo/ Guadalajara 1994–95 (Avail. 1/94)	$14.00	C028
☐ Canada 1994–95 (Avail. 4/94)	$19.00	C145	☐ Scandinavia 1993–94	$19.00	C135
☐ Caribbean 1994	$18.00	C123	☐ Scotland 1994–95 (Avail. 4/94)	$17.00	C146
☐ Carolinas/Georgia 1994–95	$17.00	C128	☐ South Pacific 1994–95 (Avail. 1/94)	$20.00	C138
☐ Colorado 1994–95 (Avail. 3/94)	$16.00	C143	☐ Spain 1993–94	$19.00	C115
☐ Cruises 1993–94	$19.00	C107	☐ Switzerland/Liechtenstein 1994–95 (Avail. 1/94)	$19.00	C139
☐ Delaware/Maryland 1994–95 (Avail. 1/94)	$15.00	C136	☐ Thailand 1992–93	$20.00	C033
☐ England 1994	$18.00	C129	☐ U.S.A. 1993–94	$19.00	C116
☐ Florida 1994	$18.00	C124	☐ Virgin Islands 1994–95	$13.00	C127
☐ France 1994–95	$20.00	C132	☐ Virginia 1994–95 (Avail. 2/94)	$14.00	C142
☐ Germany 1994	$19.00	C125	☐ Yucatán 1993–94	$18.00	C110
☐ Italy 1994	$19.00	C130			
☐ Jamaica/Barbados 1993–94	$15.00	C105			

FROMMER'S $-A-DAY GUIDES
(Guides to low-cost tourist accommodations and facilities)

		Retail Price	Code			Retail Price	Code
☐ Australia on $45	1993–94	$18.00	D102	☐ Israel on $45	1993–94	$18.00	D101
☐ Costa Rica/Guatemala/ Belize on $35	1993–94	$17.00	D108	☐ Mexico on $45	1994	$19.00	D116
☐ Eastern Europe on $30	1993–94	$18.00	D110	☐ New York on $70	1994–95 (Avail. 4/94)	$16.00	D120
☐ England on $60	1994	$18.00	D112	☐ New Zealand on $45	1993–94	$18.00	D103
☐ Europe on $50	1994	$19.00	D115	☐ Scotland/Wales on $50	1992–93	$18.00	D019
☐ Greece on $45	1993–94	$19.00	D100	☐ South America on $40	1993–94	$19.00	D109
☐ Hawaii on $75	1994	$19.00	D113	☐ Turkey on $40	1992–93	$22.00	D023
☐ India on $40	1992–93	$20.00	D010	☐ Washington, D.C. on $40	1994–95 (Avail. 2/94)	$17.00	D119
☐ Ireland on $45	1994–95 (Avail. 1/94)	$17.00	D117				

FROMMER'S CITY $-A-DAY GUIDES
(Pocket-size guides to low-cost tourist accommodations
and facilities)

		Retail Price	Code			Retail Price	Code
☐ Berlin on $40	1994–95	$12.00	D111	☐ Madrid on $50	1994–95 (Avail. 1/94)	$13.00	D118
☐ Copenhagen on $50	1992–93	$12.00	D003	☐ Paris on $50	1994–95	$12.00	D117
☐ London on $45	1994–95	$12.00	D114	☐ Stockholm on $50	1992–93	$13.00	D022

FROMMER'S WALKING TOURS
(With routes and detailed maps, these companion guides point out
the places and pleasures that make a city unique)

	Retail Price	Code		Retail Price	Code
☐ Berlin	$12.00	W100	☐ Paris	$12.00	W103
☐ London	$12.00	W101	☐ San Francisco	$12.00	W104
☐ New York	$12.00	W102	☐ Washington, D.C.	$12.00	W105

FROMMER'S TOURING GUIDES
(Color-illustrated guides that include walking tours, cultural and historic
sights, and practical information)

	Retail Price	Code		Retail Price	Code
☐ Amsterdam	$11.00	T001	☐ New York	$11.00	T008
☐ Barcelona	$14.00	T015	☐ Rome	$11.00	T010
☐ Brazil	$11.00	T003	☐ Scotland	$10.00	T011
☐ Florence	$ 9.00	T005	☐ Sicily	$15.00	T017
☐ Hong Kong/Singapore/			☐ Tokyo	$15.00	T016
Macau	$11.00	T006	☐ Turkey	$11.00	T013
☐ Kenya	$14.00	T018	☐ Venice	$ 9.00	T014
☐ London	$13.00	T007			

FROMMER'S FAMILY GUIDES

	Retail Price	Code		Retail Price	Code
☐ California with Kids	$18.00	F100	☐ San Francisco with Kids		
☐ Los Angeles with Kids			(Avail. 4/94)	$17.00	F104
(Avail. 4/94)	$17.00	F103	☐ Washington, D.C. with Kids		
☐ New York City with Kids			(Avail. 2/94)	$17.00	F102
(Avail. 2/94)	$18.00	F101			

FROMMER'S CITY GUIDES
(Pocket-size guides to sightseeing and tourist accommodations and
facilities in all price ranges)

	Retail Price	Code		Retail Price	Code
☐ Amsterdam 1993–94	$13.00	S110	☐ Montréal/Québec		
☐ Athens 1993–94	$13.00	S114	City 1993–94	$13.00	S125
☐ Atlanta 1993–94	$13.00	S112	☐ Nashville/Memphis		
☐ Atlantic City/Cape			1994–95 (Avail. 4/94)	$13.00	S141
May 1993–94	$13.00	S130	☐ New Orleans 1993–94	$13.00	S103
☐ Bangkok 1992–93	$13.00	S005	☐ New York 1994 (Avail.		
☐ Barcelona/Majorca/Minorca/			1/94)	$13.00	S138
Ibiza 1993–94	$13.00	S115	☐ Orlando 1994	$13.00	S135
☐ Berlin 1993–94	$13.00	S116	☐ Paris 1993–94	$13.00	S109
☐ Boston 1993–94	$13.00	S117	☐ Philadelphia 1993–94	$13.00	S113
☐ Budapest 1994–95 (Avail.			☐ San Diego 1993–94	$13.00	S107
2/94)	$13.00	S139	☐ San Francisco 1994	$13.00	S133
☐ Chicago 1993–94	$13.00	S122	☐ Santa Fe/Taos/		
☐ Denver/Boulder/Colorado			Albuquerque 1993–94	$13.00	S108
Springs 1993–94	$13.00	S131	☐ Seattle/Portland 1994–95	$13.00	S137
☐ Dublin 1993–94	$13.00	S128	☐ St. Louis/Kansas		
☐ Hong Kong 1994–95			City 1993–94	$13.00	S127
(Avail. 4/94)	$13.00	S140	☐ Sydney 1993–94	$13.00	S129
☐ Honolulu/Oahu 1994	$13.00	S134	☐ Tampa/St.		
☐ Las Vegas 1993–94	$13.00	S121	Petersburg 1993–94	$13.00	S105
☐ London 1994	$13.00	S132	☐ Tokyo 1992–93	$13.00	S039
☐ Los Angeles 1993–94	$13.00	S123	☐ Toronto 1993–94	$13.00	S126
☐ Madrid/Costa del			☐ Vancouver/Victoria 1994–		
Sol 1993–94	$13.00	S124	95 (Avail. 1/94)	$13.00	S142
☐ Miami 1993–94	$13.00	S118	☐ Washington, D.C. 1994		
☐ Minneapolis/St.			(Avail. 1/94)	$13.00	S136
Paul 1993–94	$13.00	S119			

SPECIAL EDITIONS

	Retail Price	Code		Retail Price	Code
☐ Bed & Breakfast Southwest	$16.00	P100	☐ Caribbean Hideaways	$16.00	P103
☐ Bed & Breakfast Great American Cities (Avail. 1/94)	$16.00	P104	☐ National Park Guide 1994 (avail. 3/94)	$16.00	P105
			☐ Where to Stay U.S.A.	$15.00	P102

Please note: if the availability of a book is several months away, we may have back issues of guides to that particular destination. Call customer service at (815) 734-1104.